# The Growth

# and Development

# of Logistics

# Personnel

Council of Logistics Management
2805 Butterfield Road, Oak Brook, IL 60523-1170   (630) 574-0985
Fax # (630) 574-0989   E-Mail: clmadmin@clml.org   Web Site: www.clml.org

# The Growth and Development of Logistics Personnel

**Mississippi State University**

**Principal Investigators**

Stephen A. LeMay,
Professor of Marketing
College of Business and Industry
Mississippi State University

Jon C. Carr
Research Scientist
Social Science Research Center
Mississippi State University

**Researchers**

Jeffery A. Periatt
Assistant Professor of Marketing
School of Business
Auburn University Montgomery

Roger D. McMahon, Jr.
Assistant Professor of Marketing
Pepperdine University

**Editor**

Kara A. Keller
Social Science Research Center
Mississippi State University

Social Science Research Center
P.O. Box 5287
Miss. St. Univ., MS 39762
Web site: www.ssrc.mstate.edu

# Preface

This book resulted from the contributions of many: the managers in the firms listed above gave their time and allowed us to disrupt operations, and the employees spent enormous amounts of time and energy completing survey questionnaires and giving interviews; the Council of Logistics Management staff fielded countless phone calls, organized crucial meetings, and advised us on difficult issues; the project committee pointed to valuable resources, identified participants, and kept us on track; the staff at the Social Sciences Research Center and the College of Business and Industry worked around the absentmindedness of at least one of the researchers, kept the budget, arranged travel, and lifted our spirits.

In particular, I wish to thank three dedicated research professionals–Jon C. Carr, Jeffery A. Periatt, and Roger D. McMahon, Jr.–who devoted countless hours to research and writing. Other thanks go to Kara A. Keller, our editor, who made sure that the language was, in fact, English; Carol J. White, who arranged our frantic travel schedules; Vicki M. Mann and Vergie M. Bash, who kept the academic home fires alight; Arthur G. Cosby, Director of the Social Sciences Research Center, who supported us throughout this project; Ronald D. Taylor, Chair of the Department of Marketing, Qualitative Analysis, and Business Law, who scheduled around project demands; Scott Sloan, Vice President of Operations, Leach Company, who gave insight and directed us to outstanding firms; and Ed Wamble of East Mississippi Community College, who gave us training modules and advice on sources.

We wish to thank the Council of Logistics Management for its sponsorship of this research, with special thanks to Elaine Winter and Toni Fatigato for their support. The oversight committee for this research project is also due special

i

thanks: Richard F. Whitney, Chairperson; Alex C. Metz, President, Hunt, Ltd.; John H. Littell, Director of Distribution, Architectural Finishes, PPG Industries, Inc.; Karen Galena, Vice President, Logistics, Hub Group, Inc.; James R. Stock, Professor, Marketing and Logistics, University of South Florida; Elaine M. Winter, Director of Communication and Research, Council of Logistics Management; Toni M. Fatigato, Project Coordinator, Council of Logistics Management. Their guidance contributed greatly to the value of the project.

Finally, we wish to thank Elizabeth LeMay, Michelle Carr, and Melanie Earles. They tolerated our obsession with the project throughout the research and writing.

Thank you all.

Stephen A. LeMay, Jon C. Carr, Jeffery A. Periatt, and Roger D. McMahon
June 23, 1999

Acknowledgments
We wish to thank the following firms for providing information for this research:

Action/Lane Industries
Alply, Inc.
American Nonwovens Corporation
Averitt Logistics
Autozone, Inc.
BancorpSouth/Bank of Mississippi
BankBoston
Bill's Dollar Stores, Inc.
Brunswick/US Marine
Cardinal Logistics Management
C. H. Robinson Company
CRST Logistics
Digital Commerce Ltd.
The Dow Chemical Company
Eastman Chemical Company
Eastman Kodak Company
Ferguson Enterprises, Inc.
Ferry Transportation, Inc.
Frito-Lay, Inc.
Garan Manufacturing Corp.
GATX Logistics, Inc.
Hallmark Cards, Inc.
Harris-Teeter, Inc.

Honda Parts Distribution
Howard Industries, Inc.
Hub Group, Inc.
Lapham-Hickey Steel
Leach Company
Lee Hardeman Associates
Lowe's Inc.
Mervyn's Inc.
Microtek Medical, Inc.
Newsprint South, Inc.
Ohio Distribution and Warehousing
Owens-Illinois Labels Inc.
PPG Industries, Inc.
Pitney Bowes Management Services
Provia Software (formerly Haushahn)
The Pfaltzgraff Company
RR Donnelley Logistics Services
Royal Trucking
Service Merchandise, Inc.
Shepherd's Industrial Training Services, Inc.

**Table of Contents**

# The Growth and Development of Logistics Personnel

*I've got to get my managers to stop managing things and start managing people.*
    *—Retailing vice-president of logistics*

*Human resources gave me a training video tape to watch. When I went out to the stocking area, my supervisor told me I didn't have time to watch it. He had me stocking small parts in an area I never really understood. I quit three weeks later.*
    *—Purchasing manager and former stocking associate*

This chapter explains the research project, "The Growth and Development of Logistics Personnel." The project was driven by the growing importance of human resource issues in logistics and by the need to understand logistics jobs, career paths, and personal development in terms of job requirements, competencies, and training needs. This chapter describes eight themes uncovered in the research, the research methods, instruments, and analytical techniques used on the project, and briefly summarizes the remainder of the book.

# Key Findings and Takeaways

**1** The structure of logistics organizations today is not the structure of the past–or the structure of tomorrow. Logistics managers must create organizations that adapt quickly to rapid change and quickly add to the organizational knowledge base.

**2** Training should develop a common view of the logistics system and its role in the firm, share or expand job knowledge, and refresh or enhance job skills. Logistics managers should leverage relationships with multiple training sources to meet the complex and diverse training needs of the logistics organization.

**3** Firms can no longer guarantee long term employment and most employees expect to change jobs and firms several times before they retire. Firms that offer employability and personal development will attract a larger, better qualified labor pool.

**4** Human resource issues will dominate logistics for the foreseeable future–especially growth and development. Developing people pays off in logistics performance, employee retention, motivation, and morale. The best logistics organizations invest significant amounts of time, effort, and money in training. Logistics managers should view training as an investment, not a cost.

**5** Operating and executive level jobs in logistics are expanding and taking on new tasks, even as technology and competitive pressure reduce the middle level of logistics organizations. Logistics managers should assure that they and their operating employees are prepared for these radical changes.

**6** Purchasing, inventory control, and customer service are diminishing as distinct functions because they are becoming part of the larger supply chain organization. Their tasks are being automated or assumed by warehousing, material control, transportation, or the executive suite. Top logistics managers must grasp strategic purchasing, inventory control, and customer service issues as these functions increase in importance but change in organizational structure.

**7** While equipment operation is the core of many logistics jobs, training needs encompass communication, human resource, and self-management skills due to the intense interaction between logisticians, their fellow employees, customers, and suppliers. When people with poor communications skills use communications technology, poor communication simply takes place more quickly over a long distance. Logistics managers must seek to train employees at all levels, including themselves, in these skills.

**8** Training for logistics jobs usually takes the form of informal on-the-job-experience (OJE)–often another way of saying trial and error. Logistics organizations cannot afford to wait for their employees to become competent–usually only partially competent at that. Logistics managers should commit to formal training systems and programs as key elements in creating organizational advantages.

### The Growth and Development of Logistics Personnel

Outsourcing, downsizing, turnover, and skill shortages characterize the employment environment now and for the foreseeable future. Employment is high and the workforce is growing at the slowest rate in U.S. history.[1] The economy offers growth opportunities that many firms cannot exploit because they lack qualified people. A manufacturer turns down a potential customer due to lack of capacity, while a retailer downsizes to improve stock prices, acknowledge market failure, or fit the workforce to current circumstances. Manufacturers and retailers outsource everything but final assembly or processing the sale, placing the burden of navigating the labor market on third parties. Every decision affects logistics jobs.

This book offers a snapshot of logistics jobs, a logistics family portrait. As with many family portraits, not everyone showed up for the picture, but the family resemblance and relationships are visible. The portrait offers traces of the family history and the family future. It shows the common themes that will affect the future–what the grandchildren may look like. More importantly, it demonstrates the effectiveness of the camera, so other pictures can be taken and compared.

The snapshot was taken with a wide-angle lens. The focus was on two questions: What do logisticians do? And how do they adapt to the future? The easy answer to this question is that logisticians move goods, manage inventory, manage change, analyze systems, buy goods, and, above all, serve customers. This answer is insufficient, as easy answers often are.

*The findings reported here are based on analysis of 632 responses to the Common Metric Questionnaire© (CMQ), 354 responses to a battery of personality and attitude scales, 35 structured interviews, and dozens of*

3

*unstructured interviews with logisticians at all levels of the organization. Logistics managers should use the results to explore, evaluate, and modify the training, growth, and development practices in their organizations.*

This chapter discusses eight themes that emerged from the results. It also summarizes the research approach and gives an overview of the remaining chapters. Technical information and data analysis supporting each chapter can be found in the appendices, which are numbered to coincide with the relevant chapters. Summaries of the technical job descriptions for each job family will be found at the back of Chapters 3-9, which discuss the traditional logistics functions. Now to the eight themes.

**Theme 1.** *The structure of logistics organizations today is not the structure of the past–or the structure of tomorrow. Logistics managers must create organizations that adapt quickly to rapid change and quickly add to the organizational knowledge base.* From the warehouse floor to the executive suite, from the driver's seat to the director's office, logisticians' jobs consist of specific tasks. The assembly of these tasks into jobs varies by industry, by firm, by level in the organization, by region, and by custom. Collectively, these tasks constitute the work of logistics.

Simple tasks wiped away by automation are replaced by complex tasks. Old tasks fall away as new tasks are added, or new tasks are added and the old tasks remain. Logisticians' jobs are a kaleidoscope of tasks tied to computers and forklifts, conveyor belts and diesel engines, keyboards and telephones—and more. The tasks change, regroup, and scatter, reflecting the rapid changes in the business environment. As the tasks regroup, the structure of the logistics organization changes, the jobs change, and the training needs change.

A competent warehouse operating employee from the 1980's could not work in a modern retail distribution center without significant retraining. The job is no longer just operating the forklift, but using computer systems, barcode scanners, and telecommunications equipment as well. The pace of change will only accelerate for core logistics workers like warehouse operating employees as they assume more tasks and greater responsibility.

Logistics managers must maintain an organizational lightness of foot never before seen, let alone expected. Job descriptions chiseled in stone and functional silos bunkered against the outside world must be relegated to the organizational history. Fluid markets and a constant stream of technological change will make the work of logistics easier and more automated, while making the logistics manager's job more complex. While information will become more readily available for decision-making, logistics managers will focus as much on incalculable human issues as on the technical and readily quantifiable.

4

Logistics performance depends on the knowledge, skills, and abilities of the people in the organization. As new people join the organization, they must become competent in their assigned tasks. As job requirements change, employees must be trained to meet the new requirements. Creating and maintaining flexible, adaptive, learning organizations demand constant training at all organizational levels.

**Theme 2.** *Training should develop a common view of the logistics system and its role in the firm, share or expand job knowledge, and refresh or enhance job skills. Logistics managers should leverage relationships with multiple training sources to meet the complex and diverse training needs of the logistics organization.*

Developing a common view of the logistics system and its role in the business does not mean forcing everyone to think in the same way. It means insuring that everyone is working with the same set of facts, looking at the same logistics network, and comprehending the nature of the business in which the firm competes. Each logistician working in a network should know the system–what gets shipped from where, to whom, by what mode of transportation, in what package, on what vehicle, and so on. Each should also understand the business, the competitive position of the firm, and role of logistics in maintaining or improving that position. When employees work together, establishing this common knowledge base improves communication and accelerates the flow of work.

The move toward transparent, enterprise-wide databases is one manifestation of an attempt to build the shared reality. If every employee can look at the same data in the same form, the level of confusion is reduced, the speed and accuracy of communication increased, and speed and accuracy of decisions improved. Among the best logistics organizations in this research, creating the common reality through information systems and training was a high priority.

When employees share a common set of facts, they understand the importance of each task. This common view of reality helps employees understand where their jobs fit in the overall scheme of work and why their tasks are important. Training may enhance job performance simply by acknowledging to the employees that the subject of the training is a critical matter.

By treating training as a pointless cost, managers attempt to save money by sending as many employees as possible to a training program–whether they need it or not. The person operating the forklift may not need the same training as the person driving a yard truck. Sending them to each other's training programs is a waste of time and serves only to annoy the employees and damage their attitudes toward training. Training in this manner is a poor investment of employee time and company money.

5

While logisticians often need to be familiar with other logistics jobs, the level of familiarity required of the person doing the job differs radically from the familiarity needed for doing related jobs. Often, training programs attempt to encompass a whole class of jobs, thus creating a program not really appropriate for anyone, wasting everyone's time. Given the nature of logistics jobs, this form of economy ill serves the organization and the field of logistics.

Many skills required in logistics jobs need frequent refreshing or enhancing. Human resource law changes as courts hand down new decisions. Supervisory techniques that were appropriate for the workforce of the 1970's may work poorly in the next millennium. Computer skills become outdated with astonishing rapidity, but few take the time to train, let alone retrain on using even the most basic software. People fall into bad habits, do things the way they have always done them, or emulate top performers whose practices are questionable. Many times these slips into unfortunate work behaviors come from ignorance–a simple lack of training.

The most effective approaches to establishing training programs and training systems use multiple sources to meet complex organizational training needs. Training sources for logistics include universities, community colleges, training firms, consultants, professional associations, and other firms. Logistics managers should work to build relationships with potential training sources to foster the growth and development of their employees.

**Theme 3.** *Firms can no longer offer long term employment and most employees expect to change jobs and firms several times before they retire. Firms that offer employability and personal development will attract a larger, better qualified labor pool.*

Even outstanding logistics organizations downsize. An organization's logistics may be excellent, but lost market share may reduce volume to the point that the firm needs fewer logisticians. Employees change jobs more frequently than in the past. They are mobile and prefer mobile benefit programs. Firms also outsource more logistics activity, reducing the need for logistics employees.

The difficulty in keeping employees or finding new employees is complicated by the changing nature of logistics work. Where once a career ladder kept an employee moving up the organization without ever leaving the functional silo, the career path for many logisticians now winds through several functions and many organizations.

Employees recognize the need to grow, just as they acknowledge that employment is probably not for life. They seek new knowledge and new skills to remain employable. Training is not necessarily driven by managers, but by employees' desire to do a better job and to better themselves. At one firm in the research, warehouse operators frequently asked management for training

6

programs to make them promotable, to improve job performance, and to make themselves more effective.

Training that enhances skills may improve job performance for the current employer. That is the intent of the training. The same training also makes the employee more attractive to other potential employers, but that will almost always be the case. Real advantages in the labor market may come from training that makes the person a better employee, whether by adding skills or making the employee a better person.

Management consultant Peter Drucker was reportedly asked what he would do to make himself a better manager. After a pause, he replied, "Learn to play the violin. . .By learning to play the violin, I become a better person. If you want to be a better manager, become a better person."

---

"We like for the employees to take courses that help them at home as much as at work. Look at it this way—if the employee has trouble at home, that trouble comes to work with him. If he manages stress better at home, he probably also manages it better at work and he doesn't bring problems from home to work with him either. If he takes a Dale Carnegie course and learns to communicate better with his wife, the company benefits from that in a lot of ways. Some people may think we do a lot of training, but it pays off."

–Manufacturing Director of Logistics

---

Growth and development are personal. Forklift drivers and warehouse planners do not grow and develop. Mike and Sally and Keanu and Latisha and Jose and Juanita grow and develop. Organizations cannot always offer them long term employment, but they can offer them personal growth and employability.

---

"We get kids right out of college. We pay well and we train students well, but it is still difficult to keep them. We're a transaction-based organization, so we have to have people who will be there, physically there. Once the new employee becomes truly productive, he or she gets hired away by some firm with less of an apparent lull in promotion. They also aren't learning anything new. They're just turning the crank on the transactions."

–3PL Vice President

---

When the training–the growth and development–are not offered, employees may leave at a tremendous cost to the firm. Turnover costs can be high, especially when the employees just reached competence. Still, logistics managers must invest in training employees, even at the risk of losing the investment.

First, employees need training to do their jobs well. Neglecting their training is counter-productive. Second, one way to improve the labor pool is to train the people in it, even if they may go to someone else. If every employer hopes to poach trained workers from another firm, no one ever trains the worker. Finally, training is an attraction, a way of bringing in better employees and increasing the chance of keeping them. The best training systems found in this research were in firms with long-term, stable workforces and very low voluntary turnover. The firm described in the best practices box is an example.

---

## BEST PRACTICES
### Training at MegaProducts

The rules for access to training programs at MegaProducts are simple—anyone who wants to attend a training program offered at MegaProducts can go. Work time may be released for job-related training and many programs are offered at times convenient to the majority of employees.

The director of logistics offered a training program on basic logistics management. The program lasted several weeks, covering the subject matter of an introductory college logistics course—with a twist—these employees could look at hands-on, directly applicable examples. Attendees included a manager newly transferred to logistics from marketing, a long time operating employee from the warehouse, and a middle manager just promoted from one functional area and now responsible for several. The text for the training was customized from a major textbook publisher. The company covered the cost for all participants.

Training was even taken beyond the walls of the organization—to suppliers and customers. Some middle managers were certified as trainers in root cause failure analysis (RCFA). They offered the course to their own employees and to customers, but they required their transportation suppliers to take the course. MegaProducts covers the expenses, but trains all its carriers worldwide in RCFA.

There were other required training courses—especially for those taking over a new job. Supervisors went through several training courses prior to promotion and consistently took new programs to maintain their skills. Some years, managers at MegaProducts spend one working day in ten in training programs.

Personal development programs were encouraged—stress management, time management, and communications skills for example. The director of logistics favors training that develops people and that affects their behavior at home and at work.

The MegaProducts approach may sound costly—but it is even more valuable. Consider these numbers. On-time delivery is over 98% worldwide for all non-rail transportation. Voluntary turnover at the operating, supervisory, and managerial levels is non-existent. Can it be claimed that these results come solely from training? Probably not, at least not in a scientific or academic sense. However, the training adds value to already valuable and valued employees. The top managers in this organization consider the training worth the investment--in the warehouse, throughout the organization, and beyond.

**Theme 4.** *Human resource issues will dominate logistics for the foreseeable future–especially growth and development. Developing people pays off in logistics performance, employee retention, motivation, and morale. The best logistics organizations invest enormous amounts of time, effort, and money, in training. Logistics managers should view training as an investment, not a cost, and inform themselves on human resource practices and human resource law.* One good example encountered in the research is described in the best practices box above. This firm employs enterprise databases and software, focuses on data integrity, and offers formal training to its employees constantly. Voluntary training programs may require an employee to use his or her own time to take the training, but it is available. Since employees increasingly recognize the importance of employability to their careers, those firms that continue to develop their people will also tend to keep them. The firm described in the box has almost no voluntary turnover and a waiting list of job applicants. It is widely regarded as the best employer in its region.

When the top logistics manager delivers his or her course in logistics, they deliver a message to every employee: this is important.

Notice, that other managers are heavily involved in training, not only within the organization, but throughout the supply chain. While it might be a pleasant thought, this multi-billion dollar organization does not spend that kind of money on training and development out of kindness. The firm spends that money because of its return on investment.

In many areas, high employment, deficient school systems, and a poor job image leave apparently good logistics jobs begging to be filled. Skilled employees leave for new employers almost at will. The desperation born of high turnover means recruitment pushes out training, so the firm's knowledge capital declines. The firm operates a revolving door; efficiency and

9

effectiveness fall, and the weight of doing even more work falls to the employees who remain.

The recruiting and retention problems afflicting the truckload motor carrier industry since deregulation now afflict other logistics functions. Retention may not be a problem for some outstanding firms, but even they have difficulty finding operating employees, supervisors, and new managers to fill new jobs based on revenue growth.

Employees can no longer be viewed as replaceable parts. When unemployment rises and employees become easier to find, this will still be true. U. S. workers carry high expectations about what they will receive from their jobs, and because of the U.S.'s relative prosperity, they can afford to remain unemployed rather than take jobs that do not meet their expectations about how they are treated, how they are paid, or what they can learn.

Training programs are recruiting and retention tools. A firm may keep well-trained, highly productive employees because they stay current in their technical skills and are made to feel important because they frequently receive training. That seems better than keeping only the employees who have no opportunity to go elsewhere because they lack skills.

Firms may have to offer training in basic skills like reading and mathematics alongside highly technical skills like statistical process control or linear programming. The range of training requirements throughout the logistics organization may be great, but it is up to the logistics manager to understand these requirements and see that they are met. Chapter 10 discusses a firm that trained poorly educated workers to become successful managers, an investment in remedial training that paid handsomely.

The logistics manager must also stay abreast of human resource practices and human resource law. The law changes as courts hand down decisions and legislative bodies pass new laws. Maintaining a gender neutral, non-discriminatory workplace is essential, if not for moral reasons, then for legal reasons. In an increasingly litigious society, it is the manager's responsibility to protect the firm from lawsuits or put the firm in the best possible position to defend itself when lawsuits come. The understanding of the law and human resource practice cannot be left exclusively to the human resource department.

**Theme 5.** *Operating and executive level jobs in logistics are expanding, taking on new tasks, even as technology and competitive pressure reduce the middle level of logistics organizations. Logistics managers should assure that they and their operating employees are prepared for these radical changes.*

Career ladders housed in functional silos have mostly disappeared in logistics. Information technology allows operating employees to manage inventory while driving a material handler, and truck drivers now get their next load from a web site instead of a dispatcher. Top managers generate their own

10

analysis from shared databases rather than wait for subordinates to perform a study and develop a report.

The shift to supply chain thinking means that the top manager negotiates the deal with a top manager from another firm, often cutting out both the sales representative and purchasing manager from the process. The transactions related to the negotiated arrangement now flow through the computer system rather than across a purchasing professional's desk. In short, there is room at the top and at the bottom, but the middle is crowded and subject to thinning out.

Many outstanding logistics organizations have already gone through significant downsizing, restructuring, and reengineering. One reason explains why: it works. Costs fall and performance improves. If reengineering advocates point to success stories, the stories often involve logistics. One music company increased on time delivery percentage during peak sales of CD's from 90% to 99% while eliminating 60% of its logistics employees. One analysis, otherwise highly critical of reengineering as practiced by most firms, cited logistics and order fulfillment as the areas where it worked consistently [2]

One view of truck drivers of the future has them working out of the cab with computers and satellite communications that link them to a source of loads and a transaction management system to handle payments and receivables. They will work directly with shippers to schedule pickups and deliveries, and use their firm to handle claims, insurance coverage, and payroll issues. They may also take advantage of discounts for medical insurance, retirement funds, and other benefits. In this scenario, the need for dispatchers diminishes, as does the need for other managerial functions. The work is all in the truck cab. While this may seem a little farfetched, some trucking companies already approach this arrangement. Regardless, there is little room in the future of logistics organizations for employees who do not handle goods or coordinate directly with suppliers and customers.

Top logistics managers must expect to assume new duties and to see new tasks performed at the operating level. That means training for the top managers and the operating employees. The organization cannot afford to wait very long for either group to become competent in a new task or achieve a new skill level. The needs are immediate and crucial to the performance of the system.

**Theme 6.** *Purchasing, inventory control, and customer service are diminishing as distinct functions. Their tasks are being automated or assumed by warehousing, material control, transportation, or the executive suite. Top logistics managers must grasp strategic purchasing, inventory control, and customer service issues as these functions increase in importance, but change in organizational structure.*

Logistics functions are merging under the heat of economic pressure fueled by the possibilities of logistics information systems (LIS). Purchasing once managed inbound inventory; in some organizations, that task now takes place through the Internet or electronic data interchange (EDI) with bar codes put on during the manufacturing process. Purchasing managers once negotiated with sales representatives; now the negotiations take place between vice presidents and above who deal in multi-year contracts, not transactions. Inventory control, inbound, outbound, and work in process, takes place through automated systems. Warehouse, material control, and production employees with scanners maintain inventory counts and initiate orders. Using e-mail and the web has allowed many in the research to reduce the number of customer service call centers and initiate plans to eliminate them entirely.

The remaining organizations in these functions also tend to be flat, reflecting Theme 5 as well as this theme. Human resource thinking must now focus on career paths, not career ladders, because someone moved the ladder.

"We used to have a career ladder in customer service. Now it's a flat organization with practically no middle level. I'm not sure where these people will go if they're going to go up."
–Manufacturing Director of Distribution

This does not mean that purchasing, customer service, or inventory control have vanished as corporate needs. Purchasing has become strategic rather than transactional. The transactions take place automatically through computer systems, but choosing partners and joining alliances is a strategic activity that involves a high level of purchasing expertise. Customer service has become ubiquitous. Customer service departments, like call centers, have become more automated, using the web and e-mail as much as or more than the telephone, so fewer people work in that function. Still, customer expectations about service are rising, so more and more employees become part of the customer service function. In a third party logistics firm, every employee could have customer service as part of his or her job description. Inventory control has also been dispersed throughout the organization. The annual or semi-annual inventory count has been replaced by cycle counting and bar coding. The inventory clerk and the forklift driver have become the same person.

These changes in organizational structure mean that logistics managers have a greater burden to understand these functions. They cannot assume that someone in another department will take care of customer service issues or handle supplier problems. It becomes their job.

**Theme 7.** *While equipment operation is the core of many logistics jobs, training needs encompass communication, human resource, and self-*

*management skills due to the intense interaction between logisticians, their fellow employees, customers, and suppliers. When people with poor communications skills use communications technology, poor communication simply takes place more quickly over a long distance. Logistics managers must seek to train employees at all levels, including themselves, in these skills.*

Logisticians operate a variety of equipment from cell phones to over-the-road trucks, from tape measures to notebook computers. Still, their job performance depends as much on how well they work together to get goods moved through the system as on how well they operate the equipment. Interaction with fellow employees, suppliers, and customers is as central to warehouse operations as driving a forklift–more central for many warehousing jobs.

The logistics system consists of computer networks, distribution centers, truck terminals, call centers, and buying centers–all run by people. The human system is the most important part of any logistics system, and it operates on communication. A person feeds data into a computer system so that it will be accessible to another person who may use it to make a decision. People can make imperfect logistics systems accomplish their purpose, but perfect technical systems are worthless without people. The most important aspect of improving the performance of logistics systems is developing the people who manage and operate the system.

Put another way, a perfectly functioning e-mail system will quickly and accurately deliver a poorly written memo that confuses the majority of recipients, while a clear, simple note on lined paper will get the message across. If the only message the dispatcher ever sends to truck drivers on the satellite communications system is 'Call dispatch,' little is gained from the technology. The logistics system will run better if logisticians supervise, communicate, recruit, negotiate, and run meetings better. It is on such interactions, as much as on the heavy truck or the railcar, that the logistics system runs.

Technology works only if people treat it as what it is–a tool. What applies to computers applies to communications technology or the weekly staff meeting–garbage in, garbage out. The better the communications and interpersonal skills of the people who use the technology and work in the highly interactive logistics environment, the better the performance of the logistics system.

Logistics managers must see that these skills rise in their organizations. The long term success of every logistics organization ultimately depends on it.

**Theme 8.** *Training for logistics jobs usually takes the form of informal on-the-job-experience (OJE)–often another way of saying trial and error.*

13

*Logistics organizations cannot afford to wait for their employees to become competent–usually only partially competent at that–through informal training. Logistics managers should commit to formal training systems and programs as key elements in creating organizational advantages.*

Experience-based training is invaluable when it is properly conducted, but too often it is left to employees who already have full-time jobs that do not include training as a duty. Most training needs in most organizations are met with OJE programs. This works well if the trainers know how to train; the training results are measured; or if the firm can wait for the employees to become marginally competent.

---

"I used to do all the training in our office. If I thought something was nonsense, I didn't teach it. I told the trainees it wasn't important and moved to the next thing I thought was important. I even trained the secretary who came on the job the day after I did. When I look back on it, I don't think I'd make the same choices now that I did then."

–Former Manufacturing Purchasing Manager

---

Time-to-competence is a crucial issue for logistics jobs now and in the future. With high turnover, outsourcing, downsizing, and skill shortages, firms need to bring employees up to speed in short order. When employees typically stay with a firm for six months, the firm cannot afford to wait a year for the employee to become worth his or her paycheck. Yet informal, unstructured training leads to exactly that–it takes longer for employees to become competent than they are likely to stay in the job.

Worse, informal training programs often lead to the perpetuation of unsafe or unproductive work practices. If forty employees work in a job, a small number of them will be regarded as the best operators. Others will learn from them, imitating their techniques and following their practices. Unfortunately, these workplace leaders often get it wrong, usually because they learned the job from predecessors who did the job the same way.

---

"When we go into a company, we watch everyone who operates a piece of equipment work for a while. We often find that the lead operators, the guys that other employees will tell you are the best, do things that are unsafe, inefficient, ineffective, or all three. Usually, they weren't trained well in the first place. Because they see themselves as knowing their jobs better than anyone, we have our hands full getting them to change."

–Training Organization President

---

Formal training programs offer a significant contrast to the informal, unstructured training programs. They recognize the importance of the jobs included in the training, underscore the critical nature of the information they convey, and bring employees much more quickly to competence than informal programs. Effective formal training depends on following simple principles. First, the training should be appropriate for those attending the program. It should inform employees on how to do their jobs better, how to get promoted, or how to improve their performance. It should not teach them to do a job they will never do or give them information they can never use. Second, results should be measured. Many industrial training programs use far more exacting standards than do college courses. One trainer measured six areas related to equipment operation for manufacturing employees, requiring that the trainees earn at least a 90 percent score in all six areas to pass the course. Five 99s and one 89 meant failure. These are tough standards that emphasize to those taking the certification that the material is important.

Building a series of relationships and developing training skills to meet training needs rapidly will place additional demands on logistics managers These demands must be met to maintain or develop successful logistics organizations.

## Themes Summary

Collectively, these themes mean that logistics organizations cannot take the growth and development of logistics personnel lightly. Training should be more formal and systematic to bring employees to competence quickly in a field where tasks are changing, jobs are changing, and the available workforce is changing. Adaptation is the watchword when the only certainty is uncertainty. Logistics managers must assume responsibility for developing training relationships and working with human resource professionals to build the human side of logistics systems.

## Overview of the Research

The principal exploration of organizational and individual growth and development needs took place in forty-three outstanding logistics organizations. These organizations included manufacturers, asset-based third parties, non-asset-based third parties, retailers, and financial institutions. They ranged in size from 15 to more than 100,000 employees. Each organization was recommended for the research based on outstanding performance in overall logistics or in one or more logistics functions. The principal participating organizations are listed at the front of the book.

The results of the research are based on the analysis of data from 632 responses to the CMQ, a 3,000+ item job classification survey, and 354 responses to scales that measure personality, customer orientation, market orientation, and need for cognition. Formal phenomenological interviews were conducted with 35 top logistics managers and informal interviews were conducted with a broad range of logisticians. These instruments and their administration are discussed briefly below. Appendix 1 explains how to interpret the tables in Appendices 2-9.

### Research Instruments–Description and Administration

The research used five survey questionnaires, formal interviews, and informal interviews to gather data. With a few minor exceptions, the surveys were administered in person, either one-on-one or in groups. The exceptions, fewer than ten, were administered by mail. The interviews were all conducted in person during site visits.

*Common Metric Questionnaire©*. The participants will testify to the difficulty of completing this instrument.  Like all job classification questionnaires, it is detailed and tedious. Responses to the CMQ reveal the knowledge and skills absolutely critical to job performance, how often they are used, and how they were obtained.  The responses also show the basic activities associated with a job, whether it is attending meetings, lifting heavy objects, or interacting with people inside and outside the firm.  Analysis classifies these specific results into 80 dimensions and four domains.  The domains are interpersonal, decision-making, mechanical/physical, and work context. This detailed questionnaire helps determine competencies, job requirements, and training needs for each job family in the analysis.(For more about the CMQ, please see Appendix 1.) The 80 dimensions can also be further reduced to 17 second order factors (See Appendices 1 and 2).

*The NEO-Five Factor Inventory (NEO-FFI)*.  The NEO-FFI is a personality scale consisting of 60 items that measure five  personality factors: neuroticism, extroversion, openness, agreeableness, and conscientiousness. Results from this instrument may help in fitting people to jobs or in building compatible teams.

*Customer Orientation*. Customer orientation means adopting the customer's perspective.  The high scores suggest that the respondent approaches his or her job with the idea of satisfying the customers or clients and building long term relationships with them.

*Market Orientation*. Where customer orientation measures individual orientation toward customers, this scale measures the respondent's perception of the organization's market orientation.  Market orientation includes the generation of intelligence on customers' current and future needs, the dissemination of this intelligence throughout the organization, and the organization's responsiveness to the intelligence.[3]

*Phenomenological Interviews*. These interviews were conducted with top logistics managers.  They were asked to describe what it is like to do their jobs, to give examples of meaningful experiences, and to describe their work. Many of the interviews were tape recorded and transcribed.  The transcripts

16

were analyzed to identify phenomena common to the experience of the interview subjects.

*Informal Interviews.* In visiting distribution centers, corporate headquarters, manufacturing plants, call centers, and terminals, the researchers spoke to a variety of logisticians at all levels. These conversations added greatly to the understanding and interpretation of the research data.

*Site Visits.* The researchers visited distribution centers handling everything from groceries to bulk chemicals, medical supplies to auto parts; manufacturing firms with cross organizational Kanban systems and union welders with self-managed inventories; third parties juggling special projects involving tens of thousands of retail outlets; retailers turning $100 million in inventory 20 times annually through one distribution center; and firms delivering service in three hours against an industry standard of three days. The researchers visited more than 75 plants, headquarters, distribution centers, call centers, and terminals to administer questionnaires and conduct interviews.

## Overview of the Book

The remainder of the book consists of nine chapters and ten appendices. The appendices are numbered to coincide with the chapters they support. For example, additional information on topics in Chapter 1 is found in Appendix 1 and so on.

Chapter 1 explains the research and outlines eight themes on logistics growth and development that emerged from the analysis. Appendix 1 gives details on the research methods used in this project.

Chapter 2, Growth, Development, and the Changing Nature of Logistics Jobs, reports the results of an additional survey of 192 firms on training and human resource practices in logistics. It also puts the results of the research in the context of the human resource environment and explains how the process used in this research may be used in an organization. Appendix 2 reports summary results from the analysis of CMQ data, which provides a foundation for much of the discussion in the chapter.

Chapters 3-9 deal with the research results for specific logistics functions. The corresponding appendices contain tables of scores on the significant job dimensions for each of the 22 job families discussed in the chapters. The explanation of the scores is found in the section of Appendix 1 that discusses the CMQ.

Chapter 3, Broad Responsibility Senior Managers, discusses this one job family. It reports on the results of the phenomenological interviews and the surveys. It describes the need for broadly-based knowledge and skills training for top logistics managers and points out that too much of their training is OJE, especially in areas where they frequently make decisions.

17

Chapter 4, Logistics Information Systems(LIS), discusses two job families: LIS technicians and LIS managers. It outlines competencies and job requirements; it covers survey results, quotes from informal interviews, and places the LIS function in the context of the future of logistics organizations. It also shows the training needed to move from LIS technician to LIS manager–largely interpersonal skills development.

Chapter 5, Warehousing, describes six job families: warehouse operating employees, warehouse clerks, warehouse supervisors, warehouse administrative support, warehouse planning support, and warehouse managers. This chapter discusses interactions, competencies, job requirements, and training needs for each job family. It also discusses the degree to which these jobs are assuming more tasks and greater responsibility in the shifting world of logistics organizations.

Chapter 6, Transportation, discusses four job families: loaders, motor carrier operating employees, transportation support, and traffic managers. Unlike in other functions, the four job families are not closely tied to one another. Motor carrier operating employees are assuming more and more duties, to the point that job analysis produced few differences between the truck driver's job and the dispatcher's job. Loaders are classified in this function based on their need for highly specific knowledge of transportation modes; otherwise, they might have been included in warehousing. Transportation support also requires highly specific knowledge of transportation processes. Traffic managers perform primarily operational tasks, playing a critical role in tactical decision-making for logistics organizations.

Chapter 7, Material and Inventory Control, discusses four job families: inventory specialists, production managers, inventory and material managers, and supply chain managers. These job families often overlap with production jobs and reflect the movement of logistics tasks to the operating level. Many tasks once associated with purchasing are now found on the manufacturing floor.

Chapter 8, Purchasing, discusses two job families: buyers/purchasing agents and purchasing managers. These job families reflect the traditional purchasing function, but the chapter puts them in the context of the changing logistics environment. The number of people working in these job families has declined and will continue to decline in the foreseeable future as firms move toward supply chain management and tasks shift to the warehouse, manufacturing plant, and the executive suite.

Chapter 9, Customer Service, discusses three job families: customer service representatives, customer service supervisors, and customer service managers. As with purchasing, this function is flattening and many of the tasks once associated with it are being automated or are shifting to other logistics functions.

Chapter 10, Training Systems and Sources, outlines a detailed approach to identifying the right source of training to meet the training needs identified in Chapters 3-9. The chapter walks the reader through the process of picking the right training program, the right content, and the right means to access training. Appendix 10 shows sample training modules and how to develop a training program, and lists some sources of sources for training. The sample training modules cover developing a training plan, kanban, shipping and overall logistics.

## Final Comments

This project measured knowledge requirements and activities in a broad spectrum of logistics jobs. It also examined the logisticians themselves, their personalities and their perceptions. It outlined training needs for the job families found in the analysis. It did not cover every logistics job, but included a cross section from every organizational level and from a variety of organizations. Armed with these results, methods for applying them, and the ability to create new, internal analyses, logistics managers will be better equipped to deal with some of the most difficult problems they face—developing themselves and the people who work for them.

No corporate secrets are revealed here. No magic swords are pulled from stones. Rather, this book demonstrates a process, messy and difficult at times, for identifying competencies, job requirements, and training needs. The results will affect recruitment, selection, turnover, training, growth, and development of logistics personnel.

1. Bureau of Labor Statistics, www.stats.bls.gov/datahome.htm, consulted May 1, 1999.

2. John Micklethwait & Adrian Woolridge, The Witch Doctors: *Making Sense of the Management Gurus,* (New York: Random House, 1997), p. 133.

3. Ajay K. Kohli & Bernard J. Jaworski. (1990). *Market Orientation: The Construct, Research Propositions, and Managerial Implications.* Journal of Marketing, 54, 1-18.

# Growth, Development, and the Nature of Logistics Jobs

*Our choicest plans have fallen through,*
*Our airiest castles tumbled over,*
*Because of the lines we neatly drew,*
*And later neatly stumbled over.*
*–Piet Hein, Grooks*

*This chapter discusses the human resource environment for logistics organizations, describes key human resource practices in 192 logistics organizations, justifies the need for more formal training in logistics, explains the overall training needs for logistics organizations, and interprets the summary results of the CMQ in terms of the transformation of logistics organizations and jobs. CMQ summary data for the 22 job families can be found in Appendix 2.*

---

## Key Findings and Takeaways

**1** The human resource environment for logistics has changed, partly because of the recent economic boom, but more because of fundamental economic and cultural forces that act on all functions and all jobs, not just logistics.

---

**2** Logistics functions are consolidating, bringing tasks into the core functions of transportation, warehousing, and material control. This process is facilitated by Logistics Information Systems (LIS) and motivated by cost reduction and potential increases in customer service.

**3** Logistics managers will need knowledge-based technical competence, cross-functional experience, collaborative interpersonal skills, and self-management skills to manage logistics organizations in the future. Operating employees will require many skills currently associated with management as organizations eliminate organizational levels and assign more interpersonal tasks to the warehouse floor, the production line, and the vehicle.

**4** Logistics organizations use limited sources of training and sometimes neglect formal training to the detriment of the organizations and the people who work in them.

**5** Logisticians need structured, formal training because of the shortage of fully prepared workers and the relative failure of unstructured, informal training. Formal training shortens the time it takes an employee to become competent in a task. The more complex the job, the more tasks involved, the greater the value of formal training.

### Growth, Development, and the Nature of Logistics Jobs

Major organizational change initiatives affect logistics jobs and careers. Usually undertaken to control costs, risk, service quality, or output, change initiatives like downsizing, delayering, cost reduction, and LIS implementation sometimes have undesirable effects on jobs, careers, and the people who hold them. Increased stress, anxiety, distrust, and sense of disempowerment combine with decreased self-efficacy and self-esteem to produce negative work behaviors ranging from absenteeism to a focus on organizational politics over job performance.[1]

Jobs have never been stable over time. As technology, markets, cultures, and economies change, so does the nature of work, in general and in logistics. The driving force behind the current transformation in logistics jobs appears to be information technology (IT), but bear in mind that IT influences behavior in the context of market globalization, organizational change, and changes in workforce culture. IT and other technologies offer new and more sophisticated tools to do the work of logistics, but people must still be prepared to use these tools.

21

The logistics system, regardless of its technological development, performs within the limits of the knowledge, skills, and abilities of the people who manage and operate the system. If jobs change rapidly in the face of rapid technological change, then people must adapt rapidly to new jobs and new tasks. In short, they must quickly grow and develop.

Training is a central element in the growth and development of logistics personnel. Well-trained employees perform near miracles in productivity, responsiveness to customers, and creativity. Poorly trained employees fail to perform, develop, or stay with the firm. Despite its centrality to improved performance, firms neglect training partly because of short-term time pressures to get work out today, and partly because of the assumption that more employees can be found if current employees leave or cannot perform up to standards. In effect, training is too much trouble and the firm can always get someone else to do the job.

This chapter describes the current human resource environment, summarizes the results of a survey of logistics organizations' human resource practices, justifies formal training on the basis of human behavior and costs, and places the overall CMQ results in the context of training needs for the logistics job families.

*The human resource environment for logistics has changed, partly because of the recent economic boom, but more because of fundamental economic and cultural forces that act on all functions and all jobs, not just logistics.*

Key elements in the human resource environment include: organizational structure; jobs, careers, and career systems; the nature of the workforce; and legal issues. Changes in organizational structure are apparent in logistics organizations and in the results of this research. These changes directly affect jobs, careers, and career systems at all organizational levels. Changes in the nature of the workforce affect how organizations approach the job market and alter the implied contract between workers and organizations. Finally, no discussion of the human resource environment is complete without a discussion of legal issues which range from the definition of an employee to sexual harassment and the creation of gender neutral work environments.

## Organizational Structure

Rapid change, rapid change, rapid change–these words have become a mantra for discussing organizations of the future. Theory says organizations will move from traditional hierarchical structures to network organizations to cellular organizations that hardly fit any definition of an organization.[2] Where the traditional logistics organizations consisted of functional silos like purchasing, customer service, warehousing, and traffic, each containing a defined career ladder, the cellular organization may consist of a truck driver linked to a web site and connected to customers by cellular telephones or other telecommunications equipment. Many times the functional silos offered the security that goes with a visible, well-defined career ladder and protection from the political battles of the organization's upper levels. Like missile silos, they were well bunkered against intrusion. Network and cellular organizations do not offer protection from political battles or environmental shifts.

Drawing organizational lines is hazardous under these conditions. The functional silos no longer offer security and the career ladders inside the silos have become step-ladders at best. The bunkers are gone and the walls have mostly collapsed. While network organizations may be largely theoretical and exist in only a few industries, this was also true of the traditional hierarchical organization. Few firms will exactly match the academic notions of the future organization, just as few match the theoretical, traditional form.

One researcher described the new organization this way:

In the new paradigm, the organization is portrayed as a network of connected goals and structures, with a lean central core servicing various units, alliances, and outsourced functions. Managers' roles are those of portfolio specialists, whose value consists in their mastery and experience of the diverse elements essential to the business. . . The new contract is that managers will adapt to the changing needs of the company. The company undertakes to add value to employees by helping them acquire portable and marketable skills–employability. Employability replaces security. Self-determination is the underlying principle governing the organization, and in this spirit, individuals manage their own careers. Flattened hierarchies mean that developmental mobility is lateral rather than vertical. The risks attendant upon this vision are stress caused by the inherent ambiguity of the changing organization, conflict from competing objectives, and overload from unscheduled demands. Anarchy and inefficiency are threats, if individuals really act empowered and determine their own destinies.[3]

Some organizations will embrace the new, network structure while others will cling to their traditional approaches, quite likely with equal success.

What is clear about organizational structures, regardless of the label applied to them, is that they will be flatter than in the past. Sometimes referred to as delayering, the flattening of logistics organizations is most visible in customer service, purchasing, and inventory management. It shows to a lesser degree in transportation and LIS. Delayering increases the managerial span of control and should be accompanied by increased subordinate self-management.

Unfortunately, many subordinates are unwilling, unprepared, or ill-equipped to take on these new duties, and many managers hedge against the broad reclassification of jobs by maintaining old reporting lines to keep managerial control.[4] Empowerment becomes fiction in these circumstances, especially in the absence of preparatory training and development programs.

The dramatic impact of IT on the nature of work cannot be overestimated. IT enables workers to take on tasks that once involved countless others. Simple matters have been automated and communication on complex matters simplified. Employees at the lowest level of the traditional organizational chart have access to databases that also influence the CEO's strategic decision process. Giving broad authority to the person who looks the customer in the eye, talks to the customer on the phone, or handles and delivers the goods, makes good business sense. In logistics, a truck driver can call a customer to reschedule a delivery or a pick up, rather than call the dispatcher, who then calls customer service, who then calls the customer. The home office should be informed, but the driver is often in the best position to solve a problem. If goods are damaged, the receiving clerk or the yard worker who unloads the goods is likely to know it first. He or she can send an effective message to the supplier about replacement shipments and damage claims as readily as a manager. They have the information at hand and the technology to send the message.

Getting to the point of giving broad authority to operating employees is problematic, however. Just because something can be done, does not mean it will be done, even if it is a good idea. Giving employees more authority is hardly a new notion. Like some other intriguing notions, it is rare in practice, not because it has been tried and found wanting, but because it has been found difficult and not tried. What pushes logistics organizations toward this flatter structure is economic necessity–cost reduction and improved customer service. In an environment where transactions take place in nanoseconds, customers want quick responses to queries and to orders.

---

"We had a six-week order cycle for nearly twenty years. Now our customers want it reduced, but not by a few days. They want ten days, which we are not sure we can pull off. We cut out a week by reducing our production cycle from two weeks to one week, but we're still working on how to consolidate loads out of the distribution centers, how to process the orders and set up the production schedules faster, and how to shorten the transit time for each load. We want to meet our customers' requests. We know we have to, but we're trying to do this in a way that we can all afford."

–Manufacturing Vice President of Transportation

---

At times, operating level workers could solve this kind of problem but lack the opportunity. What must be eliminated is the wait for approval, along with unnecessary steps in logistics processes. These are often what motivates delayering–the flattening of the logistics organization. With delayering, as with other major organizational changes, the effects on jobs, careers, and career systems are often ignored until damage has been done. The next section discusses these changes, along with their impact on logistics jobs and careers.

## Jobs, Careers, and Career Systems

Logistics managers should anticipate a broader span of control and more self-management by operating employees and resign themselves to accepting the change. Skills once reserved to managers are becoming key elements of supervisory, staff, and operating jobs. Logistics operating jobs are no longer just physical but knowledge-based, a point widely acknowledged and confirmed in this research.[5] Organizations must recognize that all employees need self-expression and development in their jobs, not just managers. The effects that flatter organizations, unfulfilling jobs, and downsizing have on blue collar workers have long been known: absenteeism, turnover, restriction of output, and union activities. Combating these effects has become a task for logistics and human resource managers.[6]

The frustration experienced by managers and white-collar workers in the downsizing and reengineering of the 1980s and 1990s mirrors what blue-collar operating employees have experienced for decades. Organizations demand loyalty, but seldom give it, seeming to focus more on short term stock prices than on long-term delivery of goods and services by loyal, well-trained employees and managers. Organizations now offer employability, not secure employment. This implied contractual change profoundly affects jobs, career paths, and career systems.

Five types of career systems appear in logistics organizations: efficient, neglected, restricted, mechanistic, and political.[7] Efficient systems allocate employees to positions according to their abilities. The goal of the career system is to maintain the efficiency of the internal labor market. This meritocracy has one major shortcoming; few organizations meet the preconditions for efficient, human capital systems. They require complex, well-understood role demands, knowledge of relevant skills sets, overriding collective goals, and high visibility of job-related attributes, fit, and performance. They can lead to individualism, short-term focus, and risk aversion; they also incur high transaction and maintenance costs, which may make them cost prohibitive in many organizations. In neglected career systems, organizations let the internal labor market take care of itself. They make no serious attempt to manage it, leaving the vacancy chain to draw the next person from the vertical pecking order into the next available position. Such systems induce superstitions about what it takes to gain promotion, when in actuality, individuals' actions have no affect on the system.

In restricted career systems, promotions are driven by criteria over which the employee has no control. Working in a function, purchasing for example, may promote or end a career in these systems. Evidence of restricted career systems in operation includes the problems experienced by women, minorities, and older workers. Mechanistic or ladder systems base advancement on length of service, which is highly correlated with age. Such systems are intended to be developmental, recognizing skills accumulated over time. Political systems use tournaments to assign promotions. Employees joust for a position, often unaware that they are involved in a competition. Losers are often disqualified from future competitions in this game of ambiguous rules and uncertain outcomes.

Because logistics organizations are in transition, old and new career systems co-exist, often side-by-side in the same organization. Logistics career systems tend to be political, restricted, or neglected. Many organizations continue to rely on their traditional system, whatever it is, because the value of moving toward efficient systems is not clear and the preconditions are difficult to meet. Considerable evidence says the traditionalists may be right. The new systems are not demonstrably better than the old.[8]

One difficulty with all the career systems is the effect of the flattened organization. When obvious career ladders disappear, career paths become horizontal rather than vertical. True promotions, movements up the organizational ladder, become increasingly rare. There simply are very few positions to move into. When delayering takes place, employees are thrown off their career ladders and are likely to suffer from severe self-doubt. They thought they were going someplace, but now there is no place to go.

Horizontal career paths also become self-managed and usually extend outside the current organization. Managerial careers require a knowledge-based specialty, cross-functional experience, collaborative leadership, self-management skills, flexibility, and integrity.[9] Since the value of knowledge bases tends to erode with time, the successful career manager will move to increase learning and growth opportunities. One LIS technician, a former student in logistics at Mississippi State, began his career in a distribution center, became product supply manager, and now develops software applications for logistics–all in the same organization in just over seven years. His chances of becoming LIS manager are good because of his knowledge of LIS, experience in the distribution network of the organization, and demonstrated interpersonal skills. However, his promotion still depends on the career system in the large manufacturing firm that employs him. The good news is the breadth of his experience probably makes him employable in almost any logistics organization.

If mid-level jobs have disappeared from the flattened logistics organization, the remaining managers, supervisors, and operating employees have assumed their tasks. Two of the key findings bear discussion in the context of the human resource environment and jobs.

*Logistic functions are consolidating, bringing tasks into the core functions of transportation, warehousing, and material control. This process is facilitated by LIS and motivated by cost reduction and potential increases in customer service.*

Regardless of the labels placed on the jobs, the tasks associated with logistics are being performed by fewer people in flatter and narrower organizations. Tasks traditionally associated with inventory control, purchasing, and customer service are being performed by warehousing, material control, transportation, and executive functions, as well as by customers and suppliers. Production workers perform material control tasks and truck drivers dispatch themselves from a web site. As logistics organizations condense around the LIS, more information flows to the worker, offering the possibility that the worker can take on more responsibility.

Reengineering has demonstrably worked in logistics organizations. One record company, the music company mentioned in chapter one, reduced costs, increased revenues, and improved customer service during peak sales for CDs from 90% to 99% by reengineering logistics and order fulfillment. Transportation costs per CD fell by 30% and productivity at distribution centers increased by 70%. Not all successful reengineering programs call for significant downsizing. Corning is cited as having reengineered many of its processes without major layoffs or firings. The cost reductions and service improvements at Corning came from process improvements, not reduced payrolls.[10] One manager interviewed in this research pointed out that customer service in his manufacturing organization once had a career ladder, but is now a flat organization with little opportunity for vertical movement.

While firms reduce employment in one area, they may increase it in another. Eighty percent of the distribution centers visited in this research were seeking employees, trying to control turnover, and attempting to grow faster than the available workforce would allow. Discussions with managers at other distribution centers and warehouses support this finding: while reducing the workforce in purchasing and customer service, firms are hiring warehouse workers, supervisors, and entry level managers. Those that were not actively seeking new employees were organizations with slower growth or significant losses in market share.

In manufacturing plants, line production workers frequently take responsibility for managing inventory at their workstations. They maintain inventory counts, retrieve materials, and return rejected materials. With bar code readers, they also maintain parts inventories as they run welding

27

machines and other operational equipment.  So, while this research found many tasks moving to material control, it also found material control merging with production at the operating level.

At the managerial level, supply chain managers now work on the connections between their firm's suppliers and its customers. While this book treats supply chain managers as the upper level of material control, the job could also be classed with purchasing.  In fact, any managerial position not directly involved with supervising operations that physically move goods, might correctly be called supply chain manager.   If material control, warehousing, and transportation are catching all the operating tasks, supply chain managers are catching all the non-operating tasks including inventory planning, supplier relationships, and customer relationships. They usually have some oversight of operating tasks, since many work in manufacturing plants.

*Logistics managers will need knowledge-based technical competence, cross-functional experience, collaborative interpersonal skills, and self-management skills to manage logistics organizations in the future. Operating employees will require many skills currently associated with management as organizations reduce the number of levels in their company structure and assign interpersonal tasks to the warehouse floor, the production line, and the vehicle.*

The linear thinking that commits managers so completely to the hierarchical system is tied to the myth of the generic manager whose growth is reflected in increasingly broad responsibility, regardless of technical skill or functional background. Like the nested Russian dolls, managers at the bottom of the hierarchy are simply miniatures of those higher in the organization. The idea is that a good manager can manage anything using a common set of managerial skills.

This form of career advancement will continue to have a home, but in fewer organizations and with fewer steps upward.  If Asea Brown Boveri (ABB), a manufacturing firm based in Zurich, can generate $29 billion in annual revenue while operating in 140 countries with only four levels in its organization, firms in  less traditional industries are likely to operate flat organizations as well.[11]  Other approaches to career development include focusing on the development of highly specialized skills in one area, making major moves across specialties and disciplines, and moving from one career field to another every three-to-five years.[12]

Those who anchor their careers on security and stability will have severe problems in the work world of the near future.  As organizations shift from offering employment security to offering employability, the employee must rely less on the organization and more on himself or herself.  Those who anchor their careers on autonomy should easily find comfort in the new environment, assuming they have the fundamental wherewithal to maintain their autonomy. The secure early retiree and those with solid financial standing will happily prosper, while those who have not yet reached this standing may have problems. The traffic manager who decides to form a trucking company must be willing and able to accept the risks that go with complete autonomy. The newly laid off mid-career manager may have serious problems maintaining this anchor. Most managers will find technical and functional competence crucial to successful navigation of the career system, but will face the problem of maintaining their skills.[13]

The new view of the organization and the career system argues for training as a major part of the contract between employees and the company. If firms offer employability over security, employees and potential employees may respond by becoming loyal and long-term because of training opportunities and firms may keep them because they are well trained. A large manufacturer, a participant in this research, demonstrated this through its heavy commitment to training in a highly traditional structure (see best practices box in chapter 1). This firm demonstrated the value of well-developed training programs by offering the opportunity for training to all employees. Regardless of organizational or career structure, more firms will benefit from extensive training programs such as this.

However, the nature of the operating employee has changed, especially the new entrant into the workforce. The human resource environment no longer acts in accord with the assumptions on which many logistics organizations have based their human resources practices; examples include life-long employment and static job activities.

### The Nature of the Workforce

Firms need qualified employees regardless of the economic environment. In times of low unemployment, firms still downsize, just as in times of high unemployment, firms still hire qualified workers. Employees at all levels understand very well the nature of their employment in most firms–it is temporary. How long temporary turns out to be may vary greatly, but few logistics employees make the assumption that employment is for their entire working life. The tendency is for firms to become employee-friendly during economic booms and employee callous during economic downturns. Neither of these views reflects well on the organizations that hold them, especially if they tend to change with the economic tide.

Low unemployment and a strong economy aggravate every aspect of human resource management. When skilled workers switch jobs, their knowledge base moves with them. In the 1990's, the labor market grew at the slowest rate in U.S. history.[14] When skilled, knowledgeable employees leave, potential replacements are few—and desired by many potential employers. The replacement may know less than the employee who left, so the level of organizational knowledge falls.

The high turnover rates that have plagued the truckload motor carrier industry since deregulation now appear throughout logistics. The dissatisfied worker finds a new job across the street the next day—or whenever he or she wants a job. The retirement of a long-term skilled employee leads to a revolving door filled with young workers who stay until they get bored, which does not take long.

This reflects a change in the worker. Most firms base their assumptions about employees on the World War II generation. Children of the depression, veterans of a horrific war, they came home to a post war economy that barely had room for them. They were happy to have jobs—period. They gave loyalty to their employers and appeared to receive it in return. As long as U.S. firms absolutely dominated world markets, they kept inventories of talented people in layers of their organizations. The firms could afford it because U.S. manufacturing dominated the globe. In 1969, 60.9% of the world's manufacturing assets were controlled by the top 200 U.S. industrial firms.[15]

The new entrants into the workforce today cannot refer to a global depression, a global war, or even the less global conflict of Vietnam. They missed the 25% unemployment of the Great Depression, the grim battles of World War II, and the social foment of Vietnam. Many grew up affluent; few experienced hunger or severe deprivation. They seek experiences, not jobs, and require leadership, not management.

They have also witnessed what happened to their parents, who lost jobs as they approached retirement, struggled through downsizing caused by radical industry restructuring, and worked jobs for which they were over-qualified just to feed the family. Many of the new entrants see corporations as callous, unfeeling, and indifferent toward workers at all levels. They fear going to work for a firm that will treat them as replaceable parts, resources to be used up and tossed aside. They offer their parents' experiences as evidence.

The new generation of workers is not lazy. The so-called Generation X created the myth of the programmer who wrote a million lines of code in a hundred sleepless hours while living on diet soda and snack food. The new generation works and works hard, but seeks explanations and looks for leadership. They have little interest in climbing a corporate ladder, if they can find one, or in spending their careers in one type of work. Instead, they want to explore different jobs and learn a variety of skills. Doing specific tasks in a specific way just because the boss wants it that way means little to them. They want to learn about themselves and express their values.[16]

They also look for loyalty, but often fail to find it. They recognize loyalty as a two-way relationship. Firms that want loyalty from employees must expect to give loyalty first. The signs of loyalty include the commitment the organization makes in the form of training and preparation for the job. One trucking company structures its growth around newly hired drivers. When the firm finds a driver that meets its qualifications, the vice president of operations takes the newly hired driver to the truck dealership that handles the firm's equipment. The driver then picks the truck and specifies some of the livability options and the truck is ordered. The driver uses another vehicle until the customized truck arrives. Not surprisingly, the firm experiences low turnover among its over-the-road drivers. Involving the driver in the truck purchase sends a powerful message about the firm's commitment to the employee.

The same kind of commitment can be reflected in training. Too often, however, logistics organizations fall down in making these training commitments. Today's logistician was yesterday's school teacher or store supervisor. The discipline has a history of drawing people who were not specifically educated in logistics and then not training them in the field.

One logistics director, a participant in this research, described how new college graduates behave in his firm. At the beginning of their careers, they learn their jobs quickly. They take on news tasks, move eagerly from one function to another, and learn to be good managers in a transaction-based firm. Then, the learning stops, the transactions become routine, and the now-well-trained employee leaves. The process, according to this informant, takes about three years. Because the organization is flat, promotion is infrequent after three years. Because growth is slower than in the recent past, new managers compare themselves to their bosses' rapid promotion, and leave.

While the portraits of new workers and World War II veterans painted here are broad, perhaps stereotypical, they still make an important point. It is the logistics manager's job to understand employees, not the other way around. Treated the way their grandfathers were treated, the new entrants will leave. Offered more growth, tempted by variety, and kept current through training, they may stay.

New entrants are not the only workers available. Women returning to careers after raising children, early retirees, career changing veterans from other fields, and the disabled offer significant potential for employment in logistics. There are also the disenfranchised, the people who have been shunted aside in the typical economy because they lacked even the most basic skills–reading, writing, and basic mathematics. However, as with the new entrants into the workforce, logistics organizations must offer them potential growth and development–employability.

Perhaps some of these groups seem like questionable sources of potential employees–the disenfranchised poor for example. One manufacturing firm currently employs just over two hundred people in a plant that ships highly technical steel products all over the world. Many of the employees were illiterate when hired. The firm operates in a Mississippi delta county where unemployment was over 20 percent for decades prior to the advent of casinos. The firm had faith in the potential of the employees, worked with local community colleges, and developed its people internally. Some of the former illiterates are now managers and supervisors. A few have completed college degrees. The firm is profitable and the product recognized for its outstanding quality.

The firm also gains undying loyalty from its investment. The employees know where they came from and who helped them to get where they are. It may be difficult to bring people from such circumstances to full employability, but it may also be worthwhile. A commitment is required. But keep in mind that firms may have little choice in the future.

Logistics is behind the curve in hiring women and minorities. Through the 1990's, 70% of new entrants into the workforce were black, Hispanic, or female[17]–but not in logistics. While over 50% of the workers in some distribution centers visited in this research were female, and over 30% were minority, these were the exceptions. Logistics jobs have tended to be male bastions at all levels.

In the current job market, firms need workers to support market and revenue growth, but cannot find them. Because of low unemployment, they hire people who are less prepared to work than they would in a softer job market, but fail to spend sufficient time, effort, and money training them to perform satisfactorily. New college and high school graduates leave their first jobs because their expectations are not met, eventually settling for positions that are no better because their expectations have become more realistic. These events are far too common and add to the cost of doing business for all firms. They not only hurt the firm that loses the employee, they may reduce the size of the labor pool for all the firms that hire for a particular job.

Potential employees who do not fit the traditional logistics profile must now be regarded as critical to the future workforce. Moral and social arguments support hiring women, minorities, the disabled, and the disenfranchised–equal work for equal pay, fairness, sharing the wealth of a wealthy nation, and so on. These arguments rarely prevail on their own; otherwise, they would never need repetition. The argument here is economic: firms cannot afford to ignore potentially valuable employees for reasons over which the employees have little or no control.

**Selected Legal Issues**

The human resource environment contains many traps, including legal traps. Logisticians should consult with the human resource experts in their organizations and with attorneys who specialize in the field. Having said that, there are some basic precautions that logistics managers should take to avoid litigation and to prepare the organization should litigation occur.

First, discrimination based on race, gender, religion, national origin, and disability, is illegal in the United States. Firms can and have been sued. Managers have been held personally liable. Not only are the organization's assets in jeopardy, the manager's personal assets are subject to judgement in cases where illegal discrimination is found. Leaving aside other moral and economic arguments, which should prevail, discrimination is organizationally and personally stupid. Those who may be indifferent to discriminatory practices need to consider the financial risk associated with their indifference.

Second, sexual harassment continues to be a problem. Since many logistics organizations are in transition, hiring more women than ever, logistics managers should maintain intense awareness of the potential problems. Again, refer to the human resource experts in the firm, but also take an active role in training and educating employees to create a gender-neutral workplace. Often, the 'villains' in the case do not know the range of acceptable behavior. A few short training sessions can avoid major problems that alienate the workforce and entangle managers in litigation, taking many hours away from productive pursuits.

Third, use selection tools carefully in the hiring process. The idea of a printed form that will help choose the right people appeals to many managers. Such tools can be useful and effective, but they must pass legal muster. Otherwise, they also open firms to lawsuits. They should be technically valid and reliable instruments to begin with. (Ask the vendor for the validation study.) Then, they must be validated within the organization that uses them. That means a firm cannot buy a selection instrument off the shelf and immediately start using it without incurring legal risk. One firm in this study uses selection instruments for its customer service, transportation, marketing employees, and entry level managers. They have several thousand observations on the instruments and can tie the scores on those instruments to tenure, performance quality, and job-related behavior. The managers find the tool useful and, because the firm has validated the questionnaires internally, the legal risk is minimal.

Finally, the valid, legal foundation for most job-related actions is job classification and analysis. Procedures similar to those followed in this study, using instruments like the CMQ, provide concrete evidence of job requirements. In hiring and firing, an employee's inability to meet job requirements is a valid foundation for not hiring someone, hiring one person over another, or dismissing someone for cause. Courts will not allow a firm or a manager to compose a job requirement from thin air. There must be evidence, which is where the CMQ and similar instruments play a role.

Perhaps it is unpleasant to consider human resource tools as a way of avoiding litigation, but the human resource environment in the U.S. is laden with potential litigation. It is better to avoid litigation than to defend against a lawsuit and better to defend successfully in a lawsuit than to lose. Logistics managers help themselves, their organizations, and their employees by staying aware of these issues and managing with them in mind.

*Logistics organizations use limited sources of training and sometimes neglect formal training to the detriment of the organizations and the people who work in them.*

A survey of 192 logistics organizations showed that few take advantage of the array of potential training sources available. Neither do they use the human resource tools available to assist in developing consistent, adaptive training programs essential to operating in the rapidly changing logistics environment. This puts these organizations in the position of needing to move quickly without the tools or the trained people to allow them to escape the downsizing/ramp-up cycle.

Table 2.1 shows the percentage of the respondents who use each general source of training. These organizations used training videos more than any other training source. Training videos are relatively inexpensive and offer convenience and control over the content of the training. Whether or not the employee learned the content of the video is never measured. Videos are usually most effective if used in conjunction with other forms of training and with testing programs.

| Table 2.1 Training Sources Used by Logistics Organizations | |
|---|---|
| **Training Source** | **% Using** |
| **Training Videos** | **60.7%** |
| **Training Firms** | **55.0%** |
| **Universities** | **41.9%** |
| **Consulting Firms** | **36.7%** |
| **Community Colleges** | **36.1%** |
| **Other Sources (e.g., internal)** | **21.8%** |
| **Web-based Training** | **12.0%** |

Training firms, ranked second on use, cost more, allow interaction between the trainer and the trainees, and include testing as part of the program in many cases. Universities and consulting firms share many of the characteristics of the training firms. Community colleges and web-based training were under-used by logistics organizations responding to this survey. The point is that logistics organizations could draw from many sources to enhance employee training, but most overlook some of the obvious. Among the sources mentioned in the 'other' category was internal training and programs offered by associations (like the Council of Logistics Management).

Among those mentioned as most valuable by the respondents, associations ranked first, universities and consulting firms second, and training firms third. However, the number of responses to this item on the survey questionnaire was small. The advantages and disadvantages of each source of training are discussed in greater detail in Chapter 10.

Of concern in these results were the low use of Web-based training and community colleges. While universities, consulting firms, and training firms compete with one another to some extent, they overlap less with the community colleges. Web-based training is potentially more flexible than videos and is accessible to the vast majority of logistics employees. It offers some of the cost advantages of the videos without their limitations. The most important point, though, is that there is far more available than logistics organizations are using. This holds true for other human resource tools that contribute to training as well.

### Job Analysis and Training Survey Results

Table 2.2 shows the responses of 192 firms to questions related to selected human resource practices related to this research. These results show that logistics organizations take insufficient advantage of the human resource tools available to them. They also reflect a lack of formal training and formal training programs. This finding is further supported by the CMQ results, which showed that the majority of logistics employees received little or no formal training on key competencies related to their jobs. (See Chapters 3-9 for more details.)

**Table 2.2**
**Job Analysis and Training Survey Results**

| Process | Percent Perform | Annuall y | Semi- Annually | Less Often |
|---|---|---|---|---|
| **Perform Training Needs Assessments** | 64% | 34% | 7% | 23% |
| **Job Analysis** | 59% | 36% | 2% | 21% |
| **Develop Training Modules** | 36% | 13% | 3% | 20% |
| **Develop Competency Models** | 23% | 11% | 1% | 11% |

Job analysis, which uses techniques similar to this research, closely examines the content of a job. It helps to make decisions about pay rates, recruitment sources, and training needs. Yet only 59 percent of logistics organizations use it, and from the responses, even they do not use it often enough. Job analysis should be performed to track changes in job requirements, qualifications, and training needs. In the current logistics environment, that means frequent job analysis makes sense because the jobs are changing so rapidly. Job analysis also provides the foundation for defense against human resource-related lawsuits, as already mentioned.

Training needs assessments, training modules, and competency models help to structure training programs and keep training relevant to the job. These survey results suggest that logistics organizations need to establish better lines of communication about the nature of the work being done at all levels. Furthermore, they need to establish better base-lines of knowledge for developing training programs.

Ninety-seven percent of the survey respondents were logistics managers who worked for firms in consumer products manufacturing, heavy equipment manufacturing, chemicals, retail sales, food processing, third parties, photographic supplies, etc. The remaining 3% were human resource managers. The respondents' firms employed between 700 and 180,000 people and had revenues between $70 million and $50 billion.

*Logisticians need structured, formal training because of the shortage of fully prepared workers and the relative failure of unstructured, informal training. Training recognizes the value of an employee's job, enhances knowledge and skills, and anticipates future promotions or job expansions. Formal training also shortens the time it takes an employee to become competent in a task. The more complex the job, the more tasks involved and the greater the value of formal training.*

Formal, structured training offers a range of advantages over informal, unstructured training. This discussion will focus on three advantages. First, it brings employees to competence more quickly than informal, unstructured training. Second, it reduces total costs associated with bringing employees to competence. Third, it allows for control of the content of the training program and measurement of the results.

Time-to-competence is crucial for all employees in all jobs, especially when employees are difficult to find and keep. Time-to-competence is defined as how long it takes an employee to reach a level of performance that justifies his or her continued employment. The longer it takes, the more costs a firm incurs in pay, inefficiency, and error.

Take two examples. A research project studied formal versus informal training on simple equipment operation. It found that employees who learned informally took four times as long to become competent as those who went through formal training.[18] The more complex the job, the greater the value of formal training. No one wants to learn how to design navigational systems for aircraft by trial and error, but that is often how logisticians learn key job tasks–even complex tasks.

---

Material control clerks at a consumer durable goods manufacturer developed their own spreadsheet-based inventory tracking system because they did not understand the firm's new mainframe inventory tracking system.

–An observation made by one of the researchers

---

The second example is more elaborate. Take a newly hired over-the-road (OTR) truck driver with two years of driving experience with another firm. The driver takes $100,000 worth of equipment and $400,000 in customer goods on the road on his or her first trip. Because the driver does not know the routes or the way around the customer distribution facility, he or she misses a scheduled drop off on Friday afternoon. The next available appointment for delivery is Tuesday. The equipment and the driver are idle for the weekend. The driver makes less money sitting than driving, and the equipment does nothing, so the capital is under utilized. The firm loses the load the truck might have moved during the idle time; either the shipper or the receiver incurs additional inventory costs; the driver's morale probably falls; and the firm incurs a service failure. The cost for one incident like this is measured in thousands of dollars.

Compare this to the experienced driver who understands customer networks, facilities, and logistics practices. The driver drops off a load on Friday, picks up the next load and drives all weekend. By Tuesday, the driver has picked up another load and is halfway to his or her next destination. No service failures, no additional inventory costs, and no problems for the driver, the carrier, or the shipper. As mentioned in Chapter 6, transportation offers adventures, but managers and employees are supposed to take the adventure out of transportation–and the unnecessary cost.

The first situation occurs because of high turnover in the truckload motor carrier industry, because of inadequate training for the newly hired driver, and inadequate communications between driver, the home office, and the customer. Larger carriers with dedicated fleets spend substantial time training drivers in the practices and systems of the customers they will serve. They generally use experienced drivers on dedicated routes for important customers. Usually, turnover among these drivers is low and the training expenses are easily justified because the knowledge is used over time. But even these large, training–oriented carriers have a hard time getting fleet-wide driver turnover below 40 percent.

One reason is that they reserve the best training programs and the best routes for drivers who have been with the firm for a while. New drivers get the left overs–the simplest training and the leftover routes. Training programs recognize drivers as important members of the firm, key personnel in a complex customer service mechanism. What applies in these instances to drivers applies as well to all aspects of logistics.

Formal training can bring the first driver to the level of the second driver more quickly if the training teaches the right material. Customer networks, facilities, and practices are rarely taught in a formal setting, but should be for transportation operations. Training programs that do not measure results often do not get results. Firms should tie training to critical job-behavior and knowledge and then measure the knowledge and behavior in a training and a job setting. Otherwise, classroom training wastes time and aggravates rather than educates the trainees.

As operating level employees assume more tasks and middle management vanishes, the operating level will need more training of the type historically given to the middle manager. Communication, supervision, customer relations, team skills, stress management, and time management all apply as well to warehouse operating employees and truck drivers as they do to supply chain managers and administrative support staff.

### Overall Results from the CMQ–Broad Hints on Training Needs

While logisticians must have technical skills, whether that means driving a forklift, driving an OTR truck, or constructing an inventory database, an overriding training need is for interpersonal skills. The technical specialty may be more easily learned than self-management skills, leadership, adaptability, integrity, and trustworthiness. In logistics jobs, the scope of meetings, interpersonal interaction, and information exchange is so great, few jobs or career fields even come close.

Looking at the 22 job families categorically, there were top managers, functional managers, administrative support staff, planning and technical support staff, and operating employees. The managers were primarily decision-makers who interacted with others to support and communicate decisions. Administrative support staff acted as clearing houses for information exchange and technical information, while planning and technical staff were heavily involved in analysis and interacted through countless meetings.

Operating employees use a limited range of equipment, although what they use, they use all the time. For most job families, the primary tools are standard office equipment–computers, telephones, faxes, and terminals. The range of equipment used is higher in plants and warehouses, where they use material handling equipment, and highest for transportation operating employees who drive trucks, use office equipment, and material handling equipment. Away from the warehouse, the production line, and the vehicle, logistics jobs are not physical. Even the operating jobs are less physical and more mechanical now than in the past.

Most logisticians do not meet the public, have little to do with government regulators, and do not entertain. They also spend relatively little time training others, a problem for most organizations. The detailed analysis of results is found in Chapters 3-9.

## Summary

The logistics human resource environment has changed because of fundamental economic and cultural forces. Logistics activities are consolidating into the core functions of transportation, warehousing, and material control. Technological innovations help this process which is motivated by the firm's need to reduce cost while maintaining customer service levels. In the future, logistics managers will need expertise in all aspects of the supply chain, and operating employees will require many skills currently associated with management. Employees will continue to gain this knowledge primarily through on-the-job experience. This method increases the time firms need to invest in developing a common logistics knowledge base and employees' time to competence.

1. Nigel Nicholson, (1996). "Career Systems in Crisis: Change and Opportunity in the Information Age," *Academy of Management Executive, 10:4 40-51.*

2. Brent Allred, Charles C. Snow, and Raymond E. Miles, (1996). "Characteristics of Managerial Careers in the 21st Century," *Academy of Management Executive, 10:4 17-27.*

3. Nicholson, p.41.

4. Nicholson, *op. cit.*

5.Jim Kelly Chairman of UPS, (Fall, 1998). "Building a Work Force for the Age of Technology," Speech before the Comstock Club, September 29, 1998. *Summarized in UPS Executive Speech Digest.*

6. L. Rubin, (1976). *Worlds of Pain.* New York: Harper–Row.

7. Nicholson, *op. cit.* The subsequent discussion is based on the Nicholson article.

8. Nicholson, *op. cit.*

9. Allred, Snow, and Miles, *op. cit.*

10. John Micklethwait and Adrian Woolridge, (1997). *The Witch Doctors: Making Sense of the Management Gurus.* New York: Random House.

11. Tom Peters, (1992). *Liberations Management.* New York: Alfred A. Knopf,.

12. Kenneth R. Brousseau, Michael J. Driver, Kristina Eneroth, and Rikard Larsson, (1996). "Career Pandemonium: Realigning Organizations and Individuals," *Academy of Management Executive 10:4, 52–66.*

13. Edgar H. Schein, (1996). "Career Anchors Revisited: Implications for Career Development in the 21st Century," *Academy of Management Executive, 10:4, 80–88.*

14. Bureau of Labor Statistics, www.stats.bls.gov/datahome.htm, consulted May 1, 1999.

15. Wallace J. Hopp and Mark L Spearman, (1996). *Factory Physics,* New York: Irwin/McGraw Hill.

16. P. Sellers, (December 12, 1994). "Don't Call Me a Slacker," *Fortune,,* 181-196.

17. Wayne F. Cascio, *Costing Human Resources: The Financial Impact of Behavior in Organizations, 3rd edition,* Boston: PWS-Kent Publishing Company.

# Broad

# Responsibility
# Senior
# Management

*If I weren't doing this, I'd be an actor.*
*–3PL Vice President*

*I can't imagine myself doing anything else.*
*–Retailing Vice President of Logistics*

*This chapter describes one job family: broad responsibility senior managers or top logistics managers. It first discusses the results of phenomenological interviews with 35 top logistics managers. It then discusses the job description, competencies, job requirements, training needs, personality, and attitude results for this job family. Among the positions included in this family are: director of global logistics, general manager, senior vice president of logistics, vice president of logistics, and president of the company. This job family took responsibility for multiple logistics functions, for an organization's entire logistics function, or the whole organization. The findings affect training strategy, career development, and career paths throughout logistics. Tables showing the technical results of the surveys appear in Appendix 3. A technical job description is at the back of the chapter.*

## Key Findings and Takeaways

*Points in the text supporting each key finding are tagged with a number in parentheses, e.g (1).*

**1** Top logistics managers are decision-makers who constantly interact with other executives, mid-level managers, supervisors, professional staff, and clerical support staff. They also interact with customers, suppliers, and other external constituents.

**2** Top logistics managers' most important decisions are human resource decisions–supervision, development, motivation, leadership, performance appraisal, staffing, organizational development, selection, and recruiting.

**3** The scope of top logistics managers' involvement in supervision and development decisions is higher than 96% of all jobs in a database of 8,000 jobs. Their involvement in operations, purchasing, and budgeting decisions is higher than for 90% of all jobs in the database.

**4** The logistics top managers' jobs require skill in communication, supervision, chairing and managing meetings, negotiations, writing and editing, and basic math.

**5** Formal training was too limited in several disciplines and skill sets identified by these managers as absolutely critical to their job performance. This included inventory control and warehousing, transportation modes, pricing, supervision and development, and decision-making. This lack of formal training suggested some of the greatest training needs.

**6** Phenomenological analysis of interviews with top logistics managers showed that in performing their jobs they embrace uncertainty, engage complexity, elicit information, enter the team game, elevate processes, and evoke human systems.

### Broad Responsibility Senior Managers

Picture a street corner entertainer juggling a mixture of Rubik's cubes, chainsaws, and jigsaw puzzles while conversing with passing friends and strangers, giving speeches to assemblies, and dancing the soft shoe in small circles. Drop a chainsaw? Pick it up while keeping the other objects in the air. Catch a puzzle? Fit a piece or make a few turns on the cube, but don't miss the next one. Pass the puzzles to passers by and gather more from them--along with an occasional running chainsaw.

This is a vision of the top logistics manager's job at its best–a constant virtuoso performance before a host of often-critical publics. The pace of the job has accelerated in the last decade. After the ferocious "re-engineering" of the early 1990's, a process that continues for some firms, there are fewer jugglers, but more to juggle. The reengineering parlance suggests a 1-2-3 rule–one person paid twice as much to do the work of three. Since logistics has been a particular and notable target of reengineering, the remaining managers must juggle more and faster.

This vision suggests that senior logisticians be trained in juggling, puzzle solving, communications, dancing the soft shoe, and keeping chainsaws turned off. It is not entirely an illusion. If juggling is analogous to organizing and coordinating, dancing to adapting, puzzle solving to, well, puzzle solving of a different type, and running chainsaws to the random threats faced by organizations, then the vision describes these jobs accurately.

Broad-responsibility senior managers (top managers) either manage more than one logistics sub-function like the director of global logistics for a large corporation or manage the entire organization like the president of a small third party. Not only do the jobs call for trained talent, they call for tremendous energy.

---

"My job requires absolute energy, requires you to be alive. The on switch has to be on every minute. There's a lot going on and you have to be able to shift gears quickly. What may have been a priority five minutes ago is not (a priority) now. The dynamics of the business are incredible. I love them, I mean I really like them. My day goes by so quickly that I leave here at the end of the day wondering what happened to the day. . .It's all really fast. If you're going to be a logistics manager, you have to have lots of energy."

–Retailing Vice President of Logistics

---

The people in these jobs dealt with issues that often make headlines–downsizing, acquisitions, and new products and services–along with the mundane supervision of the offices they occupy. After talking to these top managers, observing their operations, and assessing their performance, it appeared that a major portion of the logistics system was in excellent hands–the hands of highly skilled jugglers.

This chapter differs from others in discussing only one job family and in discussing the results of phenomenological interviews with these top managers. This chapter also discusses competencies, job requirements, training

43

needs, personality, and attitudes for this job family based on the results of the battery of survey questionnaires.

## Phenomenological Interviews

Interviews were conducted with thirty-five top logistics managers. The focus of the interviews was on the interaction between the individuals and their jobs. In a real sense, these interviews were personal, not technical or business oriented. The crucial question answered by this part of the study was: "What is it like to do your job?" The emphasis was on experiences rather than methods, and on the person rather than the organization.

Transcripts of some interviews were analyzed to identify key characteristics of the relationship between these individuals and the jobs they held. Other analysts might look at the same transcripts and produce different results, so these results are not generalizable in the same sense as the results of a well-designed survey. Nonetheless, they addressed important elements of the experience of a top logistics manager.

Seven characteristics were identified: embracing uncertainty, engaging complexity, eliciting information, entering the team game, elevating processes, evoking human systems, and entertaining puzzles. Each of these characteristics is discussed in the following sections, along with some–though by no means all–of the evidence that supports it.

## Embracing Uncertainty

Where uncertainty causes anxiety for some people, it piques the interest of top logistics managers. They not only tolerated it well, as suggested by their low test scores on neuroticism, they enjoyed it. Top managers are open to new ideas and ways of doing routine activities. They enjoy examining complex issues by breaking them into their core elements to discover how they work and if they can be improved. They may not be the first to try a new process, but once they decide to give it a try, their decision is usually based on extensive analysis. **(6)**

As one 3PL vice-president put it:

---

"I love not knowing what will happen when I go into work tomorrow. That's part of what excites me about the job. If things became the same day-in, day-out, I'd probably have to leave."

---

Another 3PL vice-president said:

> "Everyday is different. It's dynamic. It's partly the industry and partly the job. Companies are migrating toward what they want to be in logistics, but that still means change from minute to minute."

Far from adding to their anxiety, uncertainty was part of the satisfaction of work and perhaps even part of the fun for top logistics managers.

## Engaging Complexity

The top logistics managers' jobs were complex–the most complex in this study and among the more complex in industry. The top managers must design ways to engage that complexity, to meet it daily. These managers captured information, made multiple decisions, and interacted with countless people in a normal workday. The complexity came not only from the nature of the work, but also from the speed at which new work arrived. Top managers' jobs were never entirely done. Some top managers had a sense of completion at the end of the day, but most carried major issues home with them at night and on the weekend. **(6)**

One retailing vice-president put it succinctly:

> "You wear one multiple hat. You don't change hats. . .There's just so much going on, it's not a matter of 'I'm a freight dispatcher, and, oh, by the way, I'm an accountant.' It all runs together. It's all happening at one time."

A 3PL vice-president said:

> "I'll comment on how we deal with change. One thing is a lack of formality in terms of meetings or formal get-togethers so that people have a full slate of time to get things done. We try not to have standing meetings."

But this only stands as evidence of the complexity. The same retailing vice-president pointed out how he captured information. The quotation clearly relates not only to engaging complexity, but also to eliciting information. The quotation is in the first box in the next section.

**Eliciting Information**

As they became accustomed to their decision-making role, top logistics managers wanted information to come to them to support those decisions–information of a defined type, in a specific form, through a specific channel. Some used e-mail, some voice mail, some notepads, some all three, while others relied primarily on personal, face-to-face contacts. **(6)**

One vice-president described his system this way:

> "I use my phone as my notepad and I leave myself lots of messages . . .so I don't forget. I do the same thing for my staff, too. I just call their voice mail day or night and leave a message to let them know what issue is at hand. Personally, though, I like to communicate through e-mail. E-mail allows me to respond at leisure and manage my time. When you're handling volumes of phone calls, you can really waste a lot of time trying to catch people that aren't there, leaving messages and playing phone tag."

This same vice-president went on to discuss his method for tracking communications, logging information, and following up on decisions. He also discussed how he trained his subordinates to give him the information he wanted:

> " . . .whatever it is, I have to spit back a decision and (my subordinates) take it back and run with it. . .when they come to me, it's 'Okay, right now we've got to feel this thing out. We've got to make a decision real quick.' When they come to me, instead of saying, 'I've got (a problem) I don't know what to do with,' they say, 'I've got X going to Y, but the truck is broken down in Renssalear, IN. The carrier is Z. Here's the issue. Here's what I think we should do. What do you think?' This is how my people are trained to come to me."

Another top manager discussed implementing enterprise software:

> "We emphasize data integrity. We want the distribution system to be transparent when we look at it through the lens of this software. . .To make good decisions, I have to be able to rely absolutely on the information in the system. It means teaching hundreds of people world-wide the importance of getting the right numbers and other information into the system–why it's important to get it right, why we're concerned–but it has been worth it so far."

46

Whether it was through technology or through people, top managers sought information and sought it through channels they found most useful. The term elicit means to draw forth or to arrive at a conclusion by questioning–which describes how this job family deals with information.

### Entering the Team Game

Some top managers used team terminology constantly while others seemed to studiously avoid it. Either way, top logistics managers ran their operations as teams. They understood the need for interaction, especially in lean organizations, between people, between departments, and between organizations in the supply chain. Managing those interactions became more difficult for the top managers as the firms grew. Still, they understood the value of working with everyone else, even as they experienced the frustration. **(6)**

This vice-president talked about the difficulties of working with people, but the team orientation was clear. He even used sports terminology–coaching and getting the players together. **(6)**

"It's through coaching. These are the questions I ask, the obvious questions, working with them to show how to get the information, trying (to help them) understand what the vital pieces are. . . .where it becomes difficult, where it is harder to get things done, is working with other departments. Other departments obviously have their priorities and I have mine. And it's not always easy to get things done through the people . . .What is on time to them and what is on time to me are two different things. . . .So it's frustrating sometimes working with the other groups. We're a lot better at it than we used to be. We've built a lot of bridges between the groups in the last six months. If I want to change a procedure or a policy, it is really difficult, as big as we are, working with the other groups. . . .Any time I'm changing processes, it affects systems. That's a problem. So I'm changing things that touch accounting. That's a problem. All the things within my world, logistics processes, I have control, so we fix them. When we work with the others, it's more of a problem.

I contact the (vice-president) of the other division, and either through a phone call or through a meeting with him and his subordinates–whoever all the players are–get everyone together, explain my situation, explain what we're trying to accomplish, and why and how it impacts them and us. Typically, I can tie some savings to it. In manpower, dollars, time, inventory. I can always show an improvement."

A 3PL vice-president, using language laden with team-speak, said:

> "People come together in work teams associated with specific projects. It is not unusual for people to be on four or five work teams at once. Some people will be together on team A, not on B, on B and not on A. The expertise is (assembled) based on the customer."

This vice-president obviously touched on several characteristics in this segment, but the important part for this discussion was the emphasis on getting everyone together. His use of the terms "coaching" and "players" suggested an underlying team approach to the management of common problems.

A 3PL vice-president said:

> "In my job, specifically managing the managers who manage pricing, international, engineering, sales, and design, we run into new business opportunities. That means we have to evaluate continually how we apply those resources. That's everyone, together."

Again, a 3PL vice-president said:

> "An advantage of working in the fluid teams, a benefit for us, is the pretty much automatic transfer of best practice and acquired knowledge from team to team. As teams go apart and come together again, they learn lessons, and the lessons–the whole idea of a learning organization–those lessons are applied in the next project just kind of de facto because in the last one this problem came up. The next time those team members are together, when any of those problems come up on the new team, the knowledge has migrated with them. That's the best advantage. The next best advantage in a fluid work team environment like we have, it's very easy for us to step up the resources related to a specific project, or step them down. . . the parts aren't necessarily interchangeable, but people can come and go."

The emphasis on teams carried over to selection and recruiting. In fact, it tied the notion of entering the team game to the next section, evoking human systems.

A manufacturing vice president said:

> "It's a general skill, but the skill I value most is working in teams.
> Working in teams probably covers a lot of sub-skills, but what I mean
> is the ability to be fulfilled in your career by working in teams.
> That's a mind set. I'm not sure you teach that. I think you can
> enhance it, you can diagnose for it, test for it, but it is something that
> develops when you are younger. The other skills we can create. If
> you are lacking in engineering skills, in my opinion it is much easier
> to take a team player and give them technical skills than it is to take
> a technical type who is a loner and integrate them into a team
> environment."

## Evoking Human Systems

Like the surveys, the interviews reflected a strong orientation toward
human resources and the development of people, including self-development.
People can make imperfect systems work. Even a perfect system cannot make
people work. Evoking human systems means to bring out the skills, energy,
and talent of the people in the organization, to conjure them, as if by magic.
That covers the sometimes uncanny ability of the best managers to pull
together organizations that perform apparent miracles–using skills thought to
be common to all managers. **(6)**

Top logistics managers think about people constantly, in addition to
interacting with them. In interviews, human resources and their management
were the primary focus of discussion, a focus that fit with the survey results.

A 3PL vice president said:

> "Another thing we've done, we've pushed decision-making as far
> down the organization as we can so people don't have to acquire a lot
> of sign-offs. We've really flattened the organization so there's not a
> lot of hierarchy. We're not afraid to decline to work on things either.
> It's been true (since) I've been here, there are always more
> opportunities than resources... We've been able to be selective about
> individual projects, and in the larger context, markets that we're
> enamored with."

This suggested that one element in evoking human systems was to give the
people in the system autonomy within the limits of organizational needs.
Putting the right people in the right place touched on every area of supervision

and organizational development–motivation, leadership, career pathing, staffing, even performance appraisal. **(6)**

This team-oriented 3PL vice president covered many of these areas, along with recruitment and selection:

---

"It takes a very special individual–not to manage a process of self-managed teams–but the people themselves have to be the kind of people who are not necessarily lime-lighters, who can manage and influence peers without direct reporting. So what we've had to do is go out for our technical people, our business acquisition people, sales, engineering, design, pricing, functional systems design people, real estate–all the groups that are not operational groups in the company–we find people who are not only willing to work in teams but excited about working in a fluid team environment where hierarchy is not rewarded so much as team success. . .Some people have the technical skills (to work in our environment), but simply don't have the personality. So we're searching through a much smaller group. Sometimes recruiting and selecting people is one of the most daunting tasks we have.

We have very, very low turnover in sales, design, pricing, engineering; we typically have not had any trouble in terms of the number of applicants, both internal and external. We post jobs internally. It is an ethic of this company to try to promote from within. That's a stated value of this company, so we always try to do that. When we've had to go outside, we've typically been able to pick and choose. People want to come here just because of the environment. Not everybody fits, but those who fit really like it. We've built a strong, stable organization that way."

---

A 3PL president said:

---

"My people will confront me. If I'm doing something they think is wrong or that they don't understand, they'll come into my office and say 'What the hell do you think you're doing?' It keeps me in line and it keeps the lines of communication open. It would worry me if they didn't come in once in a while, especially when we're doing something new, something different, and vigorously question decisions I've made.

For all I know, they sit out there and throw dice to decide whose turn it is to jump on me, but I can tell you that it works. We've grown (over 1000%) in ten years."

---

A manufacturing vice president put it this way:

> "If you accomplish anything, it is through people. We turned this organization around, but when I say we, I don't mean just management. Sure, we had something to do with it, but it was the people out on the floor, in manufacturing and distribution, that made it work. I don't drive a forklift. I don't inspect (the product). We tried to build a way of thinking, a culture, not just a system."

In evoking human systems, top managers still focused on the business of the firm. They understood their roles as managers, not social workers, and as members of organizations with specific goals to accomplish. This came through in the interviews as elevating processes–the result of well-evoked human systems.

### Elevating Processes

In interviews, top logistics managers used the term "ramp up" for implementing new processes, opening facilities, or approaching new markets. They also applied it to process or system improvements. Perhaps elevating processes simply meant to ramp up.

These managers constantly sought to improve networks, systems, processes, procedures, and interactions, all with the goals in mind–reduce costs, improve service, integrate operations. **(6)**

Elevating processes brought fun to the job according to a retailing vice-president:

> "That's one of the fun things. I like to re-engineer the process all the time. I'm not afraid to think out of the box and (the company) is not afraid to think out of the box. We're not so defined in our rules that we have to live in fixed parameters."

A manufacturing vice-president said:

> "It's not just turning an organization around that requires improving processes. If someone had worked on improving processes all along, an organization wouldn't need turning around. You have to make every process better all the time, to re-engineer for real. We take pride in making things better, in improving processes and increasing profits, but not at the expense of people."

51

A revealing aspect of these comments was the emphasis on reengineering in the sense of redesign, not downsizing. Getting people to help elevate process performance is difficult if people think the redesign will cost them their jobs. These top managers focused on process performance, not how many jobs could be eliminated.

The problems became more complex that way, but the solutions were also more satisfying. Solving the puzzles while meeting explicit and implicit goals was another major aspect of the jobs.

### Entertaining Puzzles

Entertaining puzzles returns us to the opening vignette, the street entertainer. Entertaining puzzles means to think about them, to consider them. This element tied to pulling all of the parts together–evoking human systems, elevating processes, engaging complexity, entering the team game, and embracing uncertainty. Pulling all these parts together created the greatest puzzle for top logistics managers.

A 3PL vice-president summarized it this way:

"Eventually, it comes down to winning business. I am fulfilled when we please a customer and we get the business. Create a win-win. We can create a solution that gets us a handsome profit and helps out the customer. We have to pull everything together for this to happen–the team has to work, the environment has to be right, we have to say the right thing to the customer, and we have to deliver on what we say."

A manufacturing vice-president said:

"You work a long time, put in the hours, work with the people from everywhere in the company. There are problems, serious problems, and you have to solve them. You think about the problems, you talk about the problems, and you work together on the problems, and then put your solution in place. When it works, when you see it work, when people's jobs are better, their jobs are safe, and their lives are better, then it's really satisfying. Of course, it's never really over."

A retailing vice-president placed the puzzles in an organizational context:

"When I was a kid I rode a bicycle. I had a pair of pliers and a screwdriver in my pocket and I could fix anything on that bicycle, anything that happened, it was real easy. If I wanted to modify it and

52

take off or change the wheels, handlebars, change the seat, whatever, those were modifications I could do real quickly. Now I have a car with more advanced technology, and I can't change it. I can't change the steering wheel, I can't change the seats, I can't change a lot of those variables because it affects so many other things. Our company is the same way. (Many) years ago, when I got here, we had (over 200) stores, it was a whole lot easier to change things because there were fewer decision-makers. . . . it was real easy to go to the other guy and say, 'Hey, what if we did it this way?' And they would go, 'Oh, sure. No problem.' And we changed the process. Today, you get more into a very complex system. We have lots of systems integrated, our DCs, our stores, everything is connected by satellite, there are lots of processes in place. There are policies that we formed over the years that are necessary for business, but when you change this one little step, it affects all of these pieces, and there is a ripple effect through the whole company. It's not as easy as just saying, 'Oh, why don't we change this process.' It's not that easy now."

This vice-president entertained the nature of the puzzles he had to solve on the job, not just each puzzle as it came along. Approaching the puzzles involved the other characteristics already discussed. Engaging complexity was visible in the last quotation, as was reaching the solution through human systems. Of course, the purpose of solving puzzles was often to elevate processes, and the solutions were reached through working together in human systems.

This same vice-president brought many of these elements together (characteristics are noted in parentheses):

"It's just not easy to make changes, but we do make changes. We are constantly looking for ways to make changes (engaging complexity, embracing uncertainty). Within our group, a lot of people came through the ranks. They worked [the cash register] or as accounting clerks that used to cut checks by hand. They are the people that came up in our company and understand the workings of our company on a detailed level. They can see the workings of what we're trying to do (evoked human system, elevating processes). You need help in this area. I need help in that area. We work together on this project, we make a home run for both of us. We usually put our heads together and come up with a better solution than either of us thought of originally (entering the team game). (All together: entertaining puzzles)."

53

Phenomenological results lack the certainty and definition of encoded survey results, but these interviews added the personal, human element to the analysis of the top manager's job. These managers were complex people in complex jobs dealing with complex problems. Considering all these elements, they fit their jobs. That represents the best in human systems.

**Top Managers Job Description and Phenomenological Summary**

Decision-making dominates these jobs. More than anything else, top logistics managers make decisions, evaluate decisions, gather information for decisions, and communicate decisions. Their interaction with a wide range of people both inside and outside the firm revolve around the decisions they must make to carry out their jobs. Their interpersonal skills, knowledge of their field, and communications skills all tie to making good human resource, operations, purchasing, and budgeting decisions. **(1, 2)**

As some of the quotations in the phenomenological analysis suggest, the job can be frenetic, with one critical decision after another. Most important among these are the human resource decisions. Human resource decisions may expose the manager and the firm to legal liabilities, affect the morale and motivation of employees, and determine the future direction of the logistics organization. **(1)**

The scope of top logistics managers' involvement in supervision and development decisions is greater than 96% of the jobs in a database of 8,000 jobs. Top logistics managers' involvement in operations, purchasing, and budgeting decisions is higher than for 90% of the jobs in the database. The majority of these decisions relate to internal matters for the firm–not customers or suppliers.**(1,2,3)**

The top logistics manager must bring a broad, deep knowledge base to the decision-making table. This includes knowledge of human resources, purchasing, budgeting, accounting, marketing, warehousing, and transportation, as well as skills in negotiation, managing meetings, writing and editing, and mathematics through statistics. It also requires this knowledge from three different levels: public, industry, and firm-specific knowledge. No level can be safely neglected. **(4,5)**

The respondents in this research managed business units ranging from 15 to thousands of people. Their decisions often affected the whole firm and certainly the whole logistics organization. While mistakes may teach important lessons, the cost of poor decisions based on lack of knowledge must be and can be controlled. The degree to which top managers' knowledge base came from OJE in these crucial areas is cause for some concern. **(4,5)**

The seven phenomenological characteristics–embracing uncertainty, engaging complexity, eliciting information, entering the team game, elevating processes, evoking human systems, and entertaining puzzles–are interwoven in the decision-making. Uncertainty, complexity, and information can all have human sources. Elevating a process obviously requires operations decisions, but will be carried out through people. Evoking human systems–getting people to work together and blending people with technical systems–is founded in relating to people and making human resource decisions. As for the puzzles, they are everywhere.

### Top Managers' Competencies

Possessing the knowledge and skill to do a job is a long way from being competent at the job. Applying the knowledge in the work setting actually defines a competency. Based on survey and interview results, top managers' competencies should include those listed in Table 3-1.

The competencies listed overlap. Using development skills to build and maintain a logistics organization includes using training skills to develop managers and supervisors. However, the importance of developing managers is so great according to the survey responses and the interviews, it needed special mention.

*Use supervisory, development, recruiting, and selection skills to build and maintain a logistics organization.* This means finding the right people to fit the logistics organization and giving them the resources, including training, to do their jobs. Conceptually, it is the simplest competency. Practically, it is the most difficult. Since firms hardly offer lifetime employment and the career path of the present is far less visible than the functional career ladder of the past, the difficulty in executing this competency is clear.

*Use training skills and training resources to develop managers and supervisors to operate and manage a variety of logistics offices, facilities, and networks.* This pertains directly to the first competency, but it focuses on managers and supervisors and their development. Top managers influence the growth, training, and development of managers and supervisors through supervision and frequent contact. What top managers do with these people will permeate the organization–for good or ill.

*Use decision-making skills to manage a complex, rapidly changing operation.* The decision-making is frequent, often requiring quick analysis and a decision shortly afterward. Logistics operations encompass constant motion, constant change, and all the problems these entail. The top logistics manager makes timely decisions to maintain the logistics system in the context of constant change.

*Apply basic mathematics, statistics, accounting, budgeting, and human resource skills to establish goals and measure progress toward goals.* Since most goals are quantitative, the need for these skills is clear. However, the human resource skills are required to help the goals motivate the employees to whom they apply. Setting goals is no simple task, since they must fit not only the technical system, but also the human system.

*Use skills in managing and directing meetings to gather information for decision-making.* Meetings should contribute to decisions and to communication. It is up to the top logistics manager to invite those who should be in a meeting, and to leave out those who do not need to be there. It is also their responsibility to see that meetings run an appropriate time–long enough to cover the agenda, not so long as to waste time of the participants.

---

**Table 3-1**
**Top Logistics Managers**
**Competencies**

- **Use supervisory, development, recruiting, and selection skills to build and maintain a logistics organization**
- **Use training skills and training resources to develop managers and supervisors to operate and manage a variety of logistics offices, facilities, and networks**
- **Use decision-making skills to manage a complex, rapidly changing operation**
- **Apply basic mathematics, statistics, accounting, budgeting, and human resources to establish goals and measure progress toward goals**
- **Use skills in managing and directing meetings to gather information for decision-making**
- **Use writing and oral communication skills to report on logistics activities to corporate offices, customers, and others**
- **Apply knowledge of warehousing, inventory control, transportation, manufacturing, purchasing, and other areas specific to the firm or the industry to operations decision-making**
- **Apply knowledge of warehousing, inventory control, transportation, manufacturing, and purchasing to developing strategic plans**

---

*Use writing and oral communication skills to report on logistics activities to corporate offices, customers, and others.* Look at this competency from the perspective of its absence. Writing incomprehensible reports or no reports at all interferes with effective communication and reflects badly on the manager and the organization. Top logistics managers have

56

"public" jobs–jobs that are highly visible to a variety of constituencies. What they write and how well they write it sends messages to these constituencies about the competence of the manager and the potential effectiveness of the organization.

*Apply knowledge of warehousing, inventory control, transportation, manufacturing, purchasing, and other areas specific to the firm or the industry to operations decision-making.* These subjects surround every operations decision, since logistics systems work like spider webs–a tweak on one strand in reverberates everywhere in the web. Changes in packaging may affect purchasing, transportation, and manufacturing. A new policy at the warehouse will affect inventory control–and so on, ad infinitum. The technical knowledge of these areas must be broad and deep.

*Apply knowledge of warehousing, inventory control, transportation, manufacturing, and purchasing to developing and implementing strategies.* The same knowledge that suffuses operations decisions also covers strategy decisions. While many firms have moved away from written strategic plans, the same knowledge is still required for developing visions or encompassing concepts that govern operations and human resource decisions. The knowledge must be used more often and more quickly to adapt firms to rapid change.

### Top Managers' Job Requirements

Top managers identified, indirectly, a lengthy list of knowledge and skills used in their jobs. The first ten items in Table 3-2 are the most broadly applied knowledge and skill sets. Top managers said these items are absolutely critical to performing their jobs. The critical knowledge for top logistics managers includes budgeting, supervision and human development, strategic planning, inventory control and warehousing, selection and recruitment, writing and editing, basic mathematics, and purchasing.

A smaller percentage of the respondents considered the other items listed in the table absolutely critical to job performance. That is, when this knowledge is required, it is absolutely critical to job performance, but not every top logistics manager needs it. These items are often tied to retailing, manufacturing, or 3PLs. For example, project management is more likely to be a job requirement for top managers in 3PLs, while manufacturing management applies, obviously, to top managers in manufacturing. Remember that these responses tie directly to the respondents. Your job may differ from these results, even if you have similar duties.

**Table 3-2**
**Top Logistics Managers**
**Job Requirements**

- **Decision-making skills**
- **Chairing and using meetings**
- **Budgeting**
- **Supervision and human development**
- **Strategic Planning**
- **Inventory control and warehousing**
- **Selection and Recruitment**
- **Writing and editing**
- **Basic mathematics**
- **Purchasing**
- **Trucking**
- **Rail Transportation**
- **Marketing research and pricing**
- **Accounting**
- **Cash management**
- **Project management**
- **Manufacturing management**
- **Job analysis**
- **Benefits and workers' comp**

## Top Managers Training Needs
## Equipment Specific Skills

Top managers used and supervised the use of personal and networked computers. Only a bare majority had formal training in using computers or the associated software. Since both the computers and the software change with regularity, top managers need training on both–and retraining. One justification for this training need is time-to-competence. Struggling to understand new software takes more time than attending a seminar on its use.

Another justification is better communication with information systems professionals. Gaining a better understanding of computers, systems, and software will help greatly in working with the people who operate, install, and implement logistics information systems. As mentioned in Chapter 4, information systems professionals often lack logistics knowledge, learning logistics on the job. Top managers and information systems people communicate better if top managers better understand computer systems and their problems.

58

Top managers seldom use or directly supervise the use of forklifts or heavy trucks, but they should understand the performance of the machines that fall under their authority, however indirectly. Comparing performance of current equipment to alternatives may affect critical operations decisions, a major aspect of top managers' jobs.

---

"At least forty percent of the firms we work with don't calibrate or set-up their equipment correctly. We often find situations where employees are blamed for poor performance that is the result of faulty equipment, either in manufacturing or distribution. No one in the company knows how the equipment is supposed to work. The work is getting done, but the efficiency is lost and the employees are often frustrated. Who can blame them?"

–Training and Process Design Consultant

---

## Physical Skills

This job does not require physical skills. Some physical activity is strongly recommended to counteract having to sit too much. Corporate fitness centers and arrangements with local hospitals or health clubs have worked well for many firms. Physical activities help reduce individuals' present stress levels while increasing their ability to cope with added stresses and job complexity.

## Interpersonal Skills

Every interpersonal skill imaginable could apply to these jobs. However, top managers identified specific needs for decision-making, supervisory, team, meeting, negotiation, and communication skills.

Top managers underscored the importance of decision-making in their jobs. Like the skills of top performers in any arena such as sports, music, or engineering, critical skills in this job should be honed constantly. Michael Jordan practiced dribbling a basketball long after he learned how. Renowned concert violinists practice many hours daily and take lessons even after they appear at Carnegie Hall. Engineers routinely update their skills or rapidly fall behind changing technology. Decision-making and critical thinking skills are fundamental to top managers' jobs in the same way that dribbling is fundamental to playing guard or handling a bow is to playing the violin. Not only must top logistics managers make decisions as part of their jobs, they must continue to hone their skills through training.

Most top managers studied supervisory skills in college or in formal training programs. However, like decision-making, these skills are so important to the job that they require constant maintenance. The employees change, as does the job market. What worked in supervising twenty years ago may fail now. Also, circumstances change and supervisory methods may need to change with them. Top managers supervise constantly, and they should develop their supervisory skills constantly.

---

One firm in the research used to focus on financial incentives, but now adapts the work week to give employees more flexibility in their schedules; they have a three day work week to allow employees to hunt or spend time with their families.

–An observation of one of the researchers

---

Negotiating skills affect many aspects of a top manager's job. The obvious use of negotiating skills is with suppliers, customers, and unions, but these skills also apply to working with other upper level managers and employees to get them to buy into projects or to make changes in procedures, job duties, and so on. For top managers, negotiating is a crucial communication skill.

Top managers speak to many audiences both inside and outside their organizations. Even if a top manager rarely gives formal speeches, the training to do so helps to understand the communication process. One top manager interviewed for this project took acting classes, which goes beyond taking a speech class, but should be invaluable in communicating with a variety of audiences.

Managers in many organizations talk about teams, but do not use teams or apply the skills. Top logistics managers found the skills and concepts useful, but also applied them assiduously in self-consciously team-oriented and traditional settings. While the language of teams may become suspect, like the language of MRP or TQM, the concepts worked for these managers. But teams were more than bulletin board material in the organizations studied for this research. Top logistics managers used team skills effectively.

In jobs filled with reports, memos, and e-mails, writing and editing skills are essential and often neglected. Vague memos and e-mails cause numerous problems, including a tendency for recipients to ignore them. Poorly written reports reflect poorly on the writer and fail to accomplish their purpose–to convey information. While the top manager participants wrote well, writing and editing texts overflow with examples of poor business writing–often emanating from top managers.[1] These are among the skills requiring constant maintenance.

Top logistics managers sometimes conducted formal training programs, but more often trained subordinates informally. Training skills help in either case, but with better developed skills, top managers might put on formal, structured training programs more often. As mentioned in other chapters, formal, structured training often produces better results, especially on time-to-competence.

## Knowledge Needs

Top managers need to know it all, or so it seems. Every aspect of human resource management and logistics crept into these jobs. Unfortunately, top managers cannot spend every waking moment in training. So the list included here includes the knowledge most crucial to performing the top manager's job.

---

**Table 3-3**
**Top Managers**
**Job Training Needs**

---

*Equipment specific*
- Personal and networked computers
- Efficiency and performance of machines in their operation

*Physical skills*
- No requirements

*Interpersonal skills*
- Decision-making and critical thinking
- Supervisory skills, especially for working with mid- and upper- level managers
- Negotiating, especially with customers and suppliers
- Public speaking for large meetings and community service
- Team skills or coaching for working with peers and subordinates
- Writing and editing to improve and maintain quality of reports, memos, and e-mail
- Training skills
- Communication skills

*Knowledge Needs*
- Human resource management–legal aspects
- Human resource management–supervision, motivation, career pathing, appraisal
- Inventory control–methods, techniques, financial implications
- Warehouse operations and networks–changing technology, needs, concepts
- Purchasing–capital equipment and supplies
- Accounting, especially costing
- Budgeting–all levels
- Transportation–as required by the needs of the organization
- Firm's operating procedures, policies, practices, and goals

---

Top managers may view the legal aspects of human resources as a minefield, but part of that attitude comes from failing to understand the legal implications of their decisions. Some managers become overly cautious, while others remain oblivious to the dangers. Knowing the law will improve the human resource decisions top managers make and reduce the legal risks to the organization.

Among the parts of human resource management laced with legalities are career pathing, selection, recruiting, performance appraisal, benefits administration, and workers compensation. Often doing these things correctly also means doing them with the least possible legal risk. Consequently, it pays to learn to do them well.

Take performance appraisal as an example. Many employees view performance appraisals as useless, except to give them a raise. Accurate, timely appraisals can help job performance and give employees a clear view of their career paths and prospects. Inflated appraisal scores and poorly administered appraisal systems can endanger the resources of the firm and the individual doing the appraising.

In looking at performance appraisals in a discrimination suit, courts take numbers and their meaning seriously. In a system that rates people on a five point scale, ratings below four may be regarded as punitive by the appraiser. If, according to documentation, a three means adequate or average, the court will use the documented meaning. Even though 'everyone knows' that threes are only given to those on their way out, the judge will read the label that goes with the number.

The interpretation is apt to go like this: the ex-employee was fired, even though the performance appraisal, an overall three, showed him as adequate; therefore, he was fired for reasons unrelated to performance; the ex-employee was over 40, so it must be age discrimination. The firm may be held liable, and in discrimination cases, the manager may be held personally liable.

Based on this alone, technical knowledge of human resource law and practice would be a training need for top logistics managers. The current difficulty in finding enough qualified people at all levels makes human resource knowledge even more crucial. If a manager must work through people, he or she must have people–the right people with the right skills.

Warehousing, inventory control, purchasing, and transportation obviously make up the core knowledge of logistics. Supply-chain management, logistics information systems, and other knowledge not addressed specifically in the research could be added to the list. Astonishingly, most top logistics managers learned about one or more of these areas strictly from OJE. While the need to understand the firm's own methods is high, the firm's methods are not adequate for top managers. After all, top logistics managers may be charged with making the decision to change the methods, systems, or equipment. They should be aware of the alternatives and the methods for comparing alternatives in all areas.

Top logistics managers should know costing methods like Activity Based Costing and costing services. They should also know budgeting, although budgeting may be as much a skill as a knowledge set. With budgeting, the knowledge of the firm's methods may be the most crucial knowledge. However, formal, structured training on a firm's budgeting methods are rare. Most managers learn budgeting procedures through OJE and by trial and error.

**Chapter Summary**

Top logistics managers perform astonishing feats of juggling skill, managing rapidly changing organizations in circumstances that change just as quickly. In the process of performing these jobs, they use a broad range of knowledge in logistics, information systems, human resource management, and purchasing. They also exercise decision-making skills constantly, with much of their job-related activity focusing on gathering information, communicating, and analyzing decisions.

Viewing their jobs as experiences through phenomenological interviews produced seven characteristics of the interaction between the people and their jobs: embracing uncertainty, engaging complexity, eliciting information, entering the team game, elevating processes, evoking human systems, and entertaining puzzles. These characteristics describe the experience of working as top logistics managers.

Top managers' training needs cover a broad range of skills and knowledge. A serious concern is the degree to which training in these areas is left to OJE, which often lengthens the time to competence and relies more on trial and error than structured training programs.

1. See, Clare Kehrwald Cook, (1985). *Line by Line*, Boston: Houghton Mifflin Company. or Joseph M. Williams, (1996). *Style: Ten Lessons in Clarity and Grace* 5th edition, New York: Addison Wesley Longman, Inc.

| Table 3-4 |
| --- |
| **Broad Responsibility Senior Managers** |
| **Job Description** |
| **Example Titles:** Senior Vice President of Logistics, Vice President of Operations, President, General Manager |
| **General Job Characteristics:** *Span of Control:* managers, supervisors, and professionals report directly (12), indirect reports (329); *Budget Authority:* yes; *Licenses and Certifications:* none; *Travel:* Out of town with overnight stays (80%), and out of town travel without overnight stays (9%); *Hours:* variable, full time, seasonal; *Incentives:* receive group incentives (80%), individual (46%) |
| **Supervision:** *Supervision Received:* regular monitoring of major job duties by immediate supervisor (89%), outside auditors and government regulators (29%); *Supervision Given:* regular monitoring of major job duties for upper level managers, mid-level managers, professionals, supervisors, and clerical support staff (69%) |
| **Using Language:** Constant use of spoken and written English, including editing, composing, and report writing (100%); use database queries, macros, and other computer languages that do not produce executable programs (20%) |
| **Using the Senses:** *Use Sight for:* pictures, patterns, or graphs (80%), observing behavior of people or animals (66%), observing performance of machinery or equipment (49%), noticing changing events in the workplace (46%), details at a distance and observing quality or quantity of materials (40%), small details close up and differences in colors (37%), differences in patterns or shapes (26%); *Use Hearing for:* understanding speech (69%), noticing changing events in the workplace (29%), differences in tones or direction of a sound (26%) |
| **Decision Making:** *Human Resources Decisions:* assigning employee responsibilities (100%), increasing or decreasing the number of employees and setting or changing salaries or benefits (91%), changing work procedures (86%), changing lines of authority (63%); *Operations and Production Decisions:* evaluating the effectiveness of operations (86%), modifying or improving operations and setting short terms goals (83%), setting or changing long term goals (80%), determining equipment type or processes (49%); *Financial Decisions:* setting or changing size of budgets (91%), purchasing materials and supplies (77%), purchasing capital equipment (66%), managing investments or cash flow (34%); *Strategy Decisions:* taking on new projects (86%), changing services offered to customers (71%), shutting down operations segments or abandoning projects (49%), starting up new businesses or operations (37%), acquiring other businesses (31%), discontinuing services or products (23%) |
| **Contacts:** *Internal Contacts:* mid-level managers (89%), upper managers, clerical and support staff (83%), first line supervisors (63%), marketing and sales employees (51%), professionals and technical specialists (43%), and operations employees (40%); *External Contacts:* managers and executives (74%), suppliers (66%), customers (63%), contractors, the public or job applicants (40%), civic and charitable organizations (31%), government regulators and the press (26%) |

| Table 3-4 |
| --- |
| **Broad Responsibility Senior Managers** |
| **Job Description** |

**Meetings:** *Meetings Attended to:* informally exchange ideas, solve problems, and set policies (80%), formally exchange ideas and evaluate options and make decisions (74%), consult (66%), bargain or negotiate, resolve conflicts (60%), train or instruct (57%), evaluate people or projects (54%), formally bargain or negotiate (43%), sell or persuade (31%), coordinate work (51%); *Meetings Initiated or Chaired to:* to set policies (77%), formally exchange ideas (74%), informally exchange ideas (71%), evaluate options and make decisions (69%), solve problems (66%), consult (60%), bargain or negotiate, resolve conflicts and evaluate people or projects (57%), coordinate work (49%), train or instruct (43%), formally bargain or negotiate (31%), sell or persuade (26%)

**Required Physical Activities:** sitting for long periods(86%), walking while working (37%) coordinate fingers (29%), precise arm movements (23%)

**Use of Machines and Tools**: telephone, fax, calculators, computers (97%)

**Work context:** *Variety, Autonomy, and Interdependence:* control of work pace and schedule and learn a variety of skills (86%), depend on others to complete their work before doing their own work (69%), must complete work before others can do theirs and use a variety of skills (66%), select projects to work on (63%), produce a finished product or perform a complete service (49%); *Stressful Work Situations:* working under tight deadlines (80%), conflicting work goals (74%), working with people over whom they had no authority (60%), working with frequent distractions (46%), work in situations that are highly stressful or difficult for them (34%), and dealing with distressed people (54%). *Receiving Feedback:* From supervisors, other managers, and themselves

# Logistics Information Systems

*We feel that IS is the future of logistics management and have built our company around creating IS solutions for logistics problems.*
*–3PL Applications Manager*

*Logistics information management— Is that what I'm doing?*
*–Manufacturing In-house Systems Programmer*

This chapter describes two job families: Logistics Information Systems (LIS) managers and LIS technicians. Respondents in these job families came from logistics organizations or  firms providing IS support for logistics organizations.  This chapter describes these jobs based on scores from the CMQ. It discusses the competencies, job requirements, and training needs for each job family.  It also profiles personality, customer orientation,  market orientation, and need for cognition for these job families. These results affect the training, recruitment, and selection of LIS personnel. Tables with supporting data are in Appendix 4 and technical job descriptions are at the back of the chapter.

66

## Key Findings and Takeaways

*Points in the text supporting each key findings are tagged with a number in parentheses, e.g (1).*

**1** Firms gain competitive advantage from blending and applying public, industry, and firm- specific knowledge of LIS and logistics practices. This is the primary responsibility of LIS managers and the primary basis for their training needs.

**2** Many LIS technicians, while technical virtuosos, know little about logistics, while their functional clients know little about LIS.

**3** The career path from LIS technician to LIS manager runs through improved decision-making skills, interpersonal skills, and increased knowledge of both logistics and human resource management.

**4** LIS managers and technicians must train system users to avoid critical mistakes. Perfectly designed systems, perfectly implemented and maintained, still depend on data integrity, which depends on data entry, a task dispersed throughout the logistics function–even throughout the globe.

**5** Jumping from one computer or software mishap to another leads to inefficient LIS implementation, unnecessary frustration and stress, and more service failures. Time spent reacting to emergencies detracts from planning, problem prevention, and user training.

**6** LIS managers and technicians need training in time management and stress management. Demand for their skills usually exceeds supply by a substantial margin.

**7** LIS project management is critical to the logistics activities of the firm and to the information specialists and managers who develop and implement those projects.

## Logistics Information Systems Employees

It is difficult to say whether LIS employees more closely resemble highway engineers or the early explorers of the American continent. As highway engineers, they lay out and build the pathways for business transactions. As explorers, they hack through unexplored forests and sail

67

uncharted seas, hoping to find new worlds or new ways to wealth. Either analogy may fit at times.

Building an electronic data interchange (EDI) pathway between two firms or developing an inventory database may resemble highway construction. The methods to build both are known, and while EDI connections and databases present unique problems, the desired outcome is usually clear. But bring in global supply-chain connections, enterprise software, and point-of-sale tie-ins to transparent, company-wide databases, and suddenly the territory is entirely new. Each implementation is an adventure leading to both problems and improved performance.

The days of hang tags and paper inventory ledgers have gone the way of the three-month order cycle. Logistics information demands reach far beyond the capabilities of manual systems, and advances in information technology make it likely that any process that can be automated will soon be automated. JIT, lean manufacturing, efficient customer response, and the next, new approach to managing logistics, whatever it may be, rely on information systems (IS). Logistics has moved, in just over a decade, from the primitive backwoods of hand-cut checks to pay freight bills and 3 by 5 card files for tracking core carriers to the leading edge technology of on-board communications systems and web sites for dispatch. LISs are integral, often irreplaceable aspects of modern logistics.

---

While conducting his dissertation research on strategic information systems in the trucking industry, one of the authors interviewed the president of a small trucking firm. The president was considering putting the firm's payroll on a personal computer, but first he needed to buy one. That was 1984.

Today, drivers for that same firm, which still has fewer than 50 trucks, carry notebook computers that connect directly to the firm's web site, where they find their next loads, pick up messages from home, and check their activity log and pay records. Drivers rarely talk to dispatchers on the telephone. Most communication with dispatch takes place through the satellite communications system now built into each truck. Welcome to the new millennium.

---

The integration implicit in LIS–the combination of logistics and information systems–points to a principal finding from this research. The value of an employee who knows both information systems and logistics is inestimable. LIS employees who understand logistics implement systems more quickly and effectively, anticipate and prevent problems, and work with client functions with less disruption to operations. Many LIS employees have logistics responsibilities but lack logistics knowledge. Other logistics employees who understand IS cause fewer problems, explain problems in terms that LIS employees readily understand, and often solve their own problems. While this chapter focuses on the competencies, job requirements, and training needs of LIS managers and technicians, its findings apply to other logisticians as well.**(1)**

---

"I started off as a lead man in the shipping department . . . I started taking some night classes in network management and information systems, and before I knew it, I was putting stuff in and troubleshooting the shipping and receiving data reports. I've been here for 6 years and run all of the company's databases. I'm proud of that."

    – Manufacturing Systems Programmer

---

Some firms stepped slowly into LIS, gradually developing systems for more and more processes until they had a patchwork of systems that covered most logistics activities. This sometimes created millions of lines of undocumented code only its creators could navigate and comprehend. At other times, it created independent and incompatible systems that worked poorly together, if at all.

---

"We worked with (a multibillion dollar firm) that had 17 distinct applications for logistics. Not one of them was even remotely compatible with the others. If you wanted to use a database built for another program, it had to be retyped. We've taken nearly 3 years to pull it all together–we hope."

    –3PL Systems Analyst

---

For other companies, the leap into information technology has been less hesitant and more comprehensive. Commitments in software and hardware solutions for logistics required dedicated LIS people, with software- or hardware-specific skills. Whether these people work for 3PLs or LIS departments in a firm, the skill requirements are often unique. Sometimes firms hire employees solely for these readily identifiable skills.

---

"You know, you asked me about computerized inventory handling . . . Do you know that I was hired to run this one inventory database, just one program! I have worried sometimes that if they were to chose another vendor, I would be out of a job."

    – Manufacturing Information Specialist

---

The people in logistics information systems jobs are independent of primary logistics functions, yet integrally connected to these functions. Their understanding of logistics functions is often focused on computer operations and troubleshooting associated with "running the program." The LIS function is often just one IS activity in a full plate of activities that may include human resources, accounts payable/receivable, and the like.(2)

Despite this independence, the logistics system's reliance on information and information management makes these people crucial to logistics performance. Without 100 percent computer uptime, logistics functions slow down or even stop.(5)

---

"It used to be that if the computer hung up, or the system wouldn't print the shipping barcode labels, the shipping department would just write them in by hand, and move along . . . Now, the labels are placed during production. If the system hangs, everything stops. I didn't write the software, but I must have it running without a hitch . . . This whole place is at the mercy of this one program, and I'm responsible for it. Along with all the other things . . ."

–Manufacturing Systems Administrator

---

The problems for logistics information management are clear. First, identifying skilled LIS employees is difficult, time-consuming, and expensive because of the current job market. Second, skilled LIS employees often have little or no experience in logistics. Third, training LIS employees in logistics often is done on the job, creating piecemeal learning and less-than-ideal understanding of the broader purpose of the LIS. Finally, the upper-level LIS professional may focus less on computer operations than on the overall mission of the organization. The basis for solving these problems is systematic training to cover all levels of LIS, including those no longer under the LIS organization, notably data entry. (1,3,7)

---

"I can't tell you how important logistics is to my department. In some respects, everything we do is tied to how well we can move the material out of the warehouses. . . The computer guys under me understand this importance, and have spent a lot of their time familiarizing themselves with things like 'cases/hour' and 'load planning.' If not, we couldn't help those guys out in the field."

– 3PL Logistics Systems Director

---

This chapter discusses two job families in logistics information systems: LIS managers and LIS technicians. It gives a brief job description for each job family and discusses the competencies, job requirements, and training needs for each family. It also outlines the results of personality, customer orientation, and market orientation surveys for these employees. Both of these jobs are professional, requiring high levels of education. The operating level in LIS has largely disappeared. Data entry is automated through barcoding or EDI and is dispersed throughout the logistics organization.

## LIS Technicians Job Description

LIS technicians run the computer systems for their firms–installing systems, programming, providing system support, maintenance, and anything else needed to make the systems work. They are the troubleshooters, caught in a constant cycle of computer projects, programs, and problems. (5, 6)

As troubleshooters, they work under constant pressure to keep systems working, to get them back in operation, to meet tight deadlines for implementation, and to solve current user problems. Every user wants his or her problem solved immediately, and every logistics functional manager wants to talk about improvements to implement yesterday. Frequent interruptions and delays aggravate this stress, adding to the pressures of problem solving. (5, 6)

This can lead to a workday filled with firefights that crowd out long-term LIS improvements. Ironically, if LIS technicians take time to improve the software, they cannot service the problems the software creates. Each user's computer problem is larger, and more critical, than the last user's problem. (6)

Along with these stressors comes the ever-present need for interaction with other LIS employees, managers in other logistics departments, and clients. LIS projects and programs are both complex and difficult to implement, requiring teamwork that includes logistics employees from all areas of the organization. LIS technicians seldom have authority over the people they support and usually have little choice about the equipment or systems they use. (3)

Other evidence suggests the LIS technicians are not completely comfortable in interpersonal interactions. They scored low on measures of extroversion in a personality scale. While this tends to reinforce the "techie" stereotype, LIS technicians still work with a wide range of people to make technology decisions, solve problems, or consult. They may also see meetings as a waste of time, rather than an opportunity to gain vital knowledge, or they may lack the skills to get the maximum amount of information in the shortest possible time.

Given the potential and actual problems, the crucial question is "What does it take to do this job well?" The next section addresses this question through the competencies required to perform the LIS technician's job effectively.

## LIS Technicians Competencies

Table 4-1 shows the competencies that emerged from the data analysis and interviews with people in this job family. Each competency ties directly to knowledge or job activities the respondents identified as crucial to job performance. These competencies, collectively, distinguish this job from the jobs in the database and other jobs in the study.

*Apply knowledge of relevant software to the solution of logistics problems in the firm and in the supply chain.* LIS technicians in firms that use one enterprise software package may not need to know anything about others, but they should know everything about the one they use. Most importantly, they should know how to apply that knowledge to solving the firm's logistics problems–even when those problems come from outside the organization. As firms develop more long-standing relationships, they use more IS connections to other firms; this often means that a firm's IS problems can no longer be contained. If one firm has a problem, so do its supply chain partners. IS problems add costs and create service failures, not to mention adding to job frustration and stress for LIS employees and other logisticians in the affected area. **(4)**

A special note applies to enterprise software where databases are shared across organizational lines. Data integrity is crucial because each mistake not only reverberates throughout the system, but also becomes a part of shared reality. Special emphasis must be placed on training the people who enter the data–people who usually work in other logistics areas.**(4)**

---

"When I'm in a meeting, it is often a discussion about how we can optimize what we currently do, and make it more efficient. The managers there will have an idea on how they can save time or money, and they ask me if the system can be modified to make it happen. It's like they know what they want, but don't know how to get there, because they're not sure what the system is actually doing."

– Asset-based 3PL Systems Programmer

---

*Use project management techniques to implement new software and to install new hardware in logistics operations.* Project management techniques take into account precedence of tasks. They call for planning, the examination of time sequences for steps in implementation and installation, and organization. This helps to minimize the effect of major changes on the firm and on the supply chain. Failure to use project management techniques usually means longer than necessary disruption of operations and incomplete or inadequate implementation of systems. This simply means more fires to fight, taking more time away from planning and analysis to improve systems and repair underlying problems. **(5, 7)**

*Integrate LIS knowledge with information from users to anticipate and avoid logistics problems.* This information can come from multiple sources–informal comments, formal presentations at meetings, informal discussions, or focused task forces. Another aspect of making these systems work effectively is to assure data integrity, which means training other logisticians in data entry and in the importance of data integrity. Regardless, LIS technicians should constantly seek information that will make the logistics function work better, and which will probably make their jobs easier; LIS knowledge remains a foundation for this competency. **(2)**

*Maintain a thorough understanding of the firm's logistics practices and how they relate to LIS.* Knowing the logistics system, its goals, and methods for reaching them helps LIS technicians set priorities, avoid problems, and solve problems. Since the demands on the LIS technician's time usually exceed the time available, the most important problems must be solved first. Clients make poor sources of information about priorities, since they tend to exaggerate the importance of their own problems relative to others. **(2,6)**

Understanding the logistics system and what it is supposed to accomplish helps to avoid problems and to solve them. It also helps in communicating with logisticians in client functions.

---

**Table 4-1**
**LIS Technicians**
**Competencies**

- **Apply knowledge of relevant software to the solution of logistics problems in the firm and in the supply chain**
- **Use project management techniques to implement new software and to install new hardware in logistics operations**
- **Integrate LIS knowledge with information from users to anticipate and avoid logistics problems**
- **Maintain a thorough understanding of the firm's logistics practices and how they relate to LIS**
- **Apply training skills to keep users current on new software and hardware**
- **Use time management techniques to address problems according to their importance to the firm**
- **Maintain current knowledge of software, hardware, and systems that relate to logistics**

*Apply training skills to keep users current on new software and hardware.* The better the users of a system understand the system, the more likely they are to solve their own problems and the less likely they are to create problems through ignorance. A little training helps save a lot of time in fighting fires. Also, uninformed users ask the system to do things it cannot do, just as an LIS technician who knows nothing about logistics may get the system to do the unnecessary while overlooking the essential. Finally, perfect systems, perfectly implemented and maintained, fail if the data are wrong. The old GIGO rule still applies–garbage in, garbage out. However, data entry is no longer the exclusive arena of LIS, but dispersed throughout the logistics organization. This means assuring that what goes into excellent systems are excellent data, and user training is crucial.(**4,3**)

*Use time management techniques to address problems according to their importance to the firm.* While LIS technicians may not control priorities, their expertise is crucial. They influence priorities simply because they know how the computer system works and others do not. If LIS technicians understand the logistics system and its goals, they can argue strongly for their priorities. While computer system emergencies often take precedence, work on longer term projects should proceed in an orderly fashion. (**6**)

*Maintain current knowledge of software, hardware, and systems that relate to logistics.* LIS technicians must know how to work with the systems at the heart of their operation. The other competencies depend on this knowledge. In effect, without it an LIS technician could not be competent. Above all else, LIS technicians are just what the title indicates–technicians. Their technical competence is at the core of their job performance.(**1**)

*Summary.* These competencies depend on each other. LIS technicians cannot apply knowledge of software to the solution of logistics problems if they do not know the software or do not know logistics. The technical knowledge matters little if information about problems cannot be gathered effectively, and poor time and priority management skills eliminate the possibility of doing almost all of these things.

## LIS Technicians Job Requirements

LIS technicians must possess the knowledge and skills that will allow them to perform their jobs competently. These job requirements are precursors to competence. They come from the job classification questionnaire and include the knowledge and skills the respondents say are widely used and absolutely critical to job performance.

Table 4-2 shows the knowledge required by the respondents. Some of these requirements change with the situation, while others are constant for all LIS technicians. For example, LIS technicians in firms that never use water transportation do not need to know about water transportation, while all LIS technicians need to know computer operations. The core knowledge requirements are computer and systems related–computer operations, information/technology management, programming, database administration, and word processing. The logistics job requirements vary according to the application environment. LIS technicians working for a trucking firm will obviously need to know trucking more than they will need to know inventory control or warehousing, while those working for a retail distribution network will probably need to know more about inventory control and warehousing than about trucking. Other, obvious requirements are not listed, including basic mathematics and adequate spoken and written English.

| **Table 4-2**<br>**LIS Technicians**<br>**Job Requirements** |
| --- |
| • **Computer operations**<br>• **Information/technology management**<br>• **Programming**<br>• **Database administration**<br>• **Word processing**<br>• **Meetings and communications**<br>• **Inventory control/warehousing**<br>• **Knowledge of air/water transportation**<br>• **Knowledge of ground-based transportation** |

Putting together the competencies and job requirements leads directly to the analysis of training needs. They are discussed in the next section.

**LIS Technicians Training Needs**

In LIS technicians' jobs, time to competence is crucial. Rarely can a logistics organization wait for LIS employees to become competent by trial and error in new software or its application. Admittedly, trial and error learning will take place because each installation of new software or hardware tends to be unique. But multiple trials and multiple errors should result from the circumstances, not from lack of training or lack of knowledge, which means OJE will not suffice for training LIS technicians, especially not for those elements of the job identified as absolutely critical. Table 4-3 shows the list of training needs for LIS technicians.

Formal training in programming, computer operations, database administration, or software engineering is always necessary. The potential efficiencies of information technology can be lost through poor implementation or poor training. Under most circumstances, training in new hardware and software should be formal. Such training is likely to remain a need for the foreseeable future, but the specifics will change constantly.(3)

While LIS technicians often have excellent IS skills, they lack training in IS project management. They learn IS project management through OJE or trial and error–an expensive way to test and manage systems. This form of learning increases the disruption to operations and lengthens the time to make systems fully operational. System installation and implementation should be viewed as comprehensive programs that involve both technical and human systems. Project management skills also lie along the path from IS technician to IS manager. For an IS technician to be promotable, he or she must have project management skills. (5,7)

LIS technicians also need training in the second part of their jobs: logistics. Additional formal training for LIS technicians in logistics would improve logistics and LIS performance. LIS technicians often learn about inventory control, warehousing, trucking, and air transportation primarily through OJE. Again, while these employees come with great IS skills, melding these skills to the logistics functions of the organization remains absolutely critical to success. In some instances, LIS technicians have no idea that computerized inventory control or production scheduling represented a "logistics" activity of the firm. Training in the fundamentals of logistics, the equivalent of an introductory college course, would allow these employees to understand logistics as a distinct activity of the firm. (2)

---

**Table 4-3**
**LIS Technicians**
**Job Training Needs**

*Equipment specific*
- **All areas related to operational computer software that are relevant to the company's operation**
- **All areas related to operational computer hardware that are relevant to the company's operation**

*Interpersonal skills*
- **Stress management**
- **Meeting skills**
- **Time management**
- **Communication skills**

*Knowledge Needs*
- **Basic logistics function education**
- **Information systems project and program management**

---

So far, the discussion has centered on technical skills in IS, logistics, and project management. But these skills must be applied in a social context, through meetings, one-on-one sessions with users, suppliers, and supply chain partners. This is not the world of the stereotypical techno-geek who cannot function with or around others. Rather it is a world where conveying technical knowledge and skill is as important as possessing it.(3)

LIS technicians require basic communications skills for this job–writing a clear memo or e-mail, leaving comprehensible voice-mail messages, conversing with users, and garnering worthwhile information from meetings. Greater skills are required at the next level, so LIS technicians should work on these skills for the present and for the future.(6)

Finally, the most evident training needs were in time management and stress management. LIS technicians who constantly "fight fires" may be poor time managers. Methods for recognizing and solving these problems may not always be readily apparent to employees. The stressful aspects of the job can also be managed with training. Stress and time management skills may make a hectic workday more bearable.

### LIS Technicians Personality and Attitudes

LIS technicians were more inclined to worry than most other logistics managers and supervisors, but ranked average for the general population. They were less extroverted than most logistics managers, but not significantly less extroverted than the general population. Their scores were average on openness, agreeableness, and conscientiousness.

Their need for cognition was low, meaning that they would prefer to work on simple problems and tend to solve them using simple decision rules. Their customer orientation was among the highest scores for any group in the study, while their perception of the firm's market orientation was below average for the study.

### LIS Technicians Summary

The overall picture suggests people who are well suited to their jobs, but need to work on interpersonal skills and stress management. Their training needs stem from the high need for technical competence and frequent interaction with a broad range of fellow employees. Promotion requires development of communications, decision-making, and interpersonal skills.

### LIS Manager Job Description

The move from LIS technician to LIS manager represents a strong shift in job duties. LIS managers are more involved in decision-making than any other job family except top logistics managers. While the nature of LIS would seem to narrow the scope of LIS managers' decision-making, the pervasiveness of LIS in modern logistics brings them to the table on a wide range of decisions. LIS managers have broad responsibility for information systems implementation and management and are often heavily involved in defining the firm's technology strategy. Their responsibilities also encompass human resource decisions to a greater degree than all but four percent of the jobs in a comparison database of 8,000 jobs. LIS managers must wear two hats–one as a manager with good human resource and strategic skills, and one as a specialist, capable of fielding questions on technical matters. (1)

While most IS managers do not focus on logistics, the respondents in this study worked for logistics software firms, 3PLs, manufacturers with heavy logistics investment, and retail logistics organizations. They spent most of their work time optimizing logistics through information technology.(6)

Like LIS technicians, LIS managers work under tremendous stress and time pressures. The stress is usually born, not of an isolated problem in shipping, but of the weight of an entire logistics system riding on their recommendation. And they are well aware that they are completely accountable for that recommendation.

---

"When I became the IS Director here, I just never thought I would have to worry about databases and software again . . . Boy, was I off! I've got systems guys working for me that . . . have rewritten operational software using a different kind of compiler, and asking me if that was OK. How can I possibly make the right decision without understanding what they are talking about? And if their fix is wrong, I'm the one that will catch hell for approving it in the first place. Can you imagine getting fired for making a decision like that?"

– Manufacturing IS Application Director

---

(Standing just outside the second floor stairway of the shipping/receiving office) "You see all this (waving his hand side-to-side). . .Those people down there do one thing–ship our product. As long as the computer runs, our product goes out like clockwork. But if something is wrong, you know whose number is called first? Mine."

– Manufacturing Systems Operations Manager

---

LIS managers' involvement in business decision-making includes human resources, purchasing, budgeting, and strategic management. LIS managers often advise other operational units on technical matters, but also directly compete for resources with those units. Their decision-making profile, which so closely resembles that of the top logistics managers, distinguishes them from LIS technicians, whose involvement in decisions is not as broad or as critical to their job performance.(1)

For LIS managers, human resource decisions were of special importance. Competition for IS employees is fierce, and the cost of hiring IS employees with logistics experience is potentially prohibitive. Setting IS priorities, establishing lines of communication, and facilitating the implementation of logistics software require LIS managers to be especially adept at managing people. This people orientation at first appears counterintuitive to most LIS employees, who are more comfortable in their technical spheres of influence. Often, the LIS employees who are simultaneously technical wizards and gregarious socializers succeed beyond the ordinary.(3)

---

"After I was hired, I was told that the reason I was brought on board was for my ability to connect the technical people to the people in each of the warehouse locations. The technical IS folks were in one world, the warehousing people were in another. It had something to do with my ability to walk between both worlds, I guess."
– Retailing Director of Operations and Systems

---

**LIS Managers Competencies**

The LIS managers' competencies, shown in Table 4-4, partly reflect an elevation of skill requirements from LIS technicians; they also reflect the change in organizational level. The increased involvement in decision-making is most notable, especially for human resource decisions.

*Make systems acquisition, installation, and implementation decisions that improve logistics performance of the firm.* Knowing when system changes and upgrades are worth the time, effort, and money is crucial to LIS managers. System changes take time, cost money, and take resources away from other productive uses. Implementing enterprise software takes months or even years, so top managers turn to the LIS managers for the answer to the most important question: Is it worth it? The improvement in logistics performance, however it is measured, must justify the investment. This strongly implies that LIS managers need to know logistics as much as they need to know systems.(1)

*Coordinate LIS projects to successful completion.* This competency follows the first one. Making a good, justifiable decision regarding LIS means little if the project is not fully and successfully carried out. While major projects may require approval from the firm's general management, LIS managers usually lead the implementation because of their technical knowledge, but technical knowledge is not sufficient. Such projects require project management and human resource skills as much as technical skills.(7)

| Table 4-4 |
| LIS Managers |
| Competencies |
| --- |
| • Make systems acquisition, installation, and implementation decisions that improve logistics performance of the firm<br>• Coordinate LIS projects to successful completion<br>• Use supervisory and employee development skills to build and maintain an efficient and effective information systems workforce<br>• Use decision-making skills to improve logistics functions<br>• Maintain proficiency in technological innovations, particularly those relevant to logistics<br>• Maintain working knowledge of logistics practice in the firm and a broad understanding of logistics theory and practice<br>• Manage and organize meetings to gain crucial knowledge and make effective decisions |

*Use supervisory and employee development skills to build and maintain an efficient and effective information systems workforce.* Perhaps more than in other disciplines, LIS employees seek current skills. They want to know the newest technology, even if they later criticize it. Training becomes a motivator and an advantage to the firm. It creates an environment that attracts other specialists, helping to further build the firm's LIS knowledge base. LIS managers are crucial to establishing this environment.(3)

Other supervisory skills apply here as they apply in other fields. LIS managers should develop their own recruitment, selection, motivation, performance appraisal, and motivation skills and those of their subordinates. While LIS technicians supervise no one but themselves, in most cases, they will need these skills if they are promoted.

*Use decision-making skills to improve logistics functions.* The insights that arise from solving LIS problems easily translate to insights about logistics, assuming the LIS manager has a good understanding of the field. Their contributions to the firm should go beyond LIS to general logistics management issues. (2)

*Maintain proficiency in technological innovations, particularly those relevant to logistics.* Technology changes so rapidly that staying current is difficult and essential. LIS has made downsizing possible and profitable in logistics; so while the largest portion of the savings may have been realized in many firms, additional cost savings and significant advantages will probably be possible in the future. The LIS manager should be the first to know about the possibilities.(2)

*Maintain working knowledge of logistics practice in the firm and a broad understanding of logistics theory and practice.* This means working closely with a broad range of logisticians in the firm and staying close to changes in logistics practice. This allows the LIS managers to contribute to strategy decisions, particularly those that involve technology changes such as the use of bar codes in warehouses.(2)

*Manage and organize meetings to gain crucial knowledge and make effective decisions.* Meetings have become problematic for many managers. Meetings can be valuable or a colossal waste of time. LIS managers should reap benefits from meetings, not wasted time. (6)

### LIS Managers Job Requirements

The job requirements shown in Table 4-5 came from the list of knowledge used and the activities these managers identified as absolutely critical to their job performance. These jobs also require other obvious knowledge, skills, and abilities not in the table; these include basic mathematics and excellent written and spoken language skills.

---

**Table 4-5**
**Upper IS Managers Job Family**
**Job Requirements**

- **Information/technology management**
- **Computer operations**
- **Employee supervision and development**
- **Knowledge of the logistics function - to include inventory control, warehousing, and transportation**
- **Project management skills**
- **Meeting organization and chairing skills**
- **Operations research**

---

### LIS Managers Training Needs

LIS managers' training needs emerge from the competencies required in their jobs. Three types of knowledge plus the ability to apply them are at the heart of each competency; these are public, industry, and firm-specific.[1] Advantages accrue to firms where LIS managers possess all three types of knowledge in both LIS and logistics. Firm-specific knowledge may mean knowing something that competitors do not, while industry and public knowledge offer advantages only if applied better by one organization than by others.(1)

LIS managers' training needs begin with technical currency in software and hardware, followed closely by understanding their own logistics practices

81

or their clients' logistics practices. Industry and public technical knowledge come next, because computer hardware and software change so rapidly, along with their application in logistics. Blending logistics and LIS knowledge offers the most significant competitive advantages available to a firm, but because of rapid technological change, these advantages may be temporary.(2)

Skills in human resource management help find, recruit, supervise, and motivate the people who operate the system to the firm's advantage. Meeting, communication, training, and project management skills help to gather and disseminate crucial information. They also help reduce the isolation of LIS managers from other logisticians who find the technical aspects of LIS mysterious and intimidating. (3)

---

**Table 4-6**
**LIS Managers**
**Job Training Needs**

*Equipment specific*
• **The firm's computer hardware and software**
• **Available logistics applications**
• **Enterprise software**
• **Available hardware**
*Interpersonal skills*
• **Stress and time management**
• **Supervisory and employee development**
• **Project development and implementation**
• **Recruiting**
• **Chairing and managing meetings**
*Knowledge Needs*
• **Information systems technology management**
• **The firm's logistics practices**
• **Logistics principles and practices**
• **Computer operations management**

---

LIS managers most need training in subjects where the consequences of trial and error learning are high. This includes updated technical training in relevant hardware and software, supervision, and recruitment. Technical mistakes can disrupt logistics operations, causing service failures and frustration. Human resource management errors may mean that the firm lacks the talented people it needs to operate, maintain, and improve the system. In a tight labor market, these errors may be the most critical. While it may seem superfluous to mention training in the firm's own logistics practices, trial and error learning here can be devastating. Since the firm has the information available, formal training on this topic should be part of the over-all training program for all LIS personnel.

Poor strategic choices in LIS may significantly reduce a firm's future potential. For example, logistics firms that use multiple data bases when answering delivery questions frustrate customers as they are switched between two or more operators. Systems that fail to meet expectations will frustrate the firm's LIS and other logistics employees, and send customers to competitors whose systems work better. System choices can enhance or constrain growth, smooth or disrupt operations, and increase or decrease supply chain effectiveness and efficiency, among other things. **(4)**

These choices depend on the knowledge and skills of LIS managers. Table 4-6 shows a list of training needs that focuses on developing LIS managers who can help create competitive advantages for their firms.

### LIS Managers Personality and Attitudes

LIS managers are slightly less likely to worry than LIS technicians, but more likely to worry than other logisticians. They are slightly more open to ideas than LIS technicians, and much more extroverted. They scored close to average on conscientiousness and agreeableness. They enjoy working on complicated problems, are about average on customer orientation, and see their firms as average in market orientation. The overall picture is a stable decision-maker with a gregarious nature and a realistic, analytical view of the firm.

### LIS Managers Summary

The pervasiveness of LIS in modern logistics brings LIS managers to the table on a wide range of decisions. LIS managers have broad responsibility for defining and managing the firm's information systems. Successful LIS managers possess firm-specific, industry and public knowledge and use interpersonal and managerial skills to build and maintain an effective information systems workforce.

### Chapter Summary

LIS managers and technicians manage and run the nervous systems of the logistics organization. Their technical knowledge may be all that keeps goods flowing, so dependent on the LIS are many logistics organizations. Relentless maintenance of technical currency is crucial to these employees; however, technical knowledge is not the only important element in their jobs.

They must be technically current and capable, and they must be able to work with people throughout the logistics organization. While the IS field permits gifted programmers to hide from human contact, LIS employees cannot afford to hide from fellow logisticians. These job families interact constantly across functions in logistics and across organizational boundaries.

1. Dorothy Leonard-Barton, "Wellsprings of Knowledge: Building and Sustaining the Sources of Innovation," (Boston, 1995), p. 21, cited in John Micklethwait and Adrian Woolridge, "Witch Doctors: Making Sense of the Management Gurus," *New York: Random House,* 1997 p. 133.

| Table 4-7 |
| --- |
| **LIS Technicians** |
| **Job Description** |
| **Example Titles:** Logistics Information Specialist, Logistics Information Systems Designer, Process/System Technician, Systems Administrator, Technical Service Manager, Systems Programmer |
| **General Job Characteristics:** *Span of Control:* non-supervisory employees (1); *Budgetary Authority:* $70,000; *Licenses and Certification:* none; *Travel:* Out of town with overnight stays (25%); *Hours:* full time, same number per week; *Incentives:* receive group incentives (29%), individual (36%) |
| **Supervision:** *Supervision Received:* regular monitoring of major and minor job duties by immediate supervisor (93%); *Supervision Given:* none |
| **Using Language:** Constant use of spoken and written English, including editing, composing, and report writing (100%), use database queries, macros, and other computer languages that do not produce executable programs (57%), application development and implementation (43%) |
| **Using the Senses:** *Use Sight for:* observing small details up close (50%), observing the performance of machines or equipment and noticing changing events in the workplace (36%); *Use Hearing for:* none specifically related to job performance |
| **Decision Making:** *Human Resources Decisions:* none; *Operations and Production Decisions:* modifying or improving operations (50%), evaluating the effectiveness of operations (36%), determining equipment type or processes (29%); *Financial Decisions:* purchasing materials and supplies (29%); *Strategy Decisions:* taking on new projects (43%) |
| **Contacts:** *Internal Contacts with:* mid-level managers (79%), professionals or technical specialists and clerical support staff (71%), upper managers (64%), technical specialists with supervisory responsibility and first line supervisors (57%), marketing and sales employees (50%); *External Contacts with:* suppliers (57%), customers (50%), executives and consultants (36%) |
| **Meetings:** *Meetings Attended:* consult (93%), informally exchange information or solve problems (86%), evaluate options or make a decision (79%), formally exchange information (57%), coordinate work (46%), train or instruct (43%); *Meetings Initiated or Chaired:* informally exchange information (50%), evaluate options and make decisions or consult (36%) |
| **Required physical activities:** sit for long periods (100%) |
| **Use of machine and tools:** personal computers, multi-user computers, and peripherals (100%), standard office equipment (93%) |

| Table 4-7 |
| --- |
| LIS Technicians |
| Job Description |

**Work Context**: *Variety, Autonomy, and Interdependence:* work on shared tasks, depend on others to complete their work before doing their own work, and must complete work before others can do theirs (86%), determine the methods or equipment they use (71%), control of work pace (64%), influence work activities of others outside the organization (36%); *Stressful Work Situations:* work in situations that are highly stressful or difficult for them and working under tight deadlines (93%), working with people over whom they had no authority (79%), use a variety of different skills (71%), conflicting work goals and working with frequent distractions (64%); *Receiving Feedback:* From supervisors, other managers, and themselves

| Table 4-8 |
| --- |
| **LIS Managers** |
| **Job Description** |

**Example Titles:** Information Technology Manager, Logistics Systems and Planning Manager, Logistics Systems Application Director/Manager, Logistics Systems Architecture Director, Logistics Systems Director, Logistics Systems Project Group Manager, Systems Operations Manager

**General Job Characteristics:** *Span of Control:* managers, supervisors, and professionals reporting directly (9), indirect reports (8); *Budgetary Authority:* $3,100,000; *Licenses and Certification:* none; *Travel:* Out of town with overnight stays (25%); *Hours:* full time, same number per week; *Incentives:* receive group incentives (50%), individual (60%)

**Supervision:** *Supervision Received:* regular monitoring of major and minor job duties by immediate supervisor (100%); *Supervision Given:* regular monitoring of job duties for technical specialists and professionals (90%), technical supervisors (40%)

**Using Language:** Constant use of spoken and written English, including editing, composing, and report writing (100%); use database queries, macros, and other computer languages that do not produce executable programs (90%) application development and implementation (80%)

**Using the Senses:** *Use Sight for:* pictures, patterns, or graphs (100%), observing the performance of machines or equipment (60%); *Use Hearing for:* none specifically related to job performance

**Decision Making:** *Human Resources Decisions:* increasing or decreasing the number of employees (90%), establishing or changing lines of authority (60%), changing salaries or benefits (50%); *Operations and Production Decisions:* modifying or improving operations (70%), setting or changing short-term goals and evaluating the effectiveness of operations (60%), setting long-term goals (50%), determining equipment type or processes (40%); *Financial Decisions:* setting or changing size of budgets and purchasing capital equipment (70%); *Strategy Decisions:* taking on new projects (80%)

**Contacts:** *Internal Contacts with:* professionals or technical specialists (100%), executives, clerical support staff, marketing and sales professionals, and mid-level managers (80%), technical supervisors (60%); *External Contacts with:* customers, suppliers (90%), managers and executives (50%)

| Table 4-8<br>LIS Managers<br>Job Description |
| --- |
| **Meetings:** *Meetings Attended:* consult (100%), solve problems, formally exchange information (90%), set policies and informally exchange information (80%), resolve conflicts, persuade or sell, evaluate options or make a decision, coordinate work, evaluate people or projects (70%), train or instruct (60%); *Meetings Initiated or Chaired:* informally exchange information (90%), formally exchange information, set policies, solve problems, consult, coordinate work (80%), evaluate people or projects and evaluate options and make decisions (70%), persuade or sell, train or instruct, and resolve conflicts (60%) |
| **Required physical activities:** sit for long periods (100%) |
| **Use of machine and tools:** standard office equipment, personal computers, and mainframes or peripherals (90%) |
| **Work Context:** *Variety, Autonomy, and Interdependence:* work on shared tasks, depend on others to complete their work before doing their own work, and must complete work before others can do theirs (100%), control of work pace (80%), influence work activities of others outside the organization (70%) determine the methods or equipment they use (60%); *Stressful Work Situations:* work in situations that are highly stressful or difficult for them and working under tight deadlines (100%), conflicting work goals (80%), working with people over whom they had no authority, working with frequent distractions, and use a variety of different skills (70%); *Receiving Feedback:* From supervisors, other managers, and themselves |

# Warehousing

*I lift weights all the time.  It makes this job easy.*
*—Manufacturing Warehouse Operating Employee*

This chapter describes six job families: operating employees, lead operators, supervisors, administrative support, planning support, and managers. Respondents in these job families came from distribution centers operated by manufacturing firms, retailers, and third parties. The chapter describes these jobs based on scores from the CMQ, interviews, and other survey responses. The chapter discusses the competencies, job requirements, and training needs for each job family based on these results. It also profiles personality, customer orientation, market orientation, and need for cognition for supervisors, planning support staff, and managers. These results affect training, recruitment, retention, and selection of warehousing personnel. They also influence career paths and personal development for these key employees. Detailed data from the CMQ and personality and attitude questionnaires can be found in Appendix 5. Detailed job descriptions are included at the end of the chapter.

## Key Findings and Takeaways

*Points in the text supporting each key finding are tagged with a number in parentheses, e.g (1).*

**1** Warehouses and distribution centers are assuming more and more logistics tasks, using information systems and telecommunications to put responsibility for customer service, inventory control, and material handling on the warehouse floor.

**2** While technology has improved communications and information exchange, many operating jobs in the warehouse remain physical and require personal interaction to get goods moved.

**3** Training for warehouse operating employees focuses on mechanical skills such as how to operate the forklift or enter data into the computer, but the jobs also demand high levels of interpersonal skills.

**4** Warehouse supervisors work in managerial and operating arenas simultaneously. Consequently, their training should contain operational and managerial components.

**5** Warehouse managers often assume their duties without sufficient preparation. Relevant training often comes after they assume their duties, if then. Their jobs differ from other functional logistics managers' jobs in the level of involvement in planning and strategic decision-making. They do more than transportation, purchasing, customer service, and material control, but less than LIS or top logistics managers.

**6** Key training needs for growth and development include stress management at the operating level, training as trainers at all levels, and training in conducting meetings. More structured training for new employees would improve time to competence, problem resolution, productivity, and damage rates.

**7** Warehouse training tends to be unstructured and informal. More structured, formal programs decrease turnover and increase job satisfaction. Reliance on unstructured, informal OJE as the centerpiece for training invites high turnover, poor execution of procedures, and low morale.

**8** Long-term, programmatic training and development produce a stable workforce in the warehouse. Firms with systematic training programs for operating employees, supervisors, and managers have low turnover, capable supervisors, and savvy managers. Managers promoted too quickly without training struggled, while experience combined with training shortened the time to competence.

## Warehousing

Some warehouses hum, bringing to mind an electronic clock. Forklifts glide quietly along high stacked aisles; packages and pallets slip silently through receiving doors, racks and shipping doors. Other warehouses burst with activity, the noisy grandfather clock chiming and ticking loudly. Forklifts roar, pallets bang, steel and pipes clang from the receiving door to outbound trucks and trains. Both the clatter and the hum can move millions of dollars in inventory daily–like clockwork either way.

Warehouses and distribution centers radiate utility. Massive structures of metal, brick, and concrete suggest strongly that work takes place here–work that will continue beyond the moment. Their appearance yields other meanings, too–that this is no place for the faint of heart, the dabbler, or the dilettante.

People in six job families manage, supervise, operate, analyze, administer, and record the activity in these warehouses. These job families and the nature of the important work they perform are the subject of this chapter.

### Warehouse Operating Employees Job Description

Must be able to lift up to 75lbs and be skilled in computer operations...
  –from a want ad for a warehouse worker

This job family includes highly physical work centered around machine operation, most often forklifts and hand trucks. This work takes place in an environment that calls for frequent interaction, constant awareness of the surroundings, and heavy use of verbal and numerical information. The work also exposes these employees to hazards, although the hazards tend to be limited in scope for each job. (2)

The most important and frequent interactions are with each other, their supervisors, and lead operators–the other people on the warehouse floor. While the scope of their involvement in decision-making is limited, they contribute to human resource decisions and operations decisions frequently. The physical aspects of their jobs are at times precise and at other times gross. **(3)**

---

"We get some things in here that weigh 300lbs. They're usually awkward. They're really tough to shift around with a forklift, and you know, move just a couple of feet. A couple of us usually pick it up or slide it where it needs to be. Sometimes one guy will do it alone."

–Retailing Warehouse Operating Employee

---

This job description for operating employees contains few surprises. The job family includes receiving, shipping, stocking, and order picking. These jobs clearly depend on one another. **(3)**

---

A stock clerk at a retail distribution center pointed at a receiving clerk, a friend of hers, and said, "I have to wait on him. If he doesn't do his job, I've got nothing to do. My supervisor doesn't want to see me standing around."

---

These employees' involvement in decision-making is minimal and limited to short-term decisions on the warehouse floor. They work closely with one another and with lead operators, but most of their instructions come from supervisors and above. While managers often discuss the team concept, teamwork does not cut across organizational levels to any great extent.

A common scene for some of these employees looks something like this: drive a forklift for thirty minutes; go into the office to enter data for 15 minutes; go back into the warehouse to escort a customer on a facility tour for 15 minutes; return to the forklift; and so on. These jobs are highly physical, but also have major data entry and interpersonal duties. Warehouse operating employees also interact to carry out these duties, which requires frequent communication. **(1,3)**

### Warehouse Operating Employees Competencies

Warehouse operating employees' competencies involve machine operation and frequent interaction. These competencies are listed in table 5-1.

*Understand and apply warehouse and inventory control fundamentals in accordance with company policy.* This competency is task level knowledge and lies at the heart of these jobs. Operating employees must know the principles, policies, and procedures behind the actions they perform–as well as how to perform the actions. The knowledge includes where to store goods, how to store them, how to retrieve them, and when to take these actions.

Lifting techniques, recording data, operating material handling equipment, and communicating with fellow workers all come under this competency. Outstanding logistics organizations formally train operating employees in all of these things. Unstructured, informal approaches offer less recognition for employees and give management less control over the content of the training. **(2,7,8)**

*Understand and apply knowledge of appropriate transportation modes for loading and unloading.* This applies to operating employees involved in shipping. Working in tight places to load trailers and secure loads in vehicles of all types, knowing modal operations to the degree that they affect the job and the company, and maintaining relationships with carrier personnel could all be a part of this competency.

---

**Table 5-1**
**Warehouse Operating Employees**
**Competencies**

- **Understand and apply warehouse and inventory control fundamentals in accordance with company policy**
- **Understand and apply knowledge of appropriate transportation modes for loading and unloading**
- **Maintain data integrity and update records quickly**
- **Communicate effectively with fellow employees, supervisors, and managers to achieve short and long term goals**
- **Operate material handling equipment safely, efficiently, and effectively**
- **Operate computer and keyboard equipment effectively**
- **Lift, carry, and move objects by hand safely**
- **Maintain a calm, professional demeanor in the face of changing work demands and under a variety of situations**
- **Use basic math and reading skills effectively on the job**

---

*Maintain data integrity and update records quickly.* Data entry may be simply scanning bar codes or manually entering information into computers. The most effective employees recognize problems regardless of the system type. Accurate entry is the key to this competency, followed by problem recognition. **(1)**

*Communicate effectively with fellow employees, supervisors, and managers to achieve short and long term goals.* The important communications are usually brief, operational statements, but can involve complex information and detailed explanations. **(2)**

*Operate material-handling equipment safely, efficiently, and effectively.* Equipment operation means more than turning it on and turning the wheel. Proper function should be understood–the proper functioning of properly calibrated equipment. This goes back to assuring that the equipment is correctly set-up, calibrated, and maintained. If it is not, it will always be difficult for an employee to get the best from the equipment. **(2)**

*Operate computer and keyboard equipment effectively.* This is also crucial for data entry. As these jobs become more automated, computers and keyboards will play a larger role, while the physical aspects of the job will probably diminish, to a point. For some goods, volume will remain too low or physical manipulation will be too difficult for safe, effective automated handling. For these goods, computers and keyboards will be strictly for record keeping. **(1)**

*Lift, carry, and move objects by hand safely.* The physical nature of this job requires physical movement of goods. Carelessness and poor techniques create multiple problems. Potential injury to employees and damage to goods aside, poor training or lack of training may open a firm to legal liability. **(2)**

*Maintain a calm, professional demeanor in the face of changing work demands and under a variety of situations.* This is essential to good working relationships and reflects the high level of interpersonal skills these jobs demand.

*Use basic math and reading skills effectively on the job.* It is not enough to know these skills, they must be used on the job. These employees use these skills constantly. Note that not every employee has these skills when he or she joins a firm. Many organizations train employees in subjects like these because they did not learn them in school.

**Warehouse Operating Employees Job Requirements**

| Table 5-2<br>Warehouse Operating Employees<br>Job Requirements |
| --- |
| • **Material handling equipment operation**<br>• **Computer and keyboard use**<br>• **Data entry and scanning equipment**<br>• **Vehicle loading, load balancing**<br>• **Certification on forklifts and the like**<br>• **Firm's policies and procedures**<br>• **Basic mathematics**<br>• **Interpersonal skills** |

Forklift and other material handling equipment operation, computer operation and data entry, communication, basic math, and reading skills are all required for these jobs. Also, their knowledge base should include inventory control, warehousing, company policies and procedures, and lifting techniques. These constitute the base requirements to perform these jobs.

### Warehouse Operating Employees Training Needs

Equipment operation is the heart of these jobs, but it now combines with data entry, data management, and computer operation. While these remain the most physical of all logistics jobs, a strong back without a sound mind is of limited value to most organizations. Like the loaders (See Chapter 6), warehouse operating employees must also understand loading and unloading procedures for the vehicles used in their operations.

---

**Table 5-3**
**Warehouse Operating Employees**
**Job Training Needs**

*Equipment specific*
• **Equipment operation, including refresher training**
• **Computer operation**
• **Data entry equipment operation**
• **Vehicle loading and unloading**
*Physical skills*
• **Safe lifting techniques**
• **Strength and fitness training**
*Interpersonal skills*
• **Stress management**
• **Communication skills**
*Knowledge Needs*
• **Inventory control procedures**
• **Warehouse practices and procedures**
• **Firm's operating procedures, policies, practices, and goals**

---

The people in the warehouse asked for a fitness center in the distribution center. We would never have thought of it. I mean, these folks already work very hard, but you can see them at lunch waiting in line for the machines.

–Retailing Vice President of Logistics

Their jobs also require physical skills, notably safe lifting techniques. Physical fitness promotes safe handling procedures and reduces the likelihood of back injuries.

Stress management and communications skills help employees who work with other people constantly, a situation that fits warehouse operating employees. Warehouse operating employees need communication skills which include a set of codes adapted to routine interactions with fellow operating employees. Some firms and some employee groups in the warehouse have adopted hand signals and other simplified techniques for communicating through noise. Essential to the warehouse operating employee, though, is the basic training need of understanding and using the language clearly. (3,7,8)

Finally, these employees need an understanding of the firm's operation that goes beyond the immediate operational problem. They need a common understanding of the logistics system of the organization–the facts of the system. Failing that, they may fail to grow and develop.

### Warehouse Operating Employees Summary

Warehouse operating employees have assumed a range of tasks that go beyond using material handling equipment. While these jobs maintain their physical and mechanical nature, they have also incorporated tasks once assigned to purchasing, inventory control, and customer service.

### Warehouse Lead Operators Job Description

Warehouse lead operators perform many of the same tasks as warehouse operating employees, including driving a forklift, entering data into the computer, and moving inventory through the facility. The job families differ in emphasis. Warehouse lead operators emphasize data entry, data integrity, and computer-related equipment over the physical and mechanical, and warehouse operating employees emphasize the physical and mechanical. Also, these respondents have clear supervisory duties in many instances.

### Warehouse Lead Operators Competencies

Warehouse lead operators must have the same competencies as the warehouse operating employees, plus two more. This section will discuss only the two distinctive competencies because the discussions would be identical.

*Conduct effective operational meetings.* Warehouse lead operators regularly conduct informal meetings and attend meetings to assign work, set schedules, and solve operational problems. (6)

> "We have two meetings every shift, one at the beginning and one at the end. They never go more than five minutes. The first one tells everyone what waves of goods will come in on that shift and the second tells us what we got done."
> —Retailing Warehouse Associate

*Exercise discretion and leadership in the role of first level supervisor.* These employees assume limited supervisory roles, overseeing immediate operations and providing supervisors and managers with information about worker performance. They have no authority to change another employee's pay, job status, or annual review. Nonetheless, they are called upon to oversee the work of other workers. This means supervising with a delicate touch, because uproars disrupt the scheduled work and may cause a variety of human resource problems.

---

**Table 5-4**
**Warehouse Lead Operators**
**Additional Competencies**

- **Conducts effective operational meetings**
- **Exercises discretion and leadership in the role of first level supervisor**
- **Maintains all the same competencies as warehouse operating employees**

---

**Warehouse Lead Operators Job Requirements**

The requirements for this job again resemble warehouse operating employees. The additional job requirements stem directly from the differences between the two jobs–supervisory skills and meeting skills. The knowledge base includes one that is often overlooked–knowledge of the firm's own systems. Both operating and clerical employees need this knowledge, but the need is greater for the lead operator job family because of their larger role in information exchange and supervision. **(6)**

The meeting skills required in this job are not those associated with conducting week-long seminars but are those required to communicate with a small group in an informal setting. The meetings this group conducts and attends most often involve giving instructions, setting schedules, and discussing short term operating goals. **(7)**

| Table 5-5 |
| --- |
| Warehouse Lead Operators |
| Additional Job Requirements |
| • Firm's policies and procedures |
| • Supervisory skills |
| • Meeting skills |

### Warehouse Lead Operators Training Needs

In addition to training that warehouse operating employees require, warehouse lead operators need training in supervisory skills, meeting skills, and the firm's policies and procedures. The supervisory skills required in these jobs are rudimentary; they include how to give simple instructions without causing unnecessary conflict and how to lead a small group through basic, structured tasks. These jobs do not require training in performance evaluation or setting human resource policies. They do need to understand how to avoid discriminatory behavior and how to prevent and discourage sexual harassment. Since they work directly with operating employees, they may be in the best position to implement prevention programs. **(6,7)**

| Table 5-6 |
| --- |
| Warehouse Lead Operators |
| Additional Job Training Needs |
| *Equipment specific* |
| • Identical to warehouse operating employees |
| *Physical skills* |
| • Identical to warehouse operating employees |
| *Interpersonal skills* |
| • Identical to warehouse operating employees, plus |
| • Supervisory skills |
| • Meeting skills |
| *Knowledge Needs* |
| • Identical to warehouse operating employees |

### Warehouse Lead Operators Summary

These jobs closely resemble warehouse operating employees, but they have additional responsibilities in supervision and in conducting meetings. It is critical that they understand the firm's policies and operating procedures.

## Warehouse Administrative Employees Job Description

This job family conducts the internal business of the warehouse; office procedures, payroll, cash management, paperwork, human resource record keeping, and information exchange are among these responsibilities. These employees play a central role in administering key company policies and making critical decisions, although their primary role is in support. They attend meetings to support management decisions. These jobs make few physical demands on employees, but require a high level of interaction with a variety of fellow employees, suppliers, and customers. Many of the respondents supervised a clerical staff.

These jobs resemble transportation administrative support and customer service support in providing clerical services and a communications exchange point for other job families. They provide a reservoir of information about the organization and its administrative procedures that is crucial to decision-making in all areas.

## Warehouse Administrative Employees Competencies

Warehouse administrative employees' competencies center on processing paperwork and operating an information Kiosk. Table 5-7 shows these competencies

*Understand and apply office procedures and company policies.* Many of the tasks associated with these jobs pertain to company policies, procedures, and directives. Employees in these positions maintain personnel records, customer records, shipping documents, and regulatory compliance records. They need to be aware of the rules and regulations that underlie the records they maintain to assure their accuracy.

*Operate basic office machines effectively to maintain a smooth flow of information and essential paperwork.* These employees often play a central roll in information flow. The information they hold often affects the lives, let alone the work lives, of other employees. The machine operation can also be complex. Their acquaintance with the operation of the variety of office machines can make the work of other employees easier. Collectively, these employees should be a repository of expertise on all of these things. This competency also covers software like word processing and spreadsheets.

*Maintain data integrity and update records quickly.* Because much of the information they handle affects pay and benefits, regulatory compliance, and daily operation, accuracy and speed are important.

*Communicate effectively with fellow employees, supervisors, and managers to achieve short and long term goals.* Effective communication is crucial to every logistics job, but central to this job family. Other employees will ask questions and rely on the answers they get from these employees, so they not only need expertise, they must have the ability to convey information about that expertise to others.(6,7)

99

*Provide information to support human resource decisions and assist other employees on payroll and benefits issues.* Because of their procedural and regulatory knowledge, these employees will be consulted by managers and planners on a variety of topics. Human resource decisions and the information to support them may be the most crucial.

*Maintain a calm, professional demeanor in the face of changing work demands and under a variety of situations.* Because many of the duties associated with these jobs pertain to all the employees in the warehouse, these jobs can be stressful. These employees are sometimes pulled in multiple directions simultaneously, so it is important for them to manage themselves and to help maintain calm. **(6,7)**

*Use basic math and reading skills effectively on the job.* The paperwork these employees process often requires basic mathematics. The regulations and procedures they must comprehend are sometimes written poorly, so they must read well enough to translate the documents into the correct actions.

---

**Table 5-7**
**Warehouse Administrative Employees**
**Competencies**

---

- **Understand and apply office procedures and company policies**
- **Operate basic office machines effectively to maintain a smooth flow of information and essential paperwork**
- **Maintain data integrity and update records quickly**
- **Communicate effectively with fellow employees, supervisors, and managers to achieve short and long term goals**
- **Provide information to support human resource decisions and assist other employees on payroll and benefits issues**
- **Maintain a calm, professional demeanor in the face of changing work demands and under a variety of situations**
- **Use basic math and reading skills effectively on the job**

---

**Warehouse Administrative Employees Job Requirements**

These employees must have basic office skills including operating computers, telecommunications equipment, fax machines, copiers, calculators, and so on. They must also have good math and reading skills, a thorough understanding of office procedures, and knowledge of relevant regulations. Since they will most likely work with every employee in the warehouse, interpersonal skills are also a must.

100

| Table 5-8<br>Warehouse Administrative Employees<br>Job Requirements |
| --- |
| • Office equipment operation<br>• Computer and keyboard use<br>• Understanding of regulations and procedures<br>• Firm's policies and procedures<br>• Basic mathematics<br>• Interpersonal skills |

**Warehouse Administrative Employees Training Needs**

Administrative employee's equipment training needs cover the machines and software they use to keep information flowing and records up to date. Too often, employees are given the rudiments of equipment operation or software use and left to learn the rest by trial and error. This increases their frustration and the frustration of those who rely on them for information and assistance. These jobs usually have no major physical element.

| Table 5-9<br>Warehouse Administrative Employees<br>Job Training Needs |
| --- |
| *Equipment specific*<br>• Software use<br>• Computer operation<br>• Other office machines<br>• Telecommunications equipment<br>*Physical skills*<br>• None required<br>*Interpersonal skills*<br>• Stress management<br>• Time management<br>• Organizing skills<br>• Communication skills<br>*Knowledge Needs*<br>• Pertinent regulations<br>• Paperwork requirements<br>• Warehouse practices and procedures<br>• Firm's operating procedures, policies, practices, and goals |

Self management skills like stress management and time management help these employees work with conflicting goals and multiple demands placed on them. Organizing skills also help greatly in these jobs. Interpersonal skills, including communications, negotiations, and business writing play a vital role in these jobs. **(6,7)**

Administrative employees must know company policies, regulations relevant to their field (hazardous material, human resources, hours of operation), and office procedures. They must also know the paperwork associated with a variety of procedures.

## Warehouse Administrative Employees Summary

These are administrative jobs that may vary from firm to firm and function to function, but are central to the flow of knowledge, information, and paperwork. They manage and operate the underpinnings of the warehouse, the kinds of tasks that everyone assumes will be done.

## Warehouse Supervisors Job Description

Warehouse supervisors work in the difficult middle. They must understand and often do the work of operating and clerical employees, but also perform management tasks. These jobs are complex, requiring frequent decisions and almost constant activity. They supervise up to 60 employees, frequently attend meetings to assist with human resource decisions, and chair meetings to schedule work, resolve conflicts, and informally exchange information.

Warehouse supervisors must know everything pertaining to the warehouse operating and clerical jobs. In addition, they add a high level requirement for supervisory skills, training skills, and interpersonal skills. They also need to know about supplier and customer procedures that may affect warehouse operations.**(4,6,7,8)**

## Warehouse Supervisors Competencies

Warehouse supervisors' competencies reflect the dichotomy of the job–operations and management. Table 5-10 shows these competencies.

*Understand and apply warehouse and inventory control procedures in accordance with company policy.* This is the competency required of other warehouse floor employees, but at a higher level. Supervisors train operating employees and coordinate their work. The supervisor must know everything the operating and clerical employees and lead operators have to know, including the proper functioning of correctly calibrated equipment and data entry procedures.

*Use supervisory skills to coordinate the flow of goods through receiving, stowage, order picking, and shipping.* Though it seems obvious that supervision is central to supervisory jobs, the number of true supervisory jobs in logistics is declining. If supervision is seen as the personal oversight of the work of another, logistics supervisory jobs are diminishing rapidly in number and increasing in span of control. Supervisors must understand performance appraisal, motivation, communications, and meeting management. Since they frequently chair meetings attended by their subordinates, they must understand how to use meetings for training, conveying and gathering information, and gaining consensus. They must also understand how to run a meeting so that employees do not feel their time has been wasted.

Finally, warehouse supervisors must understand how to run a safe, efficient warehouse operation. The goods must flow through quickly to meet customer and client demands, but also employees must stay safe. Helping people in warehouses avoid injury is a major task, one with implications for the personal welfare of the employees and the financial welfare of the firm. **(4)**

---

**Table 5-10**
**Warehouse Supervisors**
**Competencies**

- **Understand and apply warehouse and inventory control procedures in accordance with company policy**
- **Use supervisory skills to coordinate the flow of goods through receiving, stowage, order picking, and shipping**
- **Apply knowledge of supplier and customer procedures to improving warehouse operations**
- **Communicate effectively with fellow employees, supervisors, and managers to achieve short and long term goals**
- **Incorporate all the competencies required of warehouse operating employees and clerical employees**

---

*Apply knowledge of supplier and customer procedures to improving warehouse operations.* Supplier and customer logistics policies and procedures can affect a warehouse operation dramatically. Warehouse supervisors must understand those procedures and policies well enough to understand the effects on his or her own operation. How well the firm adapts to these requirements may have significant customer service implications that could determine whether or not a customer stays with them. Also, efficiency and effectiveness of warehouse operations may be affected profoundly. **(4,6,7)**

*Communicate effectively with fellow supervisors, other employees, and managers to achieve short and long term goals.* This is a minor modification of the operating employees' competency. This applies to every logistics employee because of the interactive nature of the work. Logisticians do not

103

work alone, but supervisors' job performance is especially dependent on the work of others. **(4,6,7,8)**

*Incorporate all the competencies required of warehouse operating employees and clerical employees.* To train others in a job, supervisors must know what the others know and what they do not know. Supervisors not only need the same competencies as operating and clerical employees, they need these competencies at a higher level than the people who work for them.

### Warehouse Supervisors Job Requirements

Warehouse supervisors' jobs require supervisory skills, self-management skills, equipment operation, and the knowledge base of all the employees they supervise, plus a thorough understanding of the overall supply chain. The list of required job skills and knowledge is long for this job family, but that is because this is one of the most complex jobs in logistics.

| Table 5-11<br>Warehouse Supervisors<br>Job Requirements |
| --- |
| • **Material handling equipment operation**<br>• **Supervisory skills**<br>• **Computer and keyboard use**<br>• **Data entry and scanning equipment**<br>• **Vehicle loading, load balancing**<br>• **Certification on forklifts and the like**<br>• **Firm's policies and procedures**<br>• **Basic mathematics**<br>• **Interpersonal skills**<br>• **Human resource policies**<br>• **Benefits and pay policies**<br>• **Performance appraisal**<br>• **Self-management skills** |

### Warehouse Supervisors Training Needs

Warehouse supervisors' equipment training needs are extensive because they oversee and train operating and clerical employees in the use of a broad range of equipment. An important addition to this list is the understanding of the correct functioning of properly calibrated equipment. A training specialist interviewed in the course of this research pointed out that employees are often blamed for incidents caused by poorly set up or incorrectly calibrated equipment. **(4,6,7)**

> A lot of times, no one in the organization knows how the machinery is supposed to work or how to distinguish between working properly and not working properly. No one. The employees learned to use the equipment from other employees who didn't really understand the machinery either. The ignorance is passed down from one group to the next. It costs companies serous money when they don't really know what they are doing with material handling and production equipment.
>
> –President, Training Firm

Assigning this training need to supervisors is simply picking someone in the organization who ought to know how the machinery is supposed to work. The supervisor, as potentially a long term employee, seems like the best candidate for this knowledge.

---

**Table 5-12**
**Warehouse Supervisors**
**Job Training Needs**

*Equipment specific*
- **The correct functioning of properly calibrated equipment**
- **Equipment operation, including training others**
- **Computer operation**
- **Data entry equipment operation**
- **Vehicle loading and unloading**
- **Basic office machines**

*Physical skills*
- **Safe lifting techniques**
- **Strength and fitness training**

*Interpersonal skills*
- **Stress management**
- **Communication skills**
- **Supervisory skills–performance appraisal, motivation**
- **Training skills**
- **Self-management skills–stress management, organizing, time management**

*Knowledge Needs*
- **Inventory control procedures**
- **Human resource practices, policies, and laws**
- **Warehouse practices and procedures**
- **Firm's operating procedures, policies, practices, and goals**

---

Supervisors require the same physical skills as the people who work for them, although they probably will not use the skills as often. More critically, they need to understand these skills, especially safe lifting and handling.

The level and range of interpersonal skills increases dramatically for warehouse supervisors compared to operating and clerical employees. With as many as 60 employees working directly or indirectly for them, supervisors assume major human resource duties including performance appraisal, motivation, and chairing meetings. Many managers and supervisors do performance appraisal poorly because they do not know how and because they hate the process of telling someone exactly where they stand. Much of the reluctance to carry out the process correctly comes from ignorance. This is a significant training need. **(4,6,7)**

Another training need is for training as a trainer. Supervisors train operating and clerical employees almost daily. They need skills explicitly for their training role. Training should also play a role in their performance appraisal. **(4,8)**

The knowledge base required of supervisors is broad. They play a significant role in creating gender neutral and non-discriminatory work environments and constantly affect the attitudes of the employees who work for them. The critical needs cover the technical and interpersonal skills that help develop supervisors in their current jobs and prepare them for promotion.

## Warehouse Supervisors Summary

Warehouse supervisors have one of the more complex jobs in logistics. The range of skills required is broad and the knowledge requirements deep. These employees must know what their subordinates know and much of what their bosses know. The extent of the knowledge of human resource practices and law must also increase.

## Warehouse Planning Support Job Description

Warehouse planning support employees use analytical skills to make recommendations regarding purchasing, budgeting, operations, and human resource decisions. They attend and chair meetings to present and gather information that informs managerial decisions. These employees supervise few subordinates, usually one or two administrative staff members.

This job family involves a broader scope of meetings and contacts than 95% of the jobs in a database of 8,000. They use sophisticated mathematical techniques to examine operations develop presentations, and support analytical documents. These employees work with a wide variety of employees, but their primary focus is upward, to support their bosses' and upper managers' decision-making.

### Warehouse Planning Support Competencies

Table 5-13 shows the competencies for this job family. They describe a job family that requires a broad range of knowledge and significant language, mathematical, and analytical skill. These employees must also gain from and contribute to meetings because they spend time in countless meetings.

*Use analytical techniques to develop presentations and analytical documents to support managerial decisions.* Presentations and reports are the principal output of this job family, but neither is purely descriptive. These employees gather data and information to analyze and put it into a context for decision-making. The techniques may be specific to software and based on advanced statistics. They may also use spreadsheets for less specialized analysis.

*Use meetings and contacts to gather information to support analysis.* While data may come from computers, information often comes from people. The analytical skills work better when the data have viable contexts. This can come from meetings in which issues under analysis are discussed, formal interviews with key people, and conversation. Of course, these employees also use meetings to convey or exchange information.

---

**Table 5-13**
**Warehouse Planning Support**
**Competencies**

- **Use analytical techniques to develop presentations and analytical documents to support managerial decisions**
- **Use meetings and contacts to gather information to support analysis**
- **Use presentation skills to communicate analytical results to a variety of audiences, usually management**
- **Apply knowledge of purchasing, budgeting, accounting, finance and human resource management to the development of warehouse related analyses**
- **Assist upper managers and warehouse managers in the development of long term and short term goals**
- **Understand office procedures, word processing, spreadsheets, and presentation software**

---

*Use presentation skills and writing skills to communicate analytical results to a variety of audiences, usually management.* These employees must communicate the results of the analysis they conduct to warehouse managers, top managers, warehouse supervisors, suppliers, and customers. These analyses may assist a 3PL in selling a warehouse program to a customer, redesigning a retail network, or restructuring a supply chain for a manufacturing plant. Regardless of the purpose, the results will most likely go to these audiences through a presentation or a written report.

Consequently, these employees must have impeccable presentation and writing skills. They must translate technical language and results into terms comprehensible to the audience receiving a report or presentation. **(6,7)**

*Apply knowledge of purchasing, budgeting, accounting, finance, and human resource management to the development of warehouse-related analyses.* The bulk of analysis will be based on accounting and financial figures, often applied to purchasing, budgeting, and human resource decisions. These employees should know these fields well, including the common practices of the firm itself.

*Assist upper managers and warehouse managers in the development of long term and short term goals.* The kinds of analysis planning support employees conduct should help determine feasible goals. Goal setting in logistics tends to be quantitative and based on estimates of financial results, usually costs. The primary audiences for analytical reports and presentations understand costs and easily tie them to bottom line issues.

*Understand office procedures, word processing, spreadsheets, and presentation software.* These represent the toolbox for planning support staff. Word processing programs and spreadsheets are as fundamental to these employees as hammers and nails to a carpenter. They will use word processing, spreadsheets, and presentation programs constantly in an office setting. Also, any supervisory duties assigned to planning support will usually be for administrative support staff, thus, the requirement to understand office procedures.

*Apply knowledge of the firm's logistics system, policies, and procedures in analyzing the systems and networks.* Fundamental as it may seem, these employees need to know the system in which they work. Not knowing their own practices and policies may produce some interesting analysis, most of it utterly useless.**(6,7,8)**

### Warehouse Planning Support Job Requirements

The job requirements show a body of knowledge and skills used in the application of the writing, presentation, and analytical skills. These employees embody the classic support staff function, a function that found its way to the warehouse as logistics activities have consolidated. The job requirements are shown in Table 5-14.

| Table 5-14 |
|---|
| **Warehouse Planning Support** |
| **Job Requirements** |
| • Advanced mathematics |
| • Relevant modes of transportation |
| • Telecommunications |
| • Writing skills |
| • Presentation skills |
| • Meeting skills |
| • Industry and product knowledge |
| • Data modeling and spreadsheet analysis |
| • Records control |
| • Budgeting |
| • Firm's policies and procedures |
| • Purchasing |
| • Inventory control |
| • Supervisory skills |
| • Interpersonal skills |

### Warehouse Planning Support Training Needs

Because warehouse planning support employees focus on the analysis of a core logistics function, their knowledge of logistics and business processes must be broad. The training needs shown in Table 5-15 reflect that breadth, along with the training needs for the core skills the planning support employees use to apply that knowledge.

Equipment training includes the use of all office machines and software. It also includes sufficient knowledge of material handling equipment to understand its costs and effects on operations. Effective analysis of an operation demands an understanding of the equipment at a broad level, but greater detail certainly does no harm. No physical skills are required by the job, other than the ability to sit for long periods.

The skill training reflects the core competencies of the job–presentations, analysis, and report writing–and the demands placed on the employees. More analysis is always possible and usually is requested by someone. That means the demands placed on these employees require them to handle multiple projects simultaneously and maintain their sanity. Thus, time management, stress management, and project management skills are training needs.

Finally, the knowledge base is broad, and more could be added to the list by any firm, particularly industry specific knowledge and firm knowledge. Repeating a key point, these employees need to understand their own system fully and should be trained in it.

109

| Table 5-15 |
| --- |
| Warehouse Planning Support |
| Job Training Needs |

*Equipment specific*
• Office equipment operation
• Computer operation
• Analytical software
• Word processing, spreadsheets
• Operational characteristics of material handling equipment
*Physical skills*
• None required
*Interpersonal skills*
• Stress management
• Presentation skills
• Writing skills
• Team skills
• Time management
• Decision-making skills
*Knowledge Needs*
• Budgeting
• Purchasing
• Accounting
• Finance
• Purchasing
• Operations research
• Project management
• Records control and bookkeeping
• Advanced mathematics and statistics
• Transportation modal operations
• Inventory control procedures
• Warehouse practices and procedures
• Firm's operating procedures, policies, practices, and goals

**Warehouse Planning Support Summary**

This is a classic support job that requires high-level analytical skills and a broad base of business and logistics knowledge. Given the breadth of knowledge required, training should be on-going and rigorous to increase the knowledge base, analytical skills, and interpersonal skills.

## Warehouse Managers Job Description

Warehouse managers oversee facilities that govern the performance of the logistics system. Their jobs revolve around making key decisions based on information they derive from analysis, analytical reports, and interaction with their subordinates at all levels including suppliers, customers, internal clients, and upper management. They also directly and indirectly supervise 100 or more employees, a key activity that requires a range of interpersonal skills and occupies a substantial portion of their time.

The critical decisions are human resources and operations, especially establishing work procedures and determining pay and benefits. Warehouse managers must also oversee the flow of paperwork through the warehouse, assure that office procedures and policies do not interfere with serving customers or employee productivity, and resolve conflicts. They also make service-level decisions.

Managers must work in the operating facility at least part of the time, so unlike other management and support jobs, this job family has some physical requirements. These managers mingle with operating employees daily, observing machine operation and material handling. Where warehouse supervisors link operations to the warehouse office, warehouse managers link the warehouse to the rest of the logistics system. **(5)**

## Warehouse Managers Competencies

Warehouse managers' competencies encompass a broad range of knowledge and skills. Table 5-16 shows these competencies.

*Apply supervisory skills and human resource knowledge to staff and operate a distribution center or warehouse efficiently and effectively.* What top managers do for the entire logistics organization, warehouse managers must do for their piece of the organization–find the right people, put them in the right positions, and keep them focused on meeting the goals of the organization. This requires adaptability, intensity, and a high level of self-management skill.

*Apply knowledge of transportation, inventory control, warehousing, and LIS to making operational, strategic, and human resource decisions.* This means knowing logistics and applying the knowledge to the management of a key logistics function. If logistics now revolves around LIS, the primary satellites are warehouses and distribution centers. Running a good logistics system while running the warehouses poorly is simply impossible. Since the principal elements of this job are decision-making and supervision in a logistics context, the application of this knowledge to key decisions is critical.

*Use knowledge of security and safety procedures to develop policies and practices that assure safety for employees and security for the goods.* People are an essential component of warehouse operation, so their safety must be a foremost concern for warehouse managers. Warehouse operations are

111

designed to deliver the right goods to the right people in the right condition. That does not happen if goods are damaged or stolen. Consequently, managers must focus on preventing accidents, reducing shrinkage, and minimizing loss and damage.

They must also use their senses, especially their sight and hearing, to maintain their personal safety in the warehouse. This is not an office job, at least not all the time. These managers are often in the middle of operations making decisions and observing.

---

**Table 5-16**
**Warehouse Managers**
**Competencies**

- Apply supervisory skills and human resource knowledge to staff and operate a distribution center or warehouse efficiently and effectively
- Apply knowledge of transportation, inventory control, warehousing, and LIS to making operational, strategic, and human resource decisions.
- Use knowledge of security and safety procedures to develop policies and practices that assure safety for employees and security for the goods
- Understand and apply LIS knowledge to operational and strategic decisions
- Communicate effectively with employees, supervisors, and managers to develop and achieve short and long term goals
- Understand material handling equipment operation and costs
- Operate and oversee the use of office machines and equipment
- Apply knowledge of budgeting, purchasing, accounting and use basic math and reading skills effectively on the job

---

*Understand and apply LIS knowledge to operational and strategic decisions.* LIS now ties logistics elements into a system. With operating employees linked directly to global databases, planning support analyzing based on those databases, and upper managers second-guessing decisions based on the LIS, warehouse managers must understand the system and how it operates. They must be able to use it and to train others to use it. Most critically, they must use this knowledge to make operational and strategic decisions regarding the warehouse.

*Communicate effectively with employees, supervisors, and managers to develop and achieve short and long term goals.* If employees do not know the goals, it is very difficult for them to work toward the goals. The employees

112

look to the manager to direct them in activities that will lead to the accomplishment of personal and organizational goals. Ideally, the same activities will lead to both sets of goals. All supervision requires communication, so warehouse managers must communicate effectively at some level for the warehouse to function effectively. Some managers communicate better one-on-one, others to groups. Some do both extremely well. Somehow, warehouse managers must show warehouse employees the way to achieving goals.

*Understand material handling equipment operation and costs.* The warehouse manager should understand the equipment his or her employees operate well enough to discuss its use with them, assess its effectiveness, and determine the cost of its use. Replacement versus maintenance decisions rely on this knowledge, not to mention acquisition of new equipment.

*Operate and oversee the use of office machines and equipment.* Warehouse managers are responsible for a broad range of administrative and support activities. They must know the operation of most of the machines under their control and understand how it is supposed to work.

*Apply knowledge of budgeting, purchasing, accounting, transportation, and telecommunications to operational and human resource decisions.* This simply means applying special expertise and knowledge of business principles to making warehouse decisions. As managerial jobs evolve, they will rely more and more on technical expertise in the field. They may even become highly focused, but later shift focal points. Nonetheless, these key areas will remain crucial to warehouse managers.

### Warehouse Managers Job Requirements

Warehouse managers job requirements reflect the supervisory, decision-making, and operational nature of their jobs. They are managers, of course, but the key point is that they manage warehouses and distribution centers. This requires specific knowledge that must be applied in this specific context.

```
┌─────────────────────────────────────────────────────┐
│  Table 5-17                                          │
│  Warehouse Managers                                  │
│  Job Requirements                                    │
├─────────────────────────────────────────────────────┤
│                                                      │
│  • Supervisory skills                                │
│  • Decision-making skills                            │
│  • Communication skills                              │
│  • Writing skills                                    │
│  • Presentation skills                               │
│  • Meeting skills                                    │
│  • Warehousing and inventory control                 │
│  • Retail distribution                               │
│  • Industrial distribution                           │
│  • Industry and product knowledge                    │
│  • Records control                                   │
│  • Budgeting                                         │
│  • Firm's policies and procedures                    │
│  • Purchasing                                        │
│  • Human resource principles, practices, and law     │
│  • Basic mathematics                                 │
│  • LIS                                               │
│  • Safety and security practices                     │
│  • Office machinery and procedures                   │
└─────────────────────────────────────────────────────┘
```

### Warehouse Managers Training Needs

Warehouse managers have the longest list of required knowledge in the research. These managers have complete responsibility for managing facilities that employ hundreds of people, process millions of dollars in inventory weekly, and serve dozens of retail stores or customers. They are also likely candidates to become top logistics managers, partly because they already work in jobs that require a broad knowledge base. They may not need to know everything, but they come close.

One problem is that they often assume their positions with relatively little preparation. They learn about accounting, auditing, budgeting, human resource management, occupational health and safety, labor relations, and other knowledge they identified as absolutely critical to their job performance primarily from OJE. As has been pointed out and will be emphasized again, OJE is a poor centerpiece for training. It is especially poor for training managers with such broad responsibilities.

Managers' equipment-related training covers the need to understand its proper functioning when correctly calibrated and set up and its comparative cost effectiveness. It also covers the office equipment that facilitates communication, information flow, record keeping, and facility inventory. They need a working knowledge of all the equipment under their supervision.

Physical skills play a role for these managers. They spend part of most days in the warehouse. They require detailed knowledge of their own operation, so they may even perform some of the operating employees' jobs for brief periods, just to gain an understanding of the work.

Interpersonal skills are the core of these jobs. Supervision, self-management, and communication skills require constant updating, partly because it is so easy to fall into bad habits. Team skills are now linked to project management skills because managers build and participate in so many cross functional teams.

Finally, the knowledge base for this group is enormous. The major concern is that this knowledge is far too often acquired from OJE. Experience is a wonderful teacher, but only if the learned procedures and skills are correct.

Where human resource knowledge is concerned, a little knowledge could be dangerous. In college visits, untrained interviewers sometimes violate federal discrimination laws during interviews with women and minorities. Many of these interviewers are operating managers from logistics operations. If they knew the legal jeopardy they create for themselves and their firms, they would most likely avoid these potentially damaging errors. The same behavior may hold for the same managers in the field. Asking a potential employee if she is married, for example, may open a firm to a gender discrimination suit. Even if the suit is unsuccessful, the manager's time is taken up with litigation.

There are human and operating consequences for incomplete and incorrect knowledge in most of the areas on the list in Table 5-18. Some managers are trained in a few of these areas, but not in most. A few, like the managers in the organization described in the best practices box in Chapter 2, are trained in nearly all of them. Note that this extensive training is also strong preparation for promotion to upper logistics management.

**Table 5-18**
**Warehouse Managers**
**Job Training Needs**

*Equipment specific*
- Office equipment operation
- Computer operation
- Operational characteristics of material handling equipment

*Physical skills*
- Safe lifting and handling procedures
- Use of senses to maintain safety in warehouse

*Interpersonal skills*
- Stress management
- Supervisory skills
- Interpersonal communication skills
- Presentation skills
- Writing skills
- Team skills
- Time management
- Decision-making skills

*Knowledge Needs*
- Budgeting
- Purchasing
- Accounting
- Auditing
- Finance
- Purchasing
- Project management
- Security
- Occupational health and safety
- Labor relations
- Recruitment, interviewing, and selection
- Manufacturing and production
- Operations research and quality control
- Benefits and workers compensation
- Retail distribution
- Geography–local, regional, and world
- Telecommunications
- Air and motor transportation
- Job analysis and classification
- Records control and bookkeeping
- Advanced mathematics and statistics

**Warehouse Managers Summary**

Warehouse managers carry the weight of major operations with broad responsibilities and the decision-making, supervision, and interpersonal skills associated with large organizations. The knowledge base is broad and the jobs require equipment knowledge and some physical skills. The major concern in training for this job family is the degree to which OJE acts as the primary source.

**Chapter Summary**

The warehouse is a core logistics function, one that cannot be entirely automated away–at least not in the foreseeable future. Warehouse employees are assuming more and more duties once associated with other logistics functions, especially purchasing, inventory control, and customer service.

Warehouse operating employees and lead operators not only operate equipment, they enter data, maintain inventory records, and in some firms, maintain limited contact with customers and suppliers. Their duties are expanding with new technology and the blending of other logistics functions under supply chain management.

Warehouse administrative support employees assume a broad role in coordinating communications throughout the warehouse and between the warehouse, the rest of the firm, and outsiders. While many of their duties are typical of administrative and clerical jobs elsewhere, the communications role is especially critical in a warehouse.

Warehouse supervisors require detailed knowledge of operating tasks along with significant management skills. Their jobs span organizational levels and are critical to the overall performance of the logistics and warehouse operation. Their activities and training should prepare them for promotion, since there is such a close relationship between their duties and warehouse managers' duties.

Warehouse planning support employees serve a classic staff function, examining warehouse operations, networks, and facilities to improve overall logistics function. They supervise few people, require a broad knowledge base, and focus on analysis.

Warehouse managers require the broad knowledge base and interpersonal skills that not only help them manage these complex operations, but also prepare them for upper management.

The warehouse has a discernible career ladder, but the ladder only goes so far for most employees. Operating employees may be promoted to supervisor, but rarely beyond that. Entry level managers may start as supervisors and then move to management or planning support.

| Table 5-19 |
| --- |
| **Warehouse Operating Employees** |
| **Job Description** |
| **Example Titles:** Dock Clerk, Loading Associate, Materials Handler, Merchandise Handler, Merchandise Processor, Order Packer, Order Puller/Picker, Receiving Associate, Reserve Stock Handler, Warehouse Associate, Warehouse Equipment Operator, Warehouse Inventory Handler, Warehouse Pack Processing Clerk, Yard Loader |
| **General Job Characteristics:** *Span of Control:* no direct or indirect reports; *Budgetary Authority:* none; *Licenses and Certification:* some licenses are required; *Travel:* none; *Hours:* full time, variable; *Incentives:* receive group incentives (44%), individual (20%) |
| **Supervision:** *Supervision Received:* regular monitoring of major and minor job duties by immediate supervisor (94%); *Supervision Given:* none |
| **Using Language:** Constant use of spoken and written English (100%) |
| **Using the Senses:** *Use Sight for:* observing the quality or quantity of materials (76%), seeing objects to the side while looking forward and noticing changing events in the workplace (69%), observing the performance of machines or equipment (62%), differences between colors (58%), seeing objects in low light (53%), seeing objects at a distance (48%), seeing differences between objects at a distance (47%), differences in patterns or shapes (46%); *Use Hearing for:* understanding speech (72%), the direction of a sound (68%), noticing changing events in the workplace (58%), focusing on one sound among many (53%) |
| **Decision Making:** *Human Resources Decisions:* none; *Operations and Production Decisions:* none; *Financial Decisions:* none; *Strategy Decisions:* none |
| **Contacts:** *Internal Contacts with:* first-line supervisor (92%),operational employees (79%), mid-level managers (78%), clerical staff (60%), laborers (44%); *External Contacts:* none |
| **Meetings:** *Meetings Attended:* informally exchange information (76%), solve problem or train or instruct (46%), coordinate work (29%); *Meetings Initiated or Chaired:* none |
| **Required physical activities:** coordinate eyes, ears, hands and feet (93%), walk while working (80%), twist or stretch their body (76%), lift up to 50lbs by hand (75%), coordinate arms and legs (72%), make precise arm-hand movements (71%), kneel crouch, or crawl (69%), maintain balance (54%), push or pull lightweight objects (53%), move individual fingers independently, (48%), carry up to 50lbs short distances (47%) |
| **Use of machine and tools:** utility vehicles (59%), personal computers (55%), short handled tools (40%), long handled tools (36%), office equipment (29%) |

**Table 5-19**
**Warehouse Operating Employees**
**Job Description**

**Work Context**: *Variety, Autonomy, and Interdependence:* must complete work before others can do theirs (79%), control of work pace (69%), depend on others to complete their work before doing their own work (67%), use a variety of skills (48%), determine the methods or equipment they or others use (47%); *Stressful Work Situations:* perform same physical activities over and over (81%), perform same mental activities over and over (75%), work with others on shared tasks (71%), work with people over whom they had no authority (64%), deal with distressed people (51%), work with frequent distractions (47%), work on different tasks over time (46%); *Receiving Feedback:* From supervisors, other managers, and themselves

---

**Table 5-20**
**Warehouse Lead Operators**
**Job Description**

**Example Titles:** Administrative Logistics Support Associate, Leadman/Warehouse Team Supervisor, Operations Assistant, Receiving Clerk, Receiving Supervisor, Shipping Clerk, Shipping Product Supervisor, Shipping Supervisor, Team Leader, Warehouse Foreman, Warehouse Group Leader, Warehouse Material Planner, Warehouse Shipping Leader, Warehouse Supervisor, Warehousing Administrator

**General Job Characteristics:** *Span of Control:* non-supervisory employees (9); *Budgetary Authority:* $215; *Licenses and Certification:* some required; *Travel:* none; *Hours:* full time, same number per week; *Incentives:* receive group incentives (31%)

**Supervision:** *Supervision Received:* regular monitoring of major and minor job duties by immediate supervisor (100%), other employees other than immediate supervisor (41%); *Supervision Given:* regular monitoring of job duties for laborers (31%)

**Using Language:** Constant use of spoken and written English (100%)

**Using the Senses:** *Use Sight for:* observing the quality or quantity of materials (85%), seeing objects to the side while looking forward (59%), patterns, or shapes (56%), seeing objects at a distance (53%), small details of close objects (44%), observing the performance of machines or equipment (42%), differences between colors (36%); *Use Hearing for:* seeing differences between objects at a distance (58%), understanding speech (51%), noticing changing events in the workplace (44%), focusing on one sound among many (41%)

**Decision Making:** *Human Resources Decisions:* assigning employee responsibilities (44%)

**Table 5-20**
**Warehouse Lead Operators**
**Job Description**

**Contacts:** *Internal Contacts with*: mid-level managers (80%), clerical support staff (78%), first-line supervisors (76%), operations employees (75%), laborers (53%); *External Contacts*: none

**Meetings:** *Meetings Attended*: informally exchange information (71%), formally exchange ideas (54%), solve problems (54%), resolve conflicts (49%), coordinate work (42%), train or instruct (39%); *Meetings Initiated or Chaired*: coordinate work or informally exchange ideas (31%)

**Required physical activities:** walk while working (81%), stand for long periods (71%), kneel, crouch, or crawl (54%), lift up to 50lbs by hand and coordinate eyes, ears, hands and feet (53%), climb without aid of ladders or staircases (47%)

**Use of machine and tools:** standard office equipment (93%), personal computers (92%), calculators and typewriters (76%), utility vehicles (71%)

**Work Context**: Variety, Autonomy, and Interdependence*: depend on others to complete their work before doing* their own work (80%), must complete work before others can do theirs (78%), determine the methods or equipment they or others use (66%), control their own work pace (76%), learn new skills (61%), use a variety of new skills (58%); *Stressful Work Situations:* perform same mental activities over and over (81%), work on shared tasks (69%), work with people over whom they had no authority (68%), work under tight deadlines (64%), work with frequent distractions (53%), work on different tasks over time (47%); *Receiving Feedback:* From supervisors, other managers, and themselves


**Table 5-21**
**Warehouse Supervisors**
**Job Description**

**Example Titles:** Facilities Manager, Logistics Supervisor, Senior Operations Manager, Shipping Manager, Store Delivery Manager, Transportation Department Manager, Transportation Distribution Supervisor, Transportation Yard Manager, Warehouse Department Manager, Warehouse Distribution Center Supervisor, Warehouse Physical Distribution Manager, Warehouse Section Leader, Warehouse Team Manager

**General Job Characteristics:** *Span of Control:* managers, supervisors, and non-supervisory employees reporting directly (19), indirect reports (21); *Budgetary Authority:* $390,000; *Licenses and Certification:* none; *Travel:* Out of town with overnight stays (36%); *Hours:* full time, same number per week; *Incentives:* receive group incentives (46%), individual (21%)

120

| Table 5-21 |
| --- |
| **Warehouse Supervisors** |
| **Job Description** |

**Supervision:** *Supervision Received:* regular monitoring of major and minor job duties by immediate supervisor (93%), other employees other than immediate supervisor (39%); *Supervision Given:* regular monitoring of job duties for workers involved with production or processing (39%), laborers (25%)

**Using Language:** Constant use of spoken and written English (100%)

**Using the Senses:** *Use Sight for:* pictures, patterns, or graphs (68%), observing the behavior of people or animals and observing the performance of machines or equipment (61%), noticing changing events in the workplace (46%), observing the quality or quantity of materials (36%); *Use Hearing for:* understanding speech (61%), noticing changing events in the workplace (36%), identifying the direction of a sound (32%)

**Decision Making:** *Human Resources Decisions:* assigning employee responsibilities (71%), changing work procedures (68%), increasing or decreasing the number of employees (50%); *Operations and Production Decisions:* evaluating the effectiveness of operations (79%), modifying or improving operations and setting or changing short-term goals (68%), setting long-term goals (46%), determining equipment type or processes (39%); *Financial Decisions:* setting or changing size of budgets (46%), purchasing materials and supplies (36%); *Strategy Decisions:* taking on new projects (46%)

**Contacts:** *Internal Contacts with:* operations employees (57%), clerical support staff (36%); *External Contacts:* none

**Meetings:** *Meetings Attended:* solve problems, informally exchange information, and train or instruct (61%), formally exchange ideas (50%), evaluate options or make a decision and resolve conflicts (46%), set policies (43%), coordinate work (39%), evaluate people or projects (36%); *Meetings Initiated or Chaired:* consult or informally exchange ideas (43%), coordinate work or evaluate people or projects (39%), resolve conflicts (36%)

**Required physical activities:** walk while working (63%), coordinate eyes, ears, hands, and feet (46%), stand for long periods (43%)

**Use of machine and tools:** personal computers (82%), standard office equipment (64%), calculators and typewriters (61%)

| Table 5-21 |
| --- |
| **Warehouse Supervisors** |
| **Job Description** |
| **Work Context**: *Variety, Autonomy, and Interdependence:* learn new skills and control own work pace (61%), must complete work before others can do theirs and use a variety of skills (54%), complete their work before doing their own work (46%), determine the methods or equipment they use (39%), determine the methods or equipment others use (36%); *Stressful Work Situations:* work on shared tasks (75%), work under tight deadlines (57%), conflicting work goals, perform same mental activities over and over, and deal with distressed people (54%), work on different tasks over time and work on the same physical activities over and over (43%), work in situations that are highly stressful or difficult for them and working with frequent distractions (39%); *Receiving Feedback:* From supervisors, other managers, customers, and themselves |

| Table 5-22 |
| --- |
| **Warehouse Administrative Support** |
| **Job Description** |
| **Example Titles:** Administrative Assistant, Operations Manager, Project Manager, Training Director, Transportation and Logistics Product Manager, Warehouse Office Manager, Warehouse Operations Manager |
| **General Job Characteristics:** *Span of Control:* managers, supervisors, and professionals reporting directly (7), indirect reports (17); *Budgetary Authority:* $745,000; *Licenses and Certification:* none; *Travel:* Out of town with overnight stays (58%); *Hours:* full time, same number per week; *Incentives:* receive group incentives (67%), individual (42%) |
| **Supervision:** *Supervision Received:* regular monitoring of major and minor job duties by immediate supervisor (94%); *Supervision Given:* regular monitoring of job duties for first-line supervisors (42%), clerical and support staff (33%) |
| **Using Language:** Constant use of spoken and written English (100%) |
| **Using the Senses:** *Use Sight for:* pictures, patterns, or graphs (83%), observing small details, the performance of machines or equipment, noticing changing events in the workplace, and observing the quality or quantity of materials(58%), observing details of distant objects (50%); *Use Hearing for:* understanding speech (67%), noticing changing events in the workplace (50%), identifying the direction of a sound (42%) |

| Table 5-22 |
| --- |
| Warehouse Administrative Support |
| Job Description |

**Decision Making:** *Human Resources Decisions:* increasing or decreasing the number of employees, changing work procedures, or changing salaries or benefits (67%), establishing lines of authority (58%); *Operations and Production Decisions:* modifying or improving operations or evaluating the effectiveness of operations (67%), setting or changing short-term goals (50%), setting long-term goals (42%); *Financial Decisions:* purchasing materials and supplies (83%), setting or changing size of budgets (75%), purchasing capital equipment (58%); *Strategy Decisions:* taking on new projects (75%), changing services offered (42%)

**Contacts:** *Internal Contacts with:* clerical support staff (88%) first-line supervisors, mid-level managers, and upper managers (92%), operations employees (50%); *External Contacts with:* suppliers (83%), managers (75%), customers (67%), contractors and the public (58%), non-managerial employees (50%)

**Meetings:** *Meetings Attended:* informally exchange information (92%), consult, evaluate options or make a decision, or set policies (83%), formally exchange ideas or train or instruct (75%), solve problems or evaluate people or projects (67%), coordinate work (50%); *Meetings Initiated or Chaired:* informally exchange ideas, solve problems, consult, and evaluate options or make decisions (75%), formally exchange ideas or set policies (67%), train or instruct (50%)

**Required physical activities:** sit for long periods (92%)

**Use of machine and tools:** standard office equipment, personal computers, calculators and typewriters (100%)

**Work Context:** *Variety, Autonomy, and Interdependence:* must complete work before others can do theirs and use a variety of skills (83%), depend on others to complete their work before doing their own work, learn new skills, and determine the methods or equipment others use (75%), determine the methods or equipment they use (67%), control of work pace and determine what projects they work on (58%), influence work activities of others outside the organization (50%); *Stressful Work Situations:* work on shared tasks (92%), work under tight deadlines (83%), work with people over whom they had no authority or work with frequent distractions (75%), conflicting work goals (67%), work on different tasks over time (58%), deal with distressed people or performing the same mental activities over and over (50%); *Receiving Feedback:* From supervisors, other managers, and themselves

123

| **Table 5-23** |
| :--- |
| **Warehouse Planning Support** |
| **Job Description** |
| **Example Titles:** Logistics and Warehouse Engineer, Logistics Manager of Distribution, Logistics Planning Manager, Logistics Quality Director, Senior Project Manager, Warehouse Commodity Manager, Warehouse Human Resources Manager, Warehouse Inbound Logistics Manager, Warehouse Quality Manager |
| **General Job Characteristics:** *Span of Control:* managers, supervisors, and non-supervisory employees reporting directly (2), indirect reports (1); *Budgetary Authority:* 34,600,000; *Licenses and Certification:* none; *Travel:* Out of town with overnight stays (83%); *Hours:* full time, same number per week; *Incentives:* receive group incentives (42%), individual (33%) |
| **Supervision:** *Supervision Received:* regular monitoring of major and minor job duties by immediate supervisor (100%), other employees other than immediate supervisor (33%); *Supervision Given:* regular monitoring of job duties for clerical and support staff (33%) |
| **Using Language:** Constant use of spoken and written English, including editing, composing, and report writing (100%); use database queries, macros, and other computer languages that do not produce executable programs (25%) |
| **Using the Senses:** *Use Sight for:* observing the performance of machines or equipment and differences between colors, patterns, or shapes (50%), observing the quality or quantity of materials, noticing changing events in the workplace, identifying the direction of a sound, and observing the behavior of people or animals (42%); *Use Hearing for:* understanding speech (67%), noticing changing events in the workplace and the direction of a sound (42%) |
| **Decision Making:** *Human Resources Decisions*: increasing or decreasing the number of employees (67%), assigning employee responsibilities, increasing or decreasing the number of employees, and changing work procedures(50%); *Operations and Production Decisions:* modifying or improving operations (58%), evaluating the effectiveness of operations and setting long-term operational goals (50%), setting or changing short-term goals (42%); *Financial Decisions:* purchasing materials and supplies (58%), purchasing capital equipment and setting or changing size of budgets (42%); *Strategy Decisions*: taking on new projects (67%) |
| **Contacts:** *Internal Contacts with*: mid-level managers (92%), first-line supervisor and clerical support staff (83%), upper managers (67%) professionals or technical specialists with and without authority (58%); *External Contacts with*: managers (67%), suppliers and non-managerial employees (58%), contractors (50%), executives (42%) |

124

**Table 5-23**
**Warehouse Planning Support**
**Job Description**

**Meetings:** *Meetings Attended:* informally exchange information, set policies (100%), consult and solve problems (92%), evaluate options or make a decision and train or instruct (83%), coordinate work (75%), formally exchange ideas and set policies (67%), resolve conflicts or evaluate people or projects (58%); *Meetings Initiated or Chaired:* consult (92%), informally exchange ideas (83%), formally exchange ideas (75%), coordinate work or train or instruct (67%), solve problems (58%)

**Required physical activities:** sit for long periods (83%), walk while working and make precise finger movements (50%)

**Use of machine and tools:** personal computers (100%), standard office equipment (92%), calculators and typewriters (83%), mainframes or peripherals (42%)

**Work Context:** *Variety, Autonomy, and Interdependence:* must complete work before others can do theirs, influence work activities of others outside the organization, and learn new skills (83%), use a variety of skills and control own work pace (75%), determine the methods or equipment they or others use and produce a finished product or service (58%); *Stressful Work Situations:* work on shared tasks (100%), work with people over whom they had no authority (92%), work under tight deadlines (83%), work on different tasks over time and deal with conflicting work goals (75%), work with frequent distractions (50%)


**Table 5-24**
**Warehouse Managers**
**Job Description**

**Example Titles:** Distribution Supervisor, Logistics and Transportation Director, Operations Supervisor, Transportation Logistics Coordinator, Warehouse Manager, Warehouse Operations Leader, Warehouse Production Planning Manager, Warehouse Receiving Operations Manager, Warehouse Regional Manager

**General Job Characteristics:** *Span of Control:* managers, supervisors, and professionals reporting directly (17), indirect reports (123); *Budgetary Authority:* $2,300,000; *Licenses and Certification:* none; *Travel:* Out of town with overnight stays (44%); *Hours:* variable, full time; *Incentives:* receive group incentives (69%), individual (38%)

**Supervision:** *Supervision Received:* regular monitoring of major and minor job duties by immediate supervisor (94%), other employees other than immediate supervisor (38%); *Supervision Given:* regular monitoring of job duties for clerical and support staff (75%), first-line supervisors (69%), workers involved with production or processing (63%), laborers (56%), mid-level managers (31%)

| Table 5-24 |
| --- |
| **Warehouse Managers** |
| **Job Description** |

**Using Language:** Constant use of spoken and written English, including editing, composing, and report writing (100%); use database queries, macros, and other computer languages that do not produce executable programs (31%)

**Using the Senses:** *Use Sight for:* pictures, patterns, or graphs (81%), observing the performance of machines or equipment and noticing changing events in the workplace (75%), observing the behavior of people or animals (56%), observing the quality or quantity of materials (50%), differences between colors, patterns, or shapes (44%), observing and using blueprints, maps, or similar documents (38%); *Use Hearing for:* understanding speech (63%), noticing changing events in the workplace (56%)

**Decision Making:** *Human Resources Decisions:* assigning employee responsibilities (100%), changing work procedures (94%), increasing or decreasing the number of employees (88%), changing salaries or benefits and lines of authority (69%); *Operations and Production Decisions:* modifying or improving operations (100%), setting or changing short-term goals (94%), determining equipment type or processes (88%), evaluating the effectiveness of operations and setting long-term goals (81%); *Financial Decisions:* purchasing materials and supplies (81%), setting or changing size of budgets (75%), purchasing capital equipment (69%); *Strategy Decisions:* taking on new projects (69%), abandoning projects (38%), changing services offered or shutting down operations segments (31%)

**Contacts:** *Internal Contacts with:* first-line supervisor and clerical support staff (88%), mid-level managers (81%), operations employees and professionals or technical specialists (75%), upper managers (63%) laborers (56%); *External Contacts with:* managers (63%), suppliers and non-managerial employees (56%), executives (50%), customers the public, or job applicants (44%), contractors (38%)

**Meetings:** *Meetings Attended:* informally exchange information, set policies (100%), consult and formally exchange ideas (94%), solve problems, evaluate options or make a decision (88%), coordinate work (75%), evaluate people or projects and train or instruct (69%), resolve conflicts (63%); *Meetings Initiated or Chaired:* solve problems, evaluate options and make decisions and set policies (88%), informally exchange ideas (81%), coordinate work, evaluate people or projects, formally exchange ideas, or consult (75%), resolve conflicts or train or instruct (63%)

**Required physical activities:** stand or sit for long periods (69%), walk while working (63%)

**Use of machine and tools:** standard office equipment, personal computers (100%), calculators and typewriters (94%), mainframes or peripherals (56%)

126

| Table 5-24 |
| --- |
| **Warehouse Managers** |
| **Job Description** |

**Work Context**: *Variety, Autonomy, and Interdependence:* determine the methods or equipment they or others use, learn new skills (100%), control of work pace and schedule and learn a variety of skills (94%), depend on others to complete their work before doing their own work (81%), must complete work before others can do theirs and influence work activities of others outside the organization (75%), select projects to work on (69%); *Stressful Work Situations:* work under tight deadlines, work on shared tasks, conflicting work goals (88%), work with people over whom they had no authority (81%), work in situations that are highly stressful or difficult for them, work with frequent distractions, and work on different tasks over time (75%), deal with distressed people (50%)  *Receiving Feedback:* From supervisors, other managers, and themselves

# Transportation

*If it got there, a truck brought it.*
*—Unknown*

*No one cares how it gets there as long as it gets there.*
*—Trucking President*

This chapter describes four job families: traffic managers, administrative staff, loaders, and motor carrier operating employees. Respondents in these job families came from traffic, transportation operations, and transportation firms. The chapter describes these jobs based on scores from the CMQ, interviews, and other survey responses. The chapter discusses the competencies, job requirements, and training needs for each job family based on these results. It also profiles personality, customer orientation, market orientation, and need for cognition for traffic managers.

These results affect the training, recruitment, and selection of transportation personnel. Operating employee respondents worked in trucking, loaders with rail and water, administrative support in trucking and traffic, and managers primarily in traffic or motor carriage. Consequently, these job families are distinct, fitting into no clear hierarchy. They also do not represent transportation as a whole–rail, water, air, and pipeline are not represented. Supporting data are shown in Appendix 6, at the back of the book, and technical job descriptions are shown in tables at the end of the chapter.

128

# Key Findings and Takeaways

*Points in the text supporting each key finding are tagged with a
number in parentheses, e.g (1).*

**1** Transportation tends toward flatter organizations with increasing
responsibility placed on operating employees.  In trucking, dispatchers
and drivers perform many of the same tasks, one from the truck cab,
the other from the terminal or home office. This trend is driven by
information technology.

**2** Since motor carrier operating employees spend much of their work
time away from the firm, communication technology is especially
important.  Training for operating employees should extend beyond
equipment operation to its effective use. When people with poor
communications skills use communications technology, poor
communication simply takes place more quickly over a longer distance.

**3** Motor carrier operating employees require equipment training,
licensing, and certification, but also training on information
technology, satellite communication, and interpersonal skills. Loaders
require training in packaging requirements, vehicle specifications,
regulations, and customer requirements related to the cargo they
transport or ship.

**4** Traffic managers deal with both suppliers and customers to form
working partnerships, which places greater emphasis on
communications, negotiations, and interpersonal skills.

**5** Motor carrier operating employees deal with customers' and suppliers'
warehousing employees–contact that can improve or detract from these
valuable relationships.

**6** Traffic managers frequently make purchasing, budgeting, operations,
and human resources decisions.  Put simply, they need training in all of
these area, most importantly in human resource management.

**7** Recruitment and retention of operating employees depend on training
managers, staff, loaders, and operating employees in human relations,
supervision, and communications.

**8** Loaders and operating employees contact customers more often than any other job families except customer service, suggesting training needs in sales and customer relations. Such training also encourages retention.

**9** Transportation administrative support should see its function as smoothing the work of operating employees and managers. Administrative support should act as the knowledge source for rules, regulations, laws, policies, and procedures. It should also act as a clearing house for communications.

## Transportation Employees

Transportation inspires legends, myths, and songs. After all, it is along the road, over the oceans, and in the air that true adventures take place, and where heroes come into being. Transportation is filled with legendary characters, some real and some mythical, like Hercules, Marco Polo, Columbus, Casey Jones, and Lindbergh, characters whose acts of daring and courage are the heart of adventure. In all of logistics, transportation is the only discipline tinged with romance and touched by poetry. The heroes of inventory control and warehousing, whoever they may be, remain unsung, and the legendary figures of purchasing and material management will never appear in middle school textbooks. But transportation can bring adventure.

It is removing the adventure from transportation that lies at the heart of the jobs discussed in this chapter. On-time delivery of intact goods without any mishaps lacks adventure, romance, and poetry, but it is precisely the point of transportation as a logistics function. If truck drivers, railroad engineers, marine pilots, and airline pilots are sometimes heroes, it is because something has gone badly wrong. Preventing and avoiding problems along the way leads to effective transportation and an effective logistics system–and toothpaste on the drugstore shelves, coal in fuel bins at the power plant, video games at the discount store, and parts at the manufacturing plant. While transportation is no longer the only logistics function that comes to mind, it remains the essential connector, the structure, the very bones of the logistics system.

"It almost seems stupid to say it, but we go nowhere without transportation. Warehousing is pointless and, for the most part, so is manufacturing. The goods have to get to markets. Getting them there is transportation. Without transportation, we're down in the riverbed looking for really good rocks to knock off squirrels for dinner. Transportation is the cornerstone of the economy and of modern societies."

–Retailing Vice President of Logistics

Human resource problems have seriously affected transportation since deregulation in the late 1970's and early 1980's. Turnover among truck drivers and barge crews, salary tiers for airline pilots, and changes in railroad employment all create controversy and alter the cost structures of the industry in question. Understanding the nature of the work and the changes taking place in transportation employment may help reduce the human resource costs of transportation and create a more effective system.

Trucks sitting on the fence are my biggest problem. If we can't find drivers, we don't need trucks. We know that when a driver leaves us, he can go to (another trucking company) across the street and start driving tomorrow. The driver knows that, too, so we have to give the drivers a reason to stay with us–a reason we can afford.

– Trucking Company President

Changes in transportation jobs are driven by technology, economic conditions, and the nature of the workforce. Globalization, intermodalism, and off-shore manufacturing–all intimately connected–influence the work of transportation. They underscore the need to train operating employees on communications and computer equipment, in interpersonal skills, and regulatory compliance; to find employees with these skills, or who can readily acquire them; and to find and train managers who can keep, develop, and train these employees–a need for supervisory skills that is daunting.

This chapter discusses four transportation job families: operating employees, loaders, administrative staff, and managers. It does not cover all transportation jobs, but focuses on four that fit in varied contexts. The role of each job family in the context of transportation and logistics is discussed, along with the competencies, job requirements, and training needs for each in the sections that follow. Data supporting these discussions are found in the tables in Appendix 6.

131

## Motor Carrier Operating Employees Job Description

Trucking dominates this discussion, but bear in mind that transportation operating employees not only drive trucks, they also operate trains, pilot ships, and fly planes. They also coordinate the movement of goods through the logistics system. Far from simply operating the vehicles, transportation operating employees increasingly direct their own work.(1)

The analysis of the survey data placed dispatchers and truck drivers in the same job family. While the two jobs differ in the equipment operated and the amount of time on the road, they differ little in interpersonal interactions, decision-making, and work context. They also share a common body of required knowledge. In short, they do much the same job, one group from the office, the other from the cab of the truck. This clustering reflects the trend toward driver self-dispatch on many loads, most commonly from the firm's web site.(1)

Driving, consequently, is good preparation for dispatching–and vice versa. These employees operate communications equipment, including telephones, satellite and other truck–born devices, and computer systems. They must also understand vehicle operation intimately–dispatchers as much as drivers. When one side of the communication fails to grasp the operating situation, problems arise that may disrupt customer service, increase employee stress, and decrease employee retention. (2)

---

"The dispatcher told the driver he could pass under the bridge. (The mapping program) said the clearance was 14' 4". The truck was 14' 2" clearance or something like that. Anyway, by the numbers on the truck and the numbers in (the mapping program), the truck should have been able to go under. The driver said he couldn't do it, because the sign on the bridge said 13' 9". The driver didn't think he could get under, even by letting air out of the tires. They argued for quite awhile, but the dispatcher insisted. The driver got angrier by the minute. Finally, he said, "All right, I'll take it under there, but you ---- , you better remember I told you it wouldn't go." About a foot under the bridge, the top of the trailer started to scrape, but the driver kept powering up and eventually pulled it through. It peeled back the top of the trailer, popped all the welds at the corners, so, yeah, that truck you saw driving down the road belonged to (my former company). It was quite a sight, with the sides sort of flopping out and the top bouncing up and down. It looked like an open sardine can."

–Former Trucking Operations Manager, on an event witnessed by one of the researchers

---

While one aspect of the job is operating and understanding equipment, the other is interpersonal–interacting constantly with customers, suppliers, the office, other drivers, and other transportation employees. The on-board technology can increase the amount and effectiveness of communications, but only if it is used well. It does not always improve communications, because

some dispatchers and drivers fail to use all of its capabilities. When dispatchers send the message "Call dispatch," the system adds little value.(2)

When they are on the road, operating employees experience horrendous stress. Driving 10 hours in heavy expressway traffic puts stress on anyone, but in an 18 wheeler with half-a-million dollars of customer freight the stress is worse. Even back in the office, the stress is high because the dispatcher feels time pressure from deadlines as much or more than the driver.(3)

These employees experience the adventure and poetry of transportation first hand. Vehicle breakdowns, adverse weather, congestion, and accidents may cause problems in the office, but the drivers must react to them first hand.

### Motor Carrier Operating Employees Competencies

Motor carrier operating employees' competencies revolve around vehicle operation, communication, and meeting customer needs. These competencies are listed in Table 6.1.

*Operate vehicles in keeping with company policy and the law, while satisfying customer requirements and minimizing costs.* Laws and regulations restrict vehicle size, weight, speed, and hours of operation. They also restrict the driver's hours, allowable emissions, packaging for some freight, and routes. Loosening these restrictions might allow a firm to serve its customers better, but the restrictions remain, presumably to serve a greater social purpose. Customer requirements may not recognize those restrictions, or transportation organizations may fear that compliance will cost them customers or business. Consequently, some pressure is placed on operating employees to violate laws and regulations to meet customer delivery schedules. Often dispatchers, customer service representatives, or sales representatives over-promise on delivery schedules, creating a quandary for the transportation organization. Based on this research, that constitutes incompetence. Put simply, operating in compliance with laws and regulations is a part of competence. Communicating with customers and helping them to adjust their expectations is another aspect of competent transportation, one usually left to managers.

This competency is complex, but it expresses the essence of the transportation operating employee's job. Failing to operate within the law may subject a firm to fines and open it to liability. The technology that now rapidly improves logistics performance will also improve the performance of regulatory agencies, especially their ability to monitor compliance to performance standards like speed limits and operating time. (3)

A common reason for failing to operate within company policies is not knowing them, a communications problem. Managers are too often guilty of changing policies that directly affect truck drivers without giving the driver adequate notice. The driver is often on the road when he or she discovers that the company no longer pays for motel rooms until 48 hours into a layover because the policy change took place after the driver left. Operating employees cannot comply with policies they do not know.(2)

Satisfying customer requirements assumes knowing those requirements, a key aspect of the next competency. This also depends on communication between customers, traffic and transportation employees, and drivers.(2, 5)

Cost minimization implies making good decisions about vehicle maintenance, routing, and operation. This often results from good working relationships between dispatchers and drivers. Poor working relationships almost invariably increase costs.

Finally, the central issue in this competence is operating the vehicle. This means understanding the equipment, using it safely and effectively. Given the complexity of most vehicles, this is no small matter.(3)

---

**Table 6-1**
**Motor Carrier Operating Employees**
**Competencies**

- **Operate vehicles in keeping with company policy and the law, while satisfying customer requirements and minimizing costs**
- **Use communications technology and interpersonal skills to understand, disseminate, and meet customer needs**
- **Maintain an understanding of delivery conditions and operating characteristics at customer sites**

---

*Use communications technology and interpersonal skills to understand, disseminate, and meet customer needs.* Motor carrier operating employees must grasp the immediate needs of clients and customers. When the customer expects a vehicle to arrive, it should be at least possible, if not probable. Staying in contact with the customer is crucial–and truck drivers and dispatchers are in constant contact with customers. They must let operations know what they learn from that contact and operations must listen. This applies in all modes of transportation, but especially in trucking where the contact between transportation employees and customer employees may be personal and frequent. (3)

One director of transportation had the point illustrated for him several years ago:

> "We had a driver, Bubba, who worked a retail route into Atlanta. He became so well-liked by the warehouse people at several of our customers, when they saw him pull into the distribution center, they would wave him to the front of the line to unload. When I visited the retailer, I handed the security guard my business card. The guard asked me if I worked for Bubba."
>
> –Manufacturing Director of Transportation

In another instance, the firm very nearly missed $20,000 in revenue because no one could find time to listen to a driver:

> The driver walked to a dispatcher's desk, only to be waved away by a dispatcher who was deep into a phone conversation. The driver moved toward another desk and was waved away again. The process continued until nearly every dispatcher had waved the driver away. The driver turned in slow circles, clearly having something important to say and no one to say it to. An observer, one of two consultants in the firm that day, walked to the driver and said, "You look like you want to tell someone something. Why don't you tell me?"
>
> The driver looked startled, sized up the observer, and said, "It's probably not a big deal, but I just dropped off a load up the street at (a customer's manufacturing plant). They've got fifteen truckloads no one has covered yet. I know we've got a lot of trucks in the yard right now, so I thought we ought to get somebody over there right away." The observer heard the driver out, then told a manager, and several trucks were dispatched immediately.
>
> –An event witnessed by one of the researchers

*Maintain an understanding of delivery conditions and operating characteristics at customer sites.* The more operating employees know about customer locations and customer practices, the more readily they can comply with customer requirements. This allows them to meet customer expectations quickly, while improving cost performance. This knowledge also reduces job frustration and contributes to employee retention. **(5)**

"One problem is having our drivers go into a large customer facility with dozens of trailers. If they haven't been there before, they have a hard time finding the one they're supposed to pull–assuming they can find the facility at all. With new drivers this can cost us two days or more because of missed appointments, or you know, getting there too late and having to lay over for the weekend."

–Manufacturing Traffic Manager

## Motor Carrier Operating Employees Job Requirements

Motor carrier operating employees must know the vehicles they operate, the communications equipment that keeps them linked to the terminal and the customer, basic mathematics, and interpersonal skills. This includes knowing relevant laws and regulations for the mode of transportation, maintaining self control in stressful situations, and disseminating information through operations about customers, suppliers, and vehicles. Vehicle operation usually requires licensing and certification. These job requirements are shown in Table 6-2.

These are the minimum knowledge and skill requirements for performing these jobs and precursors to competence. Putting together the competencies and job requirements leads directly to the analysis of training needs. They are discussed in the next section.

---

**Table 6-2**
**Motor Carrier Operating Employees**
**Job Requirements**

- **Vehicle operation**
- **Vehicle inspection**
- **Vehicle routine maintenance**
- **Vehicle loading, load balancing**
- **Licensing and certification**
- **Telecommunications equipment operation**
- **Telecommunications equipment troubleshooting**
- **Load documentation**
- **Customer facilities and networks**
- **Firm's policies and procedures**
- **Basic mathematics**
- **Interpersonal skills**

---

**Motor Carrier Operating Employees Training Needs**

Far too often, motor carrier operating employees are trained exclusively in vehicle operation. This leaves to chance–trial and error learning–skills that are central to the performance of their jobs. That includes communication skills, stress management, anger management, and customer relations. They also need to know the customer's operations, delivery conditions, facilities, and networks. Motor carrier operating employees' training needs are shown in Table 6-3. **(1,2,3,8)**

These jobs will expand in the future, accommodating more and more tasks as technology permits and encourages change. These employees have direct contact with customers, cargo, suppliers, and their own terminal and home offices. They are often in a better position to understand customer needs and match them to the firm's capabilities than anyone else. This does suggest that, in time, they will also need training in decision-making, negotiations, relationship management, and written communications.**(1,2,3,5,8)**

---

**Table 6-3**
**Motor Carrier Operating Employees**
**Job Training Needs**

*Equipment specific*
- **Vehicle operation, including refresher training**
- **Vehicle maintenance**
- **Telecommunications equipment operation**
- **Computer system operation**

*Interpersonal skills*
- **Stress management**
- **Anger management**
- **Time management**
- **Communication skills**

*Knowledge Needs*
- **Customer facilities, networks, and operations**
- **Transportation laws and regulations**
- **Firm's operating procedures, policies, and practices**

---

They are also in the best position to understand the condition of the vehicle they operate, the electronic equipment in their vehicles, and whether or not they are working properly. Consequently, their training should extend far beyond how to turn the equipment on and off and how to steer. As is the case with any employee who operates any equipment, they should be well aware of the proper functioning of a correctly calibrated and maintained piece of equipment.**(3)**

137

This is never more critical than with vehicles like over-the-road trucks, trains, tugs, barges, or airplanes. The consequences of failure are too great–to the smooth operation of the logistics system, and to life and limb. They also need training in company policies and procedures, training that should be routinely updated. Too many firms make changes while operating employees are gone and fail to keep them informed. **(3)**

Among the interpersonal skills training needs, anger management stands out for this job family. This is not to suggest that it is not needed by others, but operating employees are more likely to find themselves in situations that may turn to physical hostility. They need to understand anger in themselves and others. **(3)**

## Motor Carrier Operating Employees Summary

These jobs involve operating complex equipment and interacting with a variety of employees in their own company and with customers and suppliers. These jobs are increasing in complexity and in training needs as more tasks are pushed to the operating level–the cab of the vehicle in these cases.

The research supports the idea that these employees need training in areas reserved for managers and supervisors in the past–communications, interpersonal skills, and working with complex technology.

## Loaders Job Description

These employees load vehicles and coordinate vehicle movement in and out of major distribution facilities. They work closely with one another to load railcars, ocean containers, and trucks using forklifts, vans, hand trucks, and measuring devices. They assure the security, safety, quantity, and quality of the cargo and of each loaded vehicle. Some also act as lead operators, with some operational supervisory responsibilities and significant customer and supplier contact.

The point is, this is a job family, not a single job, so it includes some lead operators. These lead operators perform the same duties as operators, but also assume operational supervisory responsibility. **(3)**

They work closely with one another, their supervisors, and laborers inside the firm, and with customers and suppliers. Some of these employees conduct minor negotiations with carriers–getting the railcar at 3 p.m. rather than 5 p.m. or getting trailers spotted, for example. Overall, their jobs involve more meetings and contacts than 89% of the jobs in the comparison database of 8,000 jobs.**(3,8)**

Their work also involves frequent use of a variety of office machines, including personal computers, faxes, and telephones. They maintain inventory records and perform other clerical duties that require using numerical information and basic math skills. They also perform precise and heavy physical labor. Some lifting, including heavy lifting, is frequently part of these jobs. This distinguishes them from other largely clerical jobs–these employees physically check the freight, where administrative support employees process the paperwork while seldom coming in contact with the cargo.(3)

These employees sometimes supervise laborers, spend substantial time in meetings, sometimes chair meetings, oversee the activities of suppliers, and work closely with customers to identify transportation requirements and procedures.(3,8)

Because these jobs involve physical checking and personal verification of key elements in their respective supply chains, these jobs are not subject to any immediate change. The consequences of mistakes are too great–like chemical reactions between the load and the vehicle walls, which may put hazardous material into the environment or threaten human life and health.(3)

### Loaders Competencies

Loaders' competencies incorporate the need for technical competence in vehicle loading and the need for high-level communication skills. Table 6-4 lists the competencies for this job family.

*Assure that loaded cargo meets safety, security, regulatory, packaging, customs, and customer requirements.* This competency requires the application of a substantial knowledge base. It also implies knowing all of these requirements, a tall order in itself. Applying the knowledge may entail physically checking the quantity of liquid bulk loads, checking hazardous material regulations, evaluating packaging, and matching loads to freight bills and customer orders. It may include climbing onto or around vehicles to check loads, load cargo, and reposition cargo.(3)

*Operate material handling equipment efficiently and safely.* Effective use of handling equipment helps meet shipment schedules and safe operation protects both the cargo and the people working around it. A thorough understanding of correct functioning of properly calibrated equipment is essential.(3)

*Use communications skills to schedule and complete loading to meet customer needs.* These jobs involve extraordinary levels of interaction and cooperation. The loaders meet to coordinate work and to do the work. They deal with carriers on scheduling vehicles, customers on delivery schedules, and manufacturing on product availability for loading.(3)

*Maintain accurate inventory by using appropriate measuring devices.* These employees handle loads that require measurement by means other than counting, e.g. liquid bulk loads. They sometimes use technical measuring devices for inventory accuracy. Improperly measured loads can result in customer service failures or additional costs to the firm. (3)

*Use knowledge of vehicles and loading techniques used in the distribution center, manufacturing plant, or warehouse to assure a fit*

139

*between the cargo and the vehicle.* This includes inspecting vehicles to assure that they meet standards. For example, some liquid bulk chemicals cannot move in aluminum tank cars because they react with the aluminum, causing the metal to melt. This competency also implies extensive knowledge of the vehicles used by the firm, as well as extensive product knowledge.(3)

| **Table 6-4**<br>**Loaders**<br>**Competencies** |
|---|
| • **Assure that loaded cargo meets safety, security, regulatory, packaging, customs, and customer requirements**<br>• **Operate material handling equipment efficiently and safely**<br>• **Use communications skills to schedule and complete loading to meet customer needs**<br>• **Maintain accurate inventory by using appropriate measuring devices to avoid shipping and billing errors**<br>• **Use knowledge of vehicles and loading techniques used in the distribution center, manufacturing plant, or warehouse to assure a fit between the cargo and the vehicle** |

### Loaders Job Requirements

These jobs require the knowledge and skills listed in Table 6-5. As with other jobs more closely tied to distribution centers, these employees move freight out of the organization. They see that it moves to the right customer in the right vehicle in the right package in the right quantity. They perform many of the same tasks as employees in shipping at the warehouse, but with a specialized focus on rail or water transportation, in addition to trucking. (3)

| **Table 6-5**<br>**Loaders**<br>**Job Requirements** |
|---|
| • **Material handling equipment operation**<br>• **Knowledge of hazardous material handling and regulations**<br>• **Inventory record keeping and data control**<br>• **Loading procedures for vehicles in use**<br>• **Computer and office equipment operation**<br>• **Meeting skills**<br>• **Supervisory skills**<br>• **Communications skills**<br>• **Basic mathematics** |

Some loaders supervise others, so they need supervisory skills are needed. These skills also point to promotion possibilities. The requirements are needed to perform the basic tasks associated with these jobs. Loaders' job requirements are shown in Table 6-5.

Putting together the competencies and job requirements leads directly to the analysis of training needs. They are discussed in the next section. **(3)**

**Loaders Training Needs**

While many of the training needs for these jobs are obvious, the ability to apply knowledge and skills is crucial. For these employees, the methods for using the knowledge and skills are more important and more distinctive than the knowledge and skills themselves. Loaders' training needs are shown in Table 6-6. **(3)**

---

**Table 6-6**
**Loaders**
**Job Training Needs**

---

*Equipment specific*
• **Material handling equipment operation**
• **Office equipment use**
• **Working with appropriate vehicles, including matching loads and vehicles**
*Interpersonal skills*
• **Stress management**
• **Negotiations**
• **Meeting skills**
• **Communication skills**
*Knowledge Needs*
• **Customer networks and operations**
• **Transportation laws and regulations, especially hazardous material**
• **Transportation operations**
• **Inventory control procedures**
• **Product knowledge, especially for hazardous material**
• **Firm's operating procedures, policies, and practices**

---

Despite the obvious need for equipment training, many firms train operating employees, including loaders, minimally. Most rely on OJE, trial and error, and other informal approaches to training. The leading edge companies, by contrast, leave little to chance. They make certain that their employees understand how the equipment performs when it is working

141

properly and how to identify potential problems. While it lengthens training, it also helps prevent operational problems.(**3**)

These employees also need to know how to load equipment supplied by carriers. In some instances this is transparent–use the forklift to place the pallet on the floor of the truck–but not always. Connecting material handling equipment to rail tank cars requires specific training, which these employees need.(**3**)

The interpersonal training is often neglected, while some attention is paid to knowledge needs. Communications skills appear to be neglected and most commonly left to trial and error for these employees. Critical errors are unlikely based on a single misstatement, but increased frustration may be one result from too much reliance on chance learning. Stress management skills seem to apply to every operating level logistics job. This is no exception. Negotiation skills help in arranging vehicles with carriers and in coordinating with customers.(**3**)

Finally, these employees need training in the firm's policies and procedures. Too many firms allow employees to learn about policies and policy changes by chance. While it is not as critical, nor is it as likely to be flagrant with these employees as it often is for motor carrier operating employees, periodic overviews of policy and procedure changes are a good idea.(**3**)

Because these employees often handle hazardous material, product knowledge is critical. The product knowledge must match knowledge of hazardous material regulations. Knowing customer networks and operations can help fit the firm's procedures to customer needs. Also, knowing the firm's operating procedures, while an apparent need, is one not all companies meet. The list contains knowledge needs, not knowledge it would be nice to have. No area shown here should be neglected.(**3**)


### Transportation Administrative Support Job Description

These are standard administrative jobs with a strong transportation spin. The employees conduct office administrative duties in a transportation environment. They use standard office equipment regularly, process paperwork for regulatory compliance, freight bills, and standard office communications. Their primary focus is internal. (**9**)

Their overall job fits somewhere in the middle of the comparison database of 8,000 jobs. They are involved in meetings, deal with fellow employees, and exchange information with a wide range of fellow employees, but all at about the 50th percentile in the database. (**9**)

Their knowledge needs depend heavily on the transportation modes with which they work. More than anything else, they need to know the practices, policies, procedures, and regulations that apply to the specific modes in question. Many are involved in some aspect of regulatory compliance.**(9)**

### Transportation Administrative Support Competencies

Transportation administrative support competencies center on office procedures, paperwork management, and transportation knowledge. These competencies are shown in Table 6-7.

*Process paperwork with minimal disruption to operations or customer relationships.* The paperwork is not the operation. It merely supports and documents operations, so it should never interfere with either operations or customer relationships. This means the most critical aspect of processing the documentation is accuracy–in entering data, in selecting the documents to match a transaction, and in transmitting documents to customers or to operations.**(9)**

*Maintain accurate records to assure correct material and correct bills go to the customer.* In maintaining customer relationships, this may be the most critical paperwork. Many organizations measure billing accuracy as a dimension of customer service, so explicit standards may exist, but more importantly, billing disputes can consume time better spent improving customer relationships. Serious disputes may consume management and operating employees' time, as well as adding to the administrative support workload.**(9)**

*Maintain expertise in modes of transportation operated out of their facilities.* This is a context issue for these administrative jobs. Processing paperwork may be similar across a broad range of fields, but the devils live in the details. Administrative support employees who understand their operations are likely to help improve operations and to spend time on assuring the accuracy and appropriateness of documentation.**(9)**

*Use office equipment to smooth operations and make managers' and operating employees' jobs easier.* Support positions are exactly that–support for other jobs. Beyond not interfering with customer relationships or operations, administrative support's use of standard office equipment can make operations flow more smoothly and ease the burden of details on managers–or the opposite. Good administrative support makes work easier for others, whether through use of office equipment and computers or establishing procedures that improve communication.**(9)**

*Maintain expertise on key software used in operations.* The expertise for this group should be in use of the software, not its installation or maintenance. Maintenance and installation are LIS tasks. Software to support many transportation operations is complex, so understanding the details of running it is no trivial task. The tendency is to assume that many software features can be 'figured out' on the fly, to the detriment of performance.**(9)**

*Communicate information requirements and correct paperwork processing throughout the organization, so regulations are met, procedures are followed, and customers are satisfied.* Internal problems often come from failure to understand what is necessary to process paperwork and why the paperwork is important. Administrative support employees should train those who provide information for paperwork or who complete it in the field in how to do it correctly. Not everyone will cooperate and many will still make errors, but the time spent training will improve the support function. **(9)**

| Table 6-7<br>**Transportation Administrative Support Employees**<br>**Competencies** |
| :--- |
| • **Process paperwork with minimal disruption to operations or customer relationships**<br>• **Maintain accurate records to assure correct material and correct bills go to the customer**<br>• **Maintain expertise in modes of transportation operated out of their facilities**<br>• **Use office equipment to smooth operations and make managers' and operating employees' jobs easier**<br>• **Maintain expertise on key software used in operations**<br>• **Communicate information requirements and correct paperwork processing throughout the organization, so that regulations are met, procedures are followed, and customers are satisfied** |

**Transportation Administrative Support Job Requirements**

The requirements for transportation administrative support are typical of other administrative jobs–but they include knowledge of transportation documentation and transportation office procedures. Additional knowledge of transportation is helpful, but not an absolute requirement. The job requirements are shown in Table 6-8.

| Table 6-8<br>**Transportation Administrative Support**<br>**Job Requirements** |
| :--- |
| • **Office equipment operation**<br>• **Telecommunication equipment operation**<br>• **Office processes and procedures**<br>• **Transportation documentation**<br>• **Word processing, database, and spreadsheet skills**<br>• **Expertise in firm-specific software**<br>• **Basic mathematics and language skills**<br>• **Interpersonal skills** |

Putting together the competencies and job requirements leads directly to the analysis of training needs. They are discussed in the next section.

### Transportation Administrative Support Employees Training Needs

Equipment training should go beyond simple operation to use in communications and support. Most of the equipment involves communication, which means training should include how to use it to enhance organizational communications.(9)

Interpersonal skills include self-management–stress and time management skills. Because these employees frequently deal with people who are upset, usually on the telephone, the skills are important. Communications skills must cover both written and oral communication, but oral probably should take precedence. Poor oral communications combined with poor telephone procedures disrupt transportation operations. They often cause problems for customers and for operating employees.(9)

The crucial knowledge for this group consists of office procedures, firm-specific software, management support requirements, and the firm's operating procedures, policies, and practices. These employees should act as depositories of knowledge about the routine processes and procedures of the transportation organization. Because many non-transaction related communications go through the administrative support function, they should be aware of what is going on in the organization all the time. Transportation administrative support job training needs are shown in Table 6-9. **(9)**

---

**Table 6-9**
**Transportation Administrative Support**
**Job Training Needs**

*Equipment specific*
- **Standard office equipment**
- **Telecommunications equipment operation**
- **Satellite systems**

*Interpersonal skills*
- **Stress management**
- **Time management**
- **Communication skills**

*Knowledge Needs*
- **Transportation office procedures**
- **Firm-specific software**
- **Management support requirements**
- **Firm's operating procedures, policies, and practices**

---

## Transportation Administrative Support Summary

These support positions play a crucial role in transportation operations. While the list of equipment and skills required is relatively short, the use of both the equipment and the skills can enhance or detract from transportation operations. For many firms, these employees play a major role in customer relations and customer service, as well as helping to coordinate the interaction between employees in the transportation operation.

## Traffic Managers Job Description

These managers operate the traffic and transportation functions of their firms. They assume major responsibility for operations, human resource, purchasing, and budgeting decisions. They meet frequently with a wide variety of people both inside and outside the firm. They may make decisions about acquiring vehicles, hiring operating personnel, and budgeting. They also directly supervise technicians, operating employees, and mid-level managers.

Traffic managers play a significant role in resolving conflicts, exchanging information with shippers and receivers, and conducting meetings. Traffic managers, who comprise the majority of managers in this group, also play a major role in purchasing transportation services, most often trucking services, but also other modes of transportation. They use their knowledge of the modes of transportation constantly to assure that their firm's goods move to their customers safely and on-time.(4,6)

They chair and attend meetings, mostly with supervisors, operating employees, and mid-level managers. They deal with customers on sales-related matters. Overall, the most important aspects of their jobs are related to interacting with others, human resources and operational decision-making, overseeing office activities, and exchanging information.(4,6)

### Traffic Managers Competencies

As with other logistics managers, traffic managers' competencies focus on decision-making and human resource issues. The list of competencies is shown in Table 6-10.

*Use supervisory, development, recruiting, and selection skills to build and maintain a transportation or traffic organization.* Human resource decisions tend to drive many transportation operations, especially those oriented to trucking. Recruiting and retaining drivers causes problems for many firms, a problem aggravated or eased by how well the firm recruits, retains, and trains dispatchers, managers, and support staff. The communication and supervisory skills of the manager tend to influence communication and supervision throughout the organization. The traffic manager sets the tone and helps to establish the organizational culture. Since managerial work takes place largely through other people, this is the most important single competency for traffic managers. **(4,6,7)**

---

We don't really have any trouble keeping our truck drivers. That's never been a problem. Our problem right now is the low unemployment rate in this area. For the county it's less than 2%, so we have trouble trying to get new drivers. Our pay and benefits are good, but we know that is not what keeps our drivers. It's our work environment, it's the way our dispatchers work with them. Still, that's not helping us when we're trying to get twenty new drivers for twenty new trucks.

–Manufacturing Vice President of Transportation

---

*Use training skills and resources to develop managers and supervisors to operate and manage transportation facilities.* This competency is a specific, important instance of the first. Where a firm operates several terminals or distribution centers with private fleets, the mid-level managers assume a broad range of duties. This means training and developing these managers systematically, a process that simultaneously prepares them for promotion.**(4,6,9)**

*Use decision-making skills to manage a complex, rapidly changing operation.* Transportation operations often assume a potentially nerve-wracking, frantic climate, with loads arriving and leaving, breakdowns, driver and operator problems, recruiting, and customer service problems. The transportation or traffic manager sits in the middle of this, making choices and directing others–get that truck repaired on the road, tell that driver to bring the truck in, hire this driver, offer incentives for recruiting referrals, call the customer to arrange a new delivery appointment and apologize for the service failure, and so on. They deal primarily with the exceptions, the circumstances outside the norm. A terminal manager or a dispatcher would deal with the routine situations.

This means making decisions and making them quickly. Others may or may not like the choice the manager makes, but they need for a choice to be made. Late decisions may be more disruptive than making occasional wrong choices.**(4,6)**

*Apply basic mathematics, statistics, accounting, budgeting, and human resources to measure progress toward goals.* This competency assumes that goals have been established and will help in measuring progress. Human resource knowledge is included in the list because people will make the progress. They need to know what goes into establishing and measuring the goals they are to meet. **(6)**

147

*Use skills in managing and directing meetings to gather information for decision-making, to convey information on policies and procedures, and to train transportation employees.* The commonly held belief that most meetings are a waste of time can be overcome by giving useful information and essential training as part of the meetings. Keep meetings brief, but concentrate on listening when not delivering training. Making sure that all employees know policies and procedures is not a trivial matter. This also puts some pressure on to make sure the policies and procedures make sense.(**6,7**)

---

**Table 6-10**
**Traffic Managers**
**Competencies**

- Use supervisory, development, recruiting, and selection skills to build and maintain a transportation or traffic organization
- Use training skills and resources to develop managers and supervisors to operate and manage transportation facilities
- Use decision-making skills to manage a complex, rapidly changing operation
- Apply basic mathematics, statistics, accounting, budgeting, and human resources to measure progress toward goals
- Use skills in managing and directing meetings to gather information for decision-making, to convey information on policies and procedures, and to train transportation employees
- Use writing and oral communication skills to report on traffic and transportation activities to top logistics managers and corporate offices
- Apply knowledge of transportation to operations decision-making

---

*Use writing and oral communications skills to report on traffic and transportation activities to top logistics managers and corporate offices.* Transportation is a major cost to the firm and a major logistics activity. Supporting decision-making at higher levels of the organization is a requirement for all managers at this level.

*Apply knowledge of transportation to operations decision-making.* This includes making decisions about maintenance, resource allocation, and dispatch. Operations decisions include allocating vehicles to markets, dispatching them to customers, and assuring their maintenance. This competency also ties to the first–working with people is still the core of the traffic manager's job.(**4,6**)

148

## Traffic Managers Job Requirements

To develop the competencies shown in Table 6-10, traffic managers must have the knowledge and skills shown in Table 6-11. Notice that this knowledge and these skills are operational rather than strategic.

| Table 6-11<br>Traffic Managers<br>Job Requirements |
| --- |
| • Supervisory skills<br>• Knowledge of vehicle maintenance<br>• Knowledge of modes of transportation used in firm<br>• Use standard office equipment<br>• Basic mathematics and language skills<br>• Chairing and directing meetings<br>• Decision-making skills<br>• Knowledge of LIS used in organization<br>• Knowledge of telecommunications equipment used in organization<br>• Communications skills |

Putting together the competencies and job requirements leads directly to the analysis of training needs. They are discussed in the next section.

## Traffic Managers Training Needs

Traffic managers must know how to operate all of the equipment used by the people who work for them. That does not mean they must be certified or licensed to drive or pilot the vehicles, but they must understand the equipment well enough to know when it is performing properly and when it is not. This applies to telecommunications equipment, computer systems, LIS, and the standard office equipment employed in their operation–as well as the vehicles. They should attend the formal training programs given to their employees, at least the classroom parts of the programs–as a minimum. This is part of their own professional development.     Interpersonal skills and management skills may be synonymous. Decision-making is highly interpersonal, since decisions affect people and people implement them. The need for communications skills is ubiquitous, but they are more important to transportation and traffic managers than to many other job families because of the speed of events. Miscommunication causes immediate problems for traffic managers, where other managers may have time to reconsider.

The knowledge base required of this group extends to customer networks and operations, the firm's networks and logistics operations, the firm's policies and procedures, and transportation modes, regulations, and laws. The training needs are shown in Table 6-12.

---

**Table 6-12**
**Traffic managers**
**Job Training Needs**

*Equipment specific*
- Vehicle operation and maintenance
- Standard office equipment
- Telecommunications equipment
- LIS use and trouble-shooting
- Telecommunications equipment operation and trouble shooting

*Interpersonal skills*
- Stress management
- Chairing and managing meetings
- Time management
- Training skills
- Writing skills
- Oral communication skills
- Decision-making

*Knowledge Needs*
- Customer facilities, networks, and operations
- Transportation laws and regulations
- Firm's operating procedures, policies, and practices
- Transportation modes operated or used by firm
- Transportation markets and pricing
- The firm's logistics systems and networks

---

**Traffic Managers Summary**

Traffic managers fight the logistics battle close to the front line. Their role is tactical more than strategic, but vital to the smooth operation of the system. Their training needs cover a broad range of equipment, interpersonal skills, and knowledge of transportation procedures, markets, networks, and operations. They also need a thorough understanding of how the transportation organization fits with the rest of the logistics operation.

The competencies required to perform traffic managers' jobs focus on operating and human resource decisions. Traffic managers' training needs include training skills to develop the employees that work for them, and a wide range of knowledge about options in transportation.

**Transportation Chapter Summary**

Transportation employees will continue to play a vital role in logistics operations. They will assume more and more tasks at the operating level and play more of a coordinating role in the logistics system. As transportation and other logistics functions shift to flatter organizational structures, there will also be some mixing of tasks across functional lines, with transportation as one of the core disciplines.

In keeping with these ideas, training for transportation employees at all levels will broaden to include other parts of logistics. For the moment, however, training needs in transportation tend to have an operational and functional focus. The operating level already needs more background in interpersonal skills, but that need has probably been around for some time. It just has never been acknowledged or filled.

| Table 6-13 |
| --- |
| **Motor Carrier Operating Employees** |
| **Job Description** |

**Example Titles:** Dispatcher, Dry Van, Flatbed Driver, Live Haul Driver, Local Driver, Transportation Truck Inspector

**General Job Characteristics:** *Span of Control:* none; *Budgetary Authority:* none; *Licenses and Certification:* yes; *Travel:* Out of town with overnight stays (61%); *Hours:* full time, same number per week; *Incentives:* individual (17%)

**Supervision:** *Supervision Received:* regular monitoring of major and minor job duties by immediate supervisor (100%), outside auditors and government officials (72%); *Supervision Given:* none

**Using Language:** Constant use of spoken and written English (100%)

**Using the Senses:** *Use Sight for:* observing the behavior of people or animals and using blueprints, maps, or similar documents (83%), observing the performance of machines or equipment and seeing distant objects (78%), noticing changing events in the workplace and seeing display gauges or meters (72%), seeing objects to the side while looking forward, seeing differences in distance, observing the quality or quantity of materials (67%), differences between colors (61%), detect objects in low light (50%); *Use Hearing for:* understanding speech (83%), noticing changing events in the workplace (67%), identifying the direction of a sound (56%)

**Decision Making:** *Human Resources Decisions:* none; *Operations and Production Decisions:* none; *Financial Decisions:* none; *Strategy Decisions:* none

**Contacts:** *Internal Contacts with:* clerical support staff (89%), first-line supervisors (78%), mid-level managers (67%); *External Contacts with:* customers (89%), non-managerial employees (83%), managers (72%), government or regulatory officials (61%)

**Meetings:** *Meetings Attended to:* train or instruct (78%), informally exchange information (56%); *Meetings Initiated or Chaired:* none

**Required physical activities:** sit for long periods (100%)

**Use of machine and tools:** calculators and typewriters (100%), standard office equipment (94%), heavy highway vehicles (78%), mobile manual tools (56%)

| Table 6-13 |
| --- |
| Motor Carrier Operating Employees |
| Job Description |
| **Work Context**: *Variety, Autonomy, and Interdependence:* must complete work before others can do theirs (94%), depend on others to complete their work before doing their own work (89%), use a variety of skills and control of work pace (78%), influence work activities of others outside the organization and learns new skills (67%); *Stressful Work Situations:* work under tight deadlines (100%), work with people over whom they had no authority, perform same mental and physical activities over and over (94%), work with frequent distractions (89%), deal with distressed people and work on different tasks over time (83%), work in situations that are highly stressful (72%), work on shared tasks (67%); *Receiving Feedback:* From supervisors, customers, and themselves |

| Table 6-14 |
| --- |
| Loaders |
| Job Description |
| **Example Titles:** Load Operations Specialist, Marine Transportation Planner, Railcar Loader, Railroad Dispatcher, Railroad Specialist, Transportation Loading/Shipping Coordinator, Transportation Technologist |
| **General Job Characteristics:** *Span of Control:* supervisors and non-supervisory (3); *Budgetary Authority:* none; *Licenses and Certification:* none; *Travel:* Out of town with overnight stays (27%); *Hours:* variable, full time; *Incentives:* receive group and individual incentives (64%) |
| **Supervision:** *Supervision Received:* regular monitoring of major and minor job duties by immediate supervisor (91%), outside auditors or government regulators (64%); *Supervision Given:* regular monitoring of job duties for laborers (36%) |
| **Using Language:** Constant use of spoken and written English (100%) |

| Table 6-14 |
| --- |
| Loaders |
| Job Description |

**Using the Senses:** *Use Sight for:* observing the quality or quantity of materials and small details of close objects (91%), observing the performance of machines or equipment (82%), pictures, patterns, or graphs and noticing changing events in the workplace (73%), differences between colors (64%), seeing details of distant objects or objects in bright light (55%), observing patterns, shapes, displays, or meters (45%); *Use Hearing for:* noticing changing events in the workplace or locating the direction or differences of a sound (64%), understanding loudness of a sound (45%)

**Decision Making:** *Human Resources Decisions:* changing work procedures (36%), assigning employee responsibilities (27%); *Operations and Production Decisions:* modifying or improving operations (36%); *Financial Decisions:* none; *Strategy Decisions:* none

**Contacts:** *Internal Contacts with:* mid-level managers (100%), first-line supervisors (91%), laborers and clerical support staff (82%), operations employees and professionals or technical specialists (73%); *External Contacts with:* customers or clients (55%), contractors (36%)

**Meetings:** *Meetings Attended to:* train or instruct, informally exchange information, formally exchange information, consult (91%), evaluate options or make a decision or solve problems (82%), coordinate work (73%), resolve conflicts (64%); *Meetings Initiated or Chaired:* informally exchange information (73%), evaluate options and make decisions, solve problems, resolve conflicts, and consult (64%) schedule work (55%), train or instruct (45%)

**Required physical activities:** sit for long periods (73%), precise arm-hand movements (55%), observe more than one signal and quickly choose movement needed and walk while working (45%)

**Use of machine and tools:** standard office equipment, personal computers (91%), calculators and typewriters (82%), mainframes or peripherals (73%), light highway vehicles (55%)

| Table 6-14 |
| --- |
| Loaders |
| Job Description |

| **Work Context**: *Variety, Autonomy, and Interdependence:* learn new skills (82%), depends on others to complete their work before doing their own work and must complete work before others can do theirs (73%), determine the methods or equipment they or others use (55%); *Stressful Work Situations:* working with people over whom they had no authority and working under tight deadlines (91%), work on shared tasks and perform same mental activities over and over (82%), conflicting work goals and dealing with distressed people (73%), work on different tasks over time, perform same physical activities over and over, and working with frequent distractions (64%); *Receiving Feedback:* From supervisors, and themselves |
| --- |

| Table 6-15 |
| --- |
| Transportation Administrative Support |
| Job Description |

| **Example Titles:** Administrative Assistant, Administrative Logistics Support Associate, Administrative Office Manager, Compliance and Safety Director, Export Regulations Director, Logistics Delivery Planner, Safety Manager, Traffic Analyst, Transportation Carrier Operations Manager, Transportation Clerk, Transportation Delivery Planning Supervisor, Transportation Freight Payables Clerk, Transportation Logistics Coordinator, Transportation Traffic Administrator |
| --- |
| **General Job Characteristics:** *Span of Control:* non-supervisory employees (1); *Budgetary Authority:* $485,000; *Licenses and Certification:* none; *Travel:* Out of town with overnight stays (39%); *Hours:* full time, same number per week; *Incentives:* individual (26%) |
| **Supervision:** *Supervision Received:* regular monitoring of major and minor job duties by immediate supervisor (90%), other employees other than immediate supervisor (39%); *Supervision Given:* none |
| **Using Language:** Constant use of spoken and written English (100%) |
| **Using the Senses:** *Use Sight for:* pictures, patterns, or graphs (42%), blueprints, maps, or similar documents (39%); *Use Hearing for:* understanding speech (35%) |

| Table 6-15 |
| --- |
| Transportation Administrative Support |
| Job Description |

| |
| --- |
| **Decision Making:** *Human Resources Decisions*: none; *Operations and Production Decisions:* evaluating the effectiveness of operations (23%); *Financial Decisions:* purchasing materials and supplies (29%); *Strategy Decisions*: none |
| **Contacts:** *Internal Contacts with*: clerical support staff (81%), first-line supervisor and mid-level managers (58%), upper managers (42%); *External Contacts with*: customers (48%), suppliers (39%), non-managerial employees (35%), managers (26%) |
| **Meetings:** *Meetings Attended to*: informally exchange information (68%), train or instruct (55%), solve problems, consult, formally exchange information (39%), evaluate options or make a decision (35%); *Meetings Initiated or Chaired*: none |
| **Required physical activities:** stand or sit for long periods (82%), precise finger movements (42%) |
| **Use of machine and tools:** standard office equipment (97%), personal computers (94%), calculators and typewriters (77%) |
| **Work Context**: *Variety, Autonomy, and Interdependence:* depend on others to complete their work before doing their own work (81%), control of work pace (71%), must complete work before others can do theirs (68%), learn new skills (61%), determine the methods or equipment they use (45%); *Stressful Work Situations:* work with people over whom they had no authority (74%), work on shared tasks and same mental activities over and over (65%), work under tight deadlines (52%), deal with distressed people (48%), conflicting work goals (45%); *Receiving Feedback:* From supervisors, other managers, and themselves |

| Table 6-16 |
| --- |
| **Traffic Managers** |
| **Job Description** |

**Example Titles:** National Traffic Manager, Transportation Manager, Transportation Worldwide Services Manager, Transportation Director of Import Services, Transportation Manager of Export Operations

**General Job Characteristics:** *Span of Control:* managers, supervisors, and professionals reporting directly (13), indirect reports (13); *Budgetary Authority:* $9,950,000; *Licenses and Certification:* none; *Travel:* Out of town with overnight stays (74%); *Hours:* full time, same number per week; *Incentives:* receive group incentives (63%), individual (23%)

**Supervision:** *Supervision Received:* regular monitoring of major and minor job duties by immediate supervisor (79%); *Supervision Given:* regular monitoring of job duties for first-line supervisors (60%), professional and clerical or support staff (42%)

**Using Language:** Constant use of spoken and written English, including editing, composing, and report writing (100%); use database queries, macros, and other computer languages that do not produce executable programs (26%)

**Using the Senses:** *Use Sight for:* pictures, patterns, or graphs (89%), noticing changing events in the workplace (58%), observing objects at a distance (53%), blueprints, maps and observing the behavior of people or animals (47%); *Use Hearing for:* understanding speech (58%)

**Decision Making:** *Human Resources Decisions:* changing work procedures (95%), assigning employee responsibilities or increasing or decreasing the number of employees (89%), changing salaries or benefits (63%); *Operations and Production Decisions:* evaluating the effectiveness of operations or setting or changing short-term goals (74%), setting long-term goals (68%), modifying or improving operations (58%); *Financial Decisions:* setting or changing size of budgets (95%), purchasing materials and supplies (74%), facilities management (63%); *Strategy Decisions:* taking on new projects (68%), changing services offered (37%)

**Contacts:** *Internal Contacts with:* clerical support staff (68%), first-line supervisor (63%), mid-level managers and professionals or technical specialists (53%); *External Contacts with:* managers (79%), suppliers and non-managerial employees (68%), executives (53%), customers (47%), the public or job applicants (42%)

**Meetings:** *Meetings Attended to:* solve problems (84%), informally exchange information or consult (79%), coordinate work, set policies, or formally exchange information (74%), evaluate options or make a decision or train or instruct (68%), schedule work (58%); *Meetings Initiated or Chaired to:* coordinate work or solve problems (74%), evaluate options or make decisions, consult, set policies, or informally exchange ideas (63%), formally exchange information (53%)

**Required physical activities:** sit for long periods (74%), walk while working (42%)

| Table 6-16 |
| --- |
| **Traffic Managers** |
| **Job Description** |

**Use of machine and tools:** personal computers (100%), standard office equipment (84%), calculators and typewriters (68%)

**Work Context**: *Variety, Autonomy, and Interdependence:* use a variety of skills (79%), control of work pace and determine the methods or equipment they use (74%), learn new skills and select work projects (68%), depend on others to complete their work before doing their own work and determine the methods or equipment others will use (63%), must complete work before others can do theirs (58%), influence the work of others outside the organization (53%); *Stressful Work Situations:* work on shared tasks (84%), conflicting work goals (79%), tight time pressures (68%), work with people over whom they had no authority (58%), work with frequent distractions (53%); *Receiving Feedback:* From supervisors, other managers, and themselves

# Inventory/ Material Control

*Inventory/material control function will move away from its clerical task orientation to a more analytical function.*
*—A Comparison of North American and European*
*Future Purchasing Trends[1]*

This chapter describes four job families: inventory/material control employees, inventory supervisors, production managers, and supply chain managers. The chapter describes these jobs based on scores from the CMQ. It discusses the competencies, job requirements, and training needs for each job family based on these results. It also profiles personality, customer orientation, market orientation, and need for cognition. These results affect the training, recruitment, and selection of inventory control personnel. Technical job descriptions are at the end of the chapter. Tables with supporting data are in Appendix 7.

---

### Key Findings and Takeaways

*Points in the text supporting each key finding is tagged with a number in parentheses, e.g., (1).*

---

**1** The inventory/material control function is undergoing a transformation, eliminating organizational levels and blurring the boundaries between logistics activities.

---

**2** Inventory/material control personnel acquire their job knowledge and skills primarily through on-the-job experience.

**3** Inventory specialists need to be physically competent and computer literate, or at least computer tolerant. Their computer skills reduce their physical demands and contribute to the creation of a common knowledge base.

**4** Production managers' most important decisions are in production, operations and human resources.

**5** Inventory/material control employees' primary responsibility is to manage the flow of materials through the manufacturing process by translating strategic plans into action plans that direct warehouse and manufacturing operations.

**6** Supply chain managers focus on internal processes, suggesting that organizations have not fully adopted a market orientation.

**7** Inventory/material control employees' interpersonal skills are as important to their job as their computer skills and physical abilities.

### Inventory/Materials Control Employees

The inventory/material control functions' evolution resembles that of the internal combustion engine. In the 70s, muscle cars relied on brute force to generate horsepower performance. Mechanical controls, though crude, monitored and modified fuel-air mixtures, engine timing, and spark advance. Components, while physically connected, were functionally isolated. Fine tuning the engine was difficult because knowledge about how changes in one component's settings affected other components was limited. Fine tuning on the fly in response to environmental conditions was not an option. Once the hood was down, engine settings could not be modified to deal with unexpected environmental conditions. Controls were primitive, requiring constant monitoring to obtain peak performance. While carburetor, fuel, exhaust and suspension systems required constant monitoring, repair options were limited; adjustments required a complete overhaul. For the shade tree mechanic, progress was measured by whether this modification caused the engine to blow up. Time to competence was not important because once the basics were understood, nothing changed from year-to-year. System performance was limited to measuring output–elapse times.

The inventory/material control function was similar to a muscle car engine. Instead of brute force, organizations manned many crews to provide 'horsepower.' Monitoring and control mechanisms were crude–usually paper and pencil systems. Coordination between material control and other departments was also crude. Changes were difficult to make on the fly because files were not updated promptly, and necessary paperwork was out of order or missing. Fine tuning the inventory/material control process was difficult because inventory levels' influence on other organizational processes was not understood. Modifications required a complete overhaul of the inventory management system. Standard operating procedures made timely fine tuning difficult. Responses were limited to those that did not deviate too far from standard operating procedures. Training was provided by on-the-job experience or supervised by workers thought to be the best. Time to competence was not important because the primary tool workers needed to master was their physical strength. The number of trailers/cars loaded or how many units passed through a given location were how performance was measured.(1, 2)

---

Before their recent reorganization, Alexander Doll Co. was organized around batch manufacturing principles, they stacked boxes of costume material and vinyl doll parts to the ceiling . . . More than 90,000 unfinished dolls were in inventory, and customers had to wait up to sixteen weeks for delivery. To make matters worse, when they tried to ship an order of 300 using these 90,000 pieces, they could finish less than half the dolls with materials on hand.

   –Alex Taylor III

---

Environmental conditions changed how engines were designed and manufactured. Fuel injection, superchargers, turbos, and electronic data interface replaced brute force. Fuel air mixture, engine timing, and spark advance were monitored and controlled by electronic instruments. Precision adjustments, on the fly, became possible. Electronic monitoring eliminated functional isolation. When modifications were tried, both the effect on the component and the entire system could be measured. Computers tracked numerous engine parameters identifying exactly what needed to be modified to achieve peak performance. System performance is still measured by elapsed times, but several other measures became available–fuel efficiency and pollution levels, to name two.(1, 3)

Environmental factors resulted in the modification of the inventory/material control process as well. Exchanging information electronically allowed organizations to examine their inventory management staffing needs. Because quantities and locations were tracked electronically,

161

files were updated daily and paperwork was reduced. Inventory's impact on the manufacturing process, warehousing, and transportation costs were measured to identify how changes in inventory levels affected these other processes. Time to competence became more important because now individuals not only had to master physical activities, but they also had to understand complex inventory management systems.

---

"A man leans over a freezer full of boneless chicken breasts. He swipes a hand-held computer over a bar code near the freezer. Within seconds, a computer in the home office downloads a pile of statistics: how much the store makes selling chicken breasts, how many packages it has on hand, how many are on the way to the store, and how many are sitting in freezers within a 150 mile radius."
    –Eryn Brown

---

Like the purchasing function, the inventory/material control function is in a period of evolution. Reengineering has resulted in the blurring of the lines between inventory and material control, purchasing, customer service, and warehousing. Enterprise resource planning is becoming the standard for controlling inventory throughout the supply chain.(1)

---

"When we get really good at this, we'll have infinite turns . . . our suppliers will deliver the parts we need just when we need them. We won't pay for them until we use them. The equipment we make will be paid for before it's even assembled."
    –Ray Hill

---

This chapter discusses four job families: inventory specialist, production manager, inventory supervisor, and supply chain manager. The role of each job family is discussed, along with the competencies, job requirements, and training needs for each. Data supporting this discussion is found in tables in Appendix 7.

### Inventory Specialists Job Description

Wanted: Individual strong of back, weak of mind. While extreme, this statement represents how some organizations viewed their inventory specialists. Anything was possible if you possessed excess "horsepower." Today, not only is physical fitness required, but mental ability is becoming more important. While computerization and automation reduce both the physical and mental demands, when an exception occurs, reasoning abilities are critical to maintaining operations. Inventory specialists represent the

162

current pinnacle for material handling personnel. They combine physical abilities with computer literacy to assure materials move through the organization expediently.(3)

Without inventory specialists, the flow of materials through an organization stops. This position represents the knowledge and skills required by personnel who move materials in, within, and out of the organization's physical control. The moment raw materials or component parts enter the organization, they are placed under the watchful eye of the inventory specialist. After coming in the backdoor, bar codes are scanned, entering materials into the inventory control information system. This step triggers several processes. First, quantity received is checked against quantity ordered. Second, quality control activities are done and findings communicated with the vendor and co–workers. Third, the inventory control specialist finds out the internal destination. Finally, a receiving report is generated and funds are transferred to the supplier.(5)

Inventory specialists then place the materials on a conveyor system, carry it on their backs, or lift it with a hand truck or forklift. No matter how and where it is transferred, at a minimum, they have to tell the inventory control information system that it has left receiving and is in a temporary storage location or on the production floor. Usually this task will require the inventory specialist to rescan the material and scan or enter the material's new location.(3)

They are in constant communication with the firm's information system, identifying when material left and when it was delivered. As the internal transportation network, they are influenced by bottlenecks, whirlpools, and black holes. Bottlenecks are locations where inventory flow is slow. Whirlpools represent processes that no one has optimally organized and require more handling than necessary. Black holes represent material that has entered the system, but no one knows what became of it. From the inventory specialist's perspective, poorly designed internal transportation systems create bottlenecks. Whirlpools are similar to bottlenecks. They differ because they are the result of poorly designed manufacturing processing that necessitates additional material handling. Employees who are lax about data integrity are the source of black holes.

**Inventory Specialists Competencies**
Inventory specialists' competencies involve equipment operation, physical skills, and interpersonal skills. The list of competencies is show in Table 7-1.

*Apply inventory and record control principles to assure timely delivery of materials according to company policies.* Inventory specialists are where the rubber meets the road. They are responsible for implementing the firm's inventory/material control policies. In the organization, they are the firm's carrier network. The firm's information system is analogous to transportation's dispatchers. Inventory specialists receive their "shipping manifest," pick up their load and deliver it to its destination. Their task is to assure that material arrives where it is needed, when it is needed, and is not damaged in the process. It's 4 p.m. and manufacturing is a hundred units short of being ready to ship that order today. Several manufacturing stations need raw materials, and effective inventory specialists review manufacturing needs, rank delivery order and start moving materials to where they are needed. Priorities are set according to company policies.**(3, 5)**

*Maintain data integrity by updating data files routinely.* Once a load is delivered, a competent inventory specialist updates or downloads inventory location files. Depending on the set-up, this may require placing a hand-held computer into a docking station, swiping a bar-code radioed to the network, or following the directions on a printout or LCD screen. They exercise diligence, because forgetting to scan a location or material, downloading data at inconsistent intervals, or not precisely placing material reduces operating effectiveness.**(3)**

---

"Before we had our present inventory management systems, I spent the first hour of everyday walking through the warehouse to see what I had and if it was where the system said it was. Our present tracking system reduced these walks to every few weeks."

–Manufacturing Purchasing Agent

---

| **Table 7-1**<br>**Inventory Specialists**<br>**Competencies** |
| --- |
| • **Apply inventory and record control principles to assure timely delivery of materials according to company policies**<br>• **Operate material handling equipment efficiently and safely**<br>• **Effectively communicate with fellow employees to assure materials get to where they are needed when they are needed**<br>• **Operate material handling equipment to reduce material damage**<br>• **Safely lift, carry, push, or pull material**<br>• **Maintain data integrity by updating data files routinely** |

*Effectively communicate with fellow employees to assure materials get to where they are needed when they are needed.* Drafting an award-winning proposal is not the inventory specialists' strength. However, their communication abilities are no less critical to their performance. Effective inventory specialists can defuse potential time bombs before they have a chance to detonate. It's 4 p.m. and several manufacturing stations have placed requests for materials. Each request is presented as more urgent than the one before. Through their interpersonal skills, effective inventory specialists contact manufacturing stations to discover present inventory levels. This information is used to establish delivery priorities. They then have to tell their delivery schedule to the various manufacturing stations clearly. Two factors make this interaction difficult. First, inventory specialists do not have authority and are not supervised by the people relying on their service. Second, from the manufacturing person's perspective, their needs are more critical than other manufacturing stations' needs.(5, 7)

*Operate material handling equipment to reduce material damage.* Competent inventory specialists safely operate material-handling equipment assigned to them. This requires training, skill, and patience. Training provides the rudimentary knowledge they need to operate the equipment. Skill allows them to maneuver their equipment at top speed, yet maintain control to not jeopardize co-workers. Patience tempers recklessness. Patient inventory specialists realize that taking extra time at critical junctures–when sliding forks under a pallet, or capturing a slip sheet saves time and reduces the potential for material damage. Properly operating material handling equipment allows inventory specialists to maintain delivery and manufacturing schedules. Safely operating forklifts reduces material damage and employee injuries. Inventory specialists need a thorough understanding of the equipment they commonly use.(2)

*Safely lift, carry, push, or pull material.* While inventory specialists' physical ability is not critical, they still have to lift, push, pull, or carry material for short distances. Employing proper lifting techniques means individuals can do the same volume of work at 5 p.m. as at 8 a.m. Competent inventory specialists realize that a secondary factor affecting their ability to lift safely is pacing. When weight trainers are "maxing out,' they will sandwich three to five minutes of rest between lifts. These rest periods give the body time to recuperate. Competent inventory specialists will sandwich short periods of inactivity between periods of physical exertion. Thus, they will pace themselves allowing their bodies time to recuperate and maintain a peak physical performance over a longer period.

**Inventory Specialists Job Requirements**
Inventory specialists must possess the knowledge and skills that will allow them to perform their jobs competently. These job requirements are precursors to competence. They come from the job classification questionnaire and include the knowledge and skills that the respondents say are widely used and absolutely critical to performance.

As a minimum, inventory specialists need the following knowledge and skills to do their job. Table 7-2 shows inventory specialists physical, knowledge, and skills requirements based on the degree to which they are

165

critical to the job. Inventory specialist positions are labor intensive. First, people in these jobs move materials through the organization. While forklifts reduce the physical intensity, these individuals are having to push, pull, lift and carry 10-50 lbs. almost constantly. They have to be able to evaluate their hold on objects by using their sense of touch. Awkward packaging may cause individuals to strain, extend or twist, and challenge their ability to maintain their balance. Inventory specialists have to be masters of basic mathematical skills. They could not fulfill their record and inventory control responsibilities without these skills. The importance placed on machine operations knowledge at first glance might seem out of place here, but without this knowledge, inventory specialists would be like mice running on an exercise wheel. They use their machine operations knowledge to help them set delivery priorities to their manufacturing customers.(5)

| **Table 7-2**<br>**Inventory Specialists**<br>**Job Requirements** |
|---|
| • **Physical Fitness**<br>• **Basic mathematics skills**<br>• **Computer literacy**<br>• **Interpersonal skills**<br>• **Forklift operation** |

**Inventory Specialists Training Needs**

Examining inventory specialists' responses about critical activities, knowledge, skills, and their method of learning those skills identified training needs. Production delays or shutting down a plant is unacceptable if it can be traced to poor execution resulting from personal incompetence or ignorance. Training needs are shown in Table 7-3.

At a minimum, formal training is needed to teach inventory specialists how to get to data and communicate electronically. While inventory specialists do not need proficiency in designing computer networks or computer operations, knowing how their information affects network operations enhances their diligence for maintaining data integrity. After the initial training session, computer training should focus on processes that are the exception rather than the rule. Training sessions may start with how to handle one or more exceptions followed by a discussion of routine processes. Reinforcing routine processes first results in fatigue; by the time exceptions are discussed, individuals have lost interest in the topic. By focusing on those processes less commonly used, IS personnel reduce the likelihood of receiving a phone call when inventory specialists encounter these exceptions.(3)

Training material handling personnel about manufacturing operations may seem counter intuitive. The increased adoption of enterprise resource planning systems assures that materials arrive only when they are needed. Inventory specialists that receive machine operations training will do a better job of prioritizing their schedule of activities. For example, an inventory specialist is scheduled to deliver loads to three different stations, and he or she receives an exception request for materials at another station. By knowing each station's machine operations, inventory specialists can rank their delivery schedule to reduce overall downtime. Thus, instead of dropping everything and delivering the exception, they may deliver one or two of their scheduled deliveries first, to reduce machine inactivity.(5)

---

**Table 7-3**
**Inventory Specialists**
**Job Training Needs**

*Equipment specific*
• **Fork lift certification**
• **Computer operation**
• **Machine operations**
*Physical skills*
• **Safe lifting and carrying procedures**
*Interpersonal skills*
• **Oral and written communication skills**
• **Word processing**
• **Stress management skills**
*Knowledge Needs*
• **Operations research/quality control/systems analysis**
• **Inventory control**
• **Records control**

---

**Inventory Specialists Personal Characteristics**

Within inventory/material control personnel, inventory specialists have the highest neuroticism, agreeableness and conscientiousness scores. Their extraversion and openness scores are similar to the average. These scores mean inventory specialists are calm, achievement oriented, friendly, and conservative, and they like people. They do not have to understand how or why something works to feel comfortable with using or doing the activity. In business situations, inventory specialist take actions designed to satisfy and retain customers because they do not perceive their firms to be market oriented.

**Inventory Specialists Summary**

Inventory Specialists positions represent materials handling jobs' pinnacle of evolution. Not only are these individual expected to transport material throughout the firm, they are expected to record vital information. The old adage of strong of back and weak of mind is no longer relevant here. Inventory specialists' physical abilities are enhanced by their computer proficiency.

### Inventory Supervisors Job Description

Inventory supervisors' jobs have elements of inventory specialists and production managers' jobs. Like inventory specialists, inventory managers are found in the inventory staging, warehousing, manufacturing and finished goods facilities. While they direct the activities of inventory specialists, inventory supervisors are still called on to man forklifts, hand trucks and other material handling equipment. The primary difference between inventory specialists and inventory supervisors is the latter's supervisory responsibility and decision-making domain. Like production managers, inventory supervisors are involved in making decisions that affect the manufacturing process. The major difference between these two positions is the scope of this responsibility. Inventory supervisors' decision-making domain is limited to the task level or individual production or product lines, while production managers' decision-making domain is at the manufacturing facility or strategic level.(1, 5)

Inventory supervisors translate production managers' vision into action plans carried out by inventory specialists and manufacturing employees. As translator, inventory supervisors can exercise some control over how processes will be defined and equipment will be used to achieve desired outcomes. This ability is limited because they still rely on others to complete their tasks before they can start their work and have others waiting on them to finish their job. Interdependence creates it's own problems. Stress is the primary problem created by this interdependence. Pressure to complete tasks on time, the distraction of missing or delayed raw materials, sick or injured labors or machine operators and conflicts between goals contribute to inventory supervisors' sense of stress. Environmental conditions such as temperature extremes, poor lighting, and dirty conditions complicate the inventory supervisor's ability to monitor manufacturing processes and individuals.(6)

### Inventory Supervisors Competencies

The inventory supervisors' competencies partly reflect an elevation of skill requirements from inventory specialists. They also reflect changes in organizational level. Table 7-4 shows the competencies that emerged from the data analysis. Each competency ties directly to knowledge or job activities that respondents identified as crucial to job performance. These competencies, collectively, distinguish this job from the jobs in the data base and other jobs in the study.

*Apply supervisory skills to coordinate inventory placement to increase manufacturing efficiency.* Inventory supervisors are responsible for moving raw materials to where they are needed by coordinating subordinates' activities. This responsibility requires an understanding of how materials flow through the facility. Bottlenecks present challenges to be overcome. By understanding how bottlenecks affect material flow, inventory supervisors coordinate inventory specialists to assure manufacturing processes operate smoothly.(5)

*Thoroughly understand material-handling equipment operation and company policies regarding the operation and maintenance of material-handling equipment.* Inventory supervisors must communicate the importance of properly operating equipment to their subordinates. When potential problems are identified or breakdowns occur, they should place this equipment out of service. To do less tells subordinates that safety regulations are an obstacle that can be readily ignored.

*Communicate the importance of maintaining data integrity to material-handling personnel.* The importance material handlers place on activities is proportional to the importance communicated by inventory supervisors. Inventory supervisors communicate their feelings by the actions they take and the words they use. If they are lax about updating inventory databases, material handlers will be lax as well. Notices posted on boards, signs hung overhead or on walls, and instructions to the contrary will not overcome poor practices. Effective inventory supervisors make sure their actions and instructions are consistent.(3)

*Use supervisory and employee development skills to build and maintain an efficient material control workforce.* Human resource decisions are becoming more critical to inventory, material control, and warehousing functions. Economic conditions make finding a comparable job down the street easy. Employee turnover is directly related to a supervisor's communication and supervisory abilities. A supervisor's demeanor communicates to material-handling personnel how the firm feels about them and their importance to the firm. Effective inventory supervisors positively influence material-handling personnel's trust, commitment, and the willingness to go that extra mile to satisfy a customer.(7)

*Organize, coordinate, and manage meetings to exchange information and conduct training necessary to assure information is shared with all inventory personnel.* Most meetings are perceived to be waste of time. Inventory supervisors influence this perception by the degree to which information is perceived to be relevant to participants. Taking time to develop an agenda will go a long way towards reducing meeting's negative image. No

169

amount of planning will completely eliminate the monotony. Company policies and training material are two areas where planning can enhance the meeting's effectiveness and may even teach the old dogs a new trick.

| |
|---|
| **Table 7-4**<br>**Inventory Supervisors**<br>**Competencies** |
| • **Apply supervisory skill to coordinate inventory placement to increase manufacturing efficiency**<br>• **Thoroughly understand material-handling equipment operation and company policies regarding the operation and maintenance of material-handling equipment**<br>• **Communicate the importance of maintaining data integrity to material-handling personnel**<br>• **Use supervisory and employee development skills to build and maintain an efficient material control workforce.**<br>• **Organize, coordinate, and manage meetings to exchange information and conduct training to assure information is shared with all inventory personnel**<br>• **Use decision making skills to integrate information to anticipate problems and develop contingency plans**<br>• **Maintain a thorough understanding of the firm's logistics processes to develop operational plans** |

*Use decision-making skills to integrate information to anticipate problems and develop contingency plans.* Warehouse and manufacturing facilities are similar to perpetual motion machines. Raw materials are delivered; finished goods are sent out; components are moved through manufacturing stations or through quality control processes; and material is rejected, damaged, or reworked. Each of these actions affects the firm's ability to consume, process, or expel products. Inventory supervisors must be decisive; they must quickly size up the situations, share information with production managers, and execute the resulting plan. They do this by absorbing information vital to keeping operations humming.(5)

*Maintain a thorough understanding of the firm's logistics processes to develop operational plans.* Inventory supervisors are responsible for managing the flow of material through distribution centers, raw material and finished goods warehouses, and the manufacturing process. This responsibility requires them to make decisions about equipment and human resource allocation. By having a thorough understanding, the firm's logistics

170

process inventory supervisors are able to make decisions that reduce manufacturing down time.

### Inventory Supervisors Job Requirements

Table 7-5 shows the knowledge, skills, and aptitudes required by inventory supervisors. These job requirements are absolutely critical to accomplish the main mission of the job. These included only the knowledge and skills necessary to distinguish inventory supervisors from other job families. They come from the job classification questionnaire and include the knowledge and skills respondents say are widely used and absolutely critical to job performance.

| **Table 7-5**<br>**Inventory Supervisors**<br>**Job Requirements** |
| --- |
| • **Human Resource skills: employee supervision and**<br>  **development, job analysis, occupational health and safety,**<br>  **and collective bargaining**<br>• **Knowledge areas: production management, computer**<br>  **operations, mathematics and statistics, inventory control**<br>  **warehouse, and motor transportation**<br>• **Supervisory skills**<br>• **Knowledge of manufacturing processes**<br>• **Basic mathematics, statistics, and language skills**<br>• **Ability to chair and direct meetings**<br>• **Decision making abilities**<br>• **Communication skills** |

For inventory supervisors, the most important job requirement is supervisory ability. Inventory supervisors' ability to coordinate inventory specialists influences everyone's perception about the firm's competence. Delivery delays, unanswered requests, and poor material placement reduce employees' commitment and willingness to work hard. A seamless delivery system has the opposite effect. Not only are employees willing to exert effort, their opinions of management improve.(7)

Production management, computer operations, mathematics and statistics, inventory control warehouse, and motor transportation are knowledge and skills that inventory supervisors felt they needed to possess to be successful or hold an inventory supervisor's job. Putting together the competencies and job requirements leads directly to the analysis of training needs. They are discussed in the next section.

171

**Inventory Supervisors Training Needs**

Inventory supervisors' knowledge requirements reflect their position in the firm, and derive from their need to manage the flow of material. Inventory supervisors require training on how to be supervisors. In some firms, supervisor selection is based on tenure or willingness to take on the added responsibility. Leading firms realize that length of service only indicates familiarity with company policy, and not necessarily leadership abilities. These organizations realize that investing in supervisor training reduces employee turnover and enhances their perception of management. Table 7-6 shows inventory supervisors' training needs. **(5)**

Specifically, inventory supervisors are being called on to identify inventory specialists' critical activities. Analyzing a job entails more than just standing around observing what is happening and measuring activities which may be influenced by the worker. Leading logistics organizations anticipate these limitations and provide training about how to conduct an effective job analysis.

---

As the manufacturing engineer stood next to an employee, stop watch in hand, I couldn't help notice that he kept glancing at a point further down the line. Every so often he would write something down, speak with the employee, and move to the next station. Afterward, I asked what that was all about. He laughed and said, "when I'm doing time-motion studies, I find standing next to the person I'm measuring influences how hard they work, so I stand several stations away from the one I'm actually measuring."

–observation of one of the researchers

---

Inventory supervisors must have a thorough understanding of the firm's computer system. Without this understanding, inventory supervisors are not able to adequately explain to inventory specialists why data integrity is important or how information is stored and used by the firm. Respondents suggest that they get a lot of their computer knowledge on the job. While this method may be adequate to getting the job done, it limits inventory supervisors' ability to explain to inventory specialists how the information systems work. When asked why something is done the way it is, simply answering, "that's how the system is set up," is not an adequate answer. However, without adequate training on the firm's information system, that is essentially the only answer inventory supervisors may be able to give.**(2, 3)**

| Table 7-6 |
| --- |
| Inventory Supervisors |
| Job Training Needs |

*Equipment specific*
- Personal computer
- Other keyboard equipment
- Standard office machines
- Fork lift operation

*Interpersonal skills*
- Employee supervision
- Oral and written communication skills
- Public speaking
- How to conduct effective meetings
- Stress management techniques

*Knowledge Needs*
- Production management
- Computer operations
- Employee supervision
- Motor transportation
- Inventory control and warehousing
- Occupational safety
- Job analysis
- Purchasing/procurement

**Inventory Supervisors Personal Characteristics**

Inventory supervisors have the lowest neuroticism and extraversion scores in the inventory/material control group. Their openness, agreeableness, conscientiousness, and need for cognition scores are all average. This means that difficult situations do not influence inventory supervisors. Friendly, achievement oriented, and independent may be used to describe inventory supervisors. Inventory supervisors like to understand how something works or why it is done that way only if they are interested in the topic. They have an average customer service orientation, suggesting they will not mislead their customers. Finally, inventory supervisors believe their firms are market oriented.

**Inventory Supervisors Summary**

Inventory supervisors manage the flow of materials through a production line. They are responsible for training inventory specialists on company policies and competent job performance. Their position in the firm influences material handlers perception of the firm and the quality of the firm's management. Their jobs reflect their position in the firm and include elements of inventory specialists' and production managers' jobs.

### Production Managers Job Description

Production managers coordinate the manufacturing process. Manufacturing is dependent on and influences the organization's material control infrastructure. Production managers are charged with taking inbound inventories, and transforming them into products wanted by the firm's customers. They achieve this goal by directing the activities of first-line supervisors, manufacturing engineers, mid-level managers, and clerical staff. The production manager title is misleading because they do not direct the manufacturing process, but the people who direct the manufacturing process. What this means is production managers' technical abilities are secondary to their interpersonal skills. They manage the manufacturing process by eliminating barriers that impede the manufacturing process and the development of a common knowledge base.(5)

They achieve this goal by participating in meetings where organizational and logistics functions are coordinated. Then, production managers gather their staff, evaluate their options, analyze the manufacturing process, and render a decision. This process is highly stressful given the limited time. Deadlines, problems with raw materials, and manufacturing breakdowns all contribute to the stress involved in managing the production process. Within inventory/material control, these conditions illustrate why the production managers job is the second most stressful job.

Once the job of managing is done, production managers then become cheerleaders. Through weekly meetings or daily contact with manufacturing and professional employees, and first and mid-level managers, production managers' main task is simple–identify for their subordinates how the subordinates' activities affect the organization's ability to satisfy customers.(7)

### Production Managers Competencies

Production managers' competencies partly reflect an elevation of skill requirements from inventory supervisors and inventory specialists. They also reflect changes in organizational level. The increased importance on creating a seamless manufacturing process requires a shift in focus. Table 7-7 shows the competencies that emerged for the data analysis. Each competency ties directly to knowledge or job activities that respondents identified as crucial to job performance. These competencies, collectively, distinguish this job from the jobs in the data base and other jobs in the study.

*Apply project management techniques and coordinate production resources to increase manufacturing efficiency.* Production managers do not manage individual production activities, or the manufacturing process itself.

They manage personnel whose job is to manufacture products or services. They manage the process by exchanging information, setting the goals and exercising authority on the manufacturing process. They are the final authority regarding how to use manufacturing resources. Competent production managers realize that a heavy hand is counter productive. They establish goals, allocate resources, and monitor milestones, but they rely heavily on their managers to develop strategies to achieve their goals. They gather and distribute information and expect their managers to act on it.(**4, 5**)

*Use supervisory and employee development skills to build and maintain an efficient manufacturing workforce.* Production managers should be experts at identifying individual strengths. They use this skill to identify where these strengths can be used effectively to drive the manufacturing process. They inspire confidence in their subordinates and attempt to teach them to instill confidence in the personnel they manage. Production managers are in a critical position. Through their actions, they influence manufacturing and warehouse employees' perceptions of their organization. As firms attempt to adopt a market orientation and supply chain management philosophy, production managers must "walk the walk," if manufacturing employees are to believe that these are not the latest in the series of managerial fads.(**4, 7**)

*Organize, coordinate, and manage meetings to exchange information and training consistent with the development of a common knowledge base.* Ineffective meetings hinder a production manager's ability to manage effectively. When they chair meetings, these meetings are designed to evaluate options, coordinate activities, exchange information, and provide instruction or education. To be effective, each of these activities requires the full attention of everyone present. Ineffective meetings cause participant fatigue and reduce effectiveness of future meetings. One method to increase effectiveness is to have a series of smaller, shorter meetings instead of one universal meeting. These smaller, shorter meetings reduce the likelihood of fatigue by focusing on issues relevant to the audience.(**7**)

*Use decision-making skills to integrate information to anticipate problems and develop manufacturing contingency plans.* The manufacture of most products requires the collection of hundreds of parts and the coordination of many processes. When, critical materials are delayed, or manufacturing processes go down there are a number of negative influences. Production managers can reduce the negative influences by teaching their personnel how to collect and present information. Instead of saying we have a problem, when subordinates approach the production manager they can identify the specific problem, what steps that they have taken to reduce the present impact, and potential alternatives. This training not only increases the subordinate's value to the firm, but it also reduces time to decision because the production manager is now able to endorse their solution or offer other potential solutions.(**4, 5**)

*Maintain a thorough understanding of the firm's logistics processes and how they relate to the manufacturing process.* Managing the manufacturing process requires the coordination of many processes. Information and material collection affects each of these processes. The speed with which materials and information can be retrieved influences manufacturing efficiency. Production managers reduce negative influences by understanding how potential changes will affect operations and by clearly sharing this knowledge with other managers.(7)

*Use speaking and writing abilities to express information clearly.* A production manager's job is to manage people responsible for manufacturing products. Effective production managers' speaking and writing abilities increase understanding, trust, commitment, and acceptance of the validity of the firm's goals and of their leadership abilities.(7)

| Table 7-7 |
| --- |
| **Production Managers** |
| **Competencies** |

- **Apply project management techniques and coordinate production resources to increase manufacturing efficiency**
- **Use supervisory and employee development skills to build and maintain an efficient manufacturing workforce**
- **Organize, coordinate, and manage meetings to exchange information and training consistent with the development of a common knowledge base**
- **Use decision making skills to integrate information to anticipate problems and develop manufacturing contingency plans**
- **Maintain a thorough understanding of the firm's logistics processes and how they relate to the manufacturing process**
- **Use speaking and writing abilities to express information clearly**

### Production Managers Job Requirements

Table 7-8 shows the knowledge, skills, and aptitudes required by production managers. These job requirements are absolutely critical to accomplish the main mission of the job. They include only those knowledge and skills necessary to distinguish production managers from other job families in the table. They come from the job classification questionnaire and include the knowledge and skills respondents said were widely used and absolutely critical to job performance.

Production managers are expected to coordinate manufacturing processes to satisfy customer desires while reducing manufacturing costs. Auditing, inventory and records control, manufacturing operations, and transportation

176

are the primary knowledge areas used by production managers. Production managers coordinate the internal supply chain. They rely on supervisory, decision making, and communication skills to exercise their leadership. However, without adequate strategic planning abilities their leadership abilities are compromised.

| Table 7-8 |
| :--- |
| **Production Managers** |
| **Job Requirements** |
| • **Human Resource skills: employee development, selections, and supervision**<br>• **Knowledge areas: strategic planning, accounting principles, inventory, warehouse, and manufacturing management, operations research, basic mathematics and statistics, transportation, and word processing**<br>• **Supervisory skills**<br>• **Ability to chair and direct meetings**<br>• **Decision-making abilities**<br>• **Communication skills**<br>• **Strategic planning abilities**<br>• **Knowledge of manufacturing processes**<br>• **Basic mathematics, statistics, and language skills** |

Putting together the competencies and job requirements leads directly to the analysis of training needs. They are discussed in the next section.

### Production Managers Training Needs

Twelve knowledge or skills areas are critical to production managers' jobs. Human resource, production management, mathematical and statistical ability, and transportation are the four general knowledge categories production managers need. Except for basic math and production management skills, production managers' primary source of training is on-the-job experience. This finding suggests that they learn how to develop strategic plans, motivate employees, monitor inventory level, maintain records, and gain transportation knowledge with little direction from the firm. For production managers, time to competence is critical. How often have workers been required to put in overtime because a production manager's coordination mechanism failed to deliver the desired results? Table 7-9 shows production managers' training needs. **(2)**

| Table 7-9 |
| --- |
| **Production Managers** |
| **Job Training Needs** |

*Equipment specific*
- Machine operation and maintenance
- Personal computer
- Standard office equipment
- Other keyboard equipment

*Interpersonal skills*
- Oral and written communication skills
- Public speaking
- How to conduct effective meetings
- Stress management techniques
- Decision making

*Knowledge Needs*
- Operations research/quality control/systems analysis
- Inventory control
- Records control
- Accounting practices
- Employee selection and development
- Transportation modes

Production managers' knowledge requirements reflect their position in the organization. Critical to production managers performance is knowledge in production management, strategic planning, auditing, records control, all modes of transportation, inventory and warehouse control, and employee motivation. Production management is the only knowledge area where production managers said they learned more from formal training than OJE. **(2)**

Production managers require formal training about how to electronically store, post, and distribute information. Training should focus on how computer resources can be used to optimize the manufacturing process. This requires production managers to possess knowledge about how the various computer networks interact with each other and how information is entered, stored, and retrieved.**(3)**

Production managers' competency is contingent on their ability to lead the manufacturing process. Production managers whose meetings are perceived to be a waste of time, who are not skilled public speakers, or who cannot write a coherent sentence will be unable to instill confidence in their managerial abilities. Interpersonal weaknesses need to be quickly identified and educational programs developed based on the individual's needs.**(7)**

### Production Managers Personal Characteristics

Production managers' personality scores were all average. This means they are even tempered, achievement oriented, conservative, and friendly, and they like people. They like to completely understand how things work even if understanding its operation has no influence on their life. They have the lowest average customer service score, suggesting they are not above misleading someone or promising more than they can deliver. Production managers perceive their firm to be market oriented.

### Production Managers Summary

Production managers are responsible for assuring that manufacturing processes are consistent with the firm's strategy. Through their direction, their subordinates develop and carry out action plans designed to achieve this goal. Competence in this job is based primarily on each individual's interpersonal skills and not their technical abilities. As with the other job families, production managers acquire most of their knowledge through OJE.


### Supply Chain Managers Job Description

The job of supply chain managers is to coordinate and manage the supply chain. Supply chain managers are involved in every aspect of decision making. They have final authority over managing the entire supply chain and how to employ supply chain resources.

Supply chain managers spend much time in meetings. They are in daily contact with employees working on the production floor up to the executive suite. While they have responsibility to manage the process from raw material to ultimate consumers, their primary focus is on internal processes. Decisions about production methods, factory layouts, equipment, and human resource needs are all made by supply chain managers. Supply chain managers rely on interpersonal skills and formal authority to reduce total logistics costs.

Purchasing managers and supply chain managers share many tasks. Like purchasing managers, supply chain managers spend a great deal of time in meetings exchanging information and making decisions. They receive information about regulatory constraints and customer desires and transform this information into strategies designed to propel the firm forward.(6, 7)

Supply chain managers and purchasing managers differ in four ways. First, while the role of purchasing managers is to provide recommendations and information used to make decisions, supply chain managers have decision making authority. Second, purchasing managers are more likely to meet with customers and regulatory officials, while supply chain managers are more likely to include operating employees at their meetings. Third, purchasing managers' lack of formal decision making authority increases their stress levels, while supply chain managers' stress is the result of having to make

179

decisions that affect the firm's operations and short and long-term performance. Fourth, physical location also distinguishes purchasing managers from supply chain managers. Purchasing managers included in this survey are more likely to work out of offices away from manufacturing processes, while supply chain managers' offices are usually located adjacent to the manufacturing floor. Purchasing managers and supply chain managers share many tasks. The differences between these two positions distinguish the purchasing and supply chain manager's job families.

**Supply Chain Managers Competencies**

Supply chain managers' competencies partly reflect an elevation of skill requirements from production managers. They also reflect changes in organizational level. The increased importance on creating a seamless manufacturing process from raw materials to consumer requires a shift in focus. Table 7-10 shows the competencies that emerged from the data analysis. Each competency ties directly to knowledge or job activities that respondents identified as crucial to job performance. These competencies, collectively, distinguish this job from the jobs in the data base and other jobs in the study.

*Apply project management techniques and coordinate production resources to increase organizational and supply chain efficiency.* Supply chain managers' primary role is to manage material to and through the manufacturing process. Their success influences the other supply chain members' perceptions about the firm's competence and future prospects. They manage this process by assuring that vital information is collected and routed through them. Supply chain managers' role is to develop strategies that guide daily operations. They must be able to see both the trees and the forest. Supply managers must sum up the situation and quickly make the best decision possible.**(5, 6)**

*Use supervisory and employee development skills to build and maintain an efficient managerial workforce.* Supply chain managers are required to assess the talents of the people they manage. Weaknesses need to be identified and strategies developed to provide the necessary training. Developing employees is more difficult, because of the reduction in the number of mid-level positions. Supply chain managers are in a unique position, because all logistics functional areas are usually represented in the plant. Effective supply chain managers take advantage of this variety and assign responsibilities based on their assessment.**(1)**

*Organize, coordinate, and manage meetings to exchange information and conduct training necessary to assure development of a common knowledge base and help their decision making.* Supply chain managers' meetings are designed to integrate operations with the firm's objectives. Presenting information, evaluating options, resolving disputes and making

180

decisions are the primary functions performed at these meetings. These functions do not require everybody to be present. Supply chain managers must decide whose presence is necessary and invite only those individuals. Controlling attendance like this will reduce interruptions as issues tangent to the meeting's purpose are less likely to be brought up. This reduction increases the meeting's perceived relevance and reduces participant boredom.

| Table 7-10<br>Supply Chain Managers<br>Competencies |
| --- |
| • **Apply project management techniques and coordinate production resources to increase organizational and supply chain efficiency**<br>• **Use supervisory and employee development skills to build and maintain an efficient manufacturing workforce**<br>• **Organize, coordinate, and manage meetings to exchange information and conduct training to assure development of a common knowledge base**<br>• **Use decision-making skills to identify how trends affect the supply chain's competitiveness** |

*Use decision-making skills to identify how trends affect the supply chain's competitiveness.* Supply chain managers must be astute at identifying how environmental conditions, customer wants, and supplier constraints affect the organization's performance. They must exercise decision flexibility because what may seem to be counter–productive may enhance the functioning of the supply chain.

### Supply Chain Managers Job Requirements

Table 7-5 shows the knowledge, skills, and aptitudes required by supply chain managers. They included only knowledge and skills necessary to distinguish supply chain managers from other job families. They come from the job classification questionnaire and include the knowledge and skills respondents said were widely used and absolutely critical to job performance. Putting together the competencies and job requirements leads directly to the analysis of training needs. They are discussed in the next section.

181

| Table 7-11 |
| --- |
| Supply Chain Managers<br>Job Requirements |
| • **Employee Selection**<br>• **Supervision**<br>• **Development**<br>• **Production Management**<br>• **Purchasing/ Procurement**<br>• **Basic Mathematics**<br>• **Statistics**<br>• **Language Skills**<br>• **Public Speaking**<br>• **Computer Literacy**<br>• **Ability to chair and direct meetings**<br>• **Decision making abilities**<br>• **Communication skills** |

**Supply Chain Managers Training Needs**

Supply chain managers' computer training should focus on how computers can help them make better decisions. Training should focus on how to retrieve and package information used during the decision process. For example, supply chain managers may find it useful to know how to develop query tables. These tables allows managers to extract specific information from larger databases. Supply chain managers need to know how information is stored. Understanding how information is entered, processed, and stored by the firm's information handling system will increase the quality and reduce the time necessary to implement decisions. Table 7-12 shows supply chain managers' job training needs. **(3)**

Supply chain managers rely on co-workers to carry out their decisions. While it may become necessary to rely on their formal authority, firms should provide alternatives for supply chain managers. Relying exclusively on coercive power decreases subordinates' commitment to the organization and increases their willingness to find employment elsewhere. Supply chain managers whose meetings are perceived to be a waste of time, who routinely kill conversations, or who are indecisive reduce employee commitment and other supply chain members' confidence in the organization. **(7)**

**Table 7-12**
**Supply Chain Managers**
**Job Training Needs**

*Equipment specific*
• **Personal computer**
• **Other keyboard equipment**
• **Machine operations**
• **Standard office machines**
*Interpersonal skills*
• **Oral and written communication skills**
• **Public speaking**
• **How to conduct effective meetings**
• **Stress management techniques**
*Knowledge Needs*
• **Employee selection**
• **Inventory control and warehousing**
• **Production management**
• **Operations research**
• **Strategic planning**

### Supply Chain Managers Personal Characteristics

Supply chain managers have low neuroticism and agreeableness scores. They are not usually stressed by difficult situations. Supply chain managers are extraverts. They enjoy the company of people and are usually friendly. New ideas are quickly adopted by supply chain managers because they are customer oriented and want to do all they can to satisfy customers. Supply chain managers do not perceive their firms to be market oriented.

### Supply Chain Managers Summary

Supply chain managers are similar to purchasing managers. They are both responsible for managing the flow of materials through the supply chain. Managerially, both provide input during the decision process. The key difference is that supply chain managers have greater decision-making authority. Supply chain managers' primary focus is on internal processes. This finding suggests that firms are in the early stages of adopting the supply chain management philosophy.

### Inventory/Material Control Summary

The inventory/material control function is in the middle of a major transformation. Activities are being combined with warehousing, purchasing and customer service activities. Like most of the job families, inventory/material control employees acquire most of their job knowledge through OJE. This strategy means that employees may not reach their full potential until several years have passed. Like most logistics functions, the computer has influenced inventory/material control activities. Today, all inventory/material control employees must be computer literate. But, computer literacy is just one component necessary to become competent. Inventory/material control employees rely heavily on their interpersonal skills to manage the flow of material into and out of the manufacturing process. They are responsible for translating strategic plans into action plans.

1. Joseph R. Carter and Ran Narasimham. (1999). *A Comparison of North American and European Future Purchasing Trends.* National Association of Purchasing Management Website.

| Table 7-13 |
| --- |
| Inventory Specialists |
| Job Description |

**Example titles:** Inventory Control Administrator, Inventory Control Clerk, Inventory Control Specialist, Inventory Control Supervisor, Material Control Supervisor, Production Clerk, Production Foreman, Scheduling Manager

**General Job Characteristics:** *Span of Control:* none; *Budgetary Responsibility:* none; *Licenses and Certification:* fork-lift certification; *Travel:* none; *Hours:* full-time, constant number of hours, seasonal (27%); *Incentives:* group performance (30%), individual performance (14%); *Clothing:* work clothes (80%), protective gear (25%), office attire (16%)

**Supervision:** *Supervision Received:* regular monitoring of major and minor job duties by their immediate supervisor (100%), regular monitoring of major job duties by other supervisors (32%)

**Using Language:** Constant use of oral and written English

**Using The Senses:** *Use Sight for:* observing the quantity or quality of materials or supplies (77%), extremely small details (61%), differences in patterns, shapes or color (52%), displays, gauges, meters, or measuring instruments (43%), peripheral vision, differences in the distance of objects, focusing under bright light (43%), detecting objects under low light (41%), noticing changing events (39%), patterns or graphs (36%), details of distant objects, blueprints, or maps, and observing the operation of machines or equipment (34%); *Use Hearing for:* identifying the direction of a sound or understanding the speech of people (41%), differences in tones or sound patterns, focusing on one sound among many (36%), difference in loudness (25%), noticing changing events (23%); *Use Touch for:* evaluating objects (39%)

**Decision Making:** *Financial Resources:* purchasing materials or supplies (20%)

**Contacts:** *Internal Contacts* : mid-level managers (75%), first-line supervisors (73%), production employees (70%), clerical or support staff (66%), upper-level managers (43%), marketing or sales employees (32%)

**Meetings:** *Meetings Attended to:* informally exchange information (70%), train, instruct or educate (59%), formally exchange information (43%), diagnose or solve problems (34%), coordinate or schedule work activities, resolve conflicts or disputes (23%), consult or give specialized information, (20%)

**Required Physical Activities:** walk (84%), kneel, crouch, or crawl (70%), stand for long periods (64%), sit for long periods (57%), extend, twist, or stretch (55%), lift 10-50 lbs. (50%), coordinate arms and legs (48%), push or pull 10-20 lbs. (45%), push or pull 21-50 lbs. (41%), climb without the aid of staircases (39%), climb staircases, coordinate eyes, ears, hands, and feet (34%), maintain balance (30%), make precise finger movements (23%), find objects without being able to see them, carry 10-50 lbs. for short distances, and lift, push, or pull 51-100 lbs. (20%)

| Table 7-13 |
|---|
| **Inventory Specialists** |
| **Job Description** |
| **Use of Machine and Tools:** *Office Equipment:* personal computer (77%), keyboard equipment (70%), mainframe computer (34%); *Mobile Tools and Vehicles:* fork-lift (55%); *Hand-held Tools:* measuring devices (45%), short-handled tools (32%) |
| **Environmental Conditions:** temperatures higher than 90° (70%), temperatures below 60° (61%), dirty working conditions (43%), poor lighting (34%), exposed to loud noises (32%), cramped or confined work spaces (27%) |
| **Work Context:** *Variety, Autonomy and Interdependence:* complete their job so others can start their job (86%), depend on others to complete their job so they can start theirs (73%), control their schedule (68%), learn new skills (59%), influence activities of other departments (48%), use a variety of skills (43%), determine the method they will use (36%), perform a complete service (25%), determine the methods others will use (20%); *Stressful Work Situations:* work with others to complete a task (80%), deal with people over whom they have no authority (75%), work under tight deadlines (70%), work is distracted (68%), perform a number of different tasks (64%), perform the same mental activities (57%), deal with conflicts between goals (48%), deal with stressful situations (45%), deal with people who are distressed (30%); *Receiving Feedback:* immediate supervisor (84%), self-assessment (70%), other supervisors (59%), client or customers (20%) |

| Table 7-14 |
|---|
| **Production Managers** |
| **Job Description** |
| **Example Titles:** Production Manager, Process Unit Coordinator, Production Scheduling Manager, Quality Control Manager, Retail Logistics Manager |
| **General Job Characteristics:** *Span of Control:* indirect supervision (4), direct managerial (1), direct professional (1), direct nonsupervisory (15); *Budgetary Responsibility:* yes; *Licenses and Certification:* none; *Travel:* overnight (50%); *Hours:* full-time, employee determined with seasonal changes; *Incentives:* group performance (75%), individual performance (38%); *Clothing:* Office attire (75%) |
| **Supervision:** *Supervision Received:* infrequent monitoring of major job duties by immediate supervisor (75%), and other supervisors (25%); *Supervision Given:* regular monitoring of major job duties of clerical staff (38%), and professional employees (25%) |
| **Using Language:** Constant use of oral and written English |

| Table 7-14 |
| --- |
| **Production Managers** |
| **Job Description** |

**Using the Senses:** *Use Sight for:* pictures, drawings patterns or graphs (88%), observing the quantity or quality of materials or supplies, or the operation of machines (63%), differences in patterns or shapes, observing the behaviors and actions of people, observing changing events, and blueprints, or maps (50%), differences in color, observing the physical qualities of people, displays, gauges, meters or measuring instruments (38%); *Use Hearing for:* understanding the speech of people (75%), hearing changing events, identifying the direction of a sound (38%); *Use Touch for:* detecting or evaluating objects

**Decision Making:** *Financial Resources:* purchasing materials or supplies (75%); *Human Resources:* assigning employee responsibilities (88%), changing employee salaries or number of employees (50%); *Operations and Production:* modifying or improving operations (88%), determining the type of equipment or processes used, setting or changing short-term goals establishing or changing work policies (75%), evaluating operations (50%); *Long-term Business Strategy:* adding new products or product lines, and taking on new projects (50%)

**Contacts:** *Internal Contacts:* executives (75%), mid-level managers, nonsupervisory professional employees (63%), first-line supervisors, supervisory professional employees, manufacturing employees (50%), marketing or sales employees, clerical or support staff (38%); *External Contacts:* suppliers or sales representatives (63%), managerial employees, customers or clients, contractors, subcontractors, consultants or agents (38%)

**Meetings:** *Meetings Attended to:* train, instruct or educate, coordinate or schedule activities, informally exchange information (75%), consult or give specialized information (63%), diagnose or solve problems, evaluate options or make a decision, persuade or sell (50%), formally exchange information (38%); *Meetings Initiated or Chaired to:* evaluate options or make a decision, coordinate or schedule activities (75%), informally exchange information (63%), formally exchange information, diagnose or solve problems, supervise or evaluate people or projects, train, instruct, or educate, consult or give specialized information (50%), resolve conflicts, set policies, rules, or procedures (38%)

**Required Physical Activities:** sit for long periods (75%), walk, coordinate eyes, ears, hands, and feet, climb without aid (50%), make precise arm and finger movements, move fingers independently, and maintain balance (38%)

**Use of Machine and Tools:** *Office Equipment:* personal computer (88%), standard office equipment (50%), keyboard equipment (38%)

187

| Table 7-14 |
| --- |
| **Production Managers** |
| **Job Description** |
| **Work Context**: *Variety, Autonomy and Interdependence:* complete their work before others can start theirs, depend on others to complete their work before they can start, determine the method or equipment others will use (88%), control their work schedule (75%), select the projects they will work on, determine the methods or equipment they will use, influence the activities of others (63%), learn new skills (50%), use a variety of skills (38%); *Stressful Work Situations:* work under tight time pressures (100%), work with others on projects, deal with conflicts between goals, deal with people over whom they have no authority, work is distracted by others (75%), perform the same mental activity over and over (63%), perform a number of different tasks, deal with people who are distressed or upset (50%), deal with people in situations that are highly stressful (38%); *Receiving Feedback:* immediate supervisor (75%), self monitoring or performance (63%), other employees (50%) |

| Table 7-15 |
| --- |
| **Inventory/Materials Managers** |
| **Job Description** |
| **Example Titles:** Inventory Control Manager, Inventory Management Technician, Material Manager, Production Manager, Process Manager, Production Operations Manager, Production Scheduler, Production Supervisor, Warehouse Inventory Manager |
| **General Job Characteristics:** *Span of Control:* indirect supervision (3), direct managerial employees (1), non-supervisory employees (27) *Budgetary Responsibility:* yes; *Licenses and Certification:* none; *Travel:* overnight (23%); *Hours:* full-time, constant number of hours, seasonal changes; *Incentives:* group performance (68%), individual performance (32%); *Clothing:* work clothes (68%), protective gear (36%), office attire (27%) |
| **Supervision:** *Supervision Received:* regular monitoring of major and minor job duties by their immediate supervisor (100%), regular monitoring of major job duties by other employees (45%), and regulators or government officials (27%); *Supervision Given:* constant monitoring of major and minor job duties by machine operators (73%), laborers (36%), and first-line supervisors (23%), regular monitoring of major job duties of clerical or support staff (41%) |
| **Using Language:** Constant use of oral and written English |

| Table 7-15 |
| --- |
| Inventory/Materials Managers |
| Job Description |

| |
| --- |
| **Using the Senses:** *Use Sight for:* pictures, drawings, graphs (88%), monitor events, observe the quantity and quality of materials (77%), observing people's behavior (73%), distant object details (64%), small details, differences in colors, blueprints, or maps (59%), patterns/shapes, observing machine operation (55%), displays, gauges, or measuring instruments (50%), peripheral vision (45%), in bright light, observing the qualities of people, object's distance differences (41%), objects in low light (27%); *Use Hearing for:* understanding speech (73%), identifying a sound's direction (50%), monitoring the environment (45%), hear differences in tones or sound patterns while focusing on one sound (36%), differences in loudness (32%); *Use Touch for:* evaluating objects (32%) |
| **Decision Making:** *Financial Resources:* purchasing materials or supplies (64%); *Human Resources:* assigning employee responsibilities, changing work procedures (64%), changing the number of employees (50%), changing salaries (32%), purchasing capital equipment (23%); *Operations and Production:* modifying operations (59%), evaluating operations (55%), changing short-term goals, determining the types of equipment or processes used (36%), changing long-term goals (27%); *Long-term Business Strategy:* taking on new projects (36%) |
| **Contacts:** *Internal Contacts:* manufacturing employees, first-line supervisors (91%), mid-level managers (77%), executives (64%), clerks or support staff, laborers (59%), marketing or sales employees (50%), supervisory professional employees (45%), nonsupervisory professional employees (41%); *External Contacts:* suppliers and sales representatives, customers or clients (55%), contractors, subcontractors, consultants, or agents (27%) |
| **Meetings:** *Meetings Attended to:* diagnose problems, informally exchange information (73%), give specialized information, train, instruct, or educate (68%), coordinate activities (55%), set policies (50%), evaluate options (45%), formal presentation (41%), resolve conflicts (32%); *Meetings Initiated or Chaired to:* coordinate activities, diagnose problems (59%), informally exchange information (55%), give specialized information, and set policies (41%), train, instruct, or educate, formal presentations, and resolve conflicts (36%), evaluate options, and supervise people (32%) |
| **Required Physical Activities:** climb without aid (68%), sit for long periods (59%), walk, and make precise finger movements (55%), hand eye coordination, kneel, crouch or crawl (50%), lift 10-20 lbs. (45%), stand (41%), precise arm-hand movements, and move individual fingers (36%), carry 10-20 lbs. (32%) push or pull light weights (27%) |
| **Use of Machine and Tools:** *Office Equipment:* personal computer and keyboard equipment (86%), mainframe computer (82%), standard office equipment (77%); *Mobile Tools and Vehicles:* fork-lift and hand-truck (41%); *Hand-held Tools:* measuring devices (36%), short-handled tools (27%) |

| Table 7-15 |
| --- |
| Inventory/Materials Managers |
| Job Description |

**Environmental Conditions:** exposure to temperature greater than 90° (59%), exposure to temperatures below 60° (50%), exposure to loud noises (45%), dirty working conditions (32%)

**Work Context**: *Variety, Autonomy and Interdependence:* complete their job before others can start theirs (86%), depend on others to complete their job before they can start (82%), control own schedule (77%), learn and use a variety of skills (64%), determine the method or equipment used (59%), influence other departments' work activities and determine the method or equipment they will use (55%), select their projects (45%), perform a complete service (36%); *Stressful Work Situations:* work is distracted by others (86%), work under tight deadlines, deal with conflicts between work goals or projects, work with others on shared projects (82%), deal with people over whom they have no authority (77%), perform the same mental activities over and over, perform a number of different tasks (73%), deal with people who are distressed (68%), perform the same physical activities over and over (50%), deal with situations that are highly stressful or difficult (41%), deal with illness or injury (32%); *Receiving Feedback:* immediate supervisor (86%), self-assess performance (68%), other employees (64%), customers (36%).

<br>

| Table 7-16 |
| --- |
| Supply Chain Managers |
| Job Description |

**Example Titles:** Business Supply Chain Planner, Inventory & Supply Chain Strategy Manager, Inventory Commodity Manager, Material Control Quality Manager, Operations Manager, Production Manager, Production Planning Manager

**General Job Characteristics:** *Span of Control:* indirect supervision (31), managerial employees and nonsupervisory employees reporting directly (2); *Budgetary Responsibility:* yes; *Licenses and Certification:* none; *Travel:* overnight (82%); *Hours:* full-time, individual determines, with seasonal changes; *Incentives:* group performance (82%), individual performance (55%); *Clothing:* office attire (100%)

**Supervision:** *Supervision Received:* regular monitoring of major job duties by immediate supervisor (100%), and other supervisors (55%), infrequent monitoring of major job duties by regulators (45%); *Supervision Given:* regular monitoring of major and minor job duties of first-line supervisors, and nonsupervisory professional employees (45%); regular monitoring of major job duties of clerical staff (36%)

**Using Language:** Constant use of oral and written English

| Table 7-16 |
| --- |
| **Supply Chain Managers** |
| **Job Description** |

| |
| --- |
| **Using the Senses:** *Use Sight for:* pictures, drawings, or graphs (100%), observing the quantity or quality of materials and actions of people, noticing events (82%), observing the operation of machines, and differences in color (73%), small details (62%), blueprints or maps, distant details, differences in patterns or shapes (55%), observing the physical qualities of people, and focusing under bright light (45%), detecting objects in low light (36%); *Use Hearing for:* understanding speech (73%), monitoring the environment (55%), identifying the direction of a sound (45%); *Use Touch for:* evaluating objects (45%) |
| **Decision Making:** *Financial Resources:* purchasing materials or supplies (82%), establishing budgets (55%), purchasing capital equipment (45%); *Human Resources:* assigning employee responsibilities, changing policies or procedures (91%), changing salaries (82%), changing the number of employees or lines of authority (64%); *Operations and Production:* changing short-term goals (100%), changing long-term goals (91%), evaluating the effectiveness of operations (82%), modifying operations (73%); *Long-term Business Strategy:* taking on projects (82%), shutting down operations (73%), changing the level of service, and determining the types of equipment used (55%), adding new products/product lines, or discontinuing products (36%) |
| **Contacts:**  *Internal Contacts:* upper level management (100%), clerical staff, mid-level managers, and first line supervisors (91%), nonsupervisory professional employees, manufacturing employees (64%), marketing or sales (55%), supervisory professional employees (45%);  *External Contacts:* suppliers or sales representatives (82%), managerial employees, and contractors or consultants (73%), customers or clients, and public or job applicants (64%), executives (55%), non-managerial employees (36%), |
| **Meetings:** *Meetings Attended to:* set policies, rules, or procedures, and formally present information (100%), informally exchange information, coordinate activities, resolve conflicts, and supervise or evaluate people (91%), evaluate options, give specialized information, train, educate or instruct (82%), bargain or persuade (36%); *Meetings Initiated or Chaired to:* informally exchange information (91%), evaluate options, set policies, rules or procedures (82%), coordinate activities, diagnose problems, evaluate people, formally present information, or train, instruct, or educate (73%), resolve conflicts (64%), give specialized information (55%), formally bargain (36%) |
| **Required Physical Activities:** sit for long periods (100%), climb without aids, walk (73%), move fingers independently, coordinate eyes, ears, hands, arms, feet and legs (45%), maintain balance, stand for long periods, lift and carry 10-50 lbs. (36%) |
| **Use of Machine and Tools:** *Office Equipment:* personal computer (100%), keyboard equipment (91%), standard office equipment, and mainframe computer (73%) |

191

| Table 7-16<br>Supply Chain Managers<br>Job Description |
| --- |
| **Environmental Conditions:** exposed to moving parts (45%), high temperatures, and dirty working conditions (36%) |
| **Work Context**: *Variety, Autonomy and Interdependence:* complete their task before others can start their work, rely on others to complete their task before they can start their work (100%), learn and use a variety of skills (91%), control schedule (82%), select projects they will work on (64%), influence other departments work activities, determine the method or equipment they will use (55%), determine the method or equipment others will use (45%), perform a complete service (36%), *Stressful Work Situations:* work on shared projects, deal with conflicts between goals (100%), work under tight deadlines (91%), perform different tasks over time, distracted by others, work with people over whom they have no authority (82%), deal with people who are distressed (73%), deal with situations that are highly stressful, perform the same mental activities over and over (64%); *Receiving Feedback:* immediate supervisor and other employees (100%), self-assess performance (73%), customers or clients (55%), |

192

# Purchasing

*Their expertise lies in knowing vendors and understanding how to negotiate price and terms.*
*—Bob Donath[1]*

*You are going to see most of your tactical procurement organization disappear over the next ten years.*
*—The Future of Purchasing and Supply: A Five and Ten-Year Forecast[2]*

*This chapter describes two job families: buyers/purchasing agents and purchasing managers. They represent the remnants of the traditional purchasing function, because many traditional purchasing responsibilities have been automated or shifted to other parts of logistics—notably inventory and material control. The chapter discusses competencies, job requirements, and training needs for both job families and places them in the context of current purchasing practice. It also briefly outlines personality and attitudinal results from the survey. The job family's responsibilities encompass the procurement function for the organization. The findings affect training strategy, career development, and career paths throughout the procurement function.*

193

## Key Findings and Takeaways

*Points in the text supporting each key finding are tagged with a number in parentheses, e.g., (1).*

**1** Training for purchasing professionals should reflect the shift from traditional responsibilities to an emphasis on managing internal and external relationships.

**2** Tactical purchasing professionals' training should focus on interpersonal, communication, and supervisory skills as preparation for promotion.

**3** Purchasing managers and buyers require training on producing individual and mass communication vehicles to distribute information and develop a common knowledge base.

**4** Purchasing managers and buyers develop expertise in non-purchasing disciplines primarily through trial and error.

**5** Purchasing managers and buyers need training for dealing with environmental and situational stressors–stress and time management.

**6** Purchasing managers' communications are analogous to information systems; they are vehicles used to develop a common knowledge base.

**7** Purchasing managers and buyers need additional training on office equipment to maintain and increase their productivity.

**8** Purchasing managers and buyers need training in spreadsheets, database packages, and other analytical tools, especially as their jobs change toward supply chain management.

## Purchasing Employees

When investigating a story, a reporter contacts a variety of sources to gather information. Informants' interests are served by providing information that presents them in the best light. The reporter sorts through this information and decides what and who is credible when writing a story. When a story contains unpopular information, readers vilify the reporter, not the source, because to the reader, the reporter is the source. Purchasing professionals suffer the same fate from their internal constituents, who hold them responsible for material and service failures.

Another perspective views the purchasing professionals as auctioneers in the heat of the a bidding war. They gather information, publish it, and distribute it to interested parties weeks before the event. They field questions and define the bidding structure. On the appointed day, they field bids, give reactions, and identify the winning bid. If they perceive the bids to be out-of-line, they pull the item, and the process begins again.

Acting as a reporter, the purchasing professional interviews engineering, production, warehouse, material control, inbound transportation, and accounting to identify the effect material choice, vendor selection, purchase quantity, and delivery frequency have for each department. The purchasing professional may develop specifications and identify how two or more organizational cultures and financial structures will mesh to form a supply chain. Juggling sales representatives, co-workers, and projects requires dexterity as they discover how variations in culture, financial orientation, production capacities and materials affect internal participants and the ultimate customer. Like the reporter, they are barely tolerated until their contributions to the organization are recognized.

The purchasing-reporter also investigates specifications, sifts this information, and develops solicitations for bidders or channel participants. Identifying vendors that can and will work with the organization's structure is becoming the primary job for purchasing professionals. The communiques must appeal to readers drawn by detailed technical specifications and readers drawn by the quality of the communication or the organization. Like the reporter, the purchasing professional must also inspire trust in potential sources. While sources realize that what they say is never totally "off-the-record," they must have confidence that the purchasing professional will protect their identity, and their firm's financial, manufacturing, or material secrets. They must cultivate a kinship with everyone from design engineers and sales representatives to manufacturing employees and forklift drivers.

Purchasing professionals should be desired as members of corporate teams for their technical expertise and their ability to produce solid information from meetings. Establishing trust among internal and external constituencies helps in coordinating meetings, vendor and customer visits, and negotiations.

Technical and interpersonal expertise is important to both purchasing job families. Yet companies hire untrained people to fill buyer positions and then fail to train them. Survey respondents indicated that the only knowledge or skills required to secure a lower-level purchasing position are basic mathematics and word processing. All the other knowledge and skills critical to job performance are acquired or enhanced through OJE. Most central to the issue is knowledge of purchasing, which all respondents agree is critical to purchasing professionals.(4)

Sixty-seven percent claimed they did not have to know purchasing before starting their present jobs. Eighty-three percent claimed they acquired this knowledge through OJE, while 33% said they received this knowledge through formal training. When asked how often they attended meetings to deliver or receive training, only 36% said they attended meetings for this purpose, every few months to annually. Upper-level purchasing managers' responses told a similar story. Fourteen knowledge or skills areas are shown as absolutely critical to purchasing managers' jobs. Project management, recruiting, selection, supervision, and evaluation are the only knowledge and skill areas where more managers had formal training than did not have it. This suggests very strongly that purchasing training is largely OJE, or trial and error.(4)

The emphasis on long-term, supply-chain relationships suggests that leading edge organizations have little room for the traditional purchasing job. Many of the duties associated with these jobs are also found in material and inventory control. However, data analysis clearly shows these positions as distinct from other logistics jobs. While separating purchasing from inventory and material control addresses statistical issues, the job families share many of the same functions.

---

There will always be a core nucleus procurement group, but the absolute numbers and layers will decline.
    *–The Future of Purchasing and Supply*[3]

---

Purchasing can be segmented into sourcing and execution activities.[5] Sourcing activities represent traditional purchasing while execution activities represent information and material flows.

The data analysis reflects this perspective. Buyers' primary activities center around sourcing or what is considered to be traditional purchasing functions, while purchasing managers' primary activities center on the management of information in the supply chain.

### Buyers Job Description
Buyers, as members of the buying center, coordinate the purchasing process. A buying center includes employees from all functional areas and organizational levels who have a stake in a purchase. Centers may be either reactive or proactive. Reactive buying centers employ traditional tools or processes designed to eliminate a problem with a minimum of discomfort. Proactive buying centers develop tools or processes that not only eliminate the problem, but also make its elimination a competitive advantage.

Classical functions will be eliminated as work becomes project oriented.

–Joseph R. Carter and Ran Narasimham[4]

Success requires teamwork, as buyers seldom have authority over team members and little influence over the methods used in the process. Buying centers are given responsibility for gathering information, developing and evaluating alternatives, selecting an alternative, and making the purchase. It is the buyers' role to coordinate this process by tracking vendor and material alternatives, recording the selected alternative, and expressing this information to internal and external constituents.[1]

As process coordinators, buyers work under constant pressure to keep the decision process moving. They must rely on others–manufacturing and design engineers, sales representatives, and suppliers–to develop and provide specialized information used to define the processes, help evaluation, and assure closure. Mis-communication or reliance on different knowledge bases complicate the communication. Progress halts as issues are examined and reexamined. The fact that buyers do not have formal authority impairs their ability to coordinate the decision process. Their role is limited to recommending courses of action as other buying center members make material and supplier selection decisions.[1, 2, 3, 5]

To complicate matters further, managing this process requires technical and interpersonal sophistication. Based on their trait scores, buyers may be more comfortable in reactive buying centers. They are more comfortable with simple problems and may limit their solutions to those that worked before. Their personality profile suggests that they should be competent communication specialists. When designing new tools or processes, their "openness to new experience" score suggests they reside in the early majority. Buyers are not afraid of innovation, they simply do not want to be the first to make the change.

### Buyers Competencies

Table 8-1 shows the competencies that emerged from the data analysis. Each competency ties directly to knowledge or job activities that respondents identified as crucial to job performance. These competencies, collectively, distinguish this job from the jobs in the data base and other jobs in the study.

*Apply project management and interpersonal techniques to develop a common knowledge base and coordinate buying centers and communication networks.* The movement toward the elimination of "functional silos" and non-value adding activities will require someone to manage the process. The substantive purchasing function will evolve from a process and information turnstile to an information kiosk. Instead of acting as gatekeepers, they will be called in only when clarification is needed.

---

We want to be called in to negotiate the multimillion dollar contract, not to buy pens.
    – Michele J. Flynn[5]

---

They will coordinate communication between individuals, functional areas, and organizations. In this capacity, they assure that information flows to the right recipients. The effective buyer will gather, store, and distribute information to both buying center and supply chain members so that an informed decision is made. These activities are necessary if the organization is going to adopt a market orientation.(1, 2, 3)

---

Suppliers working with several departments may communicate information once; it is the role of purchasing to assure that everyone receives this information.
    –Roberta J. Duffy[6]

---

The competent buyer not only possesses technical expertise, but also can package information suitable for consumption by a layperson. Emphasis is placed on information packaging and not interpretation. In this capacity, purchasing's role is similar to a retail sales associate. When approached, the 'customer' wants to know that purchasing can solve the problem. Any other perception reduces the perceived value of the interaction.(3)

---

We won't manage the transaction, but will have to manage the system that manages those transactions.
    –The Future of Purchasing and Supply[7]

---

**Use software packages to design communication media distributed internally and externally.** For buyers, the ability to communicate effectively in writing will increase in importance. As purchasing evolves into the supply chain management, buyers will be asked to translate customer expectations into supplier specifications. The translation will require buyers to know graphics, word-processing, and financial packages. Visual presentation of information will become more important as organizations market themselves as attractive supply chain partners. Requests for quotes will become the vehicle that attracts, influences, or reenforces the supply chain's attractiveness.(1, 2, 8)

Requests for quotes and other correspondence will be developed with the same care lavished on consumer advertising. Buyers realize that an effective visual presentation or layout will increase message clarity and effectiveness, thereby reducing misunderstandings and the reexamination of issues thought to be settled.

---

**Table 8-1**
**Buyers/Purchasing Agents**
**Competencies**

- **Apply project management and interpersonal techniques to develop a common knowledge base and coordinate buying centers and communication networks**
- **Use software packages to design communication media distributed internally and externally**
- **Apply time management techniques to address problems according to the importance for customers, suppliers, and the firm**
- **Understand customers' desires to prioritize them and to identify their effects on the design, procurement, and manufacturing processes**

---

*Understand customers' priorities and their effect on the firms' logistics practices.* Coordinating the communication network will assure customer priorities become part of the supply chain's knowledge base. Managing parallel buying centers and supply chains requires an ability to manage time and to prioritize temporal resources given customer priorities. Successful buyers not only understand how their activities affect product costs, but also how customers value these activities. This understanding helps identify where resources and tasks can be consolidated to add the most value for the customer.(3)

**Buyers Job Requirements**

Table 8-2 shows the knowledge, skills, and aptitudes required by buyers. Purchasing, inventory control, warehouse operation, records control, and accounting are the core knowledge areas required by buyers. Transportation knowledge is limited to understanding the effect alternatives have on channel timeliness. Skills include computer, interpersonal, and negotiation skills. Numerical and technical aptitudes are necessary for their liaison role. The

199

changing nature of the job will place additional emphasis on increasing purchasing professionals' technical abilities.

| Table 8-2<br>Buyers/Purchasing Agents<br>Job Requirements |
| --- |
| • **Purchasing**<br>• **Inventory control/warehousing**<br>• **Transportation**<br>• **Records control**<br>• **Accounting**<br>• **Oral and written communication skills**<br>• **Interpersonal skills**<br>• **Computer literacy**<br>• **Numerical aptitude**<br>• **Technical aptitude**<br>• **Negotiation skills** |

**Buyers Job Training Needs**

When an organization cannot meet its obligations, supply chain commitments and trust erode. Missed deadlines are unacceptable if they can be traced to poor execution resulting from ignorance or incompetence. Buyers' training needs are shown on Table 8-3.

Turning on a computer is not equivalent to starting a car. Given the keys, almost anyone can drive any car. Once a computer is turned on, the operator may not be able to do anything. Login procedures vary, software may be company specific, a newer or older version, or an unfamiliar brand. Pursuing computer competence by trial and error is common but ineffective.**(4)**

At a minimum, formal training is needed to teach buyers how to access data and communicate electronically, including networks, intranets, databases, and other application specific training. This training should include more than how to open and save files. It should include customizing screens and programs, sharing work with other software and co-workers, protecting work from accidental erasure and company assets from competitors' eyes. Buyers believe their constant use of computer hardware is critical to their jobs. Most acquire their computer expertise through on-the-job experience. But how much work is lost because employees are unaware their word processing package contains a timed backup feature?**(4, 7, 8)**

As I peered into their frustration filled eyes, I didn't have the heart to tell them that they had wasted another eight hours because they locked their computer up before I could get the file saved. After restarting their computer, I entered the program, turned on the timed back up feature, collected the data and spent the next two days re-entering data.

–Former buyer and manufacturing consultant

| Table 8-3<br>Buyers/Purchasing Agents<br>Job Training Needs |
| --- |
| *Equipment specific*<br>• **Personal computers**<br>• **Other keyboard equipment**<br>• **Standard office equipment**<br><br>*Interpersonal skills*<br>• **Oral and written communication skills**<br>• **How to conduct effective meetings**<br>• **Stress management techniques**<br><br>*Knowledge Needs*<br>• **Purchasing**<br>• **Inventory control and warehousing**<br>• **Transportation**<br>• **Records control, bookkeeping** |

Buyers should receive formal training in oral and written communication. Internally, they talk with everyone from the factory floor to the engineering labs and the executive suite. As operators of an information kiosk, their ability to communicate is critical to their effectiveness. But communication ability is just one piece of the puzzle. Project management and managing meetings are two skills that must be developed if the buyer is to be promoted. As functions and tasks are consolidated, purchasing's functional role will shift from transaction to project management. People with poor project management, and meeting skills compromise cost reduction and value adding activities. Inefficient meetings not only waste time, but reduce participants willingness to work with the buyer in the future.(1, 2)

Buyers require basic communication skills for this job including developing requests for quotes, writing a clear memo or email, leaving a comprehensive voice-mail message, talking with others, and collecting information from contacts and meetings. Exchanging information will become more important as the purchasing function becomes an information kiosk. Information transmitted in an inappropriate format becomes clutter. Greater skills are required at the next level, so buyers should sharpen these skills.(1,3)

Finally, the management of parallel supply chains and multiple buying centers requires time and stress management techniques. Successful time management techniques need to be shared as they may not be readily apparent. Identifying individual stressors and developing coping strategies reduces job stress.(5)

Based on their responses, buyers are not required to know purchasing, inventory control and warehousing, transportation, and records control/bookkeeping when they are first hired. Yet, this knowledge is considered to be absolutely critical to their job. Knowledge in these areas was acquired through OJE. Organizations cannot afford to wait for buyers to collect enough experiences to become competent. Formal training is required to reduce their time to competence.(4)

**Buyers Summary**
The overall picture for buyers is not favorable. As organizations attempt to eliminate non-value adding activities, these jobs will quickly disappear. Future buyers will need more interpersonal and project management skills. Training should focus on honing interpersonal skills because buyers exchange information frequently through diverse channels. Promotion requires development of communication, decision-making, project management, and interpersonal skills. These are also skills required for future logistics jobs, which may or may not be called purchasing.


### Purchasing Managers Job Description
The distinction between purchasing managers and buyers is in a period of transition. Buyers are primarily engaged in purchasing activities, while purchasing managers' focus is evolving from managing the purchasing function to coordinating and managing the supply chain. Purchasing managers are involved in every aspect of decision making. Their responsibility has evolved from purchasing raw materials and managing suppliers to coordinating supply chain resources designed to translate customers' desires into value laden products or services. Coordination is not limited to managing internal processes; the entire supply chain is examined to define resource allocation strategies resulting in structural integration and task consolidation. This centrality will result in more purchasing managers being tapped to run their respective organizations.[9]

The data supports this perspective. Purchasing managers attend and chair
meetings that include everyone from customers to suppliers nonsupervisory
employees. While the frequency of these meetings is not unique to the
purchasing function, the activities done are to a greater degree than 70% of the
jobs in a comparison database of 8,000 jobs. Remove customer contacts and
this number increases to almost 90%.

Based on the variety of participants and the frequency of contracts,
purchasing managers' primary role is coordinating or managing organizational
processes. Internally they are in daily contact with the production floor and
the executive suite. Formal presentations, negotiations, comments made in
passing, and personal persuasion are all used to squeeze costs, eliminate waste
and increase perceived value. Externally, they talk with customers,
government officials and suppliers to identify where their performance falls
short, is unethical, or reduces efficiency. When meetings are required,
purchasing managers are just as likely to be the marquee player as a journey-
person. Regardless of their role, these meetings are unique because they bring
together everyone who has a stake in the issue. As one scans the room, they
are likely to see a design engineer sitting next to a customer, hunkered next to
a supplier, rubbing shoulders with a production associate as they attempt to
borrow a pen from the company's chief executive officer.

Purchasing managers participate in human resource, supply chain
management, and strategic decisions. Their decision making profile closely
resembles the other logistics managers. Purchasing managers are accountable
for identifying how their activities contribute to the bottom line and increase
product/service value. They do this by adopting a market orientation–gather,
distribute and utilize information to enhance value and profitability. They
collect, translate, distribute, and store information, necessary to identify where
supply chain processes and tasks can be consolidated or optimized

For purchasing managers, human resource decisions are very important.
The expected reduction in absolute numbers along with the routinization of
tactical purchasing processes will challenge purchasing professionals'

motivational abilities. Creating structural stability, while embracing procedural change is going to challenge even the most effective purchasing manager. The burden of job analysis and employee development will become more important to the purchasing manager. An additional challenge is to determine which characteristics, technical or interpersonal, should future purchasing professionals possess.

Purchasing activities are not done in a vacuum. Managers are under constant stress to increase channel timeliness, maintain quality standards, and meet performance goals while eliminating unnecessary activities. If these factors were not enough, uncertainty about the future of the purchasing profession increases purchasing managers' stress. While many will welcome purchasing elevation to a strategic element, others will long for the good old days when the only concern was to reduce the cost of commodities purchased from last year.(5)

### Purchasing Managers Competencies

The purchasing managers' competencies partly reflect an elevation of skill requirements from buyers. They also reflect changes in organization level. The increased strategic importance placed on purchasing decisions requires a shift in focus. Today, purchasing managers are expected to identify cost reduction or avoidance opportunities and how their decisions add to the products' perceived value. Purchasing managers' competencies are shown in Table 8-4.

*Coordinate internal and external resources used to evaluate, select, and implement decisions designed to increase supply chain efficiency.* Buyers serve as information kiosks. Their primary function is to assure that information is communicated to decision makers. This focus suggests that lower level purchasing professionals engage in the first two market orientation activities. Purchasing managers, because of their decision-making responsibility, build on these two activities; they process this information to evaluate internal operations, organizational linkages, and supplier processes. These evaluations identify where tasks are duplicated, operations are inefficient, and communication breakdowns occur. These are non- value-adding activities and cost reduction opportunities. Like LIS managers, purchasing managers must determine when supply chain changes are financially justified. That means they must be adept at identifying the impact of suggested changes on each logistics activity. Cost reductions and increases must be estimated to discover "is it worth it?"

*Use supervisory and employee development skills to build and maintain an efficient and effective purchasing workforce.* As if environmental uncertainty was not enough to contend with, purchasing managers must cope with professional uncertainty as well. The purchasing function is undergoing a major transformation expected to culminate in the fragmentation of the purchasing function into two distinct processes. The first process will govern for tactical purchases or sourcing activities. The second process will manage the supply chain. Interestingly, while respondents were involved in decisions affecting all aspects of the human resource function, they felt this knowledge was not critical to their jobs. Purchasing managers will have to become more involved in human resource issues to identify skills they need to cultivate in their subordinates. Their competency will not only determine the morale of their subordinates, but also how they are viewed in the organization.

*Organize, coordinate and manage meetings to exchange information necessary to assure the decision process is successfully completed.* Meetings have become problematic for managers. Meetings can be valuable or a colossal waste of time. One strategy to reduce waste is to invite only those members whose presence is absolutely necessary to the meeting. Before the meeting, posting the agenda at a central location would allow participants to prioritize their schedules. During the meeting, discussed issues should be limited to only those identified in the agenda. Issues tangent to the meeting should be given a minimum of time. If discussion persists, it might be suggested that an additional meeting is scheduled to address this tangent issue. After the meeting, a meeting summary should also be posted at a central location to allow other team members to access information at their convenience. Purchasing managers are in a position to identify when someone's presence is critical or if a meeting report needs to be forwarded to their attention.(6)

*Maintain working knowledge of situational and environmental trends to identify effects on purchasing practices.* For the purchasing manager simply working with a broad range of logisticians is not enough. They must communicate with the entire supply chain, if they are to identify opportunities. They must be astute at identifying how logistics, manufacturing, financial, and marketing elements fit together to form the big picture.

*Understand and employ tools to identify cost trade-offs.* The ability to not only see where costs will be reduced, but also where they will increase is important. Modifying material quality or delivery frequency will reduce operating cost for some logistics activities as it increases cost for others. Successful purchasing managers will not only be able to internally identify how these costs will shift, but will be able to identify supply chain trade-offs that result in an absolute cost reduction.

| **Table 8-4**<br>**Purchasing Managers**<br>**Competencies** |
|---|
| • **Coordinate internal and external resources used to evaluate, select, and implement decisions designed to increase supply chain efficiency**<br>• **Use supervisory and employee development skills to build and maintain an efficient and effective purchasing workforce**<br>• **Organize, coordinate, and manage meetings to exchange information necessary to assure the decision process is successfully completed.**<br>• **Maintain working knowledge of situational and environmental trends to identify effects on purchasing practices**<br>• **Understand and employ tools to identify cost trade-offs** |

**Purchasing Managers Job Requirements**     The job requirements shown in Table 8-5 come from the knowledge and skills absolutely critical to accomplishing the main mission of the job. Only those knowledge areas and skills necessary to distinguish the purchasing managers' job family from other job families are included in this table. They come from the job classification questionnaire and include the knowledge and skills that the respondents say are widely used and absolutely critical to job performance. Other skills, basic mathematic and English for example, are not listed because most jobs require a rudimentary ability in these areas.

In table 8-5, the first two bullets list the knowledge which purchasing managers said were absolutely critical for their job. Unlike buyers, purchasing

206

managers feel they should possess these knowledge and skills before they started their job. Some of the requirements will change with the size of the organization and the degree to which they have adopted a market orientation and supply chain philosophy. Individuals working for larger firms will need to possess these knowledge and skills to a greater degree than individuals working for smaller organizations. The core knowledge requirements are as follows (listed by importance): employee development, writing financial and business text, purchasing, strategic planning project management, international trade, budgeting, production management, operations research, and transportation.

Putting together the competencies and job requirements leads directly to the analysis of training needs. They are discussed in the next section.

| |
|---|
| **Table 8-5**<br>**Purchasing Managers**<br>**Job Requirements** |
| • **Employee Development**<br>• **Supervision**<br>• **Selection**<br>• **Purchasing**<br>• **Strategic Planning**<br>• **Budgeting**<br>• **Banking**<br>• **Commerce**<br>• **Trade**<br>• **International Trade**<br>• **Production Management**<br>• **Operations Research**<br>• **Transportation**<br>• **Accounting**<br>• **Oral and written communication skills**<br>• **Organizational skills**<br>• **Interpersonal skills**<br>• **Negotiation ability**<br>• **Numerical aptitude**<br>• **Technical aptitude** |

### Purchasing Managers Job Training Needs

Unlike buyer/purchasing agents, purchasing managers' responses suggest that they are required to possess certain knowledge and skills before they are hired. Thirty knowledge categories were identified by respondents to be at least necessary, if not critical, for them to accomplish their job's main objective. The primary source of this knowledge was OJE; only four areas had higher formal training percentages. How often has a hammer been used to screw two pieces of wood together–the hammer being selected because it has always been used when nailing two boards together? Purchasing managers' training needs emerge from the competencies required for their job. Table 8-6 shows these training needs. (4)

Purchasing managers' knowledge requirements reflect their position within the organization. Whereas buyers require knowledge associated with managing the transaction, purchasing managers knowledge requirements derive from their need to manage financial and operation issues. Budgetary practices, purchasing principles, international commerce, employee motivation, job analysis, employee recruitment, operations research or systems analysis, and strategic planning are just a few of the fundamental competencies purchasing managers need to possess.

---

**Table 8-6**
**Job Family**
**Job Training Needs**

*Equipment specific*
• **Personal computer operation**
• **Other keyboard equipment**
• **Standard office equipment**

*Interpersonal skills*
• **Project management**
• **Organizational skills**
• **Stress management techniques**
• **Supervisory and employee development**

*Knowledge Needs*
• **Budgetary practices**
• **Human resource management**
• **International trade**
• **Inventory control or warehousing**
• **Operations research**
• **Transportation**

---

At a minimum, formal training is needed to teach purchasing managers how to electronically store, post and distribute information. The ability to post information on the company intranet allows everyone to stay informed. At this stage, rudimentary computer skills are expected. Purchasing managers require training about how computer resources can be used to optimize the decision process. Training should include more than how to store, retrieve files, or how to log on. Training should focus on getting the most out of the company's software infrastructure. Additionally, purchasing managers need to understand how data is stored. Understanding how the various systems are integrated will reduce wasted time because purchasing managers will be less likely to ask for information in a format that is nearly impossible to deliver.(3, 7, 8)

The competency of purchasing managers is contingent on their ability to manage projects. Coordinating multiple buying centers and parallel supply chains contributes to this complexity. Success will not only be measured by the decision's impact on the bottom line, but also by how well the process progressed through the various stages. Purchasing managers who bumble through meetings, short-change communication opportunities, or sidestep decisions erode other supply chain members' confidence in the organization's ability to deliver on its promises. Ineffective purchasing managers need to be identified and receive proper training.

### Buyer and Purchasing Manager Personal Characteristics

Based on their scores, there is no difference between buyers and purchasing managers' personality traits. They remain calm in difficult situations, are usually perceived as friendly, conservative, organized, and fun to be around. When sales representatives call on purchasing professionals, they better be armed with the facts because purchasing professionals base most of their decisions on objective criteria. Internally, purchasing professionals try to be customer oriented and perceive their firms to be market oriented.

### Summary

The purchasing function is in the middle of a fundamental transformation. Purchasing activities will probably splinter into two groups. One group will manage the sourcing process, while the second group will take on more responsibilities in their supply chain manager's role. Regardless of the group in which individuals find themselves, they will still need to possess several core skills. The primary knowledge or skill will be purchasing, but purchasing professionals may start to adopt characteristics usually exhibited by the company's marketing or sales personnel. In the future, the purchasing professionals will become the project management professionals. This evolution will require greater reliance on interpersonal and technical ability and to a lesser extent on purchasing ability.

1. Bob Donath,(March 29, 1999). "How to Finesse Customers who Demand Price Cuts," *Marketing New*, pp13-14.

2. Roberta J. Duffy, (1998), "The Future of Purchasing and Supply," *Purchasing Today,* 10:5.

3. Phillip L. Carter, Joseph R. Carter, Robert M. Monczka, Thomas H. Slaight, and Andrew J. Swan, (1998), "The Future of Purchasing and Supply: a Five- and Ten-Year Forecast," *National Association of Purchasing Management: Research report,* pp 1-114.

4. Robert Handfield, (September 1997), "Supply Chain Management," *Center for Advanced Purchasing Studies: Praxis research reports,* 1:1.

5. Joseph R. Carter and Ram Narsimhan, (1998), "A Comparison of North American and European Future Purchasing Trends," *National Association of Purchasing Management: Resource Article.*

6. Mary Siegfried Dozbaba, (1999), "I'm Convinced: You've got Value!" *Purchasing Today,* 10:5.

7. Roberta J. Duffy, (April, 1999), "Trail Blazing," *Purchasing Today* 10:4.

8. Carter, Carter, Monczka, Slaight, Swan, (1998).

9. Duffy, (April, 1999).

10. Duffy, (April, 1999).

11. Duffy, (April, 1999).

12. Carter, Carter, Monczka, Slaight, Swan, (1998).

13. Dozbaba, (1999).

14. Dozbaba, (1999).

| Table 8-7 |
| --- |
| **Buyer/Purchasing Agents** |
| **Job Description** |

**Example Titles:** Logistics Business Account Receivable Manager, MRO Buyer, Operations Specialist, Purchasing Agent, Purchasing Coordinator/Buyer, Supply Chain Analyst, Supply Manager, Vendor Compliance Manager

**General Job Characteristics:** *Span of Control:* none; *Budgetary responsibility:* yes; *Licenses and Certifications:* none; *Travel:* out-of-town overnight (27%); *Hours:* full-time constant number of hours; *Incentives:* group performance (55%), individual performance (36%); *Clothing:* office attire (82%)

**Supervision:** *Supervision Received:* regular monitoring of major job duties by immediate supervisor (100%), infrequent monitoring of major job duties by other employees (55%)

**Using Language:** Constant use of both oral and written English

**Using the Senses:** *Use Sight for:* observing the quantity or quality of materials or supplies (64%), pictures drawings or graphs (55%), observing the operations or performance of machines or equipment (27%); *Use Hearing for:* identifying the speech of people (27%)

**Decision Making:** *Financial Resources:* purchasing materials or supplies (45%), purchasing capital equipment or facilities (27%); *Operations and Production:* modifying or improving operations (27%)

**Contacts:** *Internal Contacts:* mid-level managers (82%), clerical or support staff (75%), first-line supervisors, non-supervisory professional/technical employees, and marketing or sales employees (45%), manufacturing employees (36%), upper-level executives, supervisory professional/technical employees, and laborers (27%); *External Contacts:* suppliers or sales representatives (91%), managerial and non-managerial employees (55%), customers or clients (36%), executives (27%)

**Meetings:** *Meetings Attended to:* informally exchange information (82%), diagnose or solve a problem, evaluate options or make a decision (55%), consult or give specialized information (45%), train, instruct, or educate (36%), formally exchange information, resolve conflicts or disputes, set policies, rules, or procedures (27%); *Meetings Initiated or Chaired to:* informally exchange information (45%), formally exchange information, or diagnose or solve problems (27%)

**Required Physical Activities:** sit for long periods (82%), precise finger movements (45%), push or pull light weights (36%), lift and carry 10-20 lbs., coordinate eyes, ears, hands and feet, kneel, crouch, crawl and walk (27%)

**Use of Machines and Tools:** *Office equipment:* standard office equipment (100%), personal computers, other keyboard equipment (91%), mainframe or multi-use computers (45%)

| Table 8-7 |
|---|
| Buyer/Purchasing Agents |
| Job Description |

| **Work Context:** *Variety, Autonomy, and Interdependence:* must complete their work before others can complete theirs (82%), depend on others to complete their work before being able to complete theirs (73%), use a variety of different skills, and learn new skills (64%), determine the methods or equipment they will use (45%), control their pace or schedule of activities, influence the activities of employees in other departments, perform a complete service and selects the projects they will work on (36%); *Stressful Work Situations:* deal with people over whom they have no formal authority (91%), perform a number of different tasks over time (82%), work under tight time pressures or deadlines, work with other employees to accomplish shared tasks or projects (73%), perform the same mental activities over and over, deal with conflicts between work goals and projects (64%), work is distracted by others (55%), deal with people in situations that are highly stressful or difficult (45%), perform the same physical activity over and over (27%); *Receiving Feedback:* receive feedback from immediate supervisor (91%), receive feedback from other employees or self-assesses their job performance (73%) |
|---|


| Table 8-8 |
|---|
| Purchasing Managers |
| Job Description |

| **Example Titles:** Corporate Purchasing Manager, Director of Procurement, Forecast Supply Chain Solutions Manager, Global Planning Manager, Supply Chain Planning Director, Supply Management Corporate Director |
|---|
| **General Job Characteristics:** *Span of Control:* reporting indirectly (31), supervisory or managerial employees (2), professional or technical employees (1), nonsupervisory reporting (2); *Budgetary Responsibility:* yes; *Licenses and Certification:* none; *Travel:* overnight out-of-town; *Hours:* constant number of hours; *Incentives:* group performance (71%), individual performance (50%), quality of employee's work (29%); *Clothing:* Office attire (100%) |
| **Supervision:** *Supervision Received:* regular monitoring of major job duties by immediate supervisor (86%), infrequent monitoring of major job duties by other employees (36%); *Supervision Given:* regular monitoring of major job duties of technical specialist or professional (57%), clerical or support staff (50%), and mid-level managers (36%), infrequent monitoring of major job duties of first-line supervisor (21%) |
| **Using Language:** *English*: Constant use of both oral and written English (100%); *Computer:* languages that do not produce executable programs (21%) |

| Table 8-8 |
| --- |
| **Purchasing Managers** |
| **Job Description** |

**Using the Senses:** *Use Sight for:* pictures, drawings or graphs (93%), blueprints, or maps (50%), observing the behaviors and actions of people, differences in colors (36%), observing the quantity or quality of materials or supplies, differences in patterns or shapes (29%); *Use Hearing for:* understanding the speech of people (50%)

**Decision Making:** *Financial Resources:* purchasing materials or supplies (71%), setting or changing the size of budgets (64%), purchasing capital equipment or facilities (57%); *Human Resources:* assigning employee responsibilities, establishing or changing work procedures or policies (71%), establishing or changing the lines of authority (64%), increasing or decreasing employee compensation (57%), increasing or decreasing the number of employees (50%); *Operations and Production:* setting or changing short-term and long-term performance goals (50%), evaluating the effectiveness, modifying or improving of operations (36%); *Strategy Decisions:* taking on new projects (71%), changing the types or levels of services (57%), discontinuing services (50%), discontinuing products (36%), abandoning projects , adding new products or product lines (29%)

**Contacts:** *Internal Contacts:* clerical and support staff, mid-level managers (79%), non-supervisory technical specialists or professionals, first-line supervisors, supervisory technical specialists or professionals (71%), upper-level executives (64%), marketing or sales employees (43%), and manufacturing employees (29%); *External Contacts:* managerial employees (86%), suppliers or sales representatives, customers, or clients (79%), executives (64%), contractors or subcontractors (50%), non-managerial employees (43%), job applicants (36%), and government or regulatory officials (29%)

**Meetings:** *Meetings Attended to*: informally exchange information, give specialized information (100%), evaluate and make a decision, formally exchange information (93%), formally bargain or negotiate, solve problems (86%), coordinate activities, resolve conflicts, set policies, rules or procedures, train, instruct, or educate (79%), supervise or evaluate people or projects (64%), persuade or sell (57%); *Meetings Initiated or Chaired to*: evaluate options or make a decision, informally exchange information (93%), consult or give specialized information, diagnose or solve problems, formally exchange information (86%), coordinate or schedule activities, formally bargain or negotiate, train, instruct, or educate (79%), set policies, rules or procedures, supervise or evaluate people or projects (71%), resolve conflicts or disputes (69%), persuade or sell (43%)

**Required Physical Activities:** sitting for long periods (93%), climb unaided (36%)

**Use of Machines and Tools:** *Office equipment*: personal computer, standard office equipment (100%), keyboard equipment (86%), mainframe computer (50%)

213

| Table 8-8 |
| --- |
| **Purchasing Managers** |
| **Job Description** |

**Work setting:** *Variety, Autonomy and Interdependence:* learn new skills (79%), complete their work before others can complete their work, depend on others to complete their work before being able to complete theirs, control their work pace or schedule (71%), use a variety of skills, and determine method or equipment they will use (64%), select projects they will work on, and influence the activities of other departments (57%), determine the equipment others will use, perform a complete service (51%); *Stressful Work Situation:* work under tight deadlines, deal with people over whom they have no formal authority (71%), work with others, deal with conflicts between different work goals or projects, perform a number of different tasks (64%), perform the same mental activity over and over, work is distracted by others (50%), deal with people in situations that are highly stressful or difficult, deal with people who are distressed or upset (43%); *Receiving Feedback:* self assessment, immediate supervisor (100%), clients or customers (79%), other employees (71%)

Customer
Service

*Customer service is used to provide exposure for new employees*
*–Director Distribution Manufacturing Company*

This chapter describes three job families: customer service representatives, customer service supervisors, and customer service managers. Respondents in these job families came from logistics organizations, firms providing support for logistics organizations and financial institutions. The chapter describes these jobs based on scores from the CMQ. It discusses the competencies, job requirements, and training needs for each job family based on these results. It also profiles personality, customer orientation, market orientation, and need for cognition for these job families. These results affect the training, recruitment, and selection for logistics personnel in these areas.

## Key Findings and Takeaways

*Points in the text supporting each key finding are tagged with a number in parentheses, e.g., (1).*

**1** The customer service function is in a period of transition. Operating employees and third parties are taking over customer service activities in firms whose customer service department cannot find ways to add value. As change permeates organizations and their supply chain, new processes for order entry and fulfillment are being introduced. The routine or reactive nature of customer service organizations is being replaced by automation and technology driven call centers.

**2** Customer service jobs are the only job families without unique activities; these jobs require proficiency in a variety of business disciplines and interpersonal skills.

**3** The customer service function serves as a transition between the firm's entry level positions and upper manager positions.

**4** Customer service personnel must apply organizational, industry, and supply chain knowledge to resolve customer issues.

**5** Organizational knowledge is acquired through on-the-job experience rather than formal training. This method lengthens time to competence.

**6** Customer service managers' knowledge and skill requirements are the broadest of all groups included in the survey.

**7** Customer service personnel rely heavily on their critical thinking abilities to address customer issues.

### Customer Service Employees

Traditionally, customer service jobs were similar to fire fighters or air traffic controllers. As fire fighters, customer service personnel were called in when customers had a complaint. The complaint came in, and they recorded pertinent information, evaluated the situation, and dispatched resources to put out the fire and rescue the firm's reputation. During the crisis, they would monitor progress and dispatch additional resources as they were needed. Afterwards, they helped evaluate what caused the crises and develop

216

contingency plans so that the problem did not reoccur. Their task was to right injustice, save people from impending doom, inspire hope, and make sure customers were satisfied. Customer service's time in the sun has passed as customer service activities are being dispersed throughout the firm.

In their air traffic role, customer service professionals were responsible for fielding customer inquiries, taking their orders and answering their questions. Like fire fighters, they recorded pertinent information, evaluated situations and dispatched resources, but this time their goal is to assure the timely and accurate delivery of cargo or information. Unlike the fire fighter, they do not react to a crisis, they evaluate operations to increase customer satisfaction, loyalty and reduce the potential for crises. In this role, customer service activities were combined with other logistics activities as new processes for order entry and fulfillment are introduced.(1)

Customer service representatives', supervisors', and managers' activities are being redistributed throughout the organization. Information technology has influenced how firms think about the customer service function. The organization's ability to instantly share information means that customers' desires are shared with employees responsible for delivering the products or services when and where customers want them. The customers ability to contact companies and order merchandise on the Internet has reduced the need to have someone manning the phone. Someday, the general public and industrial customers will both use the Internet to communicate with suppliers eliminating the need for regional and central call centers.[1]

In the meantime, consumer manufacturers are reducing the size of their call centers faster than firms marketing to other industrial customers. Customers can extract needed information from the company's data bases. Communication infrastructure advances are making it possible for customer service personnel to live on the other side of the world. Responsibility for addressing customer complaints is becoming part of the manufacturing employees' job. Supervisory and managerial employees are taking on responsibilities traditionally reserved for the material control and purchasing function. The adoption of the supply chain mentality is reflected by the degree to which customer service personnel communicate with customers and suppliers.

These statements are not intended to imply that customer service activities are decreasing in importance. The customer service function will develop two roles. The first branch will be responsible for order fulfillment or customer satisfaction. The second branch will serve as the firm's training function, assuring individuals are exposed to material and situations that enhance their managerial development. The first branch will be done by operating employees, third parties, and information technology. The second branch will provide the link between non-managerial and managerial jobs.(1, 3)

## Customer Service Representatives Job Description

After the firm's sales force, customer service representatives are the most important customer contact employees. How they deal with customer questions or issues influences whether a relationship is established, maintained, or ended. Customer inquiries are the catalyst that drives customer service representatives' jobs. Because of these inquiries, customer service representatives are involved in evaluating and offering suggestions for improving operations. This process may result in the modification of short-term objectives as promises are prioritized to minimize disruptions. Addressing customer issues requires the input from all departments and organizational levels. Success requires teamwork as customer service representatives are not supervisors and can only suggest actions.(4)

Customer service representatives are under constant pressure. This pressure is the result of having to rely on others including manufacturing and design engineers, inventory, marketing and production managers, and suppliers to provide information they can then pass on to customers. The diversity of contacts increases the likelihood for mis-communication. Customer service representatives exercise skill in communicating to assure that everyone understands what is going on.

### Customer Service Representatives Competencies

Customer service representatives' competencies revolve around their ability to coordinate between suppliers, customers, and their own firm. These competencies are shown in Table 9-1.

*Apply project management techniques and interpersonal skills to develop a common knowledge base used to coordinate the communication network.* Customer service representatives coordinate communication within and between firms. They assure that information is shared with everyone who has a stake in the issue. They gather, store, and communicate information used to make an effective decision and maintain the relationship.

*Use the firm's computer resources to address customer complaints, issues, and questions.* This skill is critical to customer service representatives' jobs. Without an adequate information system, customer service representatives could not provide the level of service customers demand. The information system is similar to owning a performance car. If the driver does not know how to extract speed from the car, they will not win the race. If customer service representatives do not know how to extract information from the firm's information network, the information system's capacity is not fully used. Competent customer service representatives apply their knowledge about the firm's databases to efficiently extract data and turn this data into useful information.(7)

*Maintain a thorough understanding of the firm's practices and how they affect customers.* Customer service representatives must know how their

218

organization operates. This knowledge is the heart of their jobs. Their ability to answer customer questions or solve their problems depends on knowledge of the firm's principles, policies, and procedures. Without this knowledge, customer service representatives may damage relationships rather than save or enhance them.(4)

*Maintain a calm professional demeanor in the face of adversity and under a variety of conditions.* The ability to remain calm when confronted by distressed customers is central to customer service representatives' jobs. How they respond affects the likelihood of maintaining a relationship with the customer.

---

**Table 9-1**
**Customer Service Representatives**
**Competencies**

- **Apply project management techniques and interpersonal skills to develop a common knowledge base used to coordinate the communication network**
- **Use the firm's computer resources to address customer complaints, issues, and questions**
- **Maintain a thorough understanding of the firm's practices and how they affect customers**
- **Maintain a calm professional demeanor in the face of adversity and under a variety of conditions**

---

**Customer Service Representatives Job Requirements**

Representatives must possess the knowledge and skills that will allow them to perform their jobs competently. These job requirements are precursors to competence. They come from the job classification questionnaire and include the knowledge and skills that the respondents say are widely used and absolutely critical to performance. These job requirements are shown in Table 9-2.

---

**Table 9-2**
**Customer Service Representatives**
**Job Requirements**

- **Oral and written communication skills**
- **Standard office equipment usage**
- **Computer literacy**
- **Mathematical aptitude**

---

Customer service representatives' primary job is to insure customer satisfaction by taking customer orders, answering questions and monitoring manufacturing processes. When hired, customer service representatives should have excellent communication skills and be comfortable with operating computers and other standard office equipment.

### Customer Service Representatives Training Needs

Customer service representatives identified several knowledge and skill areas that are necessary, if not critical, for them to accomplish their job's main mission. These knowledge and skills areas are segmented into equipment, interpersonal, and knowledge areas. The primary source of this knowledge is OJE. This method of acquiring knowledge is questionable, given their impact on customers' attitudes. OJE is similar to learning to play Monopoly by reading the rules after a token lands on a square. Eventually the game will end, but time was wasted and opportunities were missed because players did not have a complete grasp of the rules. Table 9-3 shows customer service representatives' training needs. **(5)**

---

**Table 9-3**
**Customer Service Representatives**
**Job Training Needs**

*Equipment specific*
• **Personal computer**
• **Other Keyboard equipment**
• **Standard office equipment**
• **Telecommunication equipment operation**
*Interpersonal skills*
• **Project management**
• **Organizational skills**
• **Critical thinking**
• **Oral and written communication skills**
*Knowledge needs*
• **Carrier Operations**
• **Local and regional geography**
• **Inventory control practices**
• **Records control/bookkeeping**
• **Strategic Planning**
• **Firm's marketing climate**

---

Customer service representatives require extensive computer training. Customer attitudes are influenced by the timeliness and completeness of responses. Computer expertise is necessary because any delay reflects negatively on the firm. Computer training should focus on how to effectively extract information from personal and shared databases. Knowledge about how and where information is stored enhances customer service representatives' ability to satisfy customer information needs. Closely related to computer proficiency is telecommunications proficiency. Customer service representatives should have a complete understanding of the firm's telecommunications system. Their handling and directing of calls increases the customer's perception about the firm's competence. Interpersonal skills training should focus primarily on improving critical thinking ability. Closely related to this skill are project management and organizational skills. Properly armed customer service representatives can prioritize inquires, coordinate parallel customer inquiries, and manage the inquiry process. The skills exhibited by customer service representatives communicate to co-workers and customers the importance the firm places on professionalism. Public speaking and written communication training will increase employee confidence in their ability to clearly communicate.

Customer service representatives' knowledge training should focus on the factors that influence the delivery of merchandise to customers. Transportation modes, local and regional geography, and the manufacturing process are only the tip of the iceberg. Customer service representative should be trained about every aspect of the organization if they are to perform their tasks competently.

**Customer Service Representatives Personal Characteristics**

Customer service representatives usually maintain their cool when faced with difficult situations. They are friendly but not too friendly. They are perceived to be agreeable, conservative, well organized, and achievement oriented. Customer service representatives like to tinker with processes and tools to discover how it works. They are customer oriented and perceive their firms to be market oriented.

**Customer Service Representatives Summary**

Customer service representatives have a direct impact on how the firm is perceived by its customers. Their ability to answer customer questions, coordinate departments, and solve problems requires outstanding communication skills. Their role in organizations means they experience a lot of stress, but more importantly, incompetent customer service representatives influence the stress levels of everyone they talk to. They must know about a variety of issues and how these issues influence their ability to satisfy customers. In essence, their role is to gather and record information for the organization. How well they are trained influences the quality of the information they can gather and the image customers have of the firm.

# Customer Service Supervisors Job Description

Customer service supervisors' jobs are stressful and complex because they have to deal with multiple organizations, deadlines, and production schedules. They are responsible for managing the customer service department. They supervise the process necessary to transform customer inquiries into desirable products and services.

Customer service supervisors chair meetings designed to educate customer service representatives. During these meetings, customer problems are diagnosed and prioritized. Information is used to educate customer service representatives about company policies and procedures. These meetings are also used to enhance representatives' decision making skills by illustrating how the prioritization and decision process works. When customer service supervisors are asked to attend meetings, their role is to provide information to decision makers. Customer service supervisors are the bridge between customer service representatives and the firm's other departments. They receive information from representatives and communicate this information to the affected departments. When representatives have difficulty dealing with a customer, supervisors may have to step in to save the relationship.(3, 7)

Customer service supervisors participate in financial, human resource, production, and operations decisions. Their role is to provide information used to address customer issues, modify the firm's processes, policies, and short-term goals. In the department, they are involved with establishing budgets and departmental policies, assigning employees responsibilities, and the purchasing of materials consumed by the department.(4)

Customer service supervisors' jobs are stressful. Coordinating the firm's responses contributes to this stress because supervisors do not have formal authority over the people they rely on to solve customer problems. Dealing with distressed or upset individuals contributes to their sense of stress. Another source of stress is organizational deadlines. Deadlines are established, changed, or missed as new problems are encountered and old problems are solved, eliminated, or reduced in importance.

## Customer Service Supervisors Competencies

Customer service supervisors' competencies focus on organizing information for customers and customer service representatives. Table 9-4 shows their competencies.

*Use decision-making skills to manage dynamic, complex customer desires.* Customer needs and wants are in a constant state of change. What was popular today will languish in inventory tomorrow. Customer service supervisors are responsible for monitoring customer desires and communicating these desires to co-workers. Part of this process requires them to make judgements about the long-term demand for a product or service. Product/service enhancements are justified because they reduce cost or induce customers to pay any additional cost. Customer service supervisors use of decision-making tools and skills increases the likelihood that innovations are truly revolutionary and not just a catalyst for product proliferation.(7)

---

**Table 9-4**
**Customer Service Supervisors**
**Competencies**

- Use decision making skills to manage dynamic, complex customer desires
- Apply knowledge of warehousing, inventory control, transportation, manufacturing, purchasing, and other areas specific to the supply chain
- Conduct effective operational meetings to develop a common knowledge base
- Use supervisory and employee development skills to build and maintain an efficient and effective customer service workforce

---

*Apply knowledge of warehousing, inventory control, transportation, manufacturing, purchasing, and other areas specific to the supply chain.* Within customer service departments, supervisory positions require knowledge about the firm's and supply chain's entire operation. This knowledge is necessary because supervisors not only need to direct representatives to the appropriate information source, but they also need to understand how processes come together to create the firm's product or service offering. The possession and application of this knowledge enhance the firm's reputation. Knowledge without the ability to apply it means opportunities are missed. While the role of customer service representatives is to gather information, supervisors are the first people charged with interpreting this information.(4, 7)

*Conduct effective operational meetings to develop a common knowledge base.* Effective meetings contribute to the functioning of the firm. Many meetings are perceived to be a waste of time. Customer service supervisors can contribute to a meeting's effectiveness by reviewing published agendas and organizing information to contribute. When they chair a meeting, they can increase the meeting's effectiveness by publishing and sticking to an agenda. Limiting participation to individuals who have a stake in the meeting's outcome will increase their perceived effectiveness.

*Use supervisory and employee development skills to build and maintain an efficient and effective customer service workforce.* Customer service supervisory and employee development skills have a direct impact on the organization's success. Effective supervisors will make sure subordinates receive necessary training. Part of their development responsibilities requires them to share knowledge and decision strategies. This knowledge sharing results in the development of a common knowledge base used as a guide when employees encounter new situations.

### Customer Service Supervisors Job Requirements

Customer service supervisors must possess the knowledge and skills that will allow them to perform their jobs competently. These job requirements are precursors to competence. They come from the job classification questionnaire and include the knowledge and skills that the respondents say are widely used and absolutely critical to performance. Table 9-5 shows these job requirements.

Customer service supervisors manage multiple projects requiring in-depth communication with a variety of people. This job requires excellent oral and written communication skills. Poor communication skills affect the firm by increasing the likelihood of improper machine operation, mis-communication, and poor decisions.

The diversity of knowledge required for this position reflects the diversity of the respondents. Customer service supervisors in a manufacturing facility require knowledge about occupational safety, while financial customer service supervisors require auditing and other financial knowledge. The point is that customer service supervisors must possess core knowledge and skills related to the firm's primary business to become successful.(7)

---

**Table 9-5**
**Customer Service Supervisors**
**Job Requirements**

- **Logistics function knowledge**
- **Core business knowledge**
- **Employee supervision and development**
- **Excellent oral and written communication skills**
- **Standard office equipment proficiency**
- **Ability to work independently**
- **Mathematical aptitude**
- **Ability to cope with stress**

---

### Customer Service Supervisors Training Needs

Customer service supervisors' training needs derive from their goal of providing outstanding service to customers. These training needs were identified after reviewing respondents' answers for critical activities, knowledge, skills, and the processes they used to acquire competency in each

224

of these areas. Supervisors acquired most of their knowledge through OJE; considering the power support personnel have over subordinate employees' attitudes, customer impressions, and their role in maintaining a long-term relationship, this practice is questionable. Supervisors who are not able to quickly and effectively resolve issues, who are poor leaders, or who are otherwise incompetent will increase customer and employee dissatisfaction. Table 9-6 shows customer service supervisors' job training needs. (5)

---

**Table 9-6**
**Customer Service Supervisors**
**Job Training Needs**

*Equipment specific*
• **Personal computer**
• **Other keyboard equipment**
• **Standard office equipment**
• **Telecommunications**
*Interpersonal skills*
• **Employee supervision and development**
• **Project management skills**
• **Communication skills**
*Knowledge needs*
• **Marketing/marketing research**
• **Bookkeeping**
• **Computer operations**
• **Inventory control**
• **Occupational safety and health**
• **Purchasing**
• **Auditing**
• **Budgeting**
• **Sales**
• **Operations research**
• **Accounting**
• **Job analysis**
• **Employee benefits**
• **Employee selection**
• **Strategic planning**

---

Equipment-specific formal training is needed to teach supervisors how to retrieve data and communicate electronically. They should possess an understanding of how and where information is stored. Additionally, they need to know who has access to information to correctly direct employees to these information sources. This knowledge is necessary for files stored on both personal computers and mainframe systems. A short training program on the operation of standard office equipment should also be provided. Any mistake the supervisor makes is quickly passed on to subordinates and affects customer perceptions about the firm's competence. Finally, supervisors should receive a review of how the firm's telecommunications system works since they have to direct subordinates' activities and trouble shoot the system.

Interpersonal skills center on the supervisors' abilities to manage activities. They require training about employee development and selection. Project management training would also benefit customer service supervisors. Customer issues are mini projects which require the same skills internally-initiated projects entail. Customer service supervisors who are indecisive and unable to communicate clearly, or who side step responsibility, erode customers' confidence in the supervisor's decision–making ability and the firm's competence. Because of the potential negative outcome, customer service supervisors should receive training on how to effectively communicate orally and in writing.(7)

Knowledge based training should include those area included in table 9-6. Market/marketing research, bookkeeping, and computer operations are equally important to customer service supervisors. Customer service supervisors require knowledge in a variety of areas because of the uncertainty with where service failures will occur.

### Customer Service Supervisors Personal Characteristics

Customer service supervisors are not fazed by difficult situations. They enjoy people and taking the lead in social situations. They may be perceived to be conservative, enjoying how things work presently rather than trying to set trends. Customer service supervisors are achievement oriented and usually well organized. They are customer oriented and perceive their firms to be market oriented.

### Customer Service Supervisors Summary

Customer service supervisors have the opportunity to learn and use a variety of skills. For customer service supervisors, the most important skill is their ability to communicate. These individuals are responsible for coordinating the firm's responses to a service failure. They marshal the organization's resources as they wade through data and identify potential solutions. This ability requires customer service supervisors to deal with conflicts between information, departments, organizations, and customers. They must be a jack-of-all-trades and comfortable with their position as the eye of the hurricane.

226

## Customer Service Managers Job Description

Customer service manager positions are where the focus shifts from operational issues to strategic issues. Customer service managers have more responsibility than customer service supervisors, but less than other senior level logistics managers. Customer service managers are in a unique position because their jobs require them to communicate frequently with a variety of personnel. Additionally, their knowledge base is the most complex of all the study's groups. These attributes suggest that customer service managers' knowledge and skills would contribute to their becoming supply chain managers.(3)

The decision domain of customer service managers supports this perspective. Customer service managers are involved in the same decisions as customer service supervisors. Additionally, they contribute to decisions about the firm's product lines and the communication of benefits offered by the firm's products and services. These decisions are accomplished by their involvement in evaluating and modifying manufacturing, order fulfillment, and call center processes . The frequency at which customer service managers chair meetings provides additional support for their increased responsibilities. While supervisors may attend these meetings, it is the customer service manager who normally chairs these departmental meetings. Customer service managers' jobs require them to visit with a variety of people. Through these contacts, customer desires are turned into operational plans. Formal presentations and hall meetings are used to assure that customer issues are transformed into value laden products. Their role is limited in that they usually provide information used to make the decision.

### Customer Service Managers Competencies

Customer service managers' competencies resemble those of other logistics managers. They involve effective human resource management, a broad knowledge base, and excellent communication skills. Table 9-7 shows customer service managers' competencies.

*Use supervisory, development, recruiting, and selection skills to staff a customer service organization.* The employee development skills displayed by customer service managers influence the firm's performance. Firms with competent customer service managers will have customer service supervisors and representatives who courteously and effectively handle customer inquiries. Employee turnover will be minimal and departmental climate will increase the commitment of employees to the organization.

*Use automation, decision-making skills, and emerging technologies to change communication and order fulfillment processes to increase customer satisfaction.* Customer service managers apply their knowledge of organizational policies and emerging technologies to assure that they and those under them do not promise more than the firm can deliver. They identify priorities, change communication processes, modify order fulfillment policies, and marshal resources to assure customers are satisfied. Customer service managers, like their sales counterparts are charged with identifying and implementing innovations. They are not only adept at looking at the big picture, but they are skilled in dividing it into its core components, examining interactions and piecing the picture together again.(7)

*Apply knowledge of warehousing, inventory control, transportation, manufacturing, purchasing, and other areas specific to the supply chain.* Customer service managers are information depositories. If they do not know the specifics, they must know how to attain information with a minimal effort.(4) They are experts in telecommunications and phone switch technologies. They use this knowledge to enhance supply chain relationships by using EDI to communicate inventory status and consumption forecasts to aid the flow of materials and information between partners.

---

**Table 9-7**
**Customer Service Managers**
**Competencies**

---

- **Use supervisory, development, recruiting, and selection skills to staff a customer service organization**
- **Use automation, decision-making skills, and emerging technologies to change communication and order fulfillment processes to increase customer satisfaction**
- **Apply knowledge of warehousing, inventory control, transportation, manufacturing, purchasing, and other areas specific to the supply chain**
- **Apply communication strategies to reduce the potential for misunderstandings and communication failures**
- **Create and maintain an informal climate during meetings**

---

*Apply communication strategies to reduce the potential for misunderstandings and communication failures.* Customer service managers are effective communicators. They have the ability to adapt their message to fit the listener. This is not to imply that they change their tune. Customer service managers adopt the jargon and, generally, the speaking patterns of their audience. This adaption contributes to the development of a common knowledge base.

*Create and maintain an informal climate during meetings.* Customer service managers foster information exchange by creating an informal climate that facilitates the free flow of information. They create a consultative forum focused on evaluating and resolving customer issues. This means they do not let discussions get bogged down but keep them continually moving along the intended path. Participants understand that their participation is valued as long as they stay within the bounds of the agenda.

### Customer Service Managers Job Requirements

Customer service managers must possess the knowledge and skills that will allow them to perform their jobs competently. These job requirements are precursors to competence. They come from the job classification questionnaire and include the knowledge and skills that the respondents said were widely used and absolutely critical to performance. Table 9-8 shows customer service managers' job requirements.

| Table 9-8<br>Customer Service Managers<br>Job Requirements |
| --- |
| • **Decision making skills**<br>• **Telecommunication Systems**<br>• **Transportation**<br>• **Sales**<br>• **Local and Regional Geography**<br>• **Promotion/advertising**<br>• **Marketing**<br>• **Merchandising**<br>• **Computer Operations**<br>• **Inventory Control**<br>• **Employee Supervision**<br>• **Selection and Development**<br>• **Accounting**<br>• **Budgeting**<br>• **Purchasing**<br>• **Records Control**<br>• **Data Base Operations**<br>• **Operations Research**<br>• **Oral and written communication abilities**<br>• **Mathematical aptitude** |

Customer service managers have the most diverse knowledge requirements of any group sampled. This diversity is necessary because it helps the support employee identify where the system broke down, talk with co-workers who can rectify the situation, and share progress with customers.

Knowledge about the majority of these areas is necessary if customer service managers hope to become competent.(7)

**Customer Service Managers Training Needs**

| Table 9-9 |
| --- |
| **Customer Service Managers** |
| **Job Training Needs** |

*Equipment specific*
- **Personal computer**
- **Other keyboard equipment**
- **Standard office equipment**
- **Telecommunication equipment operation**

*Interpersonal skills*
- **Project management**
- **Organizational skills**
- **Critical thinking**
- **Supervisory skills**
- **Oral and written communication skills**

*Knowledge needs*
- **Local and regional geography**
- **Telecommunication systems**
- **Transportation**
- **Sales**
- **Promotion/advertising**
- **Marketing**
- **Merchandising**
- **Computer operations**
- **Inventory control**
- **Employee supervision**
- **Employee selection and development**
- **Accounting**
- **Budgeting**
- **Purchasing**
- **Records control**
- **Data base operations**
- **Operations research**

Customer service managers' training needs derive from their goal of providing outstanding service to customers. These training needs were identified after reviewing respondents' answers for critical activities, knowledge, skills, and how they acquired competency in each of these areas. Customer service managers acquire most of their knowledge through OJE; given the power support personnel have over customer impressions and their role in maintaining the relationship, this practice is questionable. Customer service managers that are not able to quickly and effectively resolve issues will lead to customer dissatisfaction and reduce the prospects for future business. Table 9-9 shows their training needs. **(5)**

Equipment-specific formal training is needed to teach customer service managers how to retrieve data and communicate electronically. They should possess an understanding about how and where information is stored. Additionally, they need to know who has access to information to correctly direct the customers' inquiries. This knowledge is necessary for files stored on personal computers and mainframe systems. A short training program on the operation of standard office equipment should also be provided. Any mistake customer service managers make negatively affects customer perceptions about the firm's competence. Finally, customer service managers should receive a review of how the firm's telephone system works.

Customer service managers have to rely on others to accomplish their job objectives. The ability to prioritize issues and clearly tell co-workers customer issues affects whether complaints are timely handled. A thorough understanding of the firm's telecommunication and information systems will increase customer service managers' abilities to communicate effectively with co-workers and customers.

Customer service managers' knowledge-based training needs are among the greatest in the study. Knowledge-based training is necessary in all areas that contribute to the proper organizational functioning. Support personnel's responses suggest they need additional training in human resource issues such as selection and motivation. A thorough understanding of the firm's marketing climate, account system, purchasing and manufacturing capabilities would reduce customer service managers' likelihood of promising more than the firm can deliver. Customer service managers acquired most of their knowledge through OJE. The gap between knowledge gained through formal training and on-the-job experience was the survey's largest.

## Customer Service Managers Personal Characteristics

Customer service managers do not find stressful situations difficult. They are friendly, conservative, organized, and people oriented. Customer service managers like to understand how a process or tool works. They are customer oriented and perceive their firms to be market oriented.

**Customer Service Managers Summary**

Customer service managers are central figures in a highly stressful environment. They manage their firm's, its clientele's, and their own stress levels. They do this by mastering a variety of skills. They must be knowledgeable about the firm, its partners, and their co-workers' perspectives to solve problems on a day to day, if not hourly basis. Customer service managers need to master a variety of skills requires the development of formal training programs on a variety of topics. This education allows them to operate effectively and efficiently.

**Customer Service Summary**

The customer service function is in the middle of a major transformation. Activities are being combined with warehousing, purchasing and inventory/material control activities. Like most of the job families, customer service employees acquire most of their job knowledge through on-the-job experience. This strategy means that employees may not reach their full potential until several years have passed. Like most logistics functions, the computer has influenced customer service activities. Today, all customer service employees must be computer literate. But, computer literacy is just one component necessary to become competent. Customer service employees rely heavily on their interpersonal skills to address customer issues and enhance customer satisfaction.

1. Phillip A. Carter, Joseph R. Carter, Robert M. Monczka, Thomas H. Slaight and Andrew J. Swan. (1998). *The Future of Purchasing and Supply: a Five- And Ten–Year Forecast.* Tempe, AZ: NAPM.

| Table 9-10 |
| --- |
| Customer Service Representatives |
| Job Description |
| **Example Titles:** Administrative Assistant, Business Development Analyst, Business Development Manager, Business Marketing Analyst, Customer Billing Clerk, Customer Service Clerk, Customer Service Compliance Manager, Customer Service Customs Broker, Customer Service Operations Manager, Customer Service Problem Improvement, Customer Service Supervisor, Customer Solutions Supervisor, Logistics Business Accounts Receivable Manager, Manager of Special Projects, Operations Coordinator, Operations Specialist, Product Coordinator, Project Coordinator, Senior Executive Assistant, Supply Chain Coordinator, Transportation International Sales |
| **General Job Characteristics:** *Span of Control:* none; *Budget authority:* yes; *Licenses and Certifications:* none; *Travel:* overnight; *Hours:* full-time, constant; *Incentives:* group and individual (60%) |
| **Supervision:** *Supervision Received:* reviewed or directed by employees other than immediate supervisor (64%) |
| **Using Language:** constant use of oral and written English |
| **Using the Senses:** *Use Sight for:* pictures, drawings, patterns, or graphs (62% ), blueprints, maps, or similar documents (45%); *Use Hearing for:* understanding speech (49%) |
| **Decision Making:** *Human Resources:* set or change work procedures or policies (32%); *Operations and Production:* modify or improve operations (40%), set long-term goals (30%), evaluate the effectiveness of operations (28%); *Long-term Business Strategy:* adding new products (36%) |
| **Contacts:** *Internal Contacts:* mid-level managers (79%), upper level managers or executives (68%), marketing and sales employees, clerical and support staff (55%), nonsupervisory technical specialists(34%), supervisory technical specialists (30% ); *External Contacts:* customers or clients (70%), managerial employees (49%), suppliers or sales representatives (38%), executives (36%), non-managerial employees (32%) |
| **Meetings:** *Meetings Attended to:* informally exchange information (68%), give specialized information (43%), formally present information, train, instruct, or educate (40%), coordinate activities (38%), diagnose or solve problems (36%), evaluate options (28%); *Meetings Initiated or Chaired to:* informally exchange information (32%) |
| **Required Physical Activities:** sit for long periods of time (83%), precise finger movements (49%) |
| **Use of Machines and Tools:** *Office equipment:* personal computer (87%), standard office machines, keyboard equipment (83%), mainframe computers (38%) |

233

| Table 9-10 |
| --- |
| **Customer Service Representatives** |
| **Job Description** |
| **Work Context**: *Variety, Autonomy and Interdependence:* learn new skills, must complete their work before others can start theirs (62%), control their schedule of activities (60%), depend on others to complete their work before being able to start theirs (57%), determine the method or equipment they will use (43%), produce an entire finished product or service (36%); *Stressful Work Situations:* work under tight deadlines (79%), perform a number of different tasks (74%), work with other employees to accomplish shared projects (68%) , deal with people over whom they have no formal authority (66%), deal with conflicts between different goals (57%), perform the same mental activities over and over (45%); *Receiving Feedback:* immediate supervisor (89%), self-assessment (77%), clients or customers (62%), other employees (57%) |


| Table 9-11 |
| --- |
| **Customer Service Supervisors** |
| **Job Description** |
| **Example Titles:** Customer Service Account Manager, Customer Service Operations Assistant, Customer Service Product Representative, Logistics Services Supervisor, Operations Supervisor |
| **General Job Characteristics:** *Span of Control:* direct reports (33), indirect reports (23); *Budget Authority:* yes; *Licenses and Certifications:* none; *Travel:* out of town overnight travel (38%); *Hours:* full-time, constant, seasonal; *Incentives:* group performance (75%), individual performance (63%); *Work clothing:* supplied by worker (50%), uniform supplied by employer, and business suits or office attire (38%) |
| **Supervision:** *Supervision Received:* regular monitoring by their immediate supervisor (100%), and other employees (50%); *Supervision Given:* direct the activities of clerical or support staff with regular monitoring of job duties (63%), infrequently monitor manufacturing employees (63%), nonsupervisory professional employees and almost no monitoring of job duties of laborers (25%) |
| **Using Language:** *English*: constant use of oral and written English language; *Computer:* computer languages that do not produce executable programs (50%) |
| **Using the Senses:** *Use Sight for:* pictures, drawings, patterns, or graphs (88%), noticing changing events (63%), observing the quantity or quality of materials (50%), details of close objects or the operation of equipment (38%), observing the behaviors of people, differences in patterns, shapes or colors (25%); *Use Hearing for:* understanding speech (50%), identifying the direction of a sound (38%), listening for differences in loudness, tones or sound patterns, or notice changing events in the work environment, focus on one sound (25%) |

| Table 9-11 |
| --- |
| Customer Service Supervisors |
| Job Description |

**Decision Making:** *Financial Resources:* setting or changing the size of budgets (75%), purchasing materials (50%), managing investments (25%); *Human Resources:* establishing or changing the work procedures (63%), changing the numbers of employees and assigning employee responsibilities (50%); *Operations and Production:* evaluating, modifying or improving operations (88%), changing short term goals (75%), changing long term goals, determining equipment or the processes used (50%); *Long-term Business Strategy:* changing the types or levels of services offered, starting or acquiring new businesses, adding new products or product lines (25%)

**Contacts:** *Internal Contacts:* manufacturing employees (100%), clerical or support staff and laborers (50%), first line supervisors, nonsupervisory technical or professionals, mid-level managers (38%); *External Contacts:* non-managerial employees (63%), customers or clients (50%), suppliers or sales representatives (38%), contractors, subcontractors, consultants, or agents, public or job applicants, executives and managerial employees (25%)

**Meetings:** *Meetings Attended to:* informally exchange information (75%), resolve conflicts, diagnose problems, evaluate options, make decisions, give specialized advice (63%), coordinate activities, formally exchange information, train, set policies (58%), evaluate people or projects (38%); *Meetings Initiated or Chaired to:* diagnose or solve problems (63%), evaluate options, make decisions, informally exchange information, evaluate people or projects, set policies (50%), coordinate activities, resolve conflicts, formally present information (38%), persuade or sell, and train (25%)

**Required Physical Activities:** sit for long periods (50%), lift 10-20 lbs. and stand for long periods (38%), precise finger and arm-hand movements, move individual fingers, coordinate eyes, ears, hands, and feet, climb staircases, coordinate arms and legs, maintain balance, walk, and lift 21-50 lbs. (25%)

**Use of Machine and Tools:** *Office Equipment:* personal computer (100%), keyboard equipment (75%), standard office equipment (63%), mainframe computer (50%); *Mobile Tools and Vehicles:* utility vehicles (38%), highway vehicles, and. hand trucks (25%)

| Table 9-11 |
| --- |
| **Customer Service Supervisors** |
| **Job Description** |
| **Work Context**: *Variety, Autonomy and Interdependence:* control their own work pace and use a variety skills (88%), learn new skills (75%), select the projects they will work on, must complete their work before others can start theirs, depend on others to complete their work before they can start theirs (63%), determine the method or equipment they and others will use (50%), perform a complete service (38%), influence others work activities (25%); *Stressful Work Situations:* distracted by others (88%), work with other employees on shared tasks, under tight deadlines (75%), deal with people over whom they have no authority and conflicts between goals (63%), deal with people in stressful situations, and perform the same mental activity (50%), deal with injured people (38%), deal with distressed people and perform the same physical activities over and over (25%); *Receiving Feedback:* self-monitoring, and their immediate supervisor (100%), other employees (88%), clients or customers (75%) |

| Table 9-12 |
| --- |
| **Customer Service Managers** |
| **Job Description** |
| **Example Titles:** Administrative Logistics Support Associate, Business Development-Senior Director, Customer Service Branch Manager, Customer Service Loan Officer, Customer Service Manager, Customer Service Representative, Customer Service Retail Manager, Customer Service Sales, Customer Service Sales Manager, Customer Service Sales Trainer, Director of Supplemental Services, Field Sales Representative, Inside Sales Manager, Logistics Manager, Project Manager, Transportation Sales |
| **General Job Characteristics:** *Span of Control:* indirect reports (4), direct reports (2); *Budgetary Responsibility:* yes; *Licenses and Certification:* none; *Travel:* out-of-town overnight (60%), *Hours:* full-time, constant, seasonal; *Incentives:* group (88%), individual (40%); *Clothing:* office attire |
| **Supervision:** *Supervision Received:* constant monitoring of major and minor job duties by immediate supervisor (86%), by other employees (58%), and customers (26%); *Supervision Given:* regular monitor of major and minor job duties of marketing or sales employees (19%) |
| **Using Language:** *English:* constant use of oral and written English (98%); *Computer:* use computer languages that do not produce executable programs (40%) |
| **Using the Senses:** *Use Sight for:* pictures, drawings, patterns, graphs (67%), blueprints, or maps (49%), view extremely small details of close objects (33%), observing events in the work environment (30%), observing quantity or quality of materials (26%); *Use Hearing for:* understanding speech (77%), monitoring events (37%), focusing on one sound among many (33%) |

| Table 9-12 |
| --- |
| Customer Service Managers |
| Job Description |

**Decision Making:** *Financial Resources:* modifying budgets (33%); *Human Resources:* establishing work procedures (44%), assigning employee responsibilities (30%), changing employees numbers (21%); *Operations and Production:* modifying short term goals (47%), modifying long-term goals (37%), improving operations (33%), evaluating operation effectiveness (23%); *Long-term Business Strategy:* setting types of services (37%), new projects (44%)

**Contacts:** *Internal Contacts:* marketing and sales people (84%), clerical staff (81%), mid-level managers (74%), first line supervisors (53%), upper level (49%), nonsupervisory technical specialists (47%), supervisory technical specialists (26%), with operatives (21%); *External Contacts:* customers (93%), suppliers or sales reps (58%), managers (47%), non-managerial (44%), contractors or agents (30%), public (26%), and executives (23%)

**Meetings:** *Meetings Attended to:* informally exchange information (91%), train (72%), formally exchange information (67%), evaluate options (56%), set policies, and diagnose or solve problems (51%), persuade or sell (44%), coordinate activities (42%), resolve conflicts (35%), supervise or evaluate (33%), bargain or negotiate (26%); *Meetings Initiated or Chaired to:* informally exchange information (56%), formally exchange information (44%), consult (42%), persuade or sell, evaluate options and diagnose or solve problems (40%), resolve conflicts or disputes (37%), train (35%), supervise or evaluate and coordinate work (33%), set policies (28%), evaluate people or projects (26%)

**Required Physical Activities:** sit for long periods (98%), precise finger movements (51%), individual fingers move independently (49%), coordinate ears, eyes, hands, and feet (40%), climb staircases or ramps (23%)

**Use of Machine and Tools:** *Office equipment:* standard office equipment (98%), personal computer (95%), keyboard equipment (81%), mainframe computer (56%)

**Work Context:** *Variety, Autonomy and Interdependence:* control schedule (79%), learn new skills, others depend on them (74%), use a variety of skills (72%), perform a complete service (63%), select projects (49%), determine methods used (42%), determine the methods and activities of others (35%), depend on others (72%); *Stressful Work Situations:* work with others (88%), tight deadlines (86%), deal with people over whom they had no authority (81%), frequent distractions and interruptions (67%), repetitive mental activities and conflicting goals (65%), deal with people who are upset (58%), deal with people in situations that are highly stressful (51%), and repetitive physical activity (40%); *Receiving Feedback:* immediate supervisors (93%), clients and customers (79%), other employees (72%), self monitoring (86%)

# Training
# Systems and
# Sources

*To create employability security and spread work place education: support "learning alliances" to offer training, compare best practices, share success stories, and provide internships across companies.*
*–Rosabeth Moss Kanter, Worldclass*

This chapter connects the research findings to training systems and training sources. It develops six principles for logistics training: 1) training should begin by developing a common, consistent view of the logistics system for all employees; 2) communications and interpersonal skills should be central themes in any logistics training system; 3) training to develop managerial skills should be offered to operating and support personnel; 4) training should be offered to employees through a variety of channels; 5) knowledge must be kept current at all levels of the organization; and 6) training results should be measured and tied to performance appraisal for both trainers and students. The chapter describes developing training relationships and discusses key sources of training expertise. Also, it provides a list of questions to ask when choosing training programs. Appendix 10 explains how to construct a training program, offers sample training modules, and sources of information about training sources. Some of the modules and programs shown in the appendix have been used by firms participating in the research.

238

## Key Findings and Takeaways

*Points in the text supporting each key finding are tagged with a number in parentheses, e.g (1).*

**1** Logistics organizations should cultivate training relationships the same way they cultivate other supply chain relationships.

**2** Training should begin by developing a common, consistent view of the logistics system for all employees.

**3** Communications and interpersonal skills should be central themes in any logistics training system.

**4** Training to develop managerial and supervisory skills should be offered to operating and support personnel.

**5** Training should be offered to employees through a variety of sources, including community colleges, universities, training firms, web-based training, associations, and consulting firms.

**6** Knowledge must be kept current at all levels of the organization, meaning refresher courses for operating employees, updating supervisors, and re-tooling managers as new systems and new ideas develop.

**7** Training results should be measured and tied to performance appraisal for both trainers and students.

A woman walking in the woods came across a man who was chopping wood. She stood at the edge of the clearing where he worked and watched him for several minutes. He chopped furiously and sweated copiously, all the while making little progress. She realized why he made so little headway–his axe was far too dull. She walked closer and spoke to the man, who did not pause in his work.

"I hate to interrupt," she said, "but wouldn't it help if you sharpened your axe?"

Without pausing, he replied, "I don't have time to sharpen my axe. I've got to chop wood."

His attitude reflects an inappropriate but common approach to training. Sure, people need training. It would help employees. It would improve productivity, but there simply is not enough time to train. This short-sighted attitude deprives employees of opportunities for growth and development and hinders organizational productivity. It also implies that the knowledge simply is not that important.

U.S. firms spend billions annually on training, and it is not enough. Commitment to training is uneven or lacking, even as managers complain about the failure of schools and universities to assure that their graduates have mastered basic skills.[1] Because U.S. firms tend to poach trained workers, some firms also hesitate to budget for training for fear of losing their investment. This creates a vicious cycle that depletes the knowledge base of the workforce.

For logistics jobs, the primary training system is OJE, even for skills and knowledge regarded as critical to job performance. OJE is informal, uneven, and can foster poor work practices, inadequate job knowledge, and a limited range of job knowledge. OJE translates well to performing the job, assuming the content of the training is accurate and complete. Unfortunately for those firms that rely on this approach, the content is often inaccurate or incomplete. New employees learn shortcuts that defeat efficiency and effectiveness, undercut customer service, or create safety hazards.

Outstanding logistics organizations, including the majority of firms in this research, devote time, effort, and money to training. Their approach is bottom line, cost-oriented, and practical. They do not spend the money on training out of idealism, but out of pragmatism born of tangible results. They engage their employees in the training process, offering programs during work time and outside work time. Taking training courses, continuing education courses, and voluntary, in-house seminars is given high marks on annual evaluations and serious consideration in promotions. In some cases managers and executives spend ten percent of their time as students in formal training programs, about 25 working days annually. Operating and supervisory personnel spend 10-15 days annually in training, while some specialty staff spend up to 35 days annually in technical training.

Outstanding logistics organizations also build relationships with training sources. These relationships often ease the financial and time burdens of creating consistent, long-term training systems and programs. They provide knowledge, skills training, instruction, training facilities, and expertise.

This chapter describes training sources, programs, and systems used by outstanding logistics organizations to contribute to the growth and development of logistics personnel. It also discusses training relationships, including examples, and discusses the development of training modules.

## Training Sources

Outstanding logistics firms build relationships with training sources just as they build relationships with other suppliers. These firms associate themselves with universities, community colleges, consulting firms, individual consultants, training firms, professional associations, and vocational and technical centers. They draw course content and trainers from these sources, who also provide training through multiple channels. Each source of training has strengths and weaknesses, so managers must create a blend of these sources that meets critical training needs within the training budget.

*The Firm Itself.* A primary source of training content and instruction is the firm itself. For example, managers and supervisors may be trained as trainers in forklift operation, root cause failure analysis, or statistical process control. They train line employees, supervisors, and managers in their specialty. One firm extends its network of programmatic training to suppliers and customers.

These firms also emphasize training as part of the trainer's performance appraisal and give bonuses or raises based on training performance. One method that can be used is the one group pre-test, post-test design. This design measures starting knowledge, then provides training, and measures ending knowledge. Training performance is measured by looking at the difference between starting and ending scores. This enculturates training as a key skill in the logistics organization.

The firm itself is the best source of information about the firm, obviously. It may also be the best source of trainers and training for firm-specific content. As has been stressed here, firms should give the employees a broad range of information about the logistics system in which they work and a solid background in their industry. To increase the use of internal sources, employees need education on how to be trainers. Just knowing a topic well does not grant the ability to teach it, as many college students will attest.

The advantages of using internal content, trainers, and training sites are simple: the firm has control over the training process, the information relates directly to the firm, and the trainers are familiar with the firm and its practices. The disadvantages are more complicated. Training may become too focused on what the firm already does, overlooking opportunities for improvement. Training may become lax because trainers are not rewarded for their training activities or results are never measured for students.

*Other Firms.* This might be regarded as a by-product of benchmarking, but other firms may help train employees in a firm through industry consortia, regional economic development groups, or one-to-one relationships. Cross organizational teams can work toward improving work-related behavior that leads to efficiency and effectiveness. Programs like this have succeeded in places where the odds were arguably against success. (See the Best Practices Box in Chapter 10)

241

There are several disadvantages of using other firms as a training sources. Other firms may not relate closely enough to share information, or their performance or content is so poor that it is difficult to relate to the target organization. Potential partners may also be reluctant to participate because of time or trust issues.

*Universities.* Universities traditionally provide management and technical training for logistics organizations. Departments, training units, and research centers offer scheduled seminars, custom training programs, and classes on logistics, engineering, management, and supervision. Universities harbor genuine experts in these areas, along with highly skilled teachers and trainers.

The advantages of university based training include high levels of expertise, excellent androgogy (teaching to adults), and flexible programs. Disadvantages include a lack of operating level training and the need to schedule most programs around teaching schedules. Training is not the primary mission at most universities.

*Community Colleges.* Community colleges provide valuable training programs and resources to their designated regions. They are usually associated with vocational-technical schools with a well-defined operational slant. Community colleges, vocational-technical centers, and co-resident programs often give custom training programs to manufacturing plants, distribution centers, and other businesses in their regions. They may work with universities, other government agencies, and economic development groups to train workers to meet the needs of new firms. They also participate in programs to encourage firms to locate plants and distribution centers in their regions.

Community colleges usually develop programs directed at operating level and supervisory employees. Facilities may vary from antiquated to leading edge, but program offerings can be comprehensive. A web search produced 3,000 hits on training for forklift operation at community colleges. These programs often involve classroom and on-site training designed to fit a firm's needs.

The advantages of community college-based training include low cost, customization, and a broad range of programs. The disadvantages of community college-based training are few. Programs are often simple and straightforward, but then that is often what is required. They are generally not suited to training programs designed for middle and upper management, but there are exceptions.

*Training Firms.* Training firms may offer standard programs on a schedule or customized programs designed to meet a time-frame or specialized requirement. They may offer comprehensive, enterprise-wide programs or one hour, one time talks. Because understanding the logistics organization and the business are crucial foundations for training, the comprehensive programs may interest logistics managers greatly.

These comprehensive programs begin by developing a common picture of the logistics system. From that picture they generate competencies and training needs for the positions that serve in the system. The picture is literal–buildings, planes, ships, warehouses, and so on–and depicts the system in sufficient detail to allow employees to find where they fit. Training for some analytical techniques begins with a similar picture. The purpose of these pictures is assure that each employee understands the basics of the organization.

While similar approaches to training may be developed in-house or through other training sources, the comprehensive training systems have the advantage of experience in developing and using these approaches. These programs can be costly but may add more value.

One training firm encountered in the research concentrated on training operating personnel in using material control and production machinery. Prior to conducting any training, however, the trainers conduct a thorough audit of the client firm's production and material-handling operation, observe the employees who use each machine, and make recommendations to management regarding system changes that improve productivity and safety. If the changes are not made, the training firm will not conduct any training programs. So far, after thirteen years, the vast majority of clients client has made the changes, and cut costs, improved productivity, and reduced accidents as a result. The firm maintains certification records and test scores.

Their results also demonstrate the value of high standards. To pass one of their certification programs, students must score 90 percent or better on five categories of learning. An 89 percent in any one category means loss of certification. When this happens, the trainers work with the student to improve his or her knowledge in the category that caused difficulty. The employee is then given another exam and must meet the 90 percent standard. Clients speak highly of the training firm. One industrial giant has put 30,000 employees through the firm's training programs.

*Consultants.* Large consulting firms train clients in an array of topics, often on short notice. Their trainers are usually well-prepared, adept at the techniques they teach, and thorough in their approach. Independent consultants tend to specialize, but within their specialties, they offer expertise and demonstrated training skills. Consultant training may be too costly for small and medium sized companies, especially training from the large consulting firms. However, it is wise to ask. A consulting firm may wish to establish a reputation in training on a topic or in an industry. They may offer lower cost training to gain a place in a new market.

The advantages of consultants are usually their expertise, experience, and ability to deliver courses, seminars, or one-on-one training on short notice. The disadvantages, aside from cost, arise when they fail to deliver the expected quality of training, especially given the potential for a higher price.

243

*Software Sellers.* Enterprise software developers and sellers offer logistics training to support their logistics software. These programs can be comprehensive and tie directly to the LIS. These programs are often excellent, but they depend on adopting the software. The usefulness of the training is contingent on the usefulness of the program.

*Associations.* Professional associations offer seminars and conferences that fit most logistics training systems and programs. The Council of Logistics Management (CLM) annual conference and seminars serve as prime examples of such programs. One large food processing firm uses involvement in CLM as part of its management development program. As a manager's career progresses, involvement in CLM increases. Attending association sponsored seminars is part of the manager's career development plan.

In addition to the CLM, logisticians will usually find programs of interest through the American Management Association (AMA), APICS–The Educational Society for Resource Management, the National Association of Purchasing Management (NAPM), American Society of Transportation and Logistics (AST&L), the International Society of Logistics, and the American Trucking Associations, to name a few. Other more focused associations, based either in industry, or in subfunctions may also act as major sources of content or instruction. The Private Truck Council is one example.

Several associations offer member certification programs. For example, APICS–The Educational Society for Resource Management offers the Certified in Production and Inventory Management (CPIM) and the Certified in Integrated Resource Management (CIRM) programs. The CPIM provides a common knowledge base for individuals in production and inventory management. CIRM certification is for individuals requiring a cross-functional knowledge of materials management. The Materials Handling and Management Society offers two certification levels–The Certified Associate in Materials Handling (CAMH) and the Professional Certified in Materials Handling (PCMH). NAPM also offers two certification levels–The Accredited Purchasing Practitioner (APP) and the Certified Purchasing Manager (CPM). The APP is for entry level buyers engaged in the tactical or operational purchasing level, while the CPM suggests the individual possess the knowledge and skills necessary to be successful in the purchasing and supply management fields. The International Society of Logistics' certification, The Certified Professional Logistician (CPL), recognizes logistics' professional stature and cross-functional responsibilities. AST&L Certified in Transportation and Logistics designation attests to the individual's proficiency in several logistics areas. These programs are just a few of the many certification programs available to logistics professionals.

## Access to Training

Connecting employees to training programs can be a major issue. Four major techniques apply. First, an employee may be trained at his or her workstation, in a company training room, at the trainer's facilities or training center, at a hotel, or on-line. Correspondence courses on the web, teleconferences, and other forms of distance learning also apply. The key is to decide whether the training needs to come to the employee, or the employee goes to the training. This issue is assessed by examining how easily knowledge gained during training is transferred to the job. If the transfer rate is low, on site training is appropriate. When the transfer rate is high then training at special training centers or resorts can be used.

In-house training programs offer several advantages. First, economy is the primary advantage of in-house training programs because resource costs including professional trainers and facilities are minimal. Second, in-house training may have better results because instruction is more likely to be transferred from the session to the job. Third, most in-house training takes place at or near the job. This proximity may increase the individual's motivation to learn how to do their job better. Finally, in-house training programs allow the trainee to receive instant feedback. The primary disadvantage to in-house training programs is the negative affect on productivity. Experienced workers are sometimes used to supervise these training sessions, resulting in lost productivity. Another disadvantage is that products or services produced during training may be inferior.

Off site training programs offer three advantages. First, they often use professionals skilled in delivering instruction and training. Second, moving training away from the work site reduces the chance for work to distract the training sessions. Third, trainees do not have to worry about damaging production equipment or producing defective products. The primary disadvantage of off- site training is the cost associated with hiring professionals and renting training facilities. Also, with all training on company time, some productivity is lost.

## Training Systems

Ideally, each job family would have a coach who monitored employee performance, encouraged good work behavior and discouraged poor work behavior. A few firms have even re-named their supervisors and managers "coaches." This renaming process means little unless the "coach" is given the chance to spend enough time with each employee or each job family to know the training needs and prepare to meet them.

Coaching is the most customized form of training, offering immediacy and focus. Unfortunately, the ideal is difficult and widely regarded as too expensive, with notable exceptions.

# BEST PRACTICES
## Training and Success in the Mississippi Delta

The Delta region of Mississippi faced serious economic development problems as high-productivity automation displaced agricultural workers, mostly poor minorities. The displaced agricultural workers were willing to work, but lacked the skills and education required in modern manufacturing and distribution.

In 1991, six manufacturers in the region formed a consortium under the sponsorship of the U.S. Department of Agriculture, assisted by a community college, a university based consultant, the local vocational/technical center, and the Social Science Research Center at Mississippi State University. The manufacturing plants included healthcare, automotive parts, specialty metals, electrical products, heavy machinery, and food processing businesses. These firms acted as benchmarking partners for one another and for other manufacturing firms in the region. The forum did not involve direct competitors.

A survey of managers found the displaced agricultural workers more willing to work than employees in other regions, but also in serious need of training. Apprenticeship programs were developed through the community college and employees were trained in statistical process control techniques, teamwork, and leadership. The local vocational/technical center trained employees in equipment operation, although the employees themselves eventually took these duties over at most plants. The community college provided basic literacy and math courses for a significant percentage of the employees.

The results? After five years, these firms increased employment, market share, and product lines. Some plants are run by self-managed work teams, compensation in some plants is 30-50 percent based on bonuses, and employees implemented cellular manufacturing, kanban, and JIT distribution. One employee complained about the warehouse at his plant, so he was given responsibility for improving it. He did. Inventory turnover increased 35 percent, inventory accuracy by 8 percent, and warehouse productivity by 10 percent.

On specific measures, these firms parlayed their employees' extraordinary willingness to work into 18-30 percent improvements in defect rates, rework rates, scrap rates, quality, productivity, and speed of processing. The willingness to work translated easily into a willingness to learn and to be trained.

One manager said, "I've had experience in a lot of places, but the work force here, once trained, is the best I've ever had."

Consequently, training systems blend the training sources into an affordable, workable mix that, used wisely, meets most firms' and employees' training needs. The Best Practices Box above describes how one group of firms worked together to develop employees with little education, many of them illiterate, into a highly productive, effective workforce.

The firms described in the best practices box and the outstanding firms in the research used systematic training to build extraordinary logistics and manufacturing organizations. Two firms in the research have used comprehensive training programs for decades. They cannot boast the dramatic turnarounds noted in the best practices box because their performance has been outstanding all along. Their performance is sustained by relentless training, so no one ever falls behind. (See the Best Practices box in Chapter 2.)

These firms also followed a principle emphasized in this research: training should begin by developing a common, consistent view of the logistics system for all employees. The logistics organization has control over the information and people to put this principle into practice. Too many firms do not, meaning that employees at all levels perceive different logistics systems. A point of clarification–this does *not* mean that every employee should see the logistics system in the same way. A variety of perspectives can be valuable to the development and improvement of logistics systems. This means the employees should see the *same system*; they should work from a common set of facts about the system.

> "We adopted a training system that helps us work from common ground. (A training firm) worked with a cross-section of our employees to create a picture of our logistics system, a physical picture, that we could share with every employee. You can see where every job fits in the picture. After we put together the picture, we worked with employees to create a list of competencies for each job. The competencies fit the picture."
>
> –Manufacturing Director of Logistics Training

This goes beyond new employee orientation, although it certainly should be part of orientation. Often, long time employees lose sight of their role in the system as the system changes. If firms want adaptable, flexible employees, then they must maintain a concrete, fact based view of the logistics system among those employees. Clearly, outside organizations will not provide the content for this type of training, although they may facilitate creating the common view.

This training serves multiple purposes. First, it creates a foundation for other training. The organization can readily define training needs in terms of the system. Second, it eases communication. If all employees are discussing the same system, they will have fewer confused or confusing conversations. They speak the same language about the same issues if this kind of baseline training is performed. Third, it helps employees recognize the importance of the tasks they perform on the job.

Another important point arises in all of the best practices and outstanding logistics organizations: communications and interpersonal skills should be central themes in any logistics training system. Every logistics job involves interaction with other people, more so than many other jobs. Development of these skills requires a wide range of training topics; supervisory skills, time management, stress management, report writing, business writing, team building, training as trainers, and meeting skills are examples.

Take supervisory training. This could cover performance appraisal, motivation, communication, organizing, and administration. Over 90 percent of the respondents with supervisory responsibility indicated that this was critical job knowledge, but the majority gained their skills through OJE. Failing to understand and apply these skills creates major problems for logistics organizations. Supervisors can encourage or discourage turnover, for example. Dispatchers working side by side for the same firm may have vastly different levels of turnover in their part of the operation. In one firm, a dispatcher with two percent annual turnover sat next to another dispatcher with 315 percent annual turnover. Each worked with 50 drivers in an over-the-road operation. The difference between the two was simply supervisory skills. The supervisor with high turnover was dictatorial and arbitrary, while the other took a collaborative approach to employees. The supervisor with the low turnover had much higher productivity.

Training in supervisory skills helps supervisors maintain their skills and work with their subordinates better. It also prepares operating employees for promotion to supervisor. The same skills, applied in a different context, also apply to managers with supervisory responsibility. Firms often give this training to supervisors, managers, and operating employees who are in line for promotion.

Unfortunately, many logistics organizations are inconsistent in providing this training at the supervisory and operating levels. Not all firms provide supervisory training to managers, assuming that a college degree or job experience will suffice. In most degree programs, supervisory skills receive only cursory attention, if any, and job experience may as easily teach bad supervisory practice as good. The best-practice organizations involved in this research made supervisory training available to employees early in their tenure with the firm and required it when promotion was imminent.

Logistics employees who face multiple demands on their time, including supervisors, planning support, managers, and administrative support, need time management skills. These skills allow them to set priorities, focus on a task, and gain control of their work life. These skills are best applied when all employees have been trained to understand the system in which they work. Priorities are then easier to set and easier to understand. Many of these employees work where they are interrupted and new demands are placed on them constantly.

Stress management ties closely to time management. Employees who have some control of their time also have some control over the amount of stress they experience on the job. Employees need to be reminded that stress is something people feel, not some external situation. What one employee finds exceedingly stressful, another may find a matter of indifference. The ability to control time and the projects worked on may be important here.

---

Our people can say 'no' to projects and sometimes they do. If a project engineer has too many things going on, then it may make sense to turn down the next project. We don't have a problem with that. We feel like our people know how much they can handle and we certainly don't have anyone we think is slacking off. We put a lot of faith in our people and it pays off.

    –3PL Vice President

---

Since e-mail, memos, and reports represent a common way to convey business information, most logistics employees and all managers need writing skills. Regrettably, business education often fails to underscore the importance of writing skills. Many college graduates, let alone high school graduates, write poorly. Since the boss may work 2,000 miles away and see a subordinate in person only twice a year, they know their subordinates through written reports and quantitative performance measures. The ability to write a simple declarative sentence evades many managers, but it is crucial to organizational performance.

---

"The first thing I do when I bring in a new engineer is teach him or her to write a report the way I want it. They get exact instructions and I make them write a report immediately, preferably on a topic of obvious importance to the organization, not trivia. That way they get involved, and they learn how to deal with the boss."
–Telecommunications Vice President of Transportation

---

The need for team skills pervades many organizations, even those organized along traditional lines. Logistics work is collaborative by nature. It means working together, often in groups that form and reform routinely to direct attention to new projects and programs. One type of 3PL thrives on project oriented teams. Most logistics managers' career paths will pass through a 3PL or a consulting firm in the future, meaning team skills will be essential.

Operating employees may need training skills as much as managers. Training new employees should go beyond turning on the machine or entering data into the computer. Formal, structured training brings employees to competence more quickly than informal, casual training. Effective training is no accident. Just as data entry and customer service tasks have become ubiquitous, responsibility for training should be widespread in the organization. Having stated that, training effectiveness should become part of an employee's evaluation. Otherwise, if everyone is 'responsible, then no one is responsible' may become the organizational reality.

Meetings already occupy logisticians' work time. From the operations and manufacturing floor to the executive suite, everyone meets some time during the work day. The time-wasting, seemingly eternal meeting has become part of business lore. Several people encountered in this research put their pager number on the speed dialer of their cell phone so they could call themselves out of useless meetings. Yet meetings serve important collaborative, training, and information-exchange purposes. They can be effective tools when used well.

Training in meeting skills often goes too far. It details how to run a seminar or a multiple-day meeting with multiple, scheduled sessions. Far more meetings in logistics are informal meetings to assign tasks, schedule work, or informally exchange information. Such meetings should usually be brief, but frequently are not.

When more elaborate meetings are scheduled, structure and value to the participants are important. One logistics organization visited in this research put on a two-day seminar for warehouse managers and planning support staff. The vice president in charge scheduled 35 sessions for two days, with time specified for each presentation. The times ranged from one minute to 25 minutes. The meeting ran ahead of schedule, employees saw the value, and no one seemed to view the meeting as a waste of time. It had several important dimensions: structure, content, and focus among them.

Since logistics employees at all levels are apt to chair or initiate meetings, these skills are essential to the development of a logistician. Nothing is potentially more collaborative than a well run meeting.

Another key point: training to develop managerial and supervisory skills should be offered to operating and support personnel. The flat organization dictates that operating and support personnel take on responsibilities once associated with management jobs. With warehouse workers entering data, driving forklifts, and taking customers on tours of the warehouse, they must now have computer, customer service, and machine operation skills. No part of their training should be neglected.

One large organization, with over $29 billion in revenue, now has only four layers in its multinational structure. When customers have problems with the firm's heavy-duty, industrial products, they call directly the employee who built the product.[3]

Managers should bear in mind that training employees in managerial and supervisory skills will demystify these skills. Operating employees will have higher expectations of managers' application of those skills. Nonetheless, the new organizational structure and new logistics approaches force this training further down the organization. As span of control increases, managers will have less time to spend overseeing the work of each employee. It makes sense to give the employees the skills the manager might have used.

The implications, at this point, are that logistics managers should devote full time to training. That, of course, is impossible. That is where the development of training partnerships and relationships becomes so important. Where logistics managers play an important role, aside from assuming some training duties and assuring their own training, is in institutionalizing training in the organizational culture.

This raises another key point: training should be offered to employees through a variety of sources, including community colleges, universities, training firms, web-based training, associations, and consulting firms. No one source is likely to provide everything, but properly blended, the training can become part of the work life of employees at all levels.

Logistics organizations should explore and take advantage of the training resources available from local vocational/technical schools, community colleges, and universities. They should take advantage of state, federal, and local economic funding for workforce development, training, and education. The programs should be evaluated on what can be learned, not the quality of the leather in the meeting room chairs.

## Nine Questions for Choosing Training Programs

Table 10-1shows nine questions to ask when choosing or designing a training program. Training programs vary greatly in cost, time commitment, level of content, and instruction. The answers to these questions should help structure a decision about training.

| Table 10-1<br>Nine Questions for Choosing Training<br>Programs |
| --- |
| 1. What is the content?<br>2. Who will be trained?<br>3. Who will teach the course?<br>4. What is the time commitment?<br>5. Are there prerequisites?<br>6. What materials are required?<br>7. How is the course delivered?<br>8. How urgent is the training need?<br>9. What is the cost? |

## Training Modules and Training Programs

Appendix 10 contains three training modules or sections from training modules. The training modules resulted from the type of collaboration already described. The kanban training module was developed for a large manufacturing firm by the Curriculum Research Center at Mississippi State University. The Skill/Tech program at East Mississippi Community College modified the module to suit a small manufacturer that participated in this research. The module is written at the fourth grade level and was presented to employees in two classroom sessions lasting two hours each. The presenter then worked with employees at each work station to assure that they were ready to implement the program. The presenter then followed up to fine tune the program with short visits for about a month. The program significantly reduced WIP inventory in firms that boasted 99 percent plus on time delivery.

Training programs and systems should be held accountable for their results. The results should be measured and the feedback used to improve the programs. Just as firms work closely with other suppliers to improve goods and other services, measurement programs should be used to help build stronger training partners, better training programs, and more effective training systems.

## Conclusion

This research reveals the value of systematic, formal, structured training for logisticians at all levels. It also reveals the dangers of unstructured, casual, or neglected training approaches–a longer time to competence, patchwork skills, disrupted operations, communications problems, and customer service disasters among them. But the greatest danger of neglecting training lies in letting employees believe that what they do is of little consequence to the organization.

The value of training is difficult to refute, but firms still tend to avoid the investment. Training is expensive, time consuming, and risky in the sense that trained people may leave. In fact, they probably will leave withing five years. Nonetheless, training is worth it. Costs can be minimized by choosing the right content to suit each job and each person, and by creating a series of partnerships that benefit the logistics organization, and the training partners.

Training should be viewed as a logistics issue: giving the right knowledge and skill to the right person at the right time through the right medium at the right cost. This means crediting employees who train others for this work and recognizing training as a part of their jobs. It also means formalizing training to measure its results and improve its effectiveness. Otherwise, firms will not know whether the training is right in any sense.

An experiment at a university industrial manufacturing laboratory measured time to competence for two groups of twenty workers. One group received structured training in a training facility, while the other group received on-the-job instruction. The experiment's results suggest structured training is more valuable than unstructured training. The unstructured group took a little over 16 hours to become competent, while the structured group only needed about 5 hours, which represents a 72% savings in training time and time to competence. Individuals receiving structured training had lower scrap rates of approximately 70% and were more successful at solving production problems. Both training methods required about $6 per person, but when the difference in time to competence of 8 hours is factored in, it is clear that structured training offers significant benefits.[4]

Logistics managers may ignore growth and development at their peril. The informal, casual approach to training may appeal to a sense of economy, but it is a short–sighted sense. Employees should share a connom picture of the system in which they work and they should sense their own growth and development both in the job and outside the job. Logistics managers should take responsibility for the process and assure that employees develop that

253

sense. The foundation of all logistics training should be an understanding of the firm's logistics system. The primary source of content is the employee and his or her job knowledge. Employees are experts in their own jobs, at least to the extent that their level of training and their job experience developed them.

Problems arise because training is not seen as part of the trainer's job; the trainer's view of organizational, discipline, and industry issues is limited, and the trainer is not prepared to train others. The person assigned to train the new forklift driver is evaluated as a forklift driver, not a forklift driver trainer. Many excellent workers make poor trainers because they lack training skills or incentives to train others. If training is never mentioned as part of a periodic review, training skills are not taught in company or company sponsored programs, and students are not briefed on their role.

On-the-job experience is a principal form of internal training. It offers the advantage of transferring newly acquired knowledge directly to the job. It offers the disadvantage of easy misuse or casual application. Other internal approaches are formal on-the-job experience (OJE) including apprenticeships, seminars, video tapes, company trainers, corporate training centers, and universities. In large firms, internal sources may cover almost any area of knowledge and any skill.

Logistics managers face new challenges in the new millennium, which means more of the same for most of them. New challenges are old news in this tumultuous field. To meet these challenges, logistics managers will need strong allies. These include both internal and external training organizations that can meet the changing needs of the logistics organization and most importantly, well-trained colleagues and a well-trained workforce.

1. Wayne f. Cascio, (1997). *Managing Human Resources.* New York: McGraw–Hill.

2. This description is based on interviews with key people in the program and the report "Best Management practices for Manufacturing in the Mississippi Delta," *Social Research Report Series 94-1,* by Frank Hull. Social Science Research Center, January 1994. The interviews updated results from the 1994 report.

3. Tom Peters, ABB Asea Brown Boveri, Chapter 4, *Liberation Management.* New York: Alfred A. Knopf, 1992.

4. J. G. Collen, S. A. Sawein, G. R. Sisson, & R. A. Swanson (1976). "Training What's it Worth?" Training and Development Journal, 30, 17.

# APPENDIX 1

# TECHNICAL DESCRIPTION

# AND INTERPRETATION

## Discussion of Table Scores and Analysis

This appendix explains the tables in Appendices 2–9, which support the discussion and analysis in chapters 2–9. It describes how each statistic was generated and interpreted.

This research used the Common Metric Questionnaire© (CMQ) in a unique, multifirm assessment of logistics jobs. The CMQ gathers data about work behavior using a 3000+ item questionnaire. The items cover demographics, job basics, knowledge requirements, and work activities. This information is then analyzed using the Common Metric System© (CMS) a proprietary software program from PSTC, Inc.

The CMS clusters responses to the CMQ into job families. It examines the similarities and differences between responses and puts the most similar into the same job families. This statistical analysis is repeated until the responses all fit their job families well. Once the CMS identifies the job families, it generates three kinds of statistics that measure the importance of 80 job dimensions.

For each of the 80 dimensions, the CMS first develops percentage, scope and rarity scores. The percentage shows what portion of the respondents identified the items in the dimension as part of their job. For example, if 100 people were asked, "does your job require you to use personal computers," and 76 people said "yes," the percentage would be 76%. The scope score gives the ratio of actual responses to possible responses. Scope scores shows the breadth of the dimension in a job family. Scope scores range from 0–100 and are also given as a percentage. A single domain might include 50 items. When measured for a job family with 35 respondents, this means 35 x 50 possible answers. To illustrate, 10 people are asked to answer 10 questions about one domain. This means there are 100 possible answers. If each person says he or she does 4 activities, then the answer would be 40 and the percentage is 40%. The final score, rarity (which PSTC calls uniqueness) comes from comparing the scope score to scores in a database of 8000 jobs. The rarity score shows the percentage of those 8000 jobs with a lower scope score. A rarity score of 50% means that 50% of the population does more of the activities in a domain, then the job family being examined. This score also means that the job family being examined does more of the activities than 49% of the population. When examined as a group, these scores–percentage, scope and rarity–distinguish one job from other jobs.

### Decision Rules for Identifying Important Job Dimensions

The researchers agreed upon several decision rules to aid in the identification of job dimensions.

RULE 1 - A sizable percentage of respondents in that job family must have considered the dimension as "applicable" to their job.

256

This rule states that a sizable number of respondents must agree that this dimension is applicable. For example, the material handler who also fixes network computer problems would state that Office Machines is an applicable dimension. This individual represents an outlier, and a recommendation that materials handlers must be trained in network administration is nonsensical. For heavily sampled areas (warehouse operating employees, for example), the percent "applicable" might be 20%. For others, applicable could be as high as 40%. Such rules were used in each job families' job description tables, and dimension score tables. For example, in the description below, 100% of the respondents within this job family receive some level of supervision.

| Example Table<br>Example Logistics Job Family<br>Job Description |
| --- |
| Example titles: xxx,xxx,xx,xxxx,xxxx |
| General job characteristics: *Span of Control*- Managers, supervisors, and professionals reporting directly (9) ; indirect reports (8); *Budget Authority*-yes or no; *Licenses and Certifications*- None; *Travel*- Some travel is required (1-25%);*Hours*- Full-time, working the same hours per week; *Incentives*- receive individual incentives (60%), group incentives (50%); |
| Supervision: *Supervision Received*– Infrequent monitoring of major and minor job duties by immediate supervisors (100%); *Supervision Given*– Regular monitoring of major job duties for technical specialists and professional staff (90%), Regular monitoring of technical and professional supervisors (40%) |

In the example table below, 93% of the respondents indicated that "Exchanging information/consulting" was part of their job, and 50% of the respondents indicated that "Training" was part of their job. In this example 50% is the cut-off. This means 50% of the respondents had to identify this items as being part of their job to be included in the table.

| Example Job Table<br>Example Logistics Job Family<br>Domain and Dimension Scores<br><br>INTERPERSONAL DOMAIN | Percentage | Scope | Rarity |
| --- | --- | --- | --- |
| *Internal Contacts* | | | |
| Exchanging information/consulting | 93 | 36 | 96 |
| Training | 50 | 28 | 43 |

RULE 2 - The raw dimension score should be approximately 20.

The scope score shows the breadth of the dimension in a job family. A raw score of 20 indicates that those respondents which said they performed activities in this dimension perform 20% of the total number of possible activities.

| Example Table<br>Example Logistics Job Family<br>Domain and Dimension Scores | | | |
|---|---|---|---|
| **Dimension Description** | **Percentage** | **Scope** | **Rarity** |
| **INTERPERSONAL DOMAIN** | | | |
| *Internal Contacts* | | | |
| **Exchanging information/consulting** | 93 | 36 | 96 |
| **Training** | 50 | 28 | 43 |

In the example above, this job family indicates that exchanging information is done by 93% of the respondents. This family also performs 36% of the possible activities included in the exchanging information/consulting dimension. 50% of the respondents did training activities. These respondents did only 28% of the possible training activities included in the training dimension.

RULE 3 - The Rarity score should be sufficiently high to warrant investigation.

Jobs are distinguished by unique activities. The CMS© allows the researcher to test raw "scope" scores against over 8,000 jobs examined using the CMQ©. This comparison is the "rarity" score.

| Example Table<br>Example Logistics Job Family<br>Domain and Dimension Scores | | | |
|---|---|---|---|
| Dimension Description | Percentage | Scope | Rarity |
| **INTERPERSONAL DOMAIN** | | | |
| *Internal Contacts* | | | |
| **Exchanging information/consulting** | 93 | 36 | 96 |
| **Training** | 50 | 28 | 43 |

For, example, 93% of the respondents say they exchange information or consult. These people performed 36% of the activities covered by the exchange information consulting dimension. These respondents' scores were higher than the scores for 96% of the 8000 jobs examined using the CMQ®. The Rarity score provides additional information about the Scope score; knowing only the Scope score, all that can be concluded about the position is that it involves nearly 36% of all the activities that comprise the exchanging information/consulting dimension. The rarity score indicates that this is a rare Scope score; 4% or less of the 8000 jobs Common-Metric System™ database perform a higher degree of information exchange than the employees in this job family. Rare scope scores (high percentage number) mean other job families do not do the activities done by this job family. A low number means other job families do most, if not all, of the activities done by the target job family.

### Interpreting Knowledge Used
Another table important to each of the job families is the knowledge used table. Respondents indicate whether they use a particular knowledge or skill on an hourly, daily, weekly, monthly, or yearly basis.

To be included in the knowledge-used table, a large percentage of respondents had to say they used that knowledge or skill. The percent of those employees who used that knowledge was recorded as well as the frequency with which that knowledge is used.

In the example below, inventory control knowledge or skill is used on a daily basis by 76% of the respondents that said they used inventory control knowledge or skills. Additionally, 70% the respondents said they used trucking knowledge or skills constantly.

259

| Example Table<br>Example Logistics Job Family<br>Knowledge Used | | |
|---|---|---|
| **Knowledge Category** | **Used** | **By** |
| *Human Resources* | | |
| **Selection and recruitment** | **Yearly** | **36%** |
| *Management and Production* | | |
| **Inventory control and warehousing** | **Daily** | **76%** |
| *Transportation* | | |
| **Air/water** | **Constantly** | **29%** |
| **Trucking** | **Constantly** | **70%** |

The last table in Appendices 2–9 contains each job family's personnel characteristics. Information was collected using the Neuroticism, Extraversion, and Openness Five Factor Inventory (NEO-FFI) form S, need for cognition, customer orientation, market orientation scales.

The NEO-FFI is a personality scale consisting of sixty items that measure five personality factors: neuroticism, extraversion, openness, agreeableness, and conscientiousness. Scores for each factor are compared with the factor's average to identify whether the person has a high, low or average score. Need for Cognition measures individual enjoyment for doing mental puzzles. High scores suggest that the person enjoys thinking about or discovering how something works. While a low score means the individual only cares that something works and not with how it operates. Customer orientation measures the activities respondents claim to do when working with coworkers and customers. High scores mean the individual does not do things without considering how they will affect their customers. Low customer orientation scores mean the individual does not always do what is in the best interest of the customer. Market orientation measures the respondent's perception of the organization's market orientation. Market orientation includes the generation of intelligence on customers' current and future needs, the distribution of this intelligence throughout the organization, and the organization's responsiveness to the intelligence.

### Interpreting the Personal Characteristics Table

The personality, need for cognition, customer orientation, and market orientation table provides much information. In the right–hand column is the normative, the highest, and the lowest reported scores for each dimension. For example in the table below, the average score for Neuroticism has been 19.07. The highest score for this dimension is 38, while the lowest score was 4. A sample column was included in the table when space permits. This column reports the average, the highest, and the lowest score given by respondents. For example, respondents to this study had an average score of 14.5, the highest score was 40 and the lowest score was 0. To the right of this column are the job family columns. In the example below, this job family has an average score of 10.5, the highest score is 25 and the lowest score was 2.

| Table x-x<br>Job Family<br>Personality, Need for Cognition, Customer Orientation, and Market Orientation | | | | | | |
|---|---|---|---|---|---|---|
| **Dimension** | **Job Family** | | **Sample Means** | | **Normative Score** | |
| Neuroticism | 2 | 10.5 | 0 | 14.5 | 4 | 19.07 |
| | 25 | | 40 | | 38 | |

### Appendix 2

The tables in appendix 2 can be used to make cross functional comparisons. The numbers in each cell are rarity scores. These numbers come from comparing the job families' scope score to scores in the database of 8000 jobs. The rarity score shows the percentage of jobs with lower scope scores. Top logistics managers score–82 means they do more activities included under meetings/contacts than 82% of all jobs included in the 8000 job database.

Along the right side of the table is a list of seventeen items. These items are summary factors based on the 80 dimensions discussed before. These items can be used to make a quick comparison between job families.

### Summary

The goal of this section was to provide the reader with a more technical examination of how the research was conducted, and the means used to share aspects of the research with their colleagues. While technical in nature, the difficulties associated with understanding these results is compensated by the wealth of information that is provided by the CMS©. Our goal is to identify training needs and employee development for logistics personnel.

The Common Metric Questionnaire is available from Personnel Systems & Technologies Corporation (PSTC, Inc.). At http://www.pstc.com.

The NEO-PI Form S is available from Psychological Assessment Resources, Inc. At http://www.parinc.com

The need for cognition, customer and market orientation scales are available from the authors.

# APPENDIX 2

# OVERALL DOMAIN SCORES

Table 2-1

Overall Domain Scores for Top Managers, Customer Service, and Purchasing Functions

| Domain Score \ Job Family | Purchasing Manager | Purchasing Agent | Inventory Administrator | Inventory Supervisor | Production Manager | Supply Chain Manager |
|---|---|---|---|---|---|---|
| Meetings/Contacts | 93 | 51 | 40 | 68 | 81 | 97 |
| Contact with Public or Stressful Situations | 57 | 43 | 24 | 44 | 49 | 64 |
| Use of Tools/Machines/Vehicles | 2 | 16 | 26 | 32 | 6 | 31 |
| Production/Operations/HR Decision Making | 45 | 7 | 4 | 43 | 57 | 73 |
| Physical Activity or Work Environment | 16 | 19 | 42 | 51 | 31 | 40 |
| Supervision/Conflict Resolution/Training | 47 | 3 | 1 | 16 | 8 | 50 |
| Marketing, Customer, or Sales Contact | 44 | 19 | 14 | 24 | 16 | 44 |
| Bargaining/Persuading/Negotiating | 45 | 9 | 2 | 3 | 4 | 31 |
| Financial/Purchasing/Budgeting Decisions | 51 | 20 | 13 | 22 | 24 | 41 |
| Clerical/Office Activities, Information Exchange | 82 | 79 | 60 | 74 | 53 | 82 |
| Regulatory/Governmental/Media Contacts | 54 | 0 | 0 | 0 | 0 | 0 |
| Operations & Service Contacts/Supervision | 16 | 29 | 19 | 58 | 29 | 44 |
| Technical or Scientific Machine Use | 41 | 57 | 40 | 53 | 44 | 42 |
| Strategic Planning | 24 | 0 | 0 | 0 | 70 | 22 |
| Meeting with the Public or Customers | 43 | 1 | 0 | 0 | 26 | 16 |
| Product/Service Decision making or planning | 44 | 58 | 5 | 22 | 27 | 45 |
| Entertainment or Training Activities | 6 | 2 | 2 | 16 | 1 | 13 |

| Table 2-2<br>Overall Domain Scores for Top Managers, Logistics Information Systems and<br>Customer Service Functions | | | | | | |
|---|---|---|---|---|---|---|
| Job Family<br><br>Domain Score | Top Managers | LIS Technicians | LIS Managers | C. S. Representative | C. S. Supervisor | C. S. Manager |
| Meetings/Contacts | 82 | 77 | 89 | 55 | 67 | 72 |
| Contact with Public or Stressful Situations | 59 | 41 | 56 | 40 | 51 | 52 |
| Use of Tools/Machines/Vehicles | 10 | 18 | 3 | 2 | 36 | 2 |
| Production/Operations/HR Decision making | 71 | 21 | 62 | 20 | 51 | 31 |
| Physical Activity or Work Environment | 23 | 20 | 18 | 16 | 27 | 23 |
| Supervision/Conflict Resolution/Training | 53 | 9 | 51 | 3 | 33 | 16 |
| Marketing, Customer, or Sales Contact | 42 | 20 | 52 | 34 | 27 | 64 |
| Bargaining/Persuading/Negotiating | 23 | 6 | 23 | 2 | 6 | 10 |
| Financial/Purchasing/Budgeting Decisions | 56 | 12 | 40 | 9 | 29 | 18 |
| Clerical/Office Activities, Information Exchange | 73 | 77 | 76 | 69 | 59 | 79 |
| Regulatory/Governmental/Media Contacts | 13 | 0 | 1 | 1 | 0 | 26 |
| Operations & Service Contacts/Supervision | 30 | 22 | 21 | 5 | 68 | 13 |
| Technical or Scientific Machine Use | 44 | 57 | 44 | 47 | 67 | 51 |
| Strategic Planning | 63 | 0 | 96 | 16 | 42 | 17 |
| Meeting with the Public or Customers | 26 | 16 | 20 | 7 | 1 | 15 |
| Product/Service Decision making or planning | 43 | 6 | 33 | 12 | 12 | 21 |
| Entertainment or Training Activities | 21 | 2 | 19 | 3 | 15 | 6 |

| Table 2-3 Overall Domain Scores for the Warehouse Function | | | | | | |
|---|---|---|---|---|---|---|
| Job Family / Domain Score | Operational Employees | Clerks | Administrators | supervisors | Planning and Support | Managers |
| Meetings/Contacts | 41 | 50 | 83 | 69 | 95 | 93 |
| Contact with Public or Stressful Situations | 25 | 30 | 59 | 33 | 49 | 67 |
| Use of Tools/Machines/Vehicles | 11 | 20 | 12 | 10 | 19 | 34 |
| Production/Operations/HR Decision making | 28 | 20 | 51 | 52 | 33 | 81 |
| Physical Activity or Work Environment | 67 | 43 | 30 | 23 | 27 | 49 |
| Supervision/Conflict Resolution/Training | 25 | 7 | 25 | 13 | 29 | 57 |
| Marketing, Customer, or Sales Contact | 5 | 9 | 41 | 5 | 18 | 32 |
| Bargaining/Persuading/Negotiating | 2 | 3 | 4 | 3 | 18 | 14 |
| Financial/Purchasing/Budgeting Decisions | 4 | 9 | 48 | 16 | 26 | 39 |
| Clerical/Office Activities, Information Exchange | 37 | 68 | 88 | 40 | 80 | 91 |
| Regulatory/Governmental/Media Contacts | 0 | 0 | 1 | 0 | 22 | 0 |
| Operations & Service Contacts/Supervision | 32 | 48 | 31 | 39 | 14 | 59 |
| Technical or Scientific Machine Use | 45 | 48 | 47 | 37 | 35 | 54 |
| Strategic Planning | 0 | 0 | 30 | 0 | 10 | 22 |
| Meeting with the Public or Customers | 6 | 1 | 1 | 1 | 15 | 21 |
| Product/Service Decision making or planning | 0 | 5 | 26 | 18 | 18 | 26 |
| Entertainment or Training Activities | 2 | 2 | 2 | 1 | 1 | 6 |

| Table 2-4 Overall Domain Scores for the Transportation Function | | | | |
|---|---|---|---|---|
| Job Family / Domain Score | Operational Employees | Marine/Rail Employees | Administrators | Managers |
| Meetings/Contacts | 25 | 89 | 58 | 84 |
| Contact with Public or Stressful Situations | 64 | 56 | 37 | 56 |
| Use of Tools/Machines/Vehicles | 63 | 11 | 7 | 11 |
| Production/Operations/HR Decision making | 2 | 29 | 13 | 59 |
| Physical Activity or Work Environment | 44 | 58 | 17 | 22 |
| Supervision/Conflict Resolution/Training | 6 | 18 | 8 | 40 |
| Marketing, Customer, or Sales Contact | 23 | 31 | 10 | 18 |
| Bargaining/Persuading/Negotiating | 1 | 14 | 9 | 6 |
| Financial/Purchasing/Budgeting Decisions | 9 | 4 | 6 | 41 |
| Clerical/Office Activities, Information Exchange | 67 | 84 | 71 | 67 |
| Regulatory/Governmental/Media Contacts | 1 | 0 | 44 | 1 |
| Operations & Service Contacts/Supervision | 21 | 51 | 23 | 36 |
| Technical or Scientific Machine Use | 0 | 51 | 49 | 44 |
| Strategic Planning | 0 | 0 | 0 | 0 |
| Meeting with the Public or Customers | 0 | 0 | 22 | 2 |
| Product/Service Decision making or planning | 0 | 0 | 6 | 16 |
| Entertainment or Training Activities | 2 | 5 | 1 | 3 |

# APPENDIX 3

# TOP LOGISTICS MANAGERS

## Table 3-1
### Top Logistics Managers Job Family
### Domain and Dimension Scores

| Dimension Description | Percentage | Scope | Rarity |
|---|---|---|---|
| **INTERPERSONAL DOMAIN** | | | |
| *Internal Contacts* | | | |
| Exchanging information/consulting | 94 | 37 | 55 |
| Supervising professional/technical employees | 91 | 33 | 64 |
| Supervising upper-level executives | 86 | 45 | 77 |
| Training | 80 | 49 | 65 |
| Supervising mid-level managers | 77 | 36 | 77 |
| Selling or persuading | 51 | 35 | 62 |
| Supervising operative employees | 49 | 35 | 70 |
| Bargaining or negotiating | 43 | 25 | 53 |
| Supervising laborers | 40 | 43 | 44 |
| *External Contacts* | | | |
| Customers–sales related | 86 | 29 | 64 |
| Exchanging business related information | 86 | 25 | 58 |
| Supervising suppliers or contractors | 69 | 25 | 59 |
| Bargaining and negotiating | 63 | 24 | 65 |
| Resolving conflicts | 51 | 21 | 54 |
| Exchanging special interest information | 51 | 15 | 48 |

| Table 3-1 Top Logistics Managers Job Family Domain and Dimension Scores | | | |
|---|---|---|---|
| Dimension Description | Percentage | Scope | Rarity |
| Training | 34 | 28 | 59 |
| *Meetings* | | | |
| Chair meetings with non-executives | 89 | 36 | 61 |
| Attend meetings with executives | 86 | 46 | 74 |
| Attend meetings with non-executives | 86 | 40 | 61 |
| Chair meetings with executives | 71 | 41 | 74 |
| Attend meetings with non-supervisory employees | 63 | 32 | 59 |
| Chair meetings with non-supervisory employees | 63 | 31 | 58 |
| Attend meetings to bargain or persuade | 57 | 28 | 63 |
| Attend meetings with outside supervisors, technicians | 46 | 40 | 75 |
| Attend meetings with customers | 46 | 24 | 60 |
| Chair meetings with outside supervisors, technicians | 40 | 38 | 65 |
| Chair meetings to bargain or persuade | 37 | 35 | 63 |
| *Frequency Ratings for Internal and External Contacts* | | | |
| With supervisors, managers, and executives | 97 | 50 | 59 |
| Attend Meetings | 97 | 38 | 73 |
| Chair meetings | 97 | 30 | 63 |
| Business related contacts | 91 | 21 | 59 |
| With customers, marketing or sales | 74 | 53 | 51 |
| Bargaining or persuading | 49 | 32 | 68 |
| With laborers and operating employees | 46 | 40 | 40 |

## Table 3-1
### Top Logistics Managers Job Family
### Domain and Dimension Scores

| Dimension Description | Percentage | Scope | Rarity |
|---|---|---|---|
| **DECISION-MAKING DOMAIN** | | | |
| *Production, Human Resources, Financial and Strategic Decisions* | | | |
| Human resources management | 97 | 52 | 96 |
| Financial-purchasing and budgeting | 94 | 54 | 90 |
| Production/operations management | 91 | 51 | 90 |
| Strategic planning-products and services | 89 | 37 | 83 |
| Strategic planning-entire businesses | 37 | 54 | 84 |
| Financial-investment, cash | 34 | 68 | 89 |
| *Frequency Ratings for Decisions* | | | |
| Operations and human resources | 94 | 40 | 78 |
| Human resources– authority and benefits | 94 | 36 | 81 |
| Finance–purchasing and budgeting | 94 | 31 | 77 |
| Planning products and services | 89 | 21 | 72 |
| Planning for whole organization | 37 | 24 | 59 |
| **MECHANICAL/PHYSICAL DOMAIN** | | | |
| Office machines | 97 | 24 | 44 |
| *Frequency Rating for Mechanical and Physical Dimensions* | | | |
| Office machines | 97 | 78 | 55 |
| **WORK CONTEXT DOMAIN** | | | |
| Using numerical or verbal information | 97 | 33 | 39 |
| Demanding personal situations | 91 | 27 | 46 |
| Sensory input from work environment | 89 | 29 | 3 |

| Table 3-1<br>Top Logistics Managers Job Family<br>Domain and Dimension Scores | | | |
|---|---|---|---|
| Dimension Description | Percentage | Scope | Rarity |
| **OVERALL RATINGS** | | | |
| Clerical/office activities/information exchange | 100 | 46 | 73 |
| Meetings and contacts | 100 | 27 | 82 |
| Physical activity/work environment | 100 | 17 | 23 |
| Public, stressful situations | 100 | 11 | 59 |
| Production/operations/HR decision making | 97 | 44 | 71 |
| Managerial decisions: finance/purchasing/budgeting | 94 | 37 | 56 |
| Bargain/persuade/negotiate | 94 | 18 | 23 |
| Supervision, conflict resolution, training | 91 | 30 | 53 |
| Contacts: customers, sales and marketing related | 91 | 28 | 42 |
| Product/customer decision/planning | 89 | 29 | 43 |
| Meeting with public/customers | 49 | 19 | 26 |
| Blue collar/operative/service contact/supervisors | 46 | 23 | 30 |
| Strategic planning | 37 | 39 | 63 |

**Table 3-2**
**Top Logistics Managers Job Family**
**Knowledge Used**

| Knowledge Category | Used | By |
|---|---|---|
| *Finance and Accounting* | | |
| Budgeting | Weekly | 89% |
| Purchasing | Weekly | 63% |
| Accounting | Weekly | 49% |
| Commerce | Weekly | 29% |
| *Human Resources* | | |
| Supervision and development | Constantly | 86% |
| Selection and recruitment | Weekly | 71% |
| Job analysis | Monthly | 54% |
| Benefits and worker's comp | Monthly | 37% |
| *Management and Production* | | |
| Inventory control and warehousing | Daily | 74% |
| Project Management | Daily | 37% |
| Operations research | Daily | 34% |
| Manufacturing Management | Daily | 31% |
| Strategic planning | Weekly | 80% |
| *Sales and Marketing* | | |
| Retailing, wholesaling | Daily | 31% |
| Sales | Daily | 29% |
| Marketing research and pricing | Weekly | 26% |

## Table 3-2
### Top Logistics Managers Job Family
### Knowledge Used

| Knowledge Category | Used | By |
|---|---|---|
| *Geography* | | |
| Local and regional | Daily | 40% |
| World | Weekly | 23% |
| *Mathematics* | | |
| Basic | Daily | 63% |
| Algebra/statistics | Daily | 26% |
| *Communications* | | |
| Writing and editing–business text | Constantly | 71% |
| Word processing | Constantly | 49% |
| Public speaking | Weekly | 40% |
| Writing and editing–financial | Weekly | 34% |
| *Transportation* | | |
| Trucking | Daily | 57% |
| Air/water | Weekly | 43% |
| Rail | Weekly | 37% |

| Table 3-3 Top Logistics Managers Job Family Demographics | | | |
|---|---|---|---|
| **Age** | Average: 47 | | Age Range: 28-65 |
| **Education** | Some College: 17% | Bachelors Degree: 52% | Masters Degree: 27% |
| **Gender** | Male: 84% | | Female: 16% |
| **Years in Position** | 0-3 yrs: 63% | 3-5 yrs: 13% | >5 yrs: 24% |
| **Years with Firm** | 0-3 yrs: 20% | 3-5 yrs: 13% | >5 yrs: 67% |

| Table 3-4 |
|---|

**Table 3-4**
**Top Logistics Managers Job Family**
**Personality, Need for Cognition, Customer Orientation, and Market Orientation**

| Dimension | Top Managers | | Sample Means | | Normative Score | |
|---|---|---|---|---|---|---|
| Neuroticism | 2 | 10.5 | 0 | 14.5 | 4 | 19.07 |
| | 25 | | 40 | | 38 | |
| Extraversion | 22 | 33 | 11 | 31.9 | 14 | 27.69 |
| | 47 | | 47 | | 40 | |
| Openness | 18 | 26.5 | 11 | 25.9 | 14 | 27.03 |
| | 34 | | 43 | | 40 | |
| Agreeableness | 19 | 32.3 | 13 | 32.4 | 21 | 32.84 |
| | 43 | | 43 | | 45 | |
| Conscientiousness | 29 | 38.7 | 18 | 36.8 | 18 | 34.57 |
| | 47 | | 48 | | 47 | |
| Need for Cognition | -1 | 28.8 | -58 | 24.7 | -- | NA |
| | 57 | | 70 | | -- | |
| Customer Orientation[2] | 164 | 193.1 | 109 | 189.6 | 159 | 187 |
| | 216 | | 216 | | 187 | |
| Marketing Orientation[3] | 70 | 109.7 | 41 | 99.5 | -- | 97.2 |
| | 129 | | 138 | | -- | |

[1] Costa, P. T., and McCrae, R. R. (1995). NEO-PI Professional Manual. Odessa, FL: Psychological Assessment Resources, Inc.
[2] Siguaw, J. A., Brown, G., & Widing, R. E. (1994). The Influence of the Market Orientation of the Firm on Sales Force Behavior and Attitudes. Journal of Marketing Research, 31, 106-116.
[3] Siguaw, J. A., Simpson, P. M., & Baker T.L. (1998). Effects of Supplier Market Orientation on Distributor Market Orientation and the Channel Relationship: The Distributor Perspective. Journal of Marketing, 62, 99-111.

# APPENDIX 4

# LOGISTICS INFORMATION SYSTEMS

| Table 4-1 Logistics Information Systems Managers Job Family Domain and Dimension Scores | | | |
|---|---|---|---|
| Dimension Description | Percentage | Scope | Rarity |
| **INTERPERSONAL DOMAIN** | | | |
| *Internal Contacts* | | | |
| Exchanging information/consulting | 100 | 45 | 65 |
| Supervising professional technical employees | 90 | 56 | 77 |
| Training | 90 | 54 | 63 |
| Marketing/sales employees | 80 | 28 | 60 |
| Supervising mid-level employees | 80 | 26 | 66 |
| Bargaining or negotiating | 80 | 24 | 48 |
| Supervising upper-level employees | 70 | 22 | 53 |
| Resolving conflicts | 60 | 37 | 73 |
| *External Contacts* | | | |
| Exchanging business related information | 100 | 20 | 48 |
| Customers–sales related | 90 | 32 | 71 |
| Supervising suppliers or contractors | 90 | 27 | 62 |
| Bargaining and negotiating | 70 | 19 | 57 |
| Resolving conflicts | 70 | 18 | 54 |
| Training | 60 | 20 | 54 |

| Table 4-1 Logistics Information Systems Managers Job Family Domain and Dimension Scores | | | |
|---|---|---|---|
| Dimension Description | Percentage | Scope | Rarity |
| *Meetings* | | | |
| Attend meetings with non-executives | 100 | 59 | 74 |
| Attend meetings with executives | 100 | 32 | 58 |
| Chair meetings with non-executives | 90 | 56 | 75 |
| Attend meetings to bargain or persuade | 90 | 19 | 54 |
| Attend meetings with non-supervisory employees | 70 | 26 | 51 |
| Chair meetings with executives | 60 | 46 | 66 |
| Attend meetings with outside supervisors, technicians | 60 | 31 | 71 |
| Chair meetings with outside supervisors, technicians | 50 | 35 | 73 |
| Chair meetings to bargain or persuade | 50 | 27 | 57 |
| Attend meetings with customers | 50 | 19 | 55 |
| *Frequency Ratings for Internal and External Contacts* | | | |
| With supervisors, managers, and executives | 100 | 60 | 72 |
| With customers, marketing or sales | 100 | 57 | 59 |
| Attend Meetings | 100 | 45 | 81 |
| Chair meetings | 100 | 37 | 74 |
| Bargaining or persuading | 70 | 34 | 70 |

| Table 4-1 Logistics Information Systems Managers Job Family Domain and Dimension Scores | | | |
|---|---|---|---|
| Dimension Description | Percentage | Scope | Rarity |
| **DECISION-MAKING DOMAIN** | | | |
| *Production, Human Resources, Financial and Strategic Decisions* | | | |
| Human resources management | 100 | 44 | 96 |
| Financial-purchasing and budgeting | 90 | 53 | 95 |
| Strategic planning-products and services | 80 | 33 | 74 |
| Production/operations management | 70 | 55 | 90 |
| *Frequency Ratings for Decisions* | | | |
| Human resources– authority and benefits | 100 | 37 | 86 |
| Operations and human resources | 100 | 35 | 72 |
| Finance–purchasing and budgeting | 100 | 27 | 72 |
| **MECHANICAL/PHYSICAL DOMAIN** | | | |
| Office machines | 90 | 29 | 61 |
| Technical or scientific equipment | 90 | 19 | 30 |
| Precise physical activity | 60 | 36 | 37 |
| *Frequency Rating for Mechanical and Physical Dimensions* | | | |
| Office machines | 90 | 66 | 26 |
| **WORK CONTEXT DOMAIN** | | | |
| Using numerical or verbal information | 100 | 31 | 31 |
| Demanding personal situations | 100 | 20 | 38 |

| Table 4-1 Logistics Information Systems Managers Job Family Domain and Dimension Scores | | | |
|---|---|---|---|
| Dimension Description | Percentage | Scope | Rarity |
| **OVERALL RATINGS** | | | |
| Clerical/office activities/information exchange | 100 | 48 | 76 |
| Production/operations/HR decision making | 100 | 39 | 62 |
| Supervision, conflict resolution, training | 100 | 34 | 51 |
| Contacts: customers, sales and marketing related | 100 | 33 | 52 |
| Meetings and contacts | 100 | 32 | 89 |
| Managerial decisions: finance/purchasing/budgeting | 100 | 28 | 40 |
| Technical/scientific machines | 90 | 29 | 44 |
| Product/customer decision/planning | 80 | 25 | 33 |

**Table 4-2**
**Logistics Information Systems Managers Job Family**
**Knowledge Used**

| Knowledge Category | Used | By |
|---|---|---|
| *Finance and Accounting* | | |
| Accounting | Weekly | 30% |
| Budgeting | Monthly | 60% |
| Purchasing | Monthly | 60% |
| Commerce | Monthly | 20% |
| *Human Resources* | | |
| Supervision and development | Daily | 70% |
| Selection and recruitment | Monthly | 60% |
| Benefits and worker's comp | Yearly | 30% |
| *Management and Production* | | |
| Inventory control and warehousing | Daily | 40% |
| Operations research | Weekly | 70% |
| Strategic planning | Weekly | 60% |
| Project management | Weekly | 40% |
| *Sales and Marketing* | | |
| Sales | Monthly | 30% |
| Marketing research and pricing | Yearly | 40% |

**Table 4-2**
**Logistics Information Systems Managers Job Family**
**Knowledge Used**

| Knowledge Category | Used | By |
|---|---|---|
| *Computer Science* | | |
| Computer operations | Daily | 100% |
| Software engineering | Daily | 70% |
| Information/technology management | Weekly | 80% |
| Programming | Weekly | 70% |
| Database administration | Monthly | 60% |
| Network management | Monthly | 60% |
| Internet/web design | Monthly | 60% |
| Computer based training | Monthly | 40% |
| *Mathematics* | | |
| Basic | Daily | 50% |
| Algebra/statistics | Weekly | 40% |
| *Communications* | | |
| Word processing | Constantly | 60% |
| Writing and editing–business text | Daily | 90% |
| Writing and editing–financial | Weekly | 50% |
| *Transportation* | | |
| Trucking | Daily | 40% |
| Air/water | Monthly | 40% |

| Table 4-3<br>Logistics Information Systems Technicians Job Family<br>Domain and Dimension Scores | | | |
|---|---|---|---|
| Dimension Description | Percentage | Scope | Rarity |
| **INTERPERSONAL DOMAIN** | | | |
| *Internal Contacts* | | | |
| Exchanging information/consulting | 93 | 36 | 56 |
| Training | 50 | 28 | 43 |
| Marketing/sales employees | 50 | 25 | 53 |
| Supervising professional technical employees | 50 | 24 | 56 |
| *External Contacts* | | | |
| Supervising suppliers or contractors | 64 | 17 | 48 |
| *Meetings* | | | |
| Attend meetings with non-executives | 100 | 38 | 63 |
| Attend meetings with executives | 79 | 27 | 57 |
| Attend meetings with non-supervisory employees | 57 | 35 | 74 |
| Chair meetings with non-executives | 57 | 33 | 57 |
| *Frequency Ratings for Internal and External Contacts* | | | |
| Attend Meetings | 100 | 29 | 63 |
| With supervisors, managers, and executives | 93 | 50 | 59 |
| With customers, marketing or sales | 71 | 36 | 32 |
| Chair meetings | 57 | 21 | 51 |
| With laborers and operating employees | 43 | 43 | 43 |
| **DECISION-MAKING DOMAIN** | | | |
| *Production, Human Resources, Financial and Strategic Decisions* | | | |
| Production/operations management | 64 | 29 | 59 |
| Human resources management | 64 | 21 | 69 |

| Table 4-3<br>Logistics Information Systems Technicians Job Family<br>Domain and Dimension Scores | | | |
|---|---|---|---|
| Dimension Description | Percentage | Scope | Rarity |
| *Frequency Ratings for Decisions* | | | |
| Operations and human resources | 86 | 20 | 46 |
| MECHANICAL/PHYSICAL<br>DOMAIN | | | |
| Office machines | 100 | 28 | 55 |
| Technical or scientific equipment | 50 | 23 | 32 |
| *Frequency Rating for Mechanical and*<br>*Physical Dimensions* | | | |
| Office machines | 100 | 79 | 49 |
| WORK CONTEXT DOMAIN | | | |
| Using numerical or verbal<br>information | 100 | 35 | 45 |
| Demanding personal situations | 93 | 18 | 32 |
| OVERALL RATINGS | | | |
| Clerical/office activities/information<br>exchange | 100 | 47 | 77 |
| Technical/scientific machines | 50 | 35 | 57 |
| Meetings and contacts | 100 | 17 | 77 |

**Table 4-4**
**Logistics Information Systems Technicians Job Family**
**Knowledge Used**

| Knowledge Category | Used | By |
|---|---|---|
| *Human Resources* | | |
| Selection and recruitment | Yearly | 36% |
| *Management and Production* | | |
| Inventory control and warehousing | Daily | 36% |
| *Computer Science* | | |
| Programming | Constantly | 43% |
| Computer operations | Constantly | 36% |
| Information/technology management | Constantly | 29% |
| Software engineering | Daily | 43% |
| Database administration | Daily | 29% |
| *Mathematics* | | |
| Algebra/statistics | Constantly | 64% |
| Basic | Constantly | 36% |
| *Communications* | | |
| Word processing | Constantly | 60% |
| Writing and editing–business text | Weekly | 57% |
| *Transportation* | | |
| Trucking | Constantly | 50% |
| Air/water | Constantly | 29% |

| Table 4-5 | | |
|---|---|---|
| **Logistic Information Systems Job Domain** | | |
| **Demographics** | | |
| Age | Average: 42 | Age Range: 36-50 |
| Education | High School: 9%    College: 55% | Advanced Degree: 14% |
| Gender | Male: 82% | Female: 18% |
| Years with Organization | < 1 year: 23%    < 3 years: 64% | < 5 years: 73% |
| Years in Position | < 1 year: 55%    < 3 years: 91% | |

### Table 4-6
### Logistics Information Systems Job Domain
### Personality, Need for Cognition, Customer Orientation, and Market Orientation

| Dimension | IS Techs | | IS Mngrs | | Sample Means | | Norm Score | |
|---|---|---|---|---|---|---|---|---|
| Neuroticism | 9 | | 12 | | 0 | | 4 | |
| | | 19.2 | | 17.1 | | 14.5 | | 19.1 |
| | 36 | | 27 | | 40 | | 38 | |
| Extraversion | 11 | | 22 | | 11 | | 14 | |
| | | 25.7 | | 33.2 | | 31.9 | | 27.7 |
| | 35 | | 40 | | 47 | | 40 | |
| Openness | 15 | | 20 | | 11 | | 14 | |
| | | 26.8 | | 29.2 | | 25.9 | | 27 |
| | 35 | | 36 | | 43 | | 40 | |
| Agreeableness | 22 | | 24 | | 13 | | 21 | |
| | | 31.6 | | 31.9 | | 32.4 | | 32.8 |
| | 41 | | 41 | | 43 | | 45 | |
| Conscientiousness | 29 | | 30 | | 18 | | 18 | |
| | | 36.1 | | 36.1 | | 36.8 | | 34.6 |
| | 47 | | 41 | | 48 | | 47 | |
| Need for Cognition | -12 | | 18 | | -58 | | -- | |
| | | 17.7 | | 32.4 | | 24.7 | | NA |
| | 50 | | 46 | | 70 | | -- | |
| Customer Orientation | 185 | | 163 | | 109 | | 159 | |
| | | 197.2 | | 185.8 | | 189.6 | | 187 |
| | 214 | | 208 | | 216 | | 187 | |
| Marketing Orientation | 41 | | 65 | | 41 | | -- | |
| | | 91.4 | | 101.9 | | 99.5 | | 97.2 |
| | 120 | | 134 | | 138 | | -- | |

# APPENDIX 5

# WAREHOUSE

| Table 5-1<br>Warehouse Managers Job Family<br>Domain and Dimension Scores | | | |
|---|---|---|---|
| Dimension Description | Percentage | Scope | Rarity |
| **INTERPERSONAL DOMAIN** | | | |
| *Internal Contacts* | | | |
| Exchanging information/consulting | 100 | 49 | 67 |
| Supervising mid-level managers | 88 | 47 | 83 |
| Resolving conflicts | 88 | 46 | 78 |
| Supervising laborers | 81 | 34 | 59 |
| Supervising upper-level executives | 81 | 27 | 63 |
| Supervising operative employees | 75 | 56 | 81 |
| Training | 75 | 50 | 64 |
| Supervising professional/technical employees | 56 | 42 | 73 |
| Selling or persuading | 50 | 42 | 74 |
| *External Contacts* | | | |
| Exchanging business related information | 88 | 29 | 59 |
| Customers–sales related | 81 | 25 | 58 |
| Supervising suppliers or contractors | 75 | 31 | 63 |
| Resolving conflicts | 75 | 23 | 52 |
| Training | 56 | 15 | 46 |
| Bargaining and negotiating | 44 | 19 | 54 |

| Table 5-1<br>Warehouse Managers Job Family<br>Domain and Dimension Scores | | | |
|---|---|---|---|
| Dimension Description | Percentage | Scope | Rarity |
| *Meetings* | | | |
| Attend meetings with non-executives | 100 | 43 | 65 |
| Chair meetings with non-executives | 94 | 37 | 60 |
| Attend meetings with executives | 88 | 34 | 65 |
| Attend meetings with non-supervisory employees | 75 | 40 | 67 |
| Chair meetings with non-supervisory employees | 75 | 32 | 70 |
| Attend meetings to bargain or persuade | 69 | 18 | 48 |
| Attend meetings with outside supervisors, technicians | 50 | 41 | 79 |
| Chair meetings to bargain or persuade | 38 | 24 | 45 |
| Chair meetings with executives | 25 | 42 | 56 |

| Table 5-1 Warehouse Managers Job Family Domain and Dimension Scores | | | |
|---|---|---|---|
| **Dimension Description** | **Percentage** | **Scope** | **Rarity** |
| *Frequency Ratings for Internal and External Contacts* | | | |
| Attend Meetings | 100 | 56 | 88 |
| With supervisors, managers, and executives | 94 | 68 | 79 |
| Chair meetings | 94 | 53 | 87 |
| Business related contacts | 94 | 21 | 57 |
| With laborers and operating employees | 88 | 66 | 69 |
| With customers, marketing or sales | 56 | 52 | 52 |
| Bargaining or persuading | 50 | 34 | 68 |
| **DECISION-MAKING DOMAIN** | | | |
| *Production, Human Resources, Financial and Strategic Decisions* | | | |
| Production/operations management | 100 | 47 | 90 |
| Human resources management | 100 | 43 | 94 |
| Financial-purchasing and budgeting | 94 | 46 | 87 |
| Strategic planning-products and services | 81 | 24 | 62 |

| Table 5-1 Warehouse Managers Job Family Domain and Dimension Scores | | | |
|---|---|---|---|
| Dimension Description | Percentage | Scope | Rarity |
| *Frequency Ratings for Decisions* | | | |
| Operations and human resources | 100 | 60 | 92 |
| Human resources– authority and benefits | 100 | 47 | 88 |
| Finance–purchasing and budgeting | 94 | 33 | 82 |
| Planning products and services | 81 | 14 | 54 |
| MECHANICAL/PHYSICAL DOMAIN | | | |
| Office machines | 100 | 36 | 65 |
| Gross physical activities | 81 | 28 | 52 |
| Precise physical activity | 69 | 51 | 53 |
| Supervise machine operators | 69 | 23 | 60 |
| Technical or scientific equipment | 56 | 19 | 25 |
| Off-road/utility vehicles | 38 | 33 | 79 |
| Mobile tools/equipment | 31 | 20 | 55 |
| *Frequency Rating for Mechanical and Physical Dimensions* | | | |
| Office machines | 100 | 89 | 63 |
| Tool/manufacturing/vehicle operation | 75 | 20 | 64 |
| Technical/scientific machines | 56 | 47 | 5 |

| Table 5-1 Warehouse Managers Job Family Domain and Dimension Scores | | | |
|---|---|---|---|
| Dimension Description | Percentage | Scope | Rarity |
| **WORK CONTEXT DOMAIN** | | | |
| Using numerical or verbal information | 100 | 32 | 44 |
| Demanding personal situations | 94 | 40 | 65 |
| Sensory input from work environment | 94 | 40 | 54 |
| **OVERALL RATINGS** | | | |
| Clerical/office activities/information exchange | 100 | 60 | 91 |
| Production/operations/HR decision making | 100 | 50 | 81 |
| Supervision, conflict resolution, training | 100 | 37 | 57 |
| Meetings and contacts | 100 | 33 | 93 |
| Physical activity/work environment | 100 | 32 | 49 |
| Public, stressful situations | 100 | 14 | 67 |
| Blue collar/operative/service contact/supervisors | 94 | 40 | 59 |
| Managerial decisions: finance/purchasing/budgeting | 94 | 26 | 39 |
| Contacts: customers, sales and marketing related | 94 | 22 | 32 |
| Product/customer decision/planning | 81 | 19 | 26 |
| Technical/scientific machines | 56 | 33 | 54 |

**Table 5-2**
**Warehouse Managers Job Family**
**Knowledge Used**

| Knowledge Category | Used | By |
|---|---|---|
| *Finance and Accounting* | | |
| Budgeting | Weekly | 69% |
| Purchasing | Weekly | 50% |
| Accounting | Weekly | 44% |
| *Human Resources* | | |
| Supervision and development | Constantly | 100% |
| Occupational safety and health | Daily | 63% |
| Benefits and worker's comp | Weekly | 31% |
| Selection and recruitment | Monthly | 75% |
| Job analysis | Monthly | 50% |
| *Management and Production* | | |
| Inventory control and warehousing | Constantly | 94% |
| Manufacturing Management | Constantly | 31% |
| Operations research | Daily | 56% |
| Strategic planning | Weekly | 63% |
| Records control | Weekly | 44% |
| Project Management | Monthly | 31% |
| *Sales and Marketing* | | |
| Retailing, wholesaling | Constantly | 25% |

**Table 5-2**
**Warehouse Managers Job Family**
**Knowledge Used**

| Knowledge Category | Used | By |
|---|---|---|
| *Geography* | | |
| Local and regional | Daily | 50% |
| *Mathematics* | | |
| Algebra/statistics | Constantly | 75% |
| Basic | Constantly | 44% |
| *Communications* | | |
| Word processing | Constantly | 75% |
| Writing and editing–business text | Constantly | 69% |
| Telecommunications systems | Daily | 31% |
| Public speaking | Weekly | 44% |
| *Transportation* | | |
| Trucking | Daily | 69% |

**Table 5-3**
**Warehouse Planning Support Job Family**
**Domain and Dimension Scores**

| Dimension Description | Percentage | Scope | Rarity |
|---|---|---|---|
| **INTERPERSONAL DOMAIN** | | | |
| *Internal Contacts* | | | |
| Exchanging information/consulting | 100 | 33 | 52 |
| Supervising mid-level managers | 83 | 33 | 63 |
| Training | 75 | 38 | 52 |
| Resolving conflicts | 75 | 29 | 53 |
| *External Contacts* | | | |
| Supervising suppliers or contractors | 75 | 23 | 55 |
| Bargaining and negotiating | 58 | 24 | 71 |
| Customers–sales related | 50 | 25 | 54 |

| Table 5-3<br>Warehouse Planning Support Job Family<br>Domain and Dimension Scores | | | |
|---|---|---|---|
| Dimension Description | Percentage | Scope | Rarity |
| *Meetings* | | | |
| Attend meetings with non-executives | 100 | 55 | 75 |
| Chair meetings with non-executives | 92 | 46 | 71 |
| Attend meetings with outside supervisors, technicians | 92 | 41 | 79 |
| Attend meetings with executives | 92 | 39 | 70 |
| Chair meetings with outside supervisors, technicians | 83 | 29 | 58 |
| Attend meetings with non-supervisory employees | 75 | 36 | 63 |
| Chair meetings with non-supervisory employees | 75 | 32 | 67 |
| Attend meetings to bargain or persuade | 67 | 23 | 54 |
| Chair meetings with executives | 50 | 35 | 64 |

| Table 5-3 Warehouse Planning Support Job Family Domain and Dimension Scores | | | |
|---|---|---|---|
| Dimension Description | Percentage | Scope | Rarity |
| *Frequency Ratings for Internal and External Contacts* | | | |
| With supervisors, managers, and executives | 100 | 51 | 61 |
| Attend Meetings | 100 | 49 | 82 |
| Chair meetings | 92 | 34 | 70 |
| Business related contacts | 92 | 17 | 50 |
| Bargaining or persuading | 58 | 24 | 50 |
| With customers, marketing or sales | 33 | 38 | 34 |
| With laborers and operating employees | 33 | 33 | 28 |
| **DECISION-MAKING DOMAIN** | | | |
| *Production, Human Resources, Financial and Strategic Decisions* | | | |
| Human resources management | 92 | 28 | 81 |
| Financial-purchasing and budgeting | 75 | 44 | 80 |
| Strategic planning-products and services | 75 | 19 | 61 |
| Production/operations management | 67 | 40 | 80 |
| *Frequency Ratings for Decisions* | | | |
| Operations and human resources | 100 | 24 | 52 |
| Finance–purchasing and budgeting | 92 | 20 | 53 |
| Human resources– authority and benefits | 75 | 24 | 62 |

| Table 5-3 Warehouse Planning Support Job Family Domain and Dimension Scores | | | |
|---|---|---|---|
| Dimension Description | Percentage | Scope | Rarity |
| **MECHANICAL/PHYSICAL DOMAIN** | | | |
| Office machines | 100 | 20 | 45 |
| Precise physical activity | 50 | 46 | 48 |
| *Frequency Rating for Mechanical and Physical Dimensions* | | | |
| Office machines | 100 | 85 | 57 |
| **WORK CONTEXT DOMAIN** | | | |
| Using numerical or verbal information | 100 | 34 | 35 |
| Sensory input from work environment | 92 | 28 | 38 |
| Demanding personal situations | 92 | 21 | 38 |
| **OVERALL RATINGS** | | | |
| Clerical/office activities/information exchange | 100 | 48 | 80 |
| Meetings and contacts | 100 | 36 | 95 |
| Production/operations/HR decision making | 100 | 24 | 33 |
| Supervision, conflict resolution, training | 100 | 21 | 29 |
| Physical activity/work environment | 100 | 21 | 27 |
| Managerial decisions: finance/purchasing/budgeting | 92 | 19 | 26 |
| Technical/scientific machines | 42 | 25 | 35 |

**Table 5-4**
**Warehouse Planning Support Job Family**
**Knowledge Used**

| Knowledge Category | Used | By |
|---|---|---|
| *Finance and Accounting* | | |
| Accounting | Daily | 58% |
| Purchasing | Weekly | 50% |
| Budgeting | Monthly | 50% |
| *Human Resources* | | |
| Supervision and development | Weekly | 33% |
| Selection and recruitment | Yearly | 33% |
| *Management and Production* | | |
| Operations research | Daily | 67% |
| Inventory control and warehousing | Daily | 58% |
| Project Management | Weekly | 58% |
| Records control | Weekly | 33% |
| Strategic planning | Monthly | 75% |
| *Mathematics* | | |
| Algebra/statistics | Daily | 33% |
| Basic | Weekly | 33% |

**Table 5-4**
**Warehouse Planning Support Job Family**
**Knowledge Used**

| Knowledge Category | Used | By |
|---|---|---|
| *Communications* | | |
| Word processing | Constantly | 75% |
| Writing and editing–financial | Constantly | 67% |
| Writing and editing–business text | Constantly | 67% |
| Public speaking | Yearly | 42% |
| *Transportation* | | |
| Trucking | Constantly | 33% |

| Table 5-5<br>Warehouse Supervisors Job Family<br>Domain and Dimension Scores | | | |
|---|---|---|---|
| **Dimension Description** | **Percentage** | **Scope** | **Rarity** |
| **INTERPERSONAL DOMAIN** | | | |
| *Internal Contacts* | | | |
| Supervising operative employees | 57 | 51 | 80 |
| Supervising mid-level managers | 50 | 26 | 61 |
| Resolving conflicts | 50 | 22 | 48 |
| Training | 36 | 20 | 28 |
| Marketing/sales employees | 29 | 26 | 28 |
| *Meetings* | | | |
| Attend meetings with non-executives | 79 | 20 | 40 |
| Attend meetings with non-supervisory employees | 61 | 27 | 53 |
| Chair meetings with non-executives | 57 | 19 | 34 |
| Attend meetings with executives | 54 | 26 | 58 |
| Chair meetings with non-supervisory employees | 46 | 24 | 58 |
| *Frequency Ratings for Internal and External Contacts* | | | |
| Attend Meetings | 89 | 33 | 89 |
| With laborers and operating employees | 71 | 45 | 53 |
| Chair meetings | 68 | 24 | 53 |
| With supervisors, managers, and executives | 57 | 27 | 31 |

| Table 5-5<br>Warehouse Supervisors Job Family<br>Domain and Dimension Scores | | | |
|---|---|---|---|
| Dimension Description | Percentage | Scope | Rarity |
| **DECISION-MAKING DOMAIN** | | | |
| *Production, Human Resources,*<br>*Financial and Strategic Decisions* | | | |
| **Production/operations management** | 89 | 35 | 76 |
| **Human resources management** | 86 | 27 | 80 |
| **Financial-purchasing and budgeting** | 57 | 31 | 65 |
| **Strategic planning-products and services** | 50 | 18 | 60 |
| *Frequency Ratings for Decisions* | | | |
| **Operations and human resources** | 89 | 41 | 81 |
| **Human resources– authority and benefits** | 75 | 31 | 77 |
| **Planning products and services** | 50 | 13 | 55 |
| **MECHANICAL/PHYSICAL DOMAIN** | | | |
| **Office machines** | 86 | 17 | 37 |
| **Gross physical activities** | 64 | 16 | 38 |
| **Precise physical activity** | 50 | 24 | 23 |
| *Frequency Rating for Mechanical and*<br>*Physical Dimensions* | | | |
| **Office machines** | 86 | 67 | 33 |
| **Tool/manufacturing/vehicle operation** | 50 | 10 | 43 |

| Table 5-5 Warehouse Supervisors Job Family Domain and Dimension Scores | | | |
|---|---|---|---|
| Dimension Description | Percentage | Scope | Rarity |
| **WORK CONTEXT DOMAIN** | | | |
| Using numerical or verbal information | 100 | 29 | 29 |
| Sensory input from work environment | 93 | 28 | 38 |
| Demanding personal situations | 93 | 23 | 40 |
| **OVERALL RATINGS** | | | |
| Physical activity/work environment | 100 | 19 | 23 |
| Clerical/office activities/information exchange | 93 | 27 | 40 |
| Production/operations/HR decision making | 89 | 32 | 52 |
| Meetings and contacts | 89 | 15 | 69 |
| Blue collar/operative/service contact/supervisors | 75 | 26 | 39 |

**Table 5-6**
**Warehouse Supervisors Job Family**
**Knowledge Used**

| Knowledge Category | Used | By |
|---|---|---|
| *Human Resources* | | |
| Supervision and development | Constantly | 64% |
| Selection and recruitment | Yearly | 36% |
| *Management and Production* | | |
| Inventory control and warehousing | Constantly | 46% |
| Strategic planning | Daily | 36% |
| Operations research | Weekly | 29% |
| *Mathematics* | | |
| Algebra/statistics | Constantly | 57% |
| Basic | Constantly | 25% |
| *Communications* | | |
| Writing and editing–business text | Daily | 36% |
| Word processing | Daily | 36% |

**Table 5-7**
**Warehouse Administrative Support Job Family**
**Domain and Dimension Scores**

| Dimension Description | Percentage | Scope | Rarity |
|---|---|---|---|
| **INTERPERSONAL DOMAIN** | | | |
| *Internal Contacts* | | | |
| Exchanging information/consulting | 100 | 39 | 57 |
| Training | 92 | 36 | 49 |
| Supervising mid-level managers | 75 | 33 | 74 |
| Supervising operative employees | 50 | 16 | 53 |
| Marketing/sales employees | 42 | 36 | 71 |
| *External Contacts* | | | |
| Exchanging business related information | 92 | 21 | 57 |
| Supervising suppliers or contractors | 83 | 26 | 62 |
| Customers–sales related | 83 | 24 | 69 |
| Bargaining and negotiating | 67 | 16 | 53 |
| Resolving conflicts | 42 | 23 | 63 |
| *Meetings* | | | |
| Attend meetings with non-executives | 100 | 36 | 60 |
| Attend meetings with executives | 83 | 34 | 68 |
| Chair meetings with non-executives | 83 | 32 | 57 |
| Attend meetings with non-supervisory employees | 75 | 29 | 64 |
| Chair meetings with non-supervisory employees | 75 | 20 | 51 |
| Chair meetings with executives | 67 | 28 | 52 |

| Table 5-7 Warehouse Administrative Support Job Family Domain and Dimension Scores | | | |
|---|---|---|---|
| **Dimension Description** | **Percentage** | **Scope** | **Rarity** |
| *Frequency Ratings for Internal and External Contacts* | | | |
| With supervisors, managers, and executives | 100 | 57 | 68 |
| Attend Meetings | 100 | 34 | 67 |
| Business related contacts | 100 | 17 | 52 |
| Chair meetings | 83 | 29 | 66 |
| With customers, marketing or sales | 67 | 59 | 59 |
| With laborers and operating employees | 58 | 44 | 43 |
| **DECISION-MAKING DOMAIN** | | | |
| *Production, Human Resources, Financial and Strategic Decisions* | | | |
| Financial-purchasing and budgeting | 92 | 52 | 86 |
| Human resources management | 83 | 48 | 89 |
| Strategic planning-products and services | 83 | 27 | 69 |
| Production/operations management | 67 | 50 | 89 |
| Strategic planning-entire businesses | 33 | 36 | 74 |
| *Frequency Ratings for Decisions* | | | |
| Finance–purchasing and budgeting | 92 | 32 | 80 |
| Operations and human resources | 83 | 27 | 62 |
| Human resources– authority and benefits | 75 | 28 | 73 |

| Table 5-7<br>Warehouse Administrative Support Job Family<br>Domain and Dimension Scores | | | |
|---|---|---|---|
| Dimension Description | Percentage | Scope | Rarity |
| MECHANICAL/PHYSICAL DOMAIN | | | |
| Office machines | 100 | 36 | 70 |
| Precise physical activity | 75 | 29 | 28 |
| Technical or scientific equipment | 42 | 18 | 42 |
| *Frequency Rating for Mechanical and Physical Dimensions* | | | |
| Office machines | 100 | 88 | 56 |
| WORK CONTEXT DOMAIN | | | |
| Using numerical or verbal information | 100 | 32 | 40 |
| Demanding personal situations | 92 | 26 | 47 |
| Sensory input from work environment | 83 | 36 | 49 |

| Table 5-7 Warehouse Administrative Support Job Family Domain and Dimension Scores |  |  |  |
|---|---|---|---|
| Dimension Description | Percentage | Scope | Rarity |
| OVERALL RATINGS |  |  |  |
| Clerical/office activities/information exchange | 100 | 55 | 55 |
| Physical activity/work environment | 100 | 22 | 30 |
| Meetings and contacts | 100 | 22 | 83 |
| Managerial decisions: finance/purchasing/budgeting | 92 | 32 | 48 |
| Production/operations/HR decision making | 92 | 32 | 51 |
| Contacts: customers, sales and marketing related | 92 | 27 | 41 |
| Supervision, conflict resolution, training | 92 | 20 | 25 |
| Product/customer decision/planning | 83 | 20 | 26 |
| Blue collar/operative/service contact/supervisors | 58 | 23 | 31 |
| Technical/scientific machines | 42 | 30 | 47 |

**Table 5-8**
**Warehouse Administrative Support Job Family**
**Knowledge Used**

| Knowledge Category | Used | By |
|---|---|---|
| *Finance and Accounting* | | |
| Accounting | Weekly | 58% |
| Purchasing | Monthly | 58% |
| Budgeting | Yearly | 67% |
| *Human Resources* | | |
| Supervision and development | Constantly | 67% |
| Benefits and worker's comp | Weekly | 42% |
| Occupational safety and health | Monthly | 33% |
| Selection and recruitment | Yearly | 67% |
| Job analysis | Yearly | 50% |
| *Management and Production* | | |
| Records control | Weekly | 42% |
| Project Management | Weekly | 33% |
| Operations research | Weekly | 33% |
| Strategic planning | Monthly | 58% |
| Inventory control and warehousing | Monthly | 50% |
| Manufacturing Management | Monthly | 42% |

**Table 5-8**
**Warehouse Administrative Support Job Family**
**Knowledge Used**

| Knowledge Category | Used | By |
|---|---|---|
| *Mathematics* | | |
| Basic | Daily | 58% |
| Algebra/statistics | Daily | 58% |
| Advanced statistics | Weekly | 42% |
| *Communications* | | |
| Writing and editing–business text | Constantly | 92% |
| Word processing | Constantly | 92% |
| Writing and editing–financial | Daily | 50% |
| Public speaking | Weekly | 42% |
| *Transportation* | | |
| Trucking | Weekly | 75% |
| Air/water | Weekly | 50% |
| Rail | Monthly | 50% |

**Table 5-9**
**Warehouse Clerical Employees Job Family**
**Domain and Dimension Scores**

| Dimension Description | Percentage | Scope | Rarity |
|---|---|---|---|
| **INTERPERSONAL DOMAIN** | | | |
| *Internal Contacts* | | | |
| Exchanging information/consulting | 97 | 29 | 47 |
| Supervising operative employees | 75 | 32 | 62 |
| Supervising laborers | 56 | 28 | 47 |
| Resolving conflicts | 29 | 18 | 37 |
| *Meetings* | | | |
| Attend meetings with non-supervisory employees | 90 | 17 | 45 |
| Attend meetings with non-executives | 88 | 16 | 34 |
| Chair meetings with non-supervisory employees | 37 | 17 | 44 |
| *Frequency Ratings for Internal and External Contacts* | | | |
| Attend Meetings | 97 | 25 | 51 |
| With supervisors, managers, and executives | 92 | 40 | 47 |
| With laborers and operating employees | 86 | 70 | 76 |
| Chair meetings | 39 | 28 | 57 |
| With customers, marketing or sales | 32 | 33 | 27 |

313

| Table 5-9<br>Warehouse Clerical Employees Job Family<br>Domain and Dimension Scores | | | |
|---|---|---|---|
| Dimension Description | Percentage | Scope | Rarity |
| **DECISION-MAKING DOMAIN** | | | |
| *Production, Human Resources,*<br>*Financial and Strategic Decisions* | | | |
| Human resources management | 53 | 15 | 56 |
| Production/operations management | 29 | 25 | 62 |
| Financial-purchasing and budgeting | 20 | 27 | 68 |
| *Frequency Ratings for Decisions* | | | |
| Operations and human resources | 56 | 23 | 50 |
| Human resources– authority and<br>benefits | 49 | 26 | 64 |
| Finance–purchasing and budgeting | 36 | 17 | 48 |
| **MECHANICAL/PHYSICAL<br>DOMAIN** | | | |
| Office machines | 100 | 22 | 49 |
| Gross physical activities | 90 | 32 | 58 |
| Off-road/utility vehicles | 66 | 30 | 68 |
| Precise physical activity | 63 | 40 | 40 |
| *Frequency Rating for Mechanical and*<br>*Physical Dimensions* | | | |
| Office machines | 100 | 76 | 46 |
| Tool/manufacturing/vehicle operation | 78 | 11 | 49 |

| Table 5-9 Warehouse Clerical Employees Job Family Domain and Dimension Scores | | | |
|---|---|---|---|
| Dimension Description | Percentage | Scope | Rarity |
| **WORK CONTEXT DOMAIN** | | | |
| Using numerical or verbal information | 100 | 28 | 41 |
| Sensory input from work environment | 98 | 33 | 45 |
| Demanding personal situations | 88 | 24 | 42 |
| **OVERALL RATINGS** | | | |
| Clerical/office activities/information exchange | 100 | 41 | 68 |
| Physical activity/work environment | 100 | 29 | 43 |
| Blue collar/operative/service contact/supervisors | 86 | 31 | 48 |
| Production/operations/HR decision making | 59 | 17 | 20 |
| Technical/scientific machines | 29 | 30 | 48 |

**Table 5-10**
**Warehouse Clerical Employees Job Family**
**Knowledge Used**

| Knowledge Category | Used | By |
|---|---|---|
| *Human Resources* | | |
| Supervision and development | Constantly | 27% |
| *Management and Production* | | |
| Inventory control and warehousing | Constantly | 66% |
| Records control | Constantly | 24% |
| *Mathematics* | | |
| Algebra/statistics | Constantly | 78% |
| Basic | Constantly | 63% |
| *Communications* | | |
| Word processing | Constantly | 34% |
| Writing and editing–business text | Daily | 20% |
| *Transportation* | | |
| Trucking | Constantly | 31% |

316

| Table 5-11<br>Warehouse Operational Employee Job Family<br>Domain and Dimension Scores | | | |
|---|---|---|---|
| **Dimension Description** | **Percentage** | **Scope** | **Rarity** |
| **INTERPERSONAL DOMAIN** | | | |
| *Internal Contacts* | | | |
| Exchanging information/consulting | 96 | 27 | 44 |
| Supervising operative employees | 79 | 26 | 50 |
| Supervising laborers | 44 | 21 | 41 |
| *Meetings* | | | |
| Attend meetings with non-executives | 89 | 12 | 27 |
| Attend meetings with non-supervisory employees | 85 | 15 | 41 |
| *Frequency Ratings for Internal and External Contacts* | | | |
| With supervisors, managers, and executives | 96 | 36 | 42 |
| With laborers and operating employees | 92 | 62 | 68 |
| Attend meetings | 92 | 19 | 42 |
| **DECISION-MAKING DOMAIN** | | | |
| *Production, Human Resources, Financial and Strategic Decisions* | | | |
| Production/operations management | 24 | 28 | 69 |
| *Frequency Ratings for Decisions* | | | |
| Operations and human resources | 31 | 30 | 62 |
| Human resources– authority and benefits | 25 | 31 | 73 |

317

| Table 5-11<br>Warehouse Operational Employee Job Family<br>Domain and Dimension Scores | | | |
|---|---|---|---|
| Dimension Description | Percentage | Scope | Rarity |
| **MECHANICAL/PHYSICAL<br>DOMAIN** | | | |
| Precise physical activity | 99 | 56 | 56 |
| Gross physical activities | 99 | 46 | 73 |
| Hand-held tools | 60 | 11 | 43 |
| Off-road/utility vehicles | 59 | 23 | 50 |
| *Frequency Rating for Mechanical and*<br>*Physical Dimensions* | | | |
| Tool/manufacturing/vehicle operation | 96 | 11 | 50 |
| Office machines | 72 | 47 | 24 |
| **WORK CONTEXT DOMAIN** | | | |
| Using numerical or verbal<br>information | 100 | 48 | 44 |
| Sensory input from work environment | 100 | 40 | 53 |
| Demanding personal situations | 89 | 24 | 42 |
| Unpleasant or hazardous work<br>environment | 87 | 19 | 56 |

## Table 5-11
### Warehouse Operational Employee Job Family
### Domain and Dimension Scores

| Dimension Description | Percentage | Scope | Rarity |
|---|---|---|---|
| **OVERALL RATINGS** | | | |
| Physical activity/work environment | 100 | 41 | 67 |
| Clerical/office activities/information exchange | 99 | 26 | 37 |
| Meetings and contacts | 94 | 6 | 41 |
| Blue collar/operative/service contact/supervisors | 92 | 24 | 32 |
| Production/operations/HR decision making | 33 | 21 | 28 |

## Table 5-12
### Warehouse Operational Employee Job Family
### Knowledge Used

| Knowledge Category | Used | By |
|---|---|---|
| *Management and Production* | | |
| Inventory control and warehousing | Constantly | 69% |
| Records control | Constantly | 39% |
| *Mathematics* | | |
| Basic | Constantly | 85% |
| Algebra/statistics | Constantly | 66% |

319

| Table 5-13 Warehouse Job Domain Demographics | | | |
|---|---|---|---|
| Age | Average: 38 | | Age Range: 19-60 |
| Education | < High School: 10% | High School: 39% | > High School: 51% |
| Gender | Male: 73% | | Female: 21% |
| Years in Position | 0-5 yrs: 48% | 5-10 yrs: 20% | >10 yrs: 32% |
| Years with Firm | 0-5 yrs: 31% | 5-10 yrs: 20% | >10 yrs: 49% |

**Table 5-14**
**Warehouse Personnel**
**Personality, Need for Cognition, Customer Orientation, and Market Orientation**

| Dimension | Mngr | | Super | | Planning | | Admin. | | Norm Score | |
|---|---|---|---|---|---|---|---|---|---|---|
| Neuroticism | 0 / 23 | 13.7 | 2 / 26 | 14.4 | 8 / 29 | 14.9 | 3 / 35 | 15.4 | 4 / 38 | 19.07 |
| Extraversion | 26 / 42 | 32.8 | 17 / 41 | 32.5 | 27 / 35 | 31.1 | 17 / 38 | 27.8 | 14 / 40 | 27.69 |
| Openness | 18 / 41 | 26.7 | 14 / 35 | 23.8 | 17 / 30 | 23.1 | 14 / 34 | 23.7 | 14 / 40 | 27.03 |
| Agreeableness | 26 / 40 | 31.8 | 20 / 42 | 33.4 | 29 / 37 | 32.6 | 22 / 39 | 33 | 21 / 45 | 32.84 |
| Conscientiousness | 28 / 44 | 36.2 | 26 / 43 | 36.4 | 33 / 44 | 37.6 | 30 / 44 | 35.9 | 18 / 47 | 34.57 |
| Need for Cognition | -2 / 53 | 31.9 | -13 / 52 | 20.9 | -16 / 47 | 21 | -41 / 43 | 19.1 | -- / -- | NA |
| Customer Orientation | 169 / 212 | 196.2 | 140 / 215 | 187 | 109 / 210 | 180 | 165 / 216 | 191.4 | 159 / 187 | 187 |
| Marketing Orientation | 54 / 120 | 86.1 | 69 / 126 | 99.6 | 57 / 114 | 93.6 | 73 / 133 | 89.9 | -- / -- | 97.2 |

# APPENDIX 6

# TRANSPORTATION

| Table 6-1<br>Transportation Managers Job Family<br>Domain and Dimensions Scores | | | |
|---|---|---|---|
| Dimension Description | Percentage | Scope | Rarity |
| **INTERPERSONAL DOMAIN** | | | |
| *Internal Contacts* | | | |
| Exchanging information/consulting | 84 | 30 | 47 |
| Supervising mid-level managers | 79 | 31 | 69 |
| Training | 74 | 41 | 58 |
| Resolving conflicts | 63 | 29 | 61 |
| Supervising professional/technical employees | 58 | 43 | 79 |
| Selling or persuading | 37 | 22 | 46 |
| Supervising operative employees | 26 | 58 | 73 |
| Supervising laborers | 21 | 39 | 43 |
| *External Contacts* | | | |
| Exchanging business related information | 84 | 24 | 56 |
| Supervising suppliers or contractors | 63 | 23 | 57 |
| Customers–sales related | 53 | 27 | 63 |
| Bargaining and negotiating | 53 | 19 | 61 |

| Table 6-1<br>Transportation Managers Job Family<br>Domain and Dimensions Scores | | | |
|---|---|---|---|
| Dimension Description | Percentage | Scope | Rarity |
| *Meetings* | | | |
| Chair meetings with non-executives | 100 | 34 | 53 |
| Attend meetings with non-executives | 95 | 42 | 61 |
| Attend meetings with outside supervisors, technicians | 74 | 25 | 65 |
| Attend meetings with non-supervisory employees | 74 | 24 | 57 |
| Chair meetings with non-supervisory employees | 68 | 25 | 59 |
| Chair meetings with outside supervisors, technicians | 68 | 21 | 46 |
| Attend meetings with executives | 58 | 24 | 50 |
| Chair meetings to bargain or persuade | 42 | 19 | 46 |
| Chair meetings with executives | 32 | 23 | 45 |
| *Frequency Ratings for Internal and External Contacts* | | | |
| Attend Meetings | 100 | 39 | 72 |
| Chair meetings | 100 | 27 | 59 |
| Business related contacts | 89 | 23 | 62 |
| With supervisors, managers, and executives | 84 | 46 | 54 |
| With customers, marketing or sales | 53 | 33 | 27 |
| With laborers and operating employees | 42 | 46 | 49 |

| Table 6-1<br>Transportation Managers Job Family<br>Domain and Dimensions Scores | | | |
|---|---|---|---|
| Dimension Description | Percentage | Scope | Rarity |
| **DECISION-MAKING DOMAIN** | | | |
| *Production, Human Resources,*<br>*Financial and Strategic Decisions* | | | |
| Financial-purchasing and budgeting | 100 | 44 | 81 |
| Human resources management | 100 | 40 | 93 |
| Production/operations management | 74 | 47 | 87 |
| *Frequency Ratings for Decisions* | | | |
| Finance–purchasing and budgeting | 100 | 29 | 73 |
| Human resources– authority and benefits | 95 | 36 | 83 |
| Operations and human resources | 95 | 36 | 74 |
| **MECHANICAL/PHYSICAL<br>DOMAIN** | | | |
| Office machines | 100 | 20 | 40 |
| Precise physical activity | 58 | 31 | 31 |
| *Frequency Rating for Mechanical and*<br>*Physical Dimensions* | | | |
| Office machines | 100 | 77 | 45 |
| Technical/scientific machines | 42 | 45 | 5 |
| **WORK CONTEXT DOMAIN** | | | |
| Using numerical or verbal information | 100 | 32 | 28 |
| Sensory input from work environment | 95 | 27 | 36 |
| Demanding personal situations | 79 | 26 | 45 |

| Table 6-1<br>Transportation Managers Job Family<br>Domain and Dimensions Scores | | | |
|---|---|---|---|
| Dimension Description | Percentage | Scope | Rarity |
| OVERALL RATINGS | | | |
| Clerical/office activities/information exchange | 100 | 41 | 67 |
| Production/operations/HR decision making | 100 | 36 | 59 |
| Managerial decisions: finance/purchasing/budgeting | 100 | 27 | 41 |
| Meetings and contacts | 100 | 25 | 84 |
| Supervision, conflict resolution, training | 84 | 27 | 40 |
| Technical/scientific machines | 47 | 29 | 44 |
| Blue collar/operative/service contact/supervisors | 47 | 25 | 36 |

**Table 6-2**
**Transportation Managers Job Family**
**Knowledge Used**

| Knowledge Category | Used | By |
|---|---|---|
| *Finance and Accounting* | | |
| Commerce | Weekly | 37% |
| Budgeting | Monthly | 58% |
| Purchasing | Monthly | 37% |
| Accounting | Monthly | 37% |
| *Human Resources* | | |
| Supervision and development | Daily | 58% |
| Occupational safety and health | Weekly | 37% |
| Job analysis | Monthly | 42% |
| Selection and recruitment | Yearly | 68% |
| *Management and Production* | | |
| Inventory control and warehousing | Daily | 42% |
| Records control | Weekly | 37% |
| Strategic planning | Yearly | 42% |
| *Geography* | | |
| Local and regional | Daily | 47% |

**Table 6-2**
**Transportation Managers Job Family**
**Knowledge Used**

| Knowledge Category | Used | By |
|---|---|---|
| *Communications* | | |
| Writing and editing–business text | Constantly | 63% |
| Word processing | Constantly | 58% |
| Writing and editing–financial | Daily | 32% |
| *Transportation* | | |
| Trucking | Constantly | 74% |
| Air/water | Constantly | 68% |
| Rail | Constantly | 63% |

## Table 6-3
### Transportation Administrative Support Job Family
### Domain and Dimension Scores

| Dimension Description | Percentage | Scope | Rarity |
|---|---|---|---|
| **INTERPERSONAL DOMAIN** | | | |
| *Internal Contacts* | | | |
| Exchanging information/consulting | 84 | 23 | 39 |
| Supervising mid-level managers | 48 | 16 | 43 |
| *External Contacts* | | | |
| Customers–sales related | 61 | 16 | 51 |
| Training | 26 | 13 | 42 |
| *Meetings* | | | |
| Attend meetings with non-executives | 84 | 28 | 44 |
| Attend meetings with non-supervisory employees | 61 | 28 | 53 |
| Attend meetings with executives | 61 | 24 | 45 |
| Chair meetings with non-executives | 39 | 35 | 51 |
| Attend meetings with outside supervisors, technicians | 39 | 29 | 59 |
| Chair meetings with non-supervisory employees | 32 | 30 | 47 |
| Attend meetings to bargain or persuade | 26 | 23 | 50 |
| Chair meetings with outside supervisors, technicians | 23 | 39 | 56 |

| Table 6-3<br>Transportation Administrative Support Job Family<br>Domain and Dimension Scores | | | |
|---|---|---|---|
| Dimension Description | Percentage | Scope | Rarity |
| *Frequency Ratings for Internal and External Contacts* | | | |
| With supervisors, managers, and executives | 84 | 42 | 49 |
| Attend Meetings | 84 | 23 | 50 |
| With customers, marketing or sales | 52 | 39 | 34 |
| With laborers and operating employees | 23 | 49 | 50 |
| **DECISION-MAKING DOMAIN** | | | |
| *Production, Human Resources, Financial and Strategic Decisions* | | | |
| **Financial-purchasing and budgeting** | 42 | 22 | 51 |
| **Human resources management** | 39 | 17 | 60 |
| **Production/operations management** | 29 | 24 | 61 |
| *Frequency Ratings for Decisions* | | | |
| **Finance–purchasing and budgeting** | 71 | 15 | 44 |
| **Operations and human resources** | 42 | 17 | 42 |
| **MECHANICAL/PHYSICAL DOMAIN** | | | |
| Office machines | 97 | 24 | 50 |
| Precise physical activity | 65 | 33 | 34 |

| Table 6-3 Transportation Administrative Support Job Family Domain and Dimension Scores | | | |
|---|---|---|---|
| **Dimension Description** | **Percentage** | **Scope** | **Rarity** |
| *Frequency Rating for Mechanical and Physical Dimensions* | | | |
| Office machines | 97 | 87 | 69 |
| Technical/scientific machines | 42 | 48 | 5 |
| **WORK CONTEXT DOMAIN** | | | |
| Using numerical or verbal information | 100 | 27 | 33 |
| Demanding personal situations | 74 | 18 | 31 |
| **OVERALL RATINGS** | | | |
| Clerical/office activities/information exchange | 97 | 42 | 71 |
| Technical/scientific machines | 42 | 31 | 49 |

| Table 6-4<br>**Transportation Administrative Support Support Job Family**<br>**Knowledge Used** | | |
| --- | --- | --- |
| **Knowledge Category** | **Used** | **By** |
| *Human Resources* | | |
| **Supervision and development** | Weekly | 26% |
| *Management and Production* | | |
| **Inventory control and warehousing** | Constantly | 32% |
| **Records control** | Daily | 26% |
| *Geography* | | |
| **Local and regional** | Constantly | 29% |
| *Mathematics* | | |
| **Multiplication/Division** | Constantly | 68% |
| **Basic** | Constantly | 52% |
| *Communications* | | |
| **Writing and editing–business text** | Constantly | 71% |
| **Word processing** | Constantly | 71% |
| **Writing and editing–financial** | Constantly | 39% |
| *Transportation* | | |
| **Trucking** | Constantly | 71% |
| **Rail** | Constantly | 39% |
| **Air/water** | Daily | 29% |

| Table 6-5<br>Loaders Job Family<br>Domain and Dimension Scores | | | |
|---|---|---|---|
| Dimension Description | Percentage | Scope | Rarity |
| **INTERPERSONAL DOMAIN** | | | |
| *Internal Contacts* | | | |
| Exchanging information/consulting | 100 | 48 | 68 |
| Supervising laborers | 82 | 33 | 51 |
| Supervising operative employees | 73 | 39 | 65 |
| Training | 55 | 36 | 46 |
| Bargaining or negotiating | 45 | 42 | 76 |
| Supervising mid-level managers | 45 | 35 | 58 |
| Resolving conflicts | 45 | 26 | 53 |
| Supervising professional/technical employees | 36 | 34 | 56 |
| Selling or persuading | 36 | 32 | 60 |
| Marketing/sales employees | 27 | 39 | 62 |
| *External Contacts* | | | |
| Customers–sales related | 55 | 26 | 62 |
| Bargaining and negotiating | 45 | 42 | 72 |
| Supervising suppliers or contractors | 36 | 42 | 79 |

| Table 6-5<br>Loaders Job Family<br>Domain and Dimension Scores | | | |
| --- | --- | --- | --- |
| Dimension Description | Percentage | Scope | Rarity |
| *Meetings* | | | |
| Attend meetings with non-executives | 100 | 47 | 65 |
| Attend meetings with non-supervisory employees | 100 | 46 | 76 |
| Chair meetings with non-executives | 82 | 39 | 58 |
| Chair meetings with non-supervisory employees | 82 | 35 | 63 |
| *Frequency Ratings for Internal and External Contacts* | | | |
| With laborers and operating employees | 100 | 69 | 76 |
| With supervisors, managers, and executives | 100 | 53 | 62 |
| Attend Meetings | 100 | 41 | 76 |
| Chair meetings | 82 | 30 | 59 |
| With customers, marketing or sales | 64 | 49 | 49 |
| Bargaining or persuading | 55 | 25 | 47 |
| **DECISION-MAKING DOMAIN** | | | |
| *Production, Human Resources, Financial and Strategic Decisions* | | | |
| Production/operations management | 36 | 21 | 54 |
| Human resources management | 36 | 18 | 71 |

334

| Table 6-5<br>Loaders Job Family<br>Domain and Dimension Scores | | | |
|---|---|---|---|
| **Dimension Description** | **Percentage** | **Scope** | **Rarity** |
| *Frequency Ratings for Decisions* | | | |
| Operations and human resources | 36 | 29 | 62 |
| Human resources– authority and benefits | 36 | 21 | 60 |
| MECHANICAL/PHYSICAL DOMAIN | | | |
| Office machines | 91 | 26 | 58 |
| Precise physical activity | 73 | 66 | 68 |
| Light highway vehicles | 55 | 50 | 67 |
| *Frequency Rating for Mechanical and Physical Dimensions* | | | |
| Office machines | 91 | 90 | 74 |
| WORK CONTEXT DOMAIN | | | |
| Sensory input from work environment | 100 | 44 | 57 |
| Using numerical or verbal information | 100 | 37 | 64 |
| Demanding personal situations | 100 | 29 | 51 |
| Unpleasant or hazardous work environment | 100 | 23 | 52 |

| Table 6-5 Loaders Job Family Domain and Dimension Scores | | | |
|---|---|---|---|
| **Dimension Description** | **Percentage** | **Scope** | **Rarity** |
| **OVERALL RATINGS** | | | |
| Physical activity/work environment | 100 | 38 | 58 |
| Blue collar/operative/service contact/supervisors | 100 | 32 | 51 |
| Clerical/office activities/information exchange | 100 | 27 | 84 |
| Meetings and contacts | 100 | 27 | 89 |
| Public, stressful situations | 100 | 9 | 56 |
| Technical/scientific machines | 73 | 31 | 51 |
| Contacts: customers, sales and marketing related | 64 | 28 | 31 |

| Table 6-6<br>Loaders Job Family<br>Knowledge Used | | |
|---|---|---|
| **Knowledge Category** | **Used** | **By** |
| *Finance and Accounting* | | |
| **Purchasing** | Weekly | 55% |
| *Human Resources* | | |
| **Supervision and development** | Constantly | 45% |
| **Occupational safety and health** | Constantly | 27% |
| *Management and Production* | | |
| **Inventory control and warehousing** | Daily | 64% |
| **Records control** | Weekly | 64% |
| *Mathematics* | | |
| **Basic** | Constantly | 91% |
| **Multiplication/division** | Constantly | 91% |
| *Communications* | | |
| **Word processing** | Constantly | 82% |
| *Transportation* | | |
| **Rail** | Constantly | 73% |
| **Trucking** | Constantly | 36% |
| **Air/water** | Constantly | 18% |

## Table 6-7
## Motor Carrier Operating Employee Job Family
## Domain and Dimension Scores

| Dimension Description | Percentage | Scope | Rarity |
|---|---|---|---|
| **INTERPERSONAL DOMAIN** | | | |
| *Internal Contacts* | | | |
| **Exchanging information/consulting** | 100 | 32 | 50 |
| **Supervising operative employees** | 78 | 24 | 50 |
| **Supervising laborers** | 39 | 22 | 44 |
| **Training** | 33 | 22 | 32 |
| **Marketing/sales employees** | 33 | 21 | 51 |
| **Resolving conflicts** | 22 | 25 | 55 |
| *External Contacts* | | | |
| **Exchanging business related information** | 94 | 20 | 51 |
| **Customers–sales related** | 94 | 17 | 54 |
| **Exchanging special interest information** | 67 | 6 | 41 |
| **Training** | 50 | 13 | 41 |
| *Meetings* | | | |
| **Attend meetings with non-supervisory employees** | 78 | 8 | 24 |
| **Attend meetings with non-executives** | 78 | 7 | 18 |
| **Attend meetings with executives** | 61 | 10 | 38 |

| Table 6-7 Motor Carrier Operating Employee Job Family Domain and Dimension Scores | | | |
|---|---|---|---|
| **Dimension Description** | **Percentage** | **Scope** | **Rarity** |
| *Frequency Ratings for Internal and External Contacts* | | | |
| With customers, marketing or sales | 94 | 54 | 54 |
| With laborers and operating employees | 94 | 44 | 43 |
| With supervisors, managers, and executives | 94 | 41 | 48 |
| Business related contacts | 94 | 19 | 5 |
| **MECHANICAL/PHYSICAL DOMAIN** | | | |
| Office machines | 100 | 18 | 38 |
| Heavy highway vehicles | 78 | 81 | 88 |
| Precise physical activity | 78 | 29 | 29 |
| Hand-held tools | 61 | 10 | 40 |
| Mobile tools/equipment | 56 | 12 | 40 |
| *Frequency Ratings/Mechanical and Physical Dimensions* | | | |
| Tool/manufacturing/vehicle operation | 78 | 9 | 57 |
| Office machines | 100 | 66 | 34 |

**Table 6-7**
**Motor Carrier Operating Employee Job Family**
**Domain and Dimension Scores**

| Dimension Description | Percentage | Scope | Rarity |
|---|---|---|---|
| **WORK CONTEXT DOMAIN** | | | |
| Demanding personal situations | 100 | 40 | 69 |
| Sensory input from work environment | 100 | 38 | 52 |
| Using numerical or verbal information | 100 | 33 | 53 |
| Unpleasant or hazardous work environment | 94 | 24 | 66 |
| **OVERALL RATINGS** | | | |
| Clerical/office activities/information exchange | 100 | 39 | 67 |
| Physical activity/work environment | 100 | 29 | 44 |
| Contacts: customers, sales and marketing related | 100 | 19 | 23 |
| Public, stressful situations | 100 | 11 | 64 |
| Tools/machines/vehicle use | 78 | 15 | 63 |

**Table 6-8**
**Motor Carrier Operating Employee Job Family Knowledge Used**

| Knowledge Category | Used | By |
|---|---|---|
| *Geography* | | |
| Local and regional | Constantly | 89% |
| *Mathematics* | | |
| Multiplication/Division | Constantly | 100% |
| Basic | Daily | 78% |
| *Communications* | | |
| Word processing | Constantly | 83% |
| Telecommunications systems | Constantly | 78% |
| Writing and editing–business text | Daily | 22% |
| *Transportation* | | |
| Trucking | Constantly | 94% |
| Rail | Weekly | 28% |

| Table 6-9 | | | |
|---|---|---|---|
| **Transportation Job Family Domain** | | | |
| **Demographics** | | | |
| Age | Average: 40 | Age Range: 23-61 | |
| Education | High School or less:29 % | Bach Deg or less:59% | > Bach. Degree:7% |
| Gender | Male: 70% | Female: 30% | |
| Years in Position | 0-5 yrs: 88% | 5-10 yrs: 10% | >10 yrs: 2% |
| Years with Firm | 0-5 yrs: 45% | 5-10 yrs: 22% | >10 yrs: 33% |

Table 6-10
Transportation Function
Personality, Need for Cognition, Customer Orientation, and Market Orientation

| Dimension | Manager | | Admin | | SMeans | | Norm | Score |
|---|---|---|---|---|---|---|---|---|
| Neuroticism | 0 | 13.6 | 9 | 13.8 | 0 | 14.5 | 4 | 19.1 |
| | 26 | | 29 | | 40 | | 38 | |
| Extraversion | 26 | 31.1 | 23 | 30.5 | 11 | 31.9 | 14 | 27.7 |
| | 38 | | 38 | | 47 | | 40 | |
| Openness | 18 | 24.8 | 13 | 23.5 | 11 | 25.9 | 14 | 27 |
| | 33 | | 35 | | 43 | | 40 | |
| Agreeableness | 23 | 33.4 | 23 | 33.6 | 13 | 32.4 | 21 | 32.8 |
| | 43 | | 40 | | 43 | | 45 | |
| Conscientiousness | 24 | 36.1 | 26 | 35.5 | 18 | 36.8 | 18 | 34.6 |
| | 43 | | 42 | | 48 | | 47 | |
| Need for Cognition | -16 | 25.7 | -27 | 20.9 | -58 | 24.7 | -- | NA |
| | 52 | | 46 | | 70 | | -- | |
| Customer Orientation | 159 | 192.9 | 124 | 187.4 | 109 | 189 | 159 | 187 |
| | 216 | | 216 | | 216 | | 187 | |
| Marketing Orientation | 70 | 97.8 | 45 | 100.8 | 41 | 99.5 | – | 97.2 |
| | 128 | | 132 | | 138 | | -- | |

343

# APPENDIX 7

# MATERIAL CONTROL

| Table 7-1 Supply Chain Managers Job Family Domain and Dimension Scores | | | |
|---|---|---|---|
| Dimension Description | Percentage | Scope | Rarity |
| **INTERPERSONAL DOMAIN** | | | |
| *Internal Contacts* | | | |
| Exchanging information/consulting | 100 | 44 | 64 |
| Training | 91 | 51 | 64 |
| Supervising mid-level managers | 82 | 38 | 65 |
| Supervising upper-level executives | 82 | 32 | 77 |
| Resolving conflicts | 73 | 45 | 79 |
| Bargaining or negotiating | 73 | 32 | 66 |
| Supervising operative employees | 64 | 53 | 83 |
| Selling or persuading | 55 | 42 | 70 |
| Supervising professional/technical employees | 55 | 42 | 67 |
| Marketing/sales employees | 55 | 42 | 67 |
| *External Contacts* | | | |
| Exchanging business related information | 100 | 21 | 52 |
| Supervising suppliers or contractors | 91 | 31 | 71 |
| Customers–sales related | 73 | 32 | 74 |
| Bargaining and negotiating | 64 | 27 | 76 |
| Resolving conflicts | 45 | 26 | 62 |
| Training | 36 | 37 | 82 |

| Table 7-1<br>Supply Chain Managers Job Family<br>Domain and Dimension Scores | | | |
|---|---|---|---|
| Dimension Description | Percentage | Scope | Rarity |
| *Meetings* | | | |
| Attend meetings with non-executives | 100 | 59 | 79 |
| Attend meetings with executives | 100 | 54 | 82 |
| Chair meetings with non-executives | 100 | 51 | 72 |
| Attend meetings with non-supervisory employees | 91 | 57 | 86 |
| Chair meetings with non-supervisory employees | 91 | 45 | 74 |
| Chair meetings with executives | 91 | 44 | 61 |
| Attend meetings to bargain or persuade | 91 | 26 | 59 |
| Attend meetings with outside non-supervisors, technicians | 73 | 50 | 73 |
| Chair meetings with outside supervisors, technicians | 73 | 44 | 67 |
| Chair meetings to bargain or persuade | 45 | 41 | 69 |

| Table 7-1 Supply Chain Managers Job Family Domain and Dimension Scores | | | |
|---|---|---|---|
| **Dimension Description** | **Percentage** | **Scope** | **Rarity** |
| *Frequency Ratings for Internal and External Contacts* | | | |
| With supervisors, managers, and executives | 100 | 59 | 71 |
| Attend Meetings | 100 | 53 | 89 |
| Chair meetings | 100 | 43 | 80 |
| Business related contacts | 91 | 20 | 57 |
| With customers, marketing or sales | 82 | 46 | 44 |
| With laborers and operating employees | 73 | 43 | 45 |
| Bargaining or persuading | 64 | 26 | 55 |
| **DECISION-MAKING DOMAIN** | | | |
| *Production, Human Resources, Financial and Strategic Decisions* | | | |
| Production/operations management | 100 | 55 | 92 |
| Financial-purchasing and budgeting | 91 | 50 | 88 |
| Human resources management | 91 | 48 | 95 |
| Strategic planning-products and services | 91 | 40 | 80 |
| Financial-investment, cash | 18 | 80 | 93 |

| Table 7-1<br>Supply Chain Managers Job Family<br>Domain and Dimension Scores | | | |
|---|---|---|---|
| Dimension Description | Percentage | Scope | Rarity |
| *Frequency Ratings for Decisions* | | | |
| Operations and human resources | 100 | 45 | 84 |
| Finance–purchasing and budgeting | 100 | 28 | 69 |
| Human resources– authority and benefits | 91 | 40 | 85 |
| Planning products and services | 91 | 20 | 66 |
| MECHANICAL/PHYSICAL DOMAIN | | | |
| Office machines | 100 | 30 | 52 |
| Gross physical activities | 91 | 19 | 37 |
| Precise physical activity | 64 | 24 | 24 |
| *Frequency Rating for Mechanical and Physical Dimensions* | | | |
| Office machines | 100 | 80 | 56 |
| WORK CONTEXT DOMAIN | | | |
| Sensory input from work environment | 100 | 40 | 54 |
| Demanding personal situations | 100 | 36 | 61 |
| Using numerical or verbal information | 100 | 35 | 51 |

| Table 7-1<br>Supply Chain Managers Job Family<br>Domain and Dimension Scores | | | |
| --- | --- | --- | --- |
| Dimension Description | Percentage | Scope | Rarity |
| OVERALL RATINGS | | | |
| Clerical/office activities/information exchange | 100 | 54 | 82 |
| Meetings and contacts | 100 | 47 | 97 |
| Production/operations/HR decision making | 100 | 45 | 73 |
| Supervision, conflict resolution, training | 100 | 34 | 50 |
| Managerial decisions: finance/purchasing/budgeting | 100 | 29 | 41 |
| Physical activity/work environment | 100 | 27 | 40 |
| Bargain/persuade/negotiate | 100 | 24 | 32 |
| Contacts: customers, sales and marketing related | 91 | 30 | 44 |
| Product/customer decision/planning | 91 | 30 | 45 |
| Blue collar/operative/service contact/supervisors | 73 | 28 | 44 |
| Technical/scientific machines | 73 | 28 | 42 |
| Strategic planning | | | |

| Table 7-2 Supply Chain Manager Knowledge Used | | |
|---|---|---|
| **Knowledge Category** | **Used** | **By** |
| *Finance and Accounting* | | |
| **Purchasing** | Weekly | 36% |
| **Budgeting** | Yearly | 36% |
| *Human Resources* | | |
| **Supervision and development** | Daily | 73% |
| **Job analysis** | Monthly | 45% |
| **Selection and recruitment** | Monthly | 45% |
| *Management and Production* | | |
| **Inventory control and warehousing** | Constantly | 91% |
| **Manufacturing Management** | Constantly | 73% |
| **Operations research** | Weekly | 64% |
| **Strategic planning** | Weekly | 45% |
| *Mathematics* | | |
| **Basic** | Constantly | 55% |
| **Algebra/statistics** | Daily | 45% |
| *Communications* | | |
| **Word processing** | Constantly | 64% |
| **Writing and editing–business text** | Daily | 82% |
| **Writing and editing–financial** | Daily | 64% |
| **Public speaking** | Monthly | 55% |

| Table 7-2 Supply Chain Manager Knowledge Used | | |
|---|---|---|
| Knowledge Category | Used | By |
| *Transportation* | | |
| Trucking | Weekly | 45% |
| Air/water | Weekly | 36% |

| Table 7-3 Inventory/Material Supervisor Domain and Dimension Scores | | | |
|---|---|---|---|
| Dimension Description | Percentage | Scope | Rarity |
| **INTERPERSONAL DOMAIN** | | | |
| *Internal Contacts* | | | |
| Exchanging information/consulting | 95 | 40 | 58 |
| Supervising laborers | 95 | 40 | 47 |
| Supervising operative employees | 91 | 48 | 75 |
| Supervising mid-level managers | 64 | 27 | 65 |
| Marketing/sales employees | 50 | 22 | 44 |
| Training | 36 | 29 | 44 |
| Supervising upper-level executives | 32 | 14 | 60 |
| Unions, special interest groups | 18 | 36 | 65 |

| Table 7-3
Inventory/Material Supervisor
Domain and Dimension Scores | | | |
|---|---|---|---|
| Dimension Description | Percentage | Scope | Rarity |
| *External Contacts* | | | |
| Customers–sales related | 73 | 16 | 48 |
| Resolving conflicts | 59 | 18 | 43 |
| Supervising suppliers or contractors | 50 | 20 | 54 |
| Exchanging business related information | 50 | 19 | 43 |
| Bargaining and negotiating | 27 | 25 | 55 |
| *Meetings* | | | |
| Attend meetings with non-executives | 95 | 26 | 46 |
| Attend meetings with executives | 68 | 23 | 49 |
| Attend meetings with non-supervisory employees | 64 | 24 | 56 |
| Chair meetings with non-executives | 64 | 17 | 34 |
| Chair meetings with non-supervisory employees | 50 | 25 | 58 |

| Table 7-3<br>Inventory/Material Supervisor<br>Domain and Dimension Scores | | | |
|---|---|---|---|
| Dimension Description | Percentage | Scope | Rarity |
| *Frequency Ratings for Internal and*<br>*External Contacts* | | | |
| Attend Meetings | 100 | 29 | 58 |
| With laborers and operating employees | 95 | 68 | 73 |
| With supervisors, managers, and executives | 91 | 52 | 62 |
| With customers, marketing or sales | 77 | 45 | 43 |
| Chair meetings | 64 | 31 | 67 |
| Business related contacts | 64 | 14 | 39 |
| DECISION-MAKING DOMAIN | | | |
| *Production, Human Resources,*<br>*Financial and Strategic Decisions* | | | |
| Human resources management | 77 | 27 | 82 |
| Financial-purchasing and budgeting | 68 | 36 | 79 |
| Production/operations management | 68 | 35 | 77 |
| Strategic planning-products and services | 41 | 21 | 57 |
| *Frequency Ratings for Decisions* | | | |
| Operations and human resources | 82 | 33 | 65 |
| Human resources– authority and benefits | 77 | 20 | 66 |
| Finance–purchasing and budgeting | 77 | 20 | 60 |
| Planning products and services | 41 | 14 | 31 |

| Table 7-3<br>Inventory/Material Supervisor<br>Domain and Dimension Scores | | | |
| :--- | :---: | :---: | :---: |
| **Dimension Description** | **Percentage** | **Scope** | **Rarity** |
| MECHANICAL/PHYSICAL<br>DOMAIN | | | |
| Office machines | 95 | 29 | 53 |
| Gross physical activity | 86 | 21 | 42 |
| Technical or scientific equipment | 82 | 18 | 25 |
| Precise physical activity | 73 | 39 | 40 |
| Direct others tool, vehicle, or machine use | 32 | 34 | 69 |
| Off-road/utility vehicles | 27 | 19 | 41 |
| *Frequency Rating for Mechanical and Physical Dimensions* | | | |
| Office machines | 95 | 79 | 57 |
| Technical/scientific machines | 82 | 46 | 5 |
| Tool/manufacturing/vehicle operation | 55 | 22 | 64 |
| WORK CONTEXT DOMAIN | | | |
| Sensory input from work environment | 100 | 44 | 57 |
| Demanding personal situations | 100 | 36 | 59 |
| Using numerical or verbal information | 100 | 36 | 61 |
| Unpleasant or hazardous work environment | 91 | 17 | 48 |

| Table 7-3 Inventory/Material Supervisor Domain and Dimension Scores | | | |
|---|---|---|---|
| **Dimension Description** | **Percentage** | **Scope** | **Rarity** |
| OVERALL RATINGS | | | |
| Clerical/office activities/information exchange | 100 | 48 | 74 |
| Blue collar/operative/service contact/supervisors | 100 | 37 | 58 |
| Physical activity/work environment | 100 | 33 | 51 |
| Contacts: customers, sales and marketing related | 86 | 20 | 24 |
| Technical/scientific machines | 82 | 32 | 53 |
| Production/operations/HR decision making | 82 | 28 | 43 |
| Managerial decisions: finance/purchasing/budgeting | 77 | 19 | 22 |

**Table 7-4**
**Inventory/Materials Supervisor**
**Knowledge Used**

| Knowledge Category | Used | By |
|---|---|---|
| *Finance and Accounting* | | |
| Purchasing | Daily | 32% |
| *Human Resources* | | |
| Supervision and development | Constantly | 68% |
| Occupational safety and health | Constantly | 23% |
| Job analysis | Weekly | 45% |
| Selection and recruitment | Yearly | 36% |
| *Management and Production* | | |
| Inventory control and warehousing | Constantly | 95% |
| Manufacturing management | Constantly | 50% |
| Records control | Constantly | 41% |
| Operations research | Daily | 36% |
| Strategic planning | Monthly | 27% |
| *Machine Trades* | | |
| Machine operation | Constantly | 32% |
| *Materials Processing Work* | | |
| Metalworking | Daily | 27% |
| *Mathematics* | | |
| Basic | Constantly | 77% |
| Algebra/statistics | Daily | 32% |

| Table 7-4 Inventory/Materials Supervisor Knowledge Used | | |
|---|---|---|
| **Knowledge Category** | **Used** | **By** |
| *Communications* | | |
| Word processing | Constantly | 32% |
| Writing and editing–business text | Daily | 41% |
| *Transportation* | | |
| Trucking | Constantly | 23% |

| Table 7-5 Production Managers Job Family Domain and Dimension Scores | | | |
|---|---|---|---|
| **Dimension Description** | **Percentage** | **Scope** | **Rarity** |
| **INTERPERSONAL DOMAIN** | | | |
| *Internal Contacts* | | | |
| Exchanging information/consulting | 75 | 35 | 50 |
| Supervising operative employees | 50 | 35 | 68 |
| Supervising mid-level managers | 50 | 16 | 36 |
| Supervising professional/technical employees | 38 | 42 | 79 |
| Marketing/sales employees | 38 | 21 | 51 |
| Supervising laborers | 25 | 25 | 38 |

| Table 7-5<br>Production Managers Job Family<br>Domain and Dimension Scores | | | |
|---|---|---|---|
| **Dimension Description** | **Percentage** | **Scope** | **Rarity** |
| *External Contacts* | | | |
| Exchanging business related information | 75 | 14 | 36 |
| Customers–sales related | 63 | 17 | 52 |
| Supervising suppliers or contractors | 50 | 17 | 51 |
| *Meetings* | | | |
| Chair meetings with non-supervisory employees | 100 | 13 | 39 |
| Attend meetings with non-supervisory employees | 88 | 18 | 49 |
| Attend meetings with non-executives | 75 | 30 | 54 |
| Attend meetings with executives | 75 | 28 | 63 |
| Chair meetings with non-executives | 75 | 24 | 49 |
| Chair meetings with executives | 63 | 22 | 46 |
| Attend meetings with outside supervisors, technicians | 63 | 18 | 56 |
| Attend meetings with customers | 25 | 22 | 49 |

| Table 7-5 Production Managers Job Family Domain and Dimension Scores | | | |
|---|---|---|---|
| **Dimension Description** | **Percentage** | **Scope** | **Rarity** |
| *Frequency Ratings for Internal and External Contacts* | | | |
| With supervisors, managers, and executives | 100 | 44 | 52 |
| Chair meetings | 100 | 26 | 57 |
| Attend meetings | 88 | 38 | 71 |
| Business related contacts | 75 | 15 | 45 |
| With laborers and operating employees | 63 | 46 | 46 |
| With customers, marketing or sales | 63 | 42 | 38 |
| Bargaining or persuading | 63 | 15 | 53 |
| **DECISION-MAKING DOMAIN** | | | |
| *Production, Human Resources, Financial and Strategic Decisions* | | | |
| Human resources management | 100 | 28 | 82 |
| Financial-purchasing and budgeting | 100 | 27 | 67 |
| Production/operations management | 88 | 45 | 86 |
| Strategic planning-products and services | 75 | 23 | 70 |

| Table 7-5 | | | |
| Production Managers Job Family | | | |
| Domain and Dimension Scores | | | |
| Dimension Description | Percentage | Scope | Rarity |
| --- | --- | --- | --- |
| *Frequency Ratings for Decisions* | | | |
| Operations and human resources | 100 | 36 | 73 |
| Finance–purchasing and budgeting | 100 | 23 | 64 |
| Human resources– authority and benefits | 88 | 41 | 83 |
| Planning products and services | 75 | 20 | 58 |
| MECHANICAL/PHYSICAL DOMAIN | | | |
| Office machines | 88 | 19 | 37 |
| Precise physical activity | 50 | 47 | 49 |
| Gross physical activity | 50 | 21 | 47 |
| *Frequency Rating for Mechanical and Physical Dimensions* | | | |
| Office machines | 88 | 59 | 25 |
| WORK CONTEXT DOMAIN | | | |
| Using numerical or verbal information | 100 | 33 | 36 |
| Demanding personal situations | 100 | 31 | 54 |
| Sensory input from work environment | 88 | 33 | 45 |

| Table 7-5<br>Production Managers Job Family<br>Domain and Dimension Scores | | | |
|---|---|---|---|
| Dimension Description | Percentage | Scope | Rarity |
| **OVERALL RATINGS** | | | |
| Clerical/office activities/information exchange | 100 | 35 | 53 |
| Production/operations/HR decision making | 100 | 35 | 57 |
| Physical activity/work environment | 100 | 23 | 31 |
| Meetings and contacts | 100 | 19 | 81 |
| Public, stressful situations | 100 | 7 | 49 |
| Bargain/persuade/negotiate | 88 | 8 | 4 |
| Product/customer decision/planning | 75 | 22 | 27 |
| Blue collar/operative/service contact/supervisors | 63 | 22 | 29 |

| Table 7-6 Production Manager Knowledge Used | | |
|---|---|---|
| **Knowledge Category** | **Used** | **By** |
| *Finance and Accounting* | | |
| **Purchasing** | **Weekly** | **38%** |
| *Human Resources* | | |
| **Supervision and development** | **Constantly** | **88%** |
| **Selection and recruitment** | **Yearly** | **50%** |
| *Management and Production* | | |
| **Manufacturing Management** | **Constantly** | **50%** |
| **Inventory control and warehousing** | **Daily** | **50%** |
| *Mathematics* | | |
| **Basic** | **Daily** | **63%** |
| *Communications* | | |
| **Writing and editing–business text** | **Daily** | **63%** |
| **Word processing** | **Daily** | **63%** |

| Table 7-7 Inventory Administration Job Family Domain and Dimension Scores | | | |
|---|---|---|---|
| **Dimension Description** | **Percentage** | **Scope** | **Rarity** |
| **INTERPERSONAL DOMAIN** | | | |
| *Internal Contacts* | | | |
| Exchanging information/consulting | 86 | 30 | 47 |
| Supervising operative employees | 61 | 27 | 56 |
| Marketing/sales employees | 32 | 20 | 48 |
| *External Contacts* | | | |
| Exchanging business related information | 27 | 11 | 33 |
| Customers–sales related | 23 | 13 | 44 |
| Supervising suppliers or contractors | 20 | 18 | 53 |
| *Meetings* | | | |
| Attend meetings with non-executives | 95 | 14 | 30 |
| Attend meetings with non-supervisory employees | 86 | 15 | 41 |
| *Frequency Ratings for Internal and External Contacts* | | | |
| Attend Meetings | 95 | 17 | 40 |
| With supervisors, managers, and executives | 84 | 42 | 49 |
| With laborers and operating employees | 77 | 46 | 53 |
| With customers, marketing or sales | 43 | 35 | 29 |

| Table 7-7<br>Inventory Administration Job Family<br>Domain and Dimension Scores | | | |
|---|---|---|---|
| Dimension Description | Percentage | Scope | Rarity |
| **DECISION-MAKING DOMAIN** | | | |
| *Production, Human Resources, Financial and Strategic Decisions* | | | |
| **Financial-purchasing and budgeting** | 23 | 30 | 72 |
| *Frequency Ratings for Decisions* | | | |
| **Finance–purchasing and budgeting** | 30 | 18 | 48 |
| **MECHANICAL/PHYSICAL DOMAIN** | | | |
| **Gross physical activities** | 91 | 30 | 57 |
| **Office machines** | 91 | 19 | 44 |
| **Off-road/utility vehicles** | 57 | 26 | 59 |
| **Hand-held tools** | 52 | 17 | 58 |
| **Precise physical activity** | 43 | 30 | 29 |
| *Frequency Rating for Mechanical and Physical Dimensions* | | | |
| **Office machines** | 91 | 78 | 53 |
| **Tool/manufacturing/vehicle operation** | 66 | 15 | 61 |
| **Technical/scientific machines** | 34 | 44 | 5 |

| Table 7-7 Inventory Administration Job Family Domain and Dimension Scores | | | |
|---|---|---|---|
| Dimension Description | Percentage | Scope | Rarity |
| **WORK CONTEXT DOMAIN** | | | |
| Using numerical or verbal information | 100 | 31 | 50 |
| Demanding personal situations | 95 | 20 | 37 |
| Sensory input from work environment | 93 | 32 | 44 |
| Unpleasant or hazardous work environment | 93 | 17 | 52 |
| **OVERALL RATINGS** | | | |
| Clerical/office activities/information exchange | 100 | 38 | 60 |
| Physical activity/work environment | 100 | 28 | 42 |
| Meetings and contacts | 95 | 6 | 40 |
| Tools/machines/vehicle use | 66 | 8 | 26 |
| Technical/scientific machines | 34 | 27 | 40 |

| Table 7-8 Inventory Administration Knowledge Used | | |
|---|---|---|
| **Knowledge Category** | Used | By |
| *Management and Production* | | |
| **Inventory control and warehousing** | Constantly | 82% |
| **Records control** | Constantly | 48% |
| **Operations research** | Constantly | 20% |
| *Machine Trades* | | |
| **Machine Operations** | Constantly | 23% |
| *Materials Processing Work* | | |
| **Metalworking** | Constantly | 23% |
| *Mathematics* | | |
| **Basic** | Constantly | 80% |
| *Communications* | | |
| **Word processing** | Constantly | 25% |
| **Writing and editing–business text** | Constantly | 20% |

| Table 7-9<br>Material Control Job Family<br>Demographics | | | |
|---|---|---|---|
| Age | Average: 37 | | Age Range: 25-56 |
| Education | < High School: 6% | High School: 49% | >High School: 45% |
| Gender | Male: 51% | | Female: 49% |
| Years in Position | 0-3 yrs: 60% | 3-5 yrs: 23% | >5 yrs: 17% |
| Years with Firm | 0-3 yrs: 17% | 3-5 yrs: 23% | >5 yrs: 60% |

**Table 7-10**
**Inventory/Materials Control Personnel**
**Personality, Need for Cognition, Customer Orientation, and Market Orientation**

| Dimension | Admin | | Prod Mngr | | Inv Supv | | S. C. Mngr | | Norm Score | |
|---|---|---|---|---|---|---|---|---|---|---|
| Neuroticism | 10 / 28 | 17.7 | 7 / 26 | 15.4 | 5 / 24 | 12.7 | 6 / 22 | 13.6 | 4 / 38 | 19.07 |
| Extraversion | 20 / 43 | 30.4 | 16 / 44 | 29 | 26 / 38 | 32.1 | 25 / 46 | 33.5 | 14 / 40 | 27.69 |
| Openness | 12 / 32 | 24.3 | 24 / 32 | 27.2 | 11 / 37 | 25.4 | 21 / 37 | 27 | 14 / 40 | 27.03 |
| Agreeableness | 29 / 40 | 34 | 29 / 43 | 34.2 | 17 / 41 | 31.9 | 19 / 36 | 28.8 | 21 / 45 | 32.84 |
| Conscientiousness | 33 / 46 | 38.4 | 22 / 46 | 35.3 | 25 / 46 | 28.4 | 23 / 44 | 35.3 | 18 / 47 | 34.57 |
| Need for Cognition | -58 / 41 | 17.38 | -9 / 60 | 29 | -15 / 67 | 25 | 5 / 47 | 28.6 | -- / -- | NA |
| Customer Orientation | 178 / 203 | 192.6 | 115 / 202 | 170 | 117 / 216 | 185.6 | 162 / 213 | 191.8 | 159 / 187 | 187 |
| Marketing Orientation | 53 / 119 | 87 | 89 / 115 | 102 | 78 / 128 | 100.2 | 60 / 117 | 92.9 | -- / -- | 97.2 |

368

# APPENDIX 8

# PURCHASING

| Table 8-1<br>Purchasing Managers Job Family<br>Domain and Dimension Scores | | | |
|---|---|---|---|
| Dimension Description | Percentage | Scope | Rarity |
| **INTERPERSONAL DOMAIN** | | | |
| *Internal Contacts* | | | |
| Exchanging information/consulting | 100 | 60 | 44 |
| Supervising mid-level employees | 79 | 74 | 35 |
| Training | 79 | 66 | 54 |
| Supervising professional/technical employees | 71 | 68 | 37 |
| Selling or persuading | 64 | 36 | 21 |
| Supervising upper-level employees | 57 | 80 | 27 |
| Resolving conflicts | 57 | 61 | 35 |
| Marketing/sales employees | 43 | 84 | 44 |
| Supervising operative employees | 36 | 58 | 38 |
| Bargaining or negotiating | 21 | 62 | 30 |
| *External Contacts* | | | |
| Exchanging business related information | 100 | 52 | 23 |
| Customers–sales related | 86 | 72 | 31 |
| Supervising suppliers or contractors | 79 | 61 | 27 |
| Bargaining and negotiating | 79 | 56 | 20 |
| Resolving conflicts | 64 | 49 | 20 |
| Training | 57 | 48 | 21 |
| Exchanging special interest information | 50 | 51 | 12 |
| Public–nonsales related | 50 | 45 | 9 |
| Supervising business–related | 36 | 43 | 7 |

370

| Table 8-1 Purchasing Managers Job Family Domain and Dimension Scores | | | |
|---|---|---|---|
| Dimension Description | Percentage | Scope | Rarity |
| *Meetings* | | | |
| Attend meetings with outside nos-supervisors, technicians | 100 | 95 | 71 |
| Attend meetings with non-executives | 100 | 87 | 78 |
| Attend meetings to bargain or persuade | 100 | 85 | 47 |
| Attend meetings with non-supervisory employees | 100 | 78 | 52 |
| Attend meetings with executives | 100 | 73 | 49 |
| Chair meetings with non-executives | 93 | 88 | 76 |
| Chair meetings with non-supervisory employees | 93 | 85 | 56 |
| Chair meetings to bargain or persuade | 79 | 85 | 59 |
| Chair meetings with outside supervisors, technicians | 71 | 89 | 63 |
| Chair meetings with executives | 71 | 69 | 51 |
| Attend meetings with customers | 64 | 73 | 31 |
| Chair meetings with public or customers | 50 | 69 | 31 |
| Attend meetings with regulators, government or press | 21 | 83 | 34 |
| Chair meetings with regulators, government or press | 21 | 77 | 34 |

| Table 8-1<br>Purchasing Managers Job Family<br>Domain and Dimension Scores | | | |
|---|---|---|---|
| **Dimension Description** | **Percentage** | **Scope** | **Rarity** |
| *Frequency Ratings for Internal and External Contacts* | | | |
| Attend meetings | 100 | 84 | 49 |
| Bargaining or persuading | 100 | 74 | 41 |
| With supervisors, managers, and executives | 100 | 63 | 53 |
| Chair meetings | 93 | 82 | 45 |
| Business related contacts | 93 | 69 | 26 |
| With customers, marketing or sales | 86 | 43 | 45 |
| With public, press, or government officials | 57 | 35 | 13 |
| With laborers and operating employees | 36 | 35 | 36 |
| **DECISION-MAKING DOMAIN** | | | |
| Human resources management | 79 | 89 | 40 |
| Strategic planning-products and services | 79 | 85 | 37 |
| Financial-purchasing and budgeting | 71 | 95 | 60 |
| Production/operations management | 57 | 82 | 37 |
| *Frequency Ratings for Decisions* | | | |
| Finance–purchasing and budgeting | 93 | 84 | 39 |
| Operations and human resources | 86 | 57 | 25 |
| Human resources– authority and benefits | 79 | 77 | 33 |
| Planning products and services | 79 | 75 | 21 |

| Table 8-1<br>Purchasing Managers Job Family<br>Domain and Dimension Scores | | | |
|---|---|---|---|
| Dimension Description | Percentage | Scope | Rarity |
| MECHANICAL/PHYSICAL<br>DOMAIN | | | |
| Office machines | 100 | 52 | 24 |
| *Frequency Rating for Mechanical and*<br>*Physical Dimensions* | | | |
| Office machines | 100 | 65 | 87 |
| WORK CONTEXT DOMAIN | | | |
| Using numerical or verbal<br>information | 100 | 37 | 30 |
| Demanding personal situations | 79 | 40 | 22 |
| OVERALL RATINGS | | | |
| Meetings and contacts | 100 | 93 | 54 |
| Clerical/office activities/information<br>exchange | 100 | 82 | 53 |
| Public, stressful situations | 100 | 57 | 11 |
| Bargain/persuade/negotiate | 100 | 45 | 30 |
| Managerial decisions:<br>finance/purchasing/budgeting | 93 | 51 | 33 |
| Supervision, conflict resolution,<br>training | 93 | 47 | 31 |
| Contacts: customers, sales and<br>marketing related | 93 | 44 | 29 |
| Production/operations/HR decision<br>making | 86 | 45 | 29 |
| Product/service decisions, planning | 79 | 44 | 30 |
| Product/customer decision/planning | 64 | 43 | 28 |
| Technical/scientific machines | 50 | 41 | 27 |

**Table 8-2**
**Purchasing Managers**
**Knowledge Used**

| Knowledge Category | Used | By |
|---|---|---|
| *Finance and Accounting* | | |
| Purchasing | Constantly | 79 |
| Accounting | Weekly | 57 |
| Banking | Weekly | 29 |
| Commerce | Weekly | 29 |
| Budgeting | Monthly | 57 |
| Cash management | Monthly | 29 |
| Insurance | Yearly | 29 |
| *Human Resources* | | |
| Supervision and development | Daily | 57 |
| Selection and recruitment | Yearly | 64 |
| Job analysis | Yearly | 43 |
| Benefits and workers' comp. | Yearly | 29 |
| *Management and Production* | | |
| Inventory control and warehousing | Daily | 86 |
| Operations research | Weekly | 50 |
| Records control | Weekly | 21 |
| Strategic planning | Monthly | 71 |
| Project Management | Monthly | 36 |
| Manufacturing Management | Monthly | 29 |

| Table 8-2 Purchasing Managers Knowledge Used | | |
|---|---|---|
| **Knowledge Category** | **Used** | **By** |
| *Sales and Marketing* | | |
| **Marketing research and pricing** | Monthly | 57 |
| **Retailing, wholesaling** | Monthly | 43 |
| **Promotions** | Monthly | 36 |
| *Geography* | | |
| **World** | Weekly | 29 |
| *Mathematics* | | |
| **Multiplication, division,** | Constantly | 50 |
| **Addition, subtraction** | Constantly | 29 |
| **Advanced statistics** | Weekly | 36 |
| *Communications* | | |
| **Writing and editing–financial** | Daily | 57 |
| **Writing and editing–business text** | Daily | 50 |
| **Word processing** | Daily | 43 |
| **Public speaking** | Yearly | 36 |
| *Transportation* | | |
| **Trucking** | Daily | 64 |
| **Air/water** | Daily | 43 |
| **Rail** | Weekly | 36 |

| Table 8-3<br>Buyer Job Family<br>Domain and Dimension Scores | | | |
|---|---|---|---|
| Dimension Description | Percentage | Scope | Rarity |
| **INTERPERSONAL DOMAIN** | | | |
| *Internal Contacts* | | | |
| Exchanging information/consulting | 91 | 55 | 36 |
| Marketing/sales employees | 45 | 50 | 22 |
| Supervising operative employees | 36 | 53 | 25 |
| Supervising laborers | 27 | 31 | 16 |
| *External Contacts* | | | |
| Supervising suppliers or contractors | 82 | 50 | 18 |
| Exchanging business related information | 82 | 35 | 11 |
| Customers–sales related | 64 | 44 | 14 |
| Resolving conflicts | 45 | 40 | 15 |
| Bargaining and negotiating | 45 | 39 | 12 |
| Supervising business–related | 36 | 50 | 8 |

| Table 8-3 Buyer Job Family Domain and Dimension Scores | | | |
|---|---|---|---|
| **Dimension Description** | **Percentage** | **Scope** | **Rarity** |
| *Meetings Chaired or Attended* | | | |
| Attend meetings with non-executives | 100 | 42 | 24 |
| Attend meetings with non-supervisory employees | 64 | 40 | 15 |
| Chair meetings with non-executives | 45 | 47 | 24 |
| Attend meetings with executives | 45 | 33 | 12 |
| Attend meetings with outside non-supervisors, technicians | 27 | 65 | 23 |
| Attend meetings to bargain or persuade | 18 | 50 | 25 |
| *Frequency Ratings for Internal and External Contacts* | | | |
| Business related contacts | 100 | 52 | 18 |
| Attend Meetings | 100 | 45 | 21 |
| With supervisors, managers, and executives | 91 | 47 | 41 |
| With customers, marketing or sales | 82 | 29 | 34 |
| With laborers and operating employees | 45 | 63 | 58 |
| Chair meetings | 45 | 46 | 18 |
| **DECISION-MAKING DOMAIN** | | | |
| Purchasing and Budgeting | 54 | 86 | 42 |
| Production and operations management | 36 | 50 | 18 |

| Table 8-3 Buyer Job Family Domain and Dimension Scores | | | |
|---|---|---|---|
| Dimension Description | Percentage | Scope | Rarity |
| *Frequency Rating for Decision–Making Domain* | | | |
| **Purchasing and Budgeting** | 100 | 73 | 27 |
| **Production and Human Resources** | 45 | 36 | 45 |
| **MECHANICAL/PHYSICAL DOMAIN** | | | |
| **Office machines** | 100 | 63 | 28 |
| **Technical or scientific equipment** | 45 | 30 | 20 |
| *Frequency Rating for Mechanical and Physical Dimensions* | | | |
| **Office machines** | 100 | 69 | 88 |
| **Technical/scientific machines** | 45 | 5 | 48 |
| **WORK CONTEXT DOMAIN** | | | |
| **Using numerical or verbal information** | 100 | 34 | 28 |
| **Demanding personal situations** | 91 | 28 | 16 |
| **Sensory input from work environment** | 91 | 18 | 13 |
| **Unpleasant or hazardous work environment** | 45 | 35 | 11 |

| Table 8-3<br>Buyer Job Family<br>Domain and Dimension Scores | | | |
|---|---|---|---|
| Dimension Description | Percentage | Scope | Rarity |
| **OVERALL RATINGS** | | | |
| Clerical/office activities/information exchange | 100 | 79 | 47 |
| Meetings and contacts | 100 | 51 | 11 |
| Public, stressful situations | 100 | 43 | 6 |
| Technical/scientific machines | 45 | 57 | 34 |
| Blue collar/operative/service contact/supervisors | 45 | 29 | 22 |

| Table 8-4 Buyer Knowledge Used | | |
|---|---|---|
| **Knowledge Category** | **Used** | **By** |
| *Finance and Accounting* | | |
| **Purchasing** | **Constantly** | **55** |
| **Accounting** | **Weekly** | **27** |
| *Management and Production* | | |
| **Inventory control and warehousing** | **Daily** | **73** |
| **Records control** | **Weekly** | **36** |
| *Mathematics* | | |
| **Basic** | **Constantly** | **55** |
| *Transportation* | | |
| **Rail** | **Daily** | **55** |
| **Trucking** | **Weekly** | **55** |
| **Air/water** | **Weekly** | **36** |
| *Communication* | | |
| **Word Processing** | **Constantly** | **64** |
| **Writing, Editing–business text** | **Daily** | **27** |

| Table 8-5 Purchasing Job Family Domain Demographics | | | |
|---|---|---|---|
| Age | Average: 40 | | Age Range: 23-59 |
| Education | High School: 20% | College: 61% | Advanced Degree: 19% |
| Gender | | Male: 58% | Female: 42% |
| Years in Position | 0-3 yrs: 31% | 3-5 yrs: 7% | >5 yrs: 50% |
| Years with Firm | 0-3 yrs: 69% | 4-6 yrs: 19% | >7 yrs: 7% |

**Table 8-6**
**Personality, Need for Cognition, Customer Orientation, and Market Orientation**
**Purchasing Function**

| Dimension | Buyer | | Purch Mmgr | | Sample Means | | Norm Score | |
|---|---|---|---|---|---|---|---|---|
| Neuroticism | 11 / 30 | 17.3 | 8 / 18 | 13.5 | 0 / 40 | 14.5 | 4 / 38 | 19.1 |
| Extraversion | 24 / 37 | 30.1 | 20 / 41 | 30.9 | 11 / 47 | 31.9 | 14 / 40 | 27.7 |
| Openness | 21 / 35 | 25.6 | 19 / 41 | 27.1 | 11 / 43 | 25.9 | 14 / 40 | 27 |
| Agreeableness | 29 / 40 | 36.1 | 29 / 40 | 34.4 | 13 / 43 | 32.4 | 21 / 45 | 32.8 |
| Conscientiousness | 18 / 43 | 32.4 | 32 / 42 | 37.2 | 18 / 48 | 36.8 | 18 / 47 | 34.6 |
| Need for Cognition | 0 / 39 | 18.1 | -7 / 49 | 24.9 | -58 / 70 | 24.7 | -- / -- | NA |
| Customer Orientation | 169 / 206 | 188.3 | 176 / 198 | 186.6 | 109 / 216 | 189 | 159 / 187 | 187 |
| Marketing Orientation | 65 / 106 | 88.4 | 64 / 118 | 99.1 | 41 / 138 | 99.5 | – / -- | 97.2 |

382

# APPENDIX 9

# CUSTOMER SERVICE

| Table 9-1<br>Customer Service Representative Job Family<br>Domain and Dimension Scores | | | |
|---|---|---|---|
| Dimension Description | Percentage | Scope | Rarity |
| **INTERPERSONAL DOMAIN** | | | |
| *Internal Contacts* | | | |
| **Exchanging information/consulting** | 89 | 29 | 46 |
| **Marketing/sales employees** | 56 | 20 | 47 |
| **Training** | 24 | 22 | 32 |
| *External Contacts* | | | |
| **Exchanging business related information** | 84 | 13 | 35 |
| **Customers–sales related** | 76 | 23 | 63 |
| **Supervising suppliers or contractors** | 40 | 22 | 55 |
| *Meetings* | | | |
| **Attend meetings with non-executives** | 76 | 22 | 42 |
| **Attend meetings with executives** | 56 | 20 | 47 |
| **Attend meetings with non-supervisory employees** | 51 | 19 | 51 |
| *Frequency Ratings for Internal and External Contacts* | | | |
| **With customers, marketing or sales** | 91 | 55 | 57 |
| **With supervisors, managers, and executives** | 87 | 39 | 46 |
| **Attend meetings** | 78 | 21 | 49 |
| **Business related contacts** | 69 | 17 | 48 |

| Table 9-1<br>Customer Service Representative Job Family<br>Domain and Dimension Scores | | | |
|---|---|---|---|
| Dimension Description | Percentage | Scope | Rarity |
| **DECISION-MAKING DOMAIN** | | | |
| *Production, Human Resources,*<br>*Financial and Strategic Decisions* | | | |
| **Production/operations management** | 56 | 32 | 67 |
| **Human resources management** | 49 | 21 | 74 |
| **Strategic planning-products and services** | 44 | 17 | 55 |
| **Financial-purchasing and budgeting** | 29 | 26 | 64 |
| *Frequency Ratings for Decisions* | | | |
| **Operations and human resources** | 69 | 18 | 44 |
| **Finance–purchasing and budgeting** | 56 | 14 | 45 |
| **Human resources– authority and benefits** | 42 | 17 | 46 |
| **MECHANICAL/PHYSICAL DOMAIN** | | | |
| **Office machines** | 89 | 22 | 50 |
| **Precise physical activity** | 53 | 37 | 37 |
| *Frequency Rating for Mechanical and*<br>*Physical Dimensions* | | | |
| **Office machines** | 89 | 90 | 71 |

**Table 9-1**
**Customer Service Representative Job Family**
**Domain and Dimension Scores**

| Dimension Description | Percentage | Scope | Rarity |
|---|---|---|---|
| **WORK CONTEXT DOMAIN** | | | |
| Using numerical or verbal information | 98 | 30 | 31 |
| Demanding personal situations | 84 | 19 | 34 |
| Sensory input from work environment | 71 | 15 | 20 |
| **OVERALL  RATINGS** | | | |
| Public, stressful situations | 96 | 6 | 40 |
| Contacts: customers, sales and marketing related | 91 | 25 | 34 |
| Meetings and contacts | 90 | 9 | 55 |
| Technical/scientific machines | 40 | 30 | 47 |

| Table 9-2 Customer Service Representative Personnel Knowledge Used | | |
|---|---|---|
| **Knowledge Category** | **Used** | **By** |
| *Finance and Accounting* | | |
| **Accounting** | **Daily** | 16% |
| **Purchasing** | **Monthly** | 56% |
| *Management and Production* | | |
| **Records control** | **Constantly** | 24% |
| **Inventory control and warehousing** | **Daily** | 32% |
| **Strategic planning** | **Weekly** | 27% |
| *Sales and Marketing* | | |
| **Marketing research and pricing** | **Constantly** | 40% |
| **Sales** | **Constantly** | 31% |
| **Retailing, wholesaling** | **Constantly** | 22% |
| *Geography* | | |
| **Local and regional** | **Constantly** | 38% |
| *Mathematics* | | |
| **Basic** | **Constantly** | 27% |
| **Algebra/statistics** | **Daily** | 24% |

**Table 9-2**
**Customer Service Representative Personnel Knowledge Used**

| Knowledge Category | Used | By |
|---|---|---|
| *Communications* | | |
| Word processing | Constantly | 53% |
| Writing and editing–business text | Constantly | 47% |
| Writing and editing–financial | Constantly | 27% |
| *Transportation* | | |
| Trucking | Constantly | 60% |
| Rail | Constantly | 40% |
| Air/water | Weekly | 33% |

**Table 9-3**
**Customer Service Supervisor Job Family**
**Domain and Dimension Scores**

| Dimension Description | Percentage | Scope | Rarity |
|---|---|---|---|
| **INTERPERSONAL DOMAIN** | | | |
| *Internal Contacts* | | | |
| Supervising operative employees | 100 | 63 | 85 |
| Exchanging information/consulting | 100 | 24 | 37 |
| Supervising laborers | 88 | 38 | 49 |
| Resolving conflicts | 88 | 29 | 53 |
| Training | 50 | 46 | 63 |
| Supervising mid-level managers | 50 | 33 | 68 |
| Supervising professional/technical employees | 38 | 54 | 85 |
| Selling or persuading | 38 | 33 | 55 |
| Supervising upper-level executives | 25 | 25 | 82 |
| *External Contacts* | | | |
| Customers–sales related | 75 | 29 | 63 |
| Exchanging business related information | 75 | 25 | 58 |
| Resolving conflicts | 63 | 21 | 51 |
| Supervising suppliers or contractors | 50 | 26 | 70 |

| Table 9-3<br>Customer Service Supervisor Job Family<br>Domain and Dimension Scores | | | |
|---|---|---|---|
| **Dimension Description** | **Percentage** | **Scope** | **Rarity** |
| *Meetings* | | | |
| Attend meetings with non-executives | 88 | 17 | 37 |
| Chair meetings with non-executives | 63 | 26 | 52 |
| Chair meetings with non-supervisory employees | 63 | 25 | 66 |
| Attend meetings with non-supervisory employees | 50 | 28 | 48 |
| Attend meetings with executives | 50 | 28 | 68 |
| *Frequency Ratings for Internal and External Contacts* | | | |
| With laborers and operating employees | 100 | 68 | 74 |
| Attend Meetings | 100 | 36 | 62 |
| Chair meetings | 75 | 39 | 71 |
| With supervisors, managers, and executives | 63 | 43 | 51 |
| With customers, marketing or sales | 63 | 40 | 39 |
| Business related contacts | 63 | 22 | 61 |
| Bargaining or persuading | 25 | 48 | 90 |

| Table 9-3<br>Customer Service Supervisor Job Family<br>Domain and Dimension Scores | | | |
|---|---|---|---|
| Dimension Description | Percentage | Scope | Rarity |
| **DECISION-MAKING DOMAIN** | | | |
| *Production, Human Resources,*<br>*Financial and Strategic Decisions* | | | |
| Human resources management | 100 | 24 | 78 |
| Production/operations management | 88 | 44 | 89 |
| Financial-purchasing and budgeting | 88 | 23 | 53 |
| Strategic planning-entire businesses | 38 | 32 | 70 |
| Financial-investment, cash | 25 | 65 | 98 |
| *Frequency Ratings for Decisions* | | | |
| Operations and human resources | 88 | 49 | 84 |
| Finance–purchasing and budgeting | 88 | 26 | 53 |
| Human resource–authority, benefits | 75 | 26 | 67 |
| Planning products and services | 50 | 12 | 53 |
| Planning for whole organization | 38 | 26 | 51 |
| **MECHANICAL/PHYSICAL**<br>**DOMAIN** | | | |
| Office machines | 100 | 35 | 55 |
| Precise physical activity | 50 | 34 | 32 |
| Technical or scientific equipment | 50 | 27 | 40 |
| Gross physical activities | 50 | 21 | 48 |
| Off-road/utility vehicles | 38 | 33 | 79 |

| Table 9-3 | | | |
|---|---|---|---|
| Customer Service Supervisor Job Family | | | |
| Domain and Dimension Scores | | | |
| **Dimension Description** | **Percentage** | **Scope** | **Rarity** |
| *Frequency Rating for Mechanical and Physical Dimensions* | | | |
| Office machines | 100 | 72 | 50 |
| Technical/scientific machines | 50 | 50 | 5 |
| **WORK CONTEXT DOMAIN** | | | |
| Using numerical or verbal information | 100 | 32 | 42 |
| Sensory input from work environment | 100 | 24 | 32 |
| Demanding personal situations | 88 | 31 | 55 |
| **OVERALL RATINGS** | | | |
| Blue collar/operative/service contact/supervisors | 100 | 42 | 68 |
| Clerical/office activities/information exchange | 100 | 40 | 59 |
| Production/operations/HR decision making | 100 | 32 | 51 |
| Physical activity/work environment | 100 | 21 | 27 |
| Supervision, conflict resolution, training | 88 | 23 | 33 |
| Managerial decisions: finance/purchasing/budgeting | 88 | 22 | 29 |
| Contacts: customers, sales and marketing related | 75 | 21 | 27 |
| Technical/scientific machines | 50 | 39 | 67 |
| Strategic planning | 38 | 29 | 42 |

**Table 9-4**
**Customer Service Supervisor Job Family**
**Knowledge Used**

| Knowledge Category | Used | By |
|---|---|---|
| *Finance and Accounting* | | |
| Budgeting | Weekly | 38 |
| Purchasing | Weekly | 38 |
| Accounting | Weekly | 38 |
| Auditing and appraisal | Monthly | 25 |
| *Human Resources* | | |
| Selection and recruitment | Daily | 75 |
| First aid/emergency care | Daily | 25 |
| Occupational safety and health | Monthly | 75 |
| Job analysis | Monthly | 25 |
| Benefits and worker's comp | Yearly | 25 |
| Supervision and development | Yearly | 25 |
| *Management and Production* | | |
| Strategic planning | Weekly | 50 |
| Records control | Monthly | 63 |
| Operations research | Monthly | 25 |
| Inventory control and warehousing | Yearly | 63 |

**Table 9-4**
**Customer Service Supervisor Job Family**
**Knowledge Used**

| Knowledge Category | Used | By |
|---|---|---|
| *Sales and Marketing* | | |
| Sales | Yearly | 25 |
| Marketing research and pricing | Yearly | 25 |
| *Geography* | | |
| Local and regional | Monthly | 38 |
| *Mathematics* | | |
| Algebra/statistics | Monthly | 75 |
| Basic | Monthly | 38 |
| Advanced statistics | Yearly | 25 |
| *Computer* | | |
| Computer Operations | Yearly | 25 |
| *Social Sciences* | | |
| Economics | Yearly | 25 |
| *Communications* | | |
| Word processing | Monthly | 75 |
| Writing and editing–business text | Monthly | 63 |
| Public speaking | Monthly | 25 |
| Writing and editing–financial | Yearly | 50 |
| Telecommunications systems | Yearly | 25 |

| Table 9-4 Customer Service Supervisor Job Family Knowledge Used | | |
|---|---|---|
| **Knowledge Category** | **Used** | **By** |
| *Transportation* | | |
| Trucking | Monthly | 50 |


| Table 9-5 Customer Service Manager Job Family Domain and Dimension Scores | | | |
|---|---|---|---|
| **Dimension Description** | **Percentage** | **Scope** | **Rarity** |
| **INTERPERSONAL DOMAIN** | | | |
| *Internal Contacts* | | | |
| Exchanging information/consulting | 98 | 37 | 56 |
| Marketing/sales employees | 84 | 38 | 72 |
| Supervising mid-level managers | 63 | 26 | 57 |
| Training | 44 | 29 | 41 |
| Resolving conflicts | 42 | 21 | 43 |
| Bargaining or negotiating | 40 | 20 | 46 |
| Selling or persuading | 33 | 23 | 42 |
| Supervising upper-level executives | 28 | 15 | 42 |
| Entertaining | 23 | 19 | 45 |
| Supervising professional/technical employees | 21 | 28 | 56 |
| Supervising operative employees | 21 | 26 | 54 |

**Table 9-5**
**Customer Service Manager Job Family**
**Domain and Dimension Scores**

| Dimension Description | Percentage | Scope | Rarity |
|---|---|---|---|
| *External Contacts* | | | |
| Exchanging business related information | 95 | 19 | 48 |
| Customers–sales related | 93 | 37 | 80 |
| Supervising suppliers or contractors | 67 | 21 | 50 |
| Bargaining and negotiating | 67 | 15 | 47 |
| Resolving conflicts | 49 | 16 | 45 |
| Training | 47 | 12 | 36 |
| Supervising business–related | 42 | 7 | 48 |
| Entertaining | 26 | 13 | 43 |

**Table 9-5**
**Customer Service Manager Job Family**
**Domain and Dimension Scores**

| Dimension Description | Percentage | Scope | Rarity |
|---|---|---|---|
| *Meetings* | | | |
| Attend meetings with non-executives | 91 | 29 | 50 |
| Attend meetings with non-supervisory employees | 84 | 33 | 65 |
| Chair meetings with non-executives | 67 | 26 | 48 |
| Attend meetings with executives | 60 | 21 | 51 |
| Attend meetings to bargain or persuade | 58 | 1/ | 50 |
| Chair meetings with non-supervisory employees | 56 | 26 | 59 |
| Attend meetings with outside supervisors, technicians | 51 | 17 | 44 |
| Chair meetings to bargain or persuade | 40 | 19 | 40 |
| Attend meetings with customers | 33 | 17 | 49 |
| Chair meetings with executives | 21 | 25 | 44 |
| Chair meetings with outside supervisors, technicians | 21 | 22 | 49 |
| Chair meetings with public or customers | 21 | 15 | 40 |

| Table 9-5<br>Customer Service Manager Job Family<br>Domain and Dimension Scores | | | |
|---|---|---|---|
| Dimension Description | Percentage | Scope | Rarity |
| *Frequency Ratings for Internal and*<br>*External Contacts* | | | |
| With customers, marketing or sales | 100 | 76 | 79 |
| With managers, professionals, clerks | 98 | 40 | 47 |
| Attend Meetings | 95 | 28 | 60 |
| Business related contacts | 84 | 19 | 53 |
| Chair meetings | 74 | 23 | 51 |
| Bargaining or persuading | 56 | 24 | 53 |
| **DECISION-MAKING DOMAIN** | | | |
| *Production, Human Resources,*<br>*Financial and Strategic Decisions* | | | |
| Strategic planning-products and services | 56 | 19 | 57 |
| Production/operations management | 53 | 30 | 68 |
| Human resources management | 53 | 27 | 76 |
| Financial-purchasing and budgeting | 44 | 28 | 64 |
| *Frequency Ratings for Decisions* | | | |
| Finance–purchasing and budgeting | 74 | 19 | 52 |
| Operations and human resources | 63 | 26 | 55 |
| Planning products and services | 56 | 15 | 57 |
| Human resources– authority and benefits | 51 | 23 | 53 |

**Table 9-5**
**Customer Service Manager Job Family**
**Domain and Dimension Scores**

| Dimension Description | Percentage | Scope | Rarity |
|---|---|---|---|
| **MECHANICAL/PHYSICAL DOMAIN** | | | |
| Office machines | 98 | 28 | 58 |
| Technical or scientific equipment | 56 | 15 | 18 |
| *Frequency Rating for Mechanical and Physical Dimensions* | | | |
| Office machines | 98 | 90 | 73 |
| Precise physical activity | 65 | 39 | 40 |
| Technical/scientific machines | 56 | 48 | 5 |
| **WORK CONTEXT DOMAIN** | | | |
| Using numerical or verbal information | 100 | 31 | 40 |
| Sensory input from work environment | 95 | 17 | 24 |
| Unpleasant or hazardous work environment | 95 | 6 | 24 |
| Demanding personal situations | 88 | 27 | 50 |

| Table 9-5<br>Customer Service Manager Job Family<br>Domain and Dimension Scores | | | |
|---|---|---|---|
| **Dimension Description** | **Percentage** | **Scope** | **Rarity** |
| OVERALL  RATINGS | | | |
| Clerical/office activities/information exchange | 100 | 48 | 79 |
| Contacts: customers, sales and marketing related | 100 | 40 | 64 |
| Physical activity/work environment | 100 | 19 | 23 |
| External contact:  public, stressful situations | 100 | 9 | 52 |
| Meetings and contacts | 95 | 18 | 72 |
| Bargain/persuade/negotiate | 88 | 10 | 10 |
| Managerial decisions: finance/purchasing/budgeting | 74 | 15 | 18 |
| Supervision, conflict resolution, training | 70 | 14 | 16 |
| Production/operations/HR decision making | 65 | 23 | 31 |
| Technical/scientific machines | 56 | 31 | 51 |
| Product/customer decision/planning | 56 | 18 | 21 |

| Table 9-6 Customer Service Manager Personnel Knowledge Used | | |
|---|---|---|
| **Knowledge Category** | **Used** | **By** |
| *Finance and Accounting* | | |
| Budgeting | Constantly | 35 |
| Accounting | Weekly | 51 |
| Purchasing | Weekly | 26 |
| *Human Resources* | | |
| Selection and recruitment | Constantly | 28 |
| Supervision and development | Weekly | 40 |
| *Management and Production* | | |
| Inventory control and warehousing | Daily | 35 |
| Operations research | Daily | 35 |
| Records control | Monthly | 28 |
| *Sales and Marketing* | | |
| Sales | Weekly | 65 |
| Marketing research and pricing | Weekly | 51 |
| Promotion and advertising | Weekly | 23 |
| Retailing, wholesaling | Monthly | 33 |
| *Geography* | | |
| World | Daily | 26 |
| Local and regional | Monthly | 56 |

**Table 9-6**
**Customer Service Manager Personnel**
**Knowledge Used**

| Knowledge Category | Used | By |
|---|---|---|
| *Mathematics* | | |
| Basic | Monthly | 72 |
| *Communications* | | |
| Word processing | Weekly | 79 |
| Writing and editing–business text | Weekly | 67 |
| Writing and editing–financial | Weekly | 42 |
| Telecommunications systems | Yearly | 37 |
| *Transportation* | | |
| Air/water | Weekly | 40 |
| Rail | Weekly | 49 |
| Trucking | Monthly | 65 |

| Table 9-7<br>Customer Service Job Family Domain<br>Demographics | | | |
|---|---|---|---|
| Age | Average: 34 | | Age Range: 21 - 65 |
| Education | Some College: 15% | College: 55% | Advanced Degree: 10% |
| Gender | Male: 52% | | Female: 48% |
| Years in Position | 0-1 yrs: 45% | 2-3 yrs: 28% | >3 yrs: 28% |
| Years with Firm | 0-3 yrs: 58% | 4-8 yrs: 21% | >8 yrs: 21% |

**Table 9-8**
**Customer Service**
**Personality, Need for Cognition, Customer Orientation, and Market Orientation**

| Dimension | Rep | Rep Mean | Sup | Sup Mean | Mngr | Mngr Mean | Sample | Sample Means | Norm | Norm Score |
|---|---|---|---|---|---|---|---|---|---|---|
| Neuroticism | 3 / 30 | 15.7 | 6 / 25 | 13.2 | 3 / 31 | 14.7 | 0 / 40 | 14.5 | 4 / 38 | 19.1 |
| Extraversion | 20 / 43 | 32.5 | 30 / 41 | 36.4 | 17 / 46 | 33.3 | 11 / 47 | 31.9 | 14 / 40 | 27.7 |
| Openness | 14 / 36 | 25.7 | 16 / 33 | 25.6 | 13 / 43 | 25.1 | 11 / 43 | 25.9 | 14 / 40 | 27 |
| Agreeableness | 21 / 42 | 33.9 | 19 / 43 | 30.4 | 20 / 42 | 32.7 | 13 / 43 | 32.4 | 21 / 45 | 32.8 |
| Conscientiousness | 25 / 48 | 37.7 | 35 / 43 | 39.2 | 25 / 47 | 35 | 18 / 48 | 36.8 | 18 / 47 | 34.6 |
| Need for Cognition | -16 / 49 | 25.9 | 20 / 47 | 32.2 | -21 / 58 | 23.5 | -58 / 70 | 24.7 | -- / -- | NA |
| Customer Orientation | 143 / 215 | 193 | 174 / 216 | 199.3 | 139 / 216 | 190.1 | 109 / 216 | 189.6 | 159 / 187 | 187 |
| Marketing Orientation | 63 / 138 | 100.1 | 97 / 119 | 107.7 | 69 / 125 | 97.1 | 41 / 138 | 99.5 | -- / -- | 97.2 |

# APPENDIX 10

# HOW TO SET UP A TRAINING PLAN

This information was adapted from *How to Develop a Training Plan: A Resource Handbook* by Nadara Cole, (February 1997), Jackson, MS: Office of Vocational and Technical Education, Mississippi Department of Education.

# INTRODUCTION

The information presented serves as a guide to help industries construct and develop an effective training plan.

This guide gives many suggestions that a company should carefully consider when allocating time and effort to set up training. When selecting training projects, the following criteria may be helpful:
- What is the cost of this training program?
- How much time does the training program require?
- What are the potential benefits of this training program?
- Who could benefit from this training program?

## GETTING STARTED

Before starting a training program, complete the following initial steps:
- Assess your current training situation.
- Determine whether you need to make more comprehensive changes such as work restructuring, etc.
- Determine how training would fit within this larger effort.
- Form a Training Steering Team to set training policy.
- Complete a training needs assessment to determine if and to what extent training will solve existing performance problems.

## REMEMBER THAT TRAINING SHOULD BE DIRECTLY RELATED TO PERFORMANCE

The next set of steps includes the following:
- Determine personnel requirements
- Determine time requirements
- Determine financial requirements
- Determine policies and procedures
- Establish evaluation procedures
- Present to management for approval
- Develop training materials
- Deliver training
- Evaluate training

## REASONS FOR TRAINING YOUR WORKFORCE

Structured training can improve the following:
- Costs
- Safety
- Production
- Skill levels of operators
- Attitudes
- Job progression
- Job flexibility

Employee training efforts can solve many existing performance problems.

**Where should you start?**

The Training Needs Assessment is a good place to start. It can also help determine the design of the training program including the best methods of presenting the training.

The assessment must accumulate all relevant and available data for review and analysis. The Training Needs Assessment document should be formal and contain the data gathered, data analysis, observations, and recommendations. Once all necessary data are collected, analyzed, and written into an assessment report, the assessment must be validated. This is accomplished in a review with key operators, supervisors, managers, and selected staff. Complete agreement of those reviewing is not necessary, but the validity of the data collected must be assured. Any needed changes are made, and the report is updated and prepared for presentation to management. After this, the team should determine the most effective types of training.

The assessment should identify the following:
- What costs can be reduced?
- How can productivity be improved?
- How can product quality be enhanced?
- How can performance be increased?
- How ready is the workforce for training?
- How committed is management to improvement?

Items for review could include the following:

| | |
|---|---|
| • Business strategy | • Current performance |
| • Policies | • Operations |
| • Problems | • Industry standards |
| • Organizational Climate | • Regulations |

**Assessment of training needs is a lot of hard work. It takes time, commitment, and effort.**

Some methods for assessing performance and training needs include:
- Job analysis and classification (like the CMQ).
- Gathering and organizing data.
- Individual interviews with managers, supervisors, operators, technicians, quality staff, technical staff, and others.

Remember that the best training is directly related to performance! And if training is not needed, do not do it.

## Gathering and Organizing the Data

Data gathering techniques could include the following:
- Observation
- Questionnaires (like the CMQ)
- Interviews

Some essential data could include the following:

- Organizational strategy
- Organizational goals
- Customers
- Employee turnover
- Grievances/complaints
- Job analyses
- Job performance standards
- Job descriptions
- Equipment
- Safety requirements
- Incidents/accidents
- Maintenance requests
- Operations down time
- Governmental or local regulations
- Cost of quality

## PLANNING THE EMPLOYEE TRAINING PROGRAM

The Training Needs Assessment provides information for designing the employee training program. Proper design plays a leading role in the development of a program that will effectively transfer knowledge and skills.

### Management and Coordination

Line managers should take responsibility for training their employees, in conjunction with a training manager/coordinator. The coordinator will usually report to human resources.

Success depends on the knowledge, technical and interpersonal skills, and aggressiveness of the training manager/coordinator. The key to success is management's commitment to the training project.

### The Training Steering Team

Any organization that is serious about training its employees, supervisors, and managers should have a Training Steering Team. An upper level manager should head the steering team. The training manager is a permanent member of the team, while supervisors and employees should rotate on and off the team. This team functions as the policy-making body for all organizational training. Included among the steering team's responsibilities are the following:

- Set training policy
- Approve training plans
- Review training program objectives and program effectiveness
- Allocate resources
- Review training status reports
- Review initial, refresher, and supplemental ongoing training

- Communicate and build acceptance of the training program with all employees

**Types of Employee Training**

There are three categories of training:

- Initial Training: Initial training is specific to the job and should be given when an employee is newly assigned to a process.
- Refresher Training: Refresher training supports initial training by reenforcing competencies that may not be used every day, but may be used in the future.
- Supplemental Training: Supplemental training supports initial training and provides new information that updates and expands the competencies already developed.

**Initial Training**

General orientation to the company is provided on the first day of work and should include benefits, policies, procedures, and introductions. Safety and any required regulatory training are an essential part of initial training. Initial training is usually provided before the employee enters the work area and is refreshed and supplemented in the work area on a regular basis.

Whatever the state of existing training, once the training need is recognized, initial training must be provided. All new employees must get initial training on the process and job in which they will work. To be effective, this training must be structured and consistent.

Structured training is planned, scheduled, followed, and formatted. This type of training uses a performance-based training medium that is performance-based. It is also tested and delivered by a knowledgeable trainer. Structured training allows practice, requires demonstration, and provides follow-up.

Structured process and job-specific training avoids placing the new employee into a new work environment with the first available operator as a trainer. To do so may ingrain poor work habits, inconsistent performance, and poor attitudes.

**Safety and Regulatory Training**

Plants using highly hazardous chemicals are required by law to provide significant training in safety, hazardous materials, and hazardous processes. Other companies not under these mandates have adopted some of the concepts for training and safety.

Safety training should be started on the first day on the job. The training should be structured and provide testing. This training should include at least proper use and maintenance of protective equipment, location and training in use of Material Safety Data Sheets (MSDS), and first aid/CPR.

410

First day safety training may require 1 to 2 hours. First aid and CPR will likely come later, but should occur within the first 12 months on the job. It is essential that safety training be emphasized in all other training materials about the process and the job. Refresher and supplemental training is also necessary to achieve a safe workplace.

## Process Specific Training

Process specific training teaches employees how the work they are doing supports the overall process. It affects downstream processes and customers and is affected by upstream processes and suppliers. This training enables the employee to make better decisions.

Good technical training for operators should include process training. This process specific training should include all "need to know" information about the process in which the trainee is working or will work. Every operator should know how his/her activity affects the overall process of manufacturing the product, and what happens upstream and downstream from that operation. Usually, training materials have to be developed for this level of training, since process training depends on the particular firm. As such, the unique processes that reside within the organization require unique process training development. Most off-the-shelf materials will not meet this need.

Trainers must know the systems, equipment, procedures, and safety requirements in the process. These trainers should understand the overall production process with particular emphasis on the immediately preceding and succeeding processes to the one being trained. In other words, it is important to know the internal customer and the internal supplier.

## Job Specific Training

Job specific training is absolutely essential to the effective operation of any process. Effective job specific training includes certain features:
- Job specific training materials, formatted with objectives, demonstration, practice, and evaluation.
- Job specific trainers that know "how to train."
- Realistic and followed training schedules.
- Testing.
- Recognition of achievement, with qualification sign-off as each training segment is successfully completed and tested.
- Continuing planned job observation.
- Refresher and supplemental job specific training.

Job specific training may be conducted on the job in a quasi-production capacity, in a classroom, or on a specific training line in the plant. As the trainees qualify in each job training segment, they perform that segment in production under close supervision. Job specific training is generally not

411

conducted continuously all day, five days a week, but spread over a longer period, typically up to about six weeks. The training, even though provided in parts, must be scheduled in writing and followed without fail.

## Refresher Training

Refresher training is mandated for some industries that manufacture or handle highly hazardous chemicals. Refresher training must meet regulatory requirements. Although not mandated for all companies, refresher training for all employees ensures competency and integrates the latest process changes.

## Supplemental Training

Supplemental training is needed to provide additional information after the initial training. This training builds on information, competencies, and skills that the employee already has. This type of training is the basis for successful on-going training programs.

## THE TRAINING PLAN

### The Planning Procedure

The design process concludes with the development of a Training Plan. This plan must be comprehensive, precise, practical, and possible. Successful planning is usually accomplished by following a rather precise procedure including:

- Detailed analysis of the situation or a Training Needs Assessment.
- Determination of priorities.
- Determination of objectives.
- Determination of types of training and which types to use.
- Determination of manpower requirements.
- Determination of time requirements.
- Determination of financial requirements.
- Determination of constraints.
- Outline of policies and procedures.
- Establishment of measurable check-points.
- Establishment of contingency plans.

## HOW TO DEVELOP TRAINING MATERIALS

### In-House Materials

In most cases, training materials should be developed from scratch or rewritten to customize the training to the specific needs of the firm. Trainees learn more quickly and retain material longer if they relate training directly to their day-to-day life or to their specific work.

412

Some existing materials that may be modified, customized, and rewritten include the following:

- Old training manuals
- Operating procedures
- Operating manuals
- Vendor manuals
- Manufacturing specifications

- Job analysis
- Job task analysis
- Job descriptions
- Performance standards
- Engineering/maintenance manuals

## Training Materials

All training manuals in the plant should follow the same format. Courses should be made up of modules or units which are made up of lessons. It is important that lessons be formatted with the following:

- Title of Lesson should be descriptive, clear, relate to the lesson objectives, and trigger the trainee's existing knowledge on the subject.
- Objectives should describe exactly what the trainee must do to demonstrate mastery of each topic or skill.
- Introduction should capture the trainee's attention, motivate the trainee, and provide an overview of the lesson's content.
- Lesson should contain "descriptive" or "how to" information.
- Exercises should not be tests but learning aids. Such exercises provide immediate feedback to the trainee on how they are doing. Exercises should relate directly to lesson objectives.
- Summary should provide a review of lesson content, re-motivate the trainee, and preview the next lesson.

Printed materials include operator workbooks, instructor guides, models, illustrations, feedback exercises, and tests. Other training materials and aids could include the following:

- Video
- Interactive video
- CD-ROM
- Simulators

- Computer self-paced
- Written off-the-shelf
- Film
- Slides

## EVALUATING THE TRAINING

All employee training programs must be constantly evaluated to ensure that they produce and continue to produce qualified employees. Evaluation must be continuous, informal, formal, planned, documented, communicated, and result in improved employee performance. Evaluation should be designed into the training program before any training takes place.

**The Pilot Training Project**

A valuable, but often under utilized, component of employee training is the use of pilot training projects. There may be no better way to validate the training plan, curriculum, trainers, materials, and trainees than to conduct a pilot training course. The results can be used to identify opportunities for improvement or fine-tuning of all features of the program.

Pilot courses should be designed as controlled situations in which trainees' current performance on the job is measured before training and after training. The effectiveness of the training, or lack thereof, is measured in the resulting trainee performance. Pilot courses offer some answers to the ever-present question of the employee's training return on investment.

**Evaluating The Training**

There is and has been a continuing search for an accurate, direct, and simple means for deterring the dollar results of training, for example, the return on training cost. It is difficult because there are so many factors outside of training that effect performance. However, there are two basic types of training program evaluations which include the following.

- Formative Evaluations – Pilot courses are one of these. This type of evaluation measures the effectiveness of the training program during its implementation.
- Summative Evaluations – This type measures the value of the training program after trainees have completed the course.

# SAMPLE TRAINING MODULES

# KANBAN TRAINING MODULE

This module was used to train fifty employees in a small manufacturing plant in Kanban. Ed Wamble of the Skill/Tech Center at East Mississippi Community College gave the training in two, two-hour classroom sessions. He then assisted in the Kan Ban implementation at each of approximately 15 work stations - a total of eight hours.

Total cost to the firm was less than $100 for materials. According to Mr. Wamble, if another trainer had been used, the cost would still have been less than $1,000.

# INTRODUCTION

This module provides a comparison of push and pull systems in manufacturing companies. Pull systems emphasize customer demands in each step of the production process. Kanbans, or visible signals, are used by pull systems to move the product through the manufacturing process in the same rate as the product is being consumed.

## CONCEPTS OF KANBAN MODULE

Upon completion of this module, each participant should understand the following concepts:
- The meaning of push and pull systems in manufacturing.
- The meaning and importance of the use of Kanbans, or signals, to stimulate production.
- The methods of determining the number of kanbans needed in the manufacturing process, the number of pieces per kanban, and the re-order point.
- An understanding of how to create a kanban system.

### Objectives of Kanban Module

Upon completion of this module, the participant should be able to complete a summary activity concerning the following topics:
- Recognize characteristics of push systems and pull systems
- List various forms of kanban system
- Create a kanban system for a given product by determining:
  - ▸ the unit quantity needed in a kanban system
  - ▸ the number of  kanbans needed in a kanban system
  - ▸ the ROP (Re-Order Point)

### Push Systems Versus Pull Systems

Push and pull systems exist in all types of businesses that move or sell products. Understanding the purpose of the manufacturing process as either a push system or a pull system is important. With this knowledge, cell operators become better customers and suppliers inside the plant.

### Understanding Push And Pull Systems

A push system is a system in which the maker of the products determines the rate of production. Most traditional manufacturing companies can be described as push systems. The customer does not determine the production rate or the quantity of the product produced.

The term pull system describes a manufacturing system in which the customer determines the rate of production.

417

# DIFFERENCES BETWEEN PUSH AND PULL SYSTEMS
## IN RETAIL BUSINESSES

Many differences exist between pull and push systems. These differences apply to every kind of business that sells or makes a product. The ordering procedures and inventory counting procedures of a grocery store can serve as an illustration of both a push and a pull system. A small (#2 size) can of Brand X Cut Green Beans is used for this illustration.

In an old grocery store system, the store determines a standard amount of green beans for delivery each week. The sales reports over a long period show the rate of consumption for this product. For example, the average rate of consumption per week might be 10 cases containing 24 cans per case, or 240 cans. This standard amount is probably closer to 8 cases with a buffer of 2 cases "just in case." The 2 buffer cases are to make sure that the store does not run out. An inventory is taken once every 4 weeks to determine if the standard order needs adjusting.

What usually happens in this type of system? The grocery store chain features "specials" for sale at a reduced price. One of these specials happens to be Brand X Cut Green Beans. The rate of consumption goes up, and the grocery store runs out of the product because of the delay in taking inventory. To compensate for this outage, the order quantity for the green beans is increased from 10 to 14 cases. A delay in the weekly delivery causes the grocery store to run out again. To compensate for this second outage, the order quantity is increased to 16 cases. In the meantime, the rate of consumption has dropped down to 8 cases a week. Now the number of cans of green beans being ordered doubles the number of cases being consumed. The extra cases of brand X Cut Green Beans are stacked sky-high in the storage room. Because of the delay factor in taking inventory, it is several weeks before anyone realized what has happened. In eight weeks of ordering too many cases, 64 extra cases, or 1,536 cans, of Brand X Cut Green Beans are in the storage room. At 50 cents per can, the grocery store is now holding $768 in nonvalue-added inventory.

Another cost factor of this inventory is storage space. The floor space used by this extra inventory takes away space from products that are in demand. Workers must go around the extra cases as they unload trucks and move stock. There is a chance of damage to this stock. The food inside the cans runs a greater risk of spoiling.

Grocery stores also can have a pull system. For this example, a more recent grocery store system serves as an illustration. The customer walks into the grocery store and purchases 2 cans of Brand X Cut Green Beans. The cashier waves the cans over the bar-code to show the price of the green beans. This bar-code reader sends a "signal" that two cans of Brand X Cut Green Beans are removed from inventory. When enough cans are removed, another "signal" tells someone to re-order Brand X Cut Green Beans. This system removes the delay factor of taking inventory. Now, stock workers do other work like arranging displays for the customer—work that adds value to the business. This pull system stops over-ordering and reduces storage room problems. The following chart summarized the differences between push and pull systems.

| COST OR RISK FACTOR | TRADITIONAL PUSH SYSTEM | QUICK RESPONSE PULL SYSTEM |
|---|---|---|
| Risk of running out | Medium to high risk | Low to medium risk |
| Risk of over-ordering | High | Low to zero |
| Cost of controlling inventory | High | Low |
| Cost of "holding" materials | High | Low to zero |
| Inconvenience to workers | High | Low |
| Risk of damage (dents. etc.) | High | Low |
| Risk of spoilage (rust, etc.) | High | Low |

**Differences in Push and Pull Systems in Manufacturing Businesses**
These differences apply to any business that sells a product. These differences are especially important to manufacturing businesses because the cost of raw materials is higher (as a percentage of total costs) than in most retail businesses.

***Customer Demand.*** The one critical difference between push systems and pull systems for manufacturing businesses involves customer demand. A push system operates on an estimate of demand, a forecasted schedule based upon old consumption rate records. A pull system operates on **real customer demand!** Study the following chart for a comparison between Traditional and Quick Response Manufacturing Systems.

| TRADITIONAL PUSH SYSTEM | QUICK RESPONSE PULL SYSTEM |
|---|---|
| Order quantities by anticipated demand | Order quantities by real demand |
| Large batches | Small batches or "Lot Size of One" |
| Large amounts of paperwork are required to track all the inventory through the plant | A simple signal starts the movement of parts; process documentation is kept at the work center |
| Parts are sent to the next operation whether the next operation is ready for them or not | Parts are made only if the next operation needs them to meet production schedule |
| Extra inventory covers up problems in the operating system; for example, scrap is not a major problem if there are extra parts | Interferences (delays to production) and quality problems are forced to surface; one is compelled to resolve them right away |

**Push System Disadvantages.**

A push system creates many nonvalue-added tasks in traditional manufacturing plants. Tasks such as issuing jobs, stuffing folders and prints, or closing jobs on the computer are necessary because of the large amount of inventory. A large amount of paperwork is created because the company cannot see directly if the materials and products are where they should be. All this paperwork activity creates problems and something always goes wrong. There is a large margin of error in push systems. Often, workers believe that parts are in the plant that the company does not have. Or the reverse: Workers believe that parts are not in the plant when they are simply misplaced.

Extra inventory and the longer cycle times often hide manufacturing problems in a push system. When there is plenty of extra material to use, scrap material is not a major problem. Having the extra inventory and the longer cycle time per product allows the company to avoid dealing with the causes of the scrap. Causes such as defective processes or worn-out tools tend to be ignored.

Certain manufacturing problems are easier to live with if the inventory level is high and the cycle time is longer. Problems such as travel distances, lengthy setups, rework, or anything that takes longer than it should, fall into this group. The problem is that both conditions (high inventory levels and longer cycle times) hide problems that cost the company money.

The high cost of holding inventory has made many companies lower their inventory levels without doing anything about the problems that caused the high levels of the inventory. The defective aspects of the system that made so much inventory necessary are not improved. The result of lowering inventory levels without correcting the problems is often disastrous. The shortage of parts leads to an increase in overtime and increases the chance of missing shipment dates.

Before reducing the amount of inventory, each production cell should be examined to reduce its material idle times, its nonvalue-added activities, and the length of its setup operations.

## INTRODUCTION TO KANBANS IN PULL SYSTEMS

In the pull system example of the grocery store, the bar-code reader sends a "signal" to order more products. This situation is different in most manufacturing plants because each step of the manufacturing process is more complex. It is not a simple matter of unloading cans and putting them on a shelf. In a factory, the pull system may need a variety of ways to signal that more materials or parts are needed from one operation to the next.

### The Purpose of Kanban

*Kanban*, a Japanese term, means visible sign or signal. Taiichi Ohno developed the first successful pull system for Toyota Motor Company in Japan. Ohno used the term, *Kanban*, to refer to the cards he used to show when it was time to move materials from one production operation to another.

Before a reliable kanban system can be started in a manufacturing plant, it is important to know why kanbans are needed. Kanbans reduce the distance between the user and the provider of the part. Kanbans connect the suppliers (the providers) to the users (the customers) in the manufacturing process. The first step involves changing everyone's attitude about production and the steps in the production process (or sequence of operations). The production process must be thought of as a chain of customers and suppliers.

**Every production worker is both a customer and supplier to other production workers.** Operator A is the supplier to Operator B. Operator B is a customer of Operator A and the supplier to Operator C. Operator C is a customer of Operator B and the supplier to Operator D, and so on.

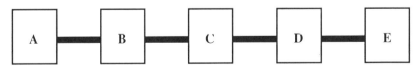

If Operator A and Operator B are next to each other, the customer (Operator B) can communicate directly with the supplier (Operator A). The "signal" or "kanban" can be an oral request. When the operators in Cell A and

Cell B are separated from each other in time, they need a system of signals to maintain this connection.

**Creating a Kaban System**

Create a kanban system to correspond to a manufacturing need. Many factories use kanban systems in the wrong way. The kanban systems do not match the production needs or the kanban system is not used in the way it was intended. Often, the result is to blame the kanban or pull the system for the failure without examining the way the kanban system was handled. Follow the steps in the chart on the next page when building a new kanban system.

| 1. Define Customer Requirements | - What is the average customer demand?<br>- How much fluctuation is there in demand?<br>- What are the customer cell's delivery requirements? |
|---|---|
| 2. Define Supplier Capacity | - What is the lead time required for delivery?<br>- What constraints exist on the supplier's ability to deliver: lengthy setups, machine capacity limitations, etc.? |
| 3. Use Kanban Selection Criteria to select or adapt the most appropriate type of kanban | In this module, see subsection D. - Types of Kanbans |
| 4. Use Customer Requirements and Supplier Capacity Limitations to determine lot sizes and re-order points | In this module, see the section Calculating Kanbans |
| 5. Precisely define and document kanban routes and their locations | Leave NO room for confusion about how the kanban is supposed to work. |

**Kanban System Considerations**

Create a kanban system to communicate a message. This message signals that something needs to be moved or something needs to be made. Consider the following points when creating or setting up a kanban system:
- The size of the object to be moved.
- How many objects will be moved.
- How much distance separates the sender and receiver.
- How much information needs to be sent.
- What kind of information needs to be sent.

These considerations only represent a starting point; there could be other considerations important to the cell. The main goal is to strive for a smooth, uninterrupted flow of the product. Strive for a processing flow that equals the rate of consumption of the product. This flow represents making only the products needed, in the quantity needed, and at the time needed.

### Types of Kanban

The kanban signals the production worker to make a product, move a product, or do both. A kanban acts like a message that has a sender and a receiver. The sender of the message is the customer or person who needs the parts. The receiver of the message is the supplier of the parts. Kanban systems can take various forms.

*Verbal.* In a verbal kanban, information is passed informally between a sender and receiver if both are located near each other. The machine operator responds to an oral request from an assembler. **Select this form if the receiver and sender of the message can hear each other without leaving their work center.**

*Containers.* Another type of signal can be the container itself. Every container holds a set quantity of the needed materials. The quantity is determined before the kanban system is put into operation. An empty container signals the operator to make or move parts. The rate of production for making parts is determined by the number of containers and how often the containers are used.

Different types of containers are used to meet a kanban need. Safety and space limitations are the only restrictions affecting the type of container selected. Select the container type that fits the kanban needs of the work center. The following examples represent different types of containers:
* Containers may be mobile (movable) or stationary (fixed in one place).
* Movable racks or shelves can hold and move a variety of parts.
* Tailor-made peg stands or egg crates can divide a variety of small parts into groups of classifications.
* Pigeon holes on an "egg-crate" board can be a signal to make or order more parts and refill the hole.
* Containers with lines or containers stacked in layers keeps on-hand quantities constant even if the rate of consumption changes. This method also can be used to adjust the on-hand quantity if the rate of consumption changes.

Be careful of uniform containers. Containers made from the same materials or the same type are confusing. Tailor-make the container by building it to hold the particular type of parts needed and only that type. By using a tailor-made container, one that is different from other containers, the chance of filling a container with the wrong parts is reduced. Use imagination in designing kanban containers.

*Squares*. Another pull signal often used is the kanban square. It is a space, or square, that acts like a kanban container. When the square is empty, it acts as a signal that it should be filled. The square can be a marked off area on a table, shelf, or shop floor. Movable containers on wheels should have a "parking space' drawn directly on the floor. Paint the outline directly on the shop floor. Paint the outline directly on the shop floor in the exact size of the container.

*Electronic*. Computer messages or faxes also can be kanbans. Usually, computer messages and faxes are not attempted within the same plant. They are often used to get materials from vendors in other plants. Materials are "pulled" from vendors by an EDI (Electronic Data Interchange) linkup.

This computer hookup between two plants reduces the paperwork involved in constantly reordering and repaying for supplies.

*Cards*. The following comparisons show how kanban cards differ in form and use:
- The card size can be large or small.
- The card can be color-coded or one color.
- The number of cards can vary from one card to several cards.
- The cards can be used from cell to cell, subplant to subplant, or plant to plant.
- The cards can contain a small amount of information or a great deal of information. How complicated the product is to make and how often the part is manufactured determine how much information is needed on the card.

Kanban cards, while they differ in several ways, tend to have similar characteristics. Kanban cards are usually pre-printed and laminated (plastic-coated). The kanban card contains the part name, the part number, the standard quantity, the name of the customer cell, and the name of the supplier cell. The simplest type of kanban card contains only a small amount of information and is used for a high-volume item.

## Calculating Kanbans
The main purpose of calculating kanbans is to bring the manufacturing process closer to Just-in-Time production. The goal of JIT production is worth striving for. Continuously improving Just-in-Time production means continuously reducing waste.

## Procedure For Calculating Kanbans

Determining the number of kanbans is not a one time activity. It may be necessary to add a small stock "buffer" to the kanban when setting up a new cell or starting a new kanban system. This small buffer compensates for problems such as change-over times, or interferences like downtime, line imbalance, and long lead times. After solving the problems, reduce the buffer stock by lowering the kanban quantity or the number of kanbans in the system.

Study the following chart to review the items that must be determined when creating a kanban system

| The Kanban Quantity | How many units of the part number or product should be in each kanban. |
|---|---|
| The Number of Kanbans | How many kanbans (cards or other signal devices) should be in the system. When using a card system, use the terms one-card, two-card, or three-card system. |

The long-term goal of any kanban system is to operate JIT (Just-in-Time). The immediate goal is to "Manage by Eye"—to know when to make a product, in the quantity needed by a visible signal. This visual sign or signal is a message from the next customer in the plant showing the parts needed. There is no set procedure to follow in determining the number of kanbans needed. Two questions, however, must be answered first. Identify the requirements of the customer; then determine the capacity of the supplier.

The operators and cells inside the plant are customers and suppliers to each other. An internal customer requirement is as important as a field customer requirement. An internal supplier capacity limitation is as important as the capacity limitation of an outside supplier or vendor. The lead-time requirement is an example of capacity limitation and presents the amount of time that the supplier needs between a request for a product and the delivery of the product.

The following charts show the type of questions that determine Customer Requirements and Supplier capacity.

**Define Customer Requirements**

| | |
|---|---|
| What is the average customer demand? | How many units per day or per week does the customer need? Look at recent history. What is the average per week, per day? |
| How much fluctuation is there in demand? | Look at the highs and lows in usage. In the recent past, how widely did the weekly usage change from the weekly average? |
| What are the customer's delivery requirements? | For example, does the customer cell not have enough storage space to receive more than a certain amount at one time? |

**Define Supplier Capacity**

| | |
|---|---|
| What is the lead time required? | How much time does the supplier cell or the supplier work center need? Are there setup considerations? Product mix? |
| What constraints exist on the supplier's ability to deliver? | For example, are the setup times at the supplier's station at present long enough that a batch must be a weekly quantity? |

The kanban system must match the supplier's capacity with the customer's requirements. If the customer cell has limited storage space or the supplier work center has long setup times, then the condition must change and the kanban system must be adjusted to fit the condition. The lengthy setup time in the supplier's operation should eventually be reduced. However, the customer and the supplier should not dictate the terms of the relationship, especially terms that would harm the other cell's operation. The kanban system must find a solution which matches the supplier's current capacity and the customer's requirements.

426

## Example of a Kanban System

Use the following charts to set up a kanban system for a company.

### Define Customer Requirements

| | |
|---|---|
| What is the average customer demand? | |
| How much fluctuation is there in demand? | |
| What are the customer's delivery requirements? | |

### Define Supplier Capacity

| | |
|---|---|
| What is the lead time required? | |
| What constraints exist on the supplier's ability to deliver? | |

### Define Re-Order Point.

After determining the customer requirement and the supplier capacity, determine the re-order point for the product which covers the product's lead time. ROP is the minimum number needed by the customer cell to make sure that the cell does not run out.

| | |
|---|---|
| The Average Weekly Usage is divided by the number of work days in the week. | |
| The Average Daily Usage is multiplied by the number of lead time days. | |

Determining the kanban quantity and the number of kanbans.

Performing this step is always different for each situation because one procedure does not always work in every situation.

# REVIEW EXERCISE

1. Name 4 cost or risk factors that improve when a company changes from a push system to a pull system.

a)_____     c)_____

b)_____     d)_____

2. Each of the following statements describes characteristics of either a push system or a pull system. Determine which type each statement describes by circling the correct answer.

| | |
|---|---|
| **Push or Pull** | 1. Order quantities for parts are based upon anticipated demand. Anticipated demand is based upon recent history of use. |
| **Push or Pull** | 2. Order quantities for parts are based upon actual sales or upon restocking parts because of the consumption of actual sales |
| **Push or Pull** | 3. Batch sizes tend to last 1 to 5 weeks, to reduce the frequency of changeovers and increase machine use. |
| **Push or Pull** | 4. Batch sizes tend to last 1 to 5 days, to reduce the lot size in downstream processes, and place a premium on reducing the length of changeovers. |
| **Push or Pull** | 5. Parts are completed for (and perhaps sent to ) the next operation, whether the next operation is ready for them or not. |
| **Push or Pull** | 6. Parts are made only if the next operation needs them to meet current production schedule. |
| **Push or Pull** | 7. Interferences like machine downtime, rework, or remakes are often compensated for by a buffer stock of parts made up in advance of the production schedule. |
| **Push or Pull** | 8. Interferences like machine downtime, rework, or remakes cause measurable production delays that must be resolved. |

3. Name the first two steps in any kanban calculation.

to define_____ and to define _____

4. Name five (5) types of kanban forms.

a) _____     d) _____

b) _____     e) _____

c) _____

5. Fill in the blank with the correct answer. The third step in kanban calculations is to define the ____, which is the minimum number of units needed in the customer cell to make sure that the cell does not run out. The final step in calculating a kanban is to determine the ____ and the _____ of____.

428

# SHIPPING TRAINING MODULE

# TERMS AND DEFINITIONS

CATEGORY: A category is a set of training materials which includes a task list for each department, written instruments, performance guides and study materials for each task.

PERFORMANCE

GUIDE: A series of steps required for performance of a task arranged in the sequence ordinarily followed.

PERFORMANCE

OBJECTIVE: A statement in precise, measurable terms of a behavior to be exhibited by a learner under specified conditions, including a standard of performance.

RELATED

INFORMATION: Related information gives more detailed information or explanation of abbreviated words or technical terms that are sometimes difficult to understand or follow.

TASK: A unit of work activity, which constitutes logical and necessary steps in the performance of a duty. A task has a definite beginning and ending point in its accomplishment and consists of two or more steps.

TASK ANALYSIS: The process of reviewing elements of a job for the purpose of improving training program content across program levels.

TOOLS AND

EQUIPMENT: The tools, equipment, and materials needed to perform a task.

A category is a set of training materials which include a task list for each department, written instruments, performance guides, and study material(s) for each task. The training materials in each category support the associate's advancement on a pay scale in each department after successful completion of the training session. The associate can also undergo cross training and advance on pay levels in other departments or all departments.

This manual is divided into three categories. Category 1 is the primary level of shipping. Category 2 is the intermediate level of shipping, while category 3 is the advanced level of shipping. Each trainee associate must learn category 1 tasks, performance guides, and objectives before proceeding to categories 2 and 3, respectively. The tasks for these categories include the following:

## CATEGORY 1

- Load the parts on the trailer with the lift truck.
- Measure the parts with a tape.
- Cut material to size.
- Determine the sizes of banding needed.
- Secure the parts to the shipment package.
- Stencil shipment package/part.
- Complete shipping tag.
- Mobile wraps the parts securely on the skid.
- Locate the parts on the scale with the lift truck.
- Address the parts.
- Determine the shipping package size.

## CATEGORY 2

- Identify the parts to be shipped.
- Determine the trailer weight capacity and distribute the weight accordingly.
- Load the parts on the trailer with the overhead crane.
- Build the fixtures to accommodate the parts for shipment.
- Develop and complete a packing list.
- Pull the parts for customer assembly per packing list.

## CATEGORY 3

- Determine the truck shipment schedule.
- Determine the type of trailer and quantity for shipment.
- Classify the freight according to the freight standards for bill of lading.
- Secure information needed to complete the bill of lading.
- Mark parts with the correct identification number.

## CATEGORY 1
**DEPARTMENT: SHIPPING**
**TASK 1:** Load the parts on the trailer with the lift truck.
**PERFORMANCE OBJECTIVE:** Given a lift truck, load the parts on the trailer with the lift truck.
**TOOLS/EQUIPMENT:** Lift truck, timbers, scale
**PERFORMANCE GUIDE:**
- Determine the weight of the packages with a scale.
- Load on the trailer according to the weight.
- Place the timber under the package to remove the lift truck jacks.

**RELATED INFORMATION:** When loading the trailer, the total weight of the trailer and the tractor must be considered so the weight will not exceed GVW limits.

The timbers are kept outside for use in removing the forks from the load. The load cannot rest on the surface. The load must be elevated for easy removal. Load van trailers from front to back.

## CATEGORY 1
## DEPARTMENT: SHIPPING
**TASK 2:** Measure the parts with a tape.

**PERFORMANCE OBJECTIVE:** Given a tape and rule, measure the parts with a tape.

**TOOLS/EQUIPMENT:** Tape, rule

**PERFORMANCE GUIDE:**
- Determine if the tape to be used is English or metric.
- Determine the number of divisions on the rule.
- Compare the graduation of the tape with the edge surface of the stock to be cut.

**RELATED INFORMATION:** The most commonly used measuring device is the 25 foot tape rule, with units of degree to 1/32 of an inch. It is read by direct comparison of the graduations with the edge or surface of the stock to be cut.

## CATEGORY 1
## DEPARTMENT: SHIPPING
**TASK 3:** Cut material to size.

**PERFORMANCE OBJECTIVE:** Given hand saw, power saw, circular saw, table saw, and tape, cut material to size.

**TOOLS/EQUIPMENT:** Hand saw, power saw, circular saw, table saw, tape

**PERFORMANCE GUIDE:**
- Measure part to be shipped with tape to determine the proper size for shipping container.
- Measure the material to be used for shipping container with tape.
- Cut the material with appropriate saw. Make sure the material is cut according to the size of the shipping container.

**RELATED INFORMATION:** The destination of the shipment and the mode of the shipment must be considered when determining the size and the type of material to be used for constructing the shipping container. Overseas shipments require a solid box.

## CATEGORY 1
## DEPARTMENT: SHIPPING
**TASK 4:** Determine the sizes of the banding needed.

**PERFORMANCE OBJECTIVE:** Given banding material and clips, determine the sizes of the banding needed.

**TOOLS/EQUIPMENT:** Banding equipment, clips

**PERFORMANCE GUIDE:**

* Weigh parts to be shipped on scale.
* Determine the size of the shipping container.
* Select proper banding according to the size of the shipping container.

**RELATED INFORMATION:** The banding material and clips are kept in the shipping department. Use 1 1/4 inch wide banding or 5/8 inch wide banding. The clips are the same as banding - 1 1/4 inch banding requires 1 1/4 inch clips. Heavy shipments and over-seas shipments should always use heavy bands.


**CATEGORY 1**

**DEPARTMENT: SHIPPING**

**TASK 5:** Secure the parts to the shipment package.

**PERFORMANCE OBJECTIVE:** Given banding equipment, bands, hammer, nails, wood sketches, lap screws, and mobile wrap, secure the parts to the shipment package.

**TOOLS/EQUIPMENT:** Banding equipment, bands, hammer, nails, wood sketches, lag screws, mobile wrap

**PERFORMANCE GUIDE:**

* Choose the correct size of banding. (See Task 4)
* Add wood sketching, if necessary, using a hammer and nails.
* Use lag screws if possible.
* Use mobile wrap if necessary.

**RELATED INFORMATION:** The parts must be secured inside the shipping container. The method of securing the part varies with each part. Electrical valves/parts must be secured so that they will be stationary inside the shipping container.

Wood sketches help to keep the part from shifting inside the shipment package. Wood sketches are attached to the shipment package with a hammer and nails. The strength of the banding material and mobile wrap add extra security to the package.


**CATEGORY 1**

**DEPARTMENT: SHIPPING**

**TASK 6:** Stencil shipment package/part.

**PERFORMANCE OBJECTIVE:** Given a complete packing list, customer bill of material, stencil machine, stencil sheets, and paint, stencil shipment package/part.

**TOOLS/EQUIPMENT:** packing list, customer bill of material, stencil machine, stencil sheets, paint

**PERFORMANCE GUIDE:**
- Check to make sure all customer markings are complete and furnished on the packing list and the bill of materials.
- Place the stencil sheets to be used for letting in the cutter.
- Cut the stencil sheet.
- Place the stencil sheet on the package and spray with a paint.

**RELATED INFORMATION:** customer determines if shipment and/or part are stenciled. Not all customers require shipments to be stenciled.

Use 1-inch stenciling sheets and stencil cutter. Black paint is most commonly used when spraying a part. Other colors may be used, depending on the color of the part. Be sure to put stencil specification on the packaging list. The following information is contained in the stencil package/part:

✓ The part number.                    ✓ The address of the customer.
✓ The item number.                    ✓ The customer P.O./job
✓ The name of the customer.             number.

**CATEGORY 1**
**DEPARTMENT: SHIPPING**
**TASK 7:** Complete shipping tag.
**PERFORMANCE OBJECTIVE:** Given a shipping tag, customer bill of material, felt pen, staple gun, and a tape, complete shipping tag.
**TOOLS/EQUIPMENT:** Shipping tag, complete packing list or customer bill of material, felt pen or marker, staple gun, tape
**PERFORMANCE GUIDE:**
- Check to make sure the address is complete with the customer's name, street address, zip code, or any other special information.
- Check packing list for special markings.
- Complete shipping tags.
- Attach shipping tags to the package with a tape or staple gun.

**RELATED INFORMATION:** Shipping tag information is found on the packing list or customer bill of materials, which are both kept in the job file in the shop. All parts in a shipment must have a shipping tag. A shipping tag will sometimes identify parts for assembly.

**CATEGORY 1**
**DEPARTMENT: SHIPPING**
**TASK 8:** Mobile wrap parts securely on the skid.
**PERFORMANCE OBJECTIVE:** Given wrapping tape and a roll of mobile wrap, wrap parts securely on the skid.
**TOOLS/EQUIPMENT:** Wrapping tape, roll of mobile wrap
**PERFORMANCE GUIDE:**
- Stretch mobile wrap around the package at lowest level for at least two turns and break the wrap.

- Wrap the top of the package completely with mobile wrap.
- Finish wrapping the sides of the package from bottom to top.

**RELATED INFORMATION:** Mobile wrap is used on loose parts on the skid to secure them for shipping. Some of these parts are too small to band. Mobile wrap is used because of its strength and durability. It is also used to protect against moisture when shipping parts such as motors.

## CATEGORY 1
## DEPARTMENT: SHIPPING
**TASK 9:** Locate the parts on the scale with the lift truck.

**PERFORMANCE OBJECTIVE:** Given extra timbers and a fork lift, locate the parts on the scale with the lift truck.

**TOOLS/EQUIPMENT:** Fork lift, extra timbers if package is larger than the scale surface

**PERFORMANCE GUIDE:**
- Make sure the scale is "0" for correct weight.
- Place extra timbers on the scale if needed and record the weight
- Place sod, pallet, crate, etc., on the scale and record the weight.
- Take total weight and subtract the weight of extra timbers to determine the correct gross weight.
- Subtract the weight of pallet, skid, or crate when empty from the gross weight to determine the net weight.

**RELATED INFORMATION:** Most scales in the industry are computerized. The accuracy of shipment weight is very important.

## CATEGORY 1
## DEPARTMENT: SHIPPING
**TASK 10:** Address the parts.

**PERFORMANCE OBJECTIVE:** Given complete packing list materials, ball point pen, address labels, customer bill of material, felt marker, and tape, address the parts.

**TOOLS/EQUIPMENT:** packing list materials, ball point pen, address labels, customer bill of material, felt maker, tape

**PERFORMANCE GUIDE:**
- Obtain the complete shipping address and information on any special makings.
- Complete the address label.
- Attach the label to the package.

**RELATED INFORMATION:** The shipping address of the customer can be found on the customer bill of material or packing list. Be sure to put the right address on each label.

Some customers require special markings on their shipments. The packing list or customer bill of materials will contain this information. Some customers also send their own bill of materials with these special markings to industry.

**CATEGORY 1**
**DEPARTMENT: SHIPPING**
**TASK 11:** Determine the shipping package size.
**PERFORMANCE OBJECTIVE:** Given a tape and a bill of material, determine the shipping package size.
**TOOLS/EQUIPMENT:** Tape, complete list or bill of material
**PERFORMANCE GUIDE:**
- Use tape to measure the width, length, and height of the parts to be shipped.
- Determine the approximate weight of shipment.
- Determine the shipping destination.

**RELATED INFORMATION:** Some customers have special shipping guidelines. Know the shipping guidelines before building a shipping crate or preparing a part to be shipped.

CATEGORY 2
DEPARTMENT: SHIPPING
TASK 1: Identify the parts to be shipped.
PERFORMANCE OBJECTIVE: Given a tape, drawings, and customer bill of materials; identify the parts to be shipped.
TOOLS/EQUIPMENT: Complete packing list or customer bill of materials, drawings, and tape
PERFORMANCE GUIDE:
• Locate parts to be shipped.
• Check parts per packing, bill of materials, or drawings using a tape or identifying part number on the piece.
RELATED INFORMATION: A tape is used to check dimensions of parts with drawings.


CATEGORY 2
DEPARTMENT: SHIPPING
TASK 2: Determine the trailer weight capacity and distribute the weight accordingly.
PERFORMANCE OBJECTIVE: Given a rule and trailer, determine the weight of the trailer and distribute the weight accordingly.
TOOLS/EQUIPMENT: Trailer, rule
PERFORMANCE GUIDE:
• Weigh parts to be loaded.
• Determine total weight to be loaded.
• Measure parts for placement on the trailer.
• Space parts equally by weight over each trailer axle.
RELATED INFORMATION: Measure length, width, and height of the parts to be loaded on the trailer. Be sure the weight of the load on the trailer is equally distributed between the two axles.


CATEGORY 2
DEPARTMENT: SHIPPING
TASK 3: Load the parts on the trailer with overhead crane.
PERFORMANCE OBJECTIVE: Given a tape, overhead crane, forklift, chains, shackles, and total assembly drawings, load the parts on the trailer with an overhead crane.
TOOLS/EQUIPMENT: Tape, overhead crane, forklift, lifting straps or chains, shackles, total assembly drawings

## PERFORMANCE GUIDE:
- Determine the total weight of the parts to be loaded.
- Measure parts to determine the center of the load to be lifted.
- Determine the distribution of the lifting devices to lift parts level – straps, chains, etc.
- Check to make sure all lifting devices are in place.
- Check to make sure the load does not exceed the lifting capacity of the cane.

**RELATED INFORMATION:** Some of the finished fabricated machinery have pre-figured lifting points provided by the customer.

Chains or cables are used for heavy loads. Shackles (crevices) should not be misplaced or twisted. The operator should check this before lifting. One snapped cable will cause others to snap causing a potentially disastrous situation.

## CATEGORY 2
## DEPARTMENT: SHIPPING
**TASK 4:** Build a fixture to accommodate the parts for shipment.

**PERFORMANCE OBJECTIVE:** Given a tape, hammer, saws, welding machine, and metal or wood, build a fixture to accommodate the parts for shipment.

**TOOLS/EQUIPMENT:** Tape, hammer, saws, welding machine, materials (metal or wood)

## PERFORMANCE GUIDE:
- Determine the shipping part sizes.
- Determine the weight for each shipment.
- Determine the number of pieces for shipment.
- Gather materials needed for fixture.
- Build a fixture to accommodate the part.

**RELATED INFORMATION:** fixture aids in grouping pieces together and keeping pieces from damaging one another. The width, length, height, and weight of a part for shipment must be determined before a proper fixture can be built.

## CATEGORY 2
## DEPARTMENT: SHIPPING
**TASK 5:** Develop and complete a packing list.

**PERFORMANCE OBJECTIVE:** Given customer bill of materials, paper, pencil, pen, or typewriter, develop and complete a packing list.

**TOOLS/EQUIPMENT:** Customer bill of materials, paper, pencil, pen, or typewriter

## PERFORMANCE GUIDE:
- Obtain correct packing list.
- Write in the part number, descriptions, size, weight, quantity, etc.
- Fill in the shipping address and any special markings.

- Determine from the customer if a detailed and master pack listing is needed.

**RELATED INFORMATION:** The packing list is developed from the bill of material provided by the customer. Accuracy of information is essential when preparing the bill of material.

**CATEGORY 2**
**DEPARTMENT: SHIPPING**
**TASK 6:** Pull the parts for customer assembly per packing list.
**PERFORMANCE OBJECTIVE:** Given a tape, boxes, sacks, and customer bill of materials, pull the parts for customer assembly per packing list.
**TOOLS/EQUIPMENT:** Tape, boxes, sacks, complete packing list or customer bill of materials with parts
**PERFORMANCE GUIDE:**
- Locate parts to be pulled.
- Identify parts from the packing list or bill of materials with parts.
- Box or pack accordingly to accommodate parts.

**RELATED INFORMATION:** Some jobs call for customer assembly of certain parts. These parts are listed on the packing list and bill of materials. They must be located and sacked/boxed for shipment.

CATEGORY 3
DEPARTMENT: SHIPPING
TASK 1: Determine the truck shipment schedule.
PERFORMANCE OBJECTIVE: Given a fax machine, telephone, and customer completed shipping instructions, determine the truck shipment schedule.
TOOLS/EQUIPMENT: Telephone, fax machine, customer completed shipping instructions
PERFORMANCE GUIDE:
• Determine the time of freight completion.
• Determine the time of parts arrival at the destination.
• Call the truck line for pickup.
RELATED INFORMATION:
Check shipping instructions to verify shipping information.

CATEGORY 3
DEPARTMENT: SHIPPING
TASK 2: Determine the type of trailer and quantity for shipment.
PERFORMANCE OBJECTIVE: Given packages and customer completed shipping instructions, determine the type of trailer and quantity for shipment.
TOOLS/EQUIPMENT: Trailer, packages, customer shipping instructions
PERFORMANCE GUIDE:
• Determine how many packages are to be shipped.
• Determine the weight of the packages.
• Determine the sizes of the packages.
• Determine customer requirements for the type of trailer.
RELATED INFORMATION: Check shipping instructions to verify shipping information.

CATEGORY 3
DEPARTMENT: SHIPPING
TASK 3: Classify the freight according to the freight standards for bill of lading.
PERFORMANCE OBJECTIVE: Given customer bill of materials and National Motor Freight Classification book, classify the freight according to the freight standards for bill of lading.
TOOLS/EQUIPMENT: Customer bill of materials, National Motor Freight Classification Book

**PERFORMANCE GUIDE:**
- Obtain the packing and list and determine how to ship. (Use full truck or L.T.L.)
- Crate the shipment in the most cost effective way.
- Find the description of the parts to be shipped in the customer information book.
- Record freight class on bill of lading.

**RELATED INFORMATION:** Less than Truck Load (L.T.L.) means partial trailer. Be sure to know the type of freight in order to obtain the freight class.

**CATEGORY 3**
**DEPARTMENT: SHIPPING**
**TASK 4:** Secure information to complete the bill of lading.
**PERFORMANCE OBJECTIVE:**
Given customer P.O. number and bill of materials, secure information to complete the bill of lading.
**TOOLS/EQUIPMENT:** Customer bill of materials, customer P.O. number
**PERFORMANCE GUIDE:**
- Check for the correct shipping address.
- Determine the freight classification.
- Determine the mode of shipment.
- Determine the shipping date.
- Determine the weight of the parts
- Determine the size of the parts.

**RELATED INFORMATION:** The bill of lading contains freight classification, destination, and number of pieces, weight, customer P.O. number, and truck line.

**CATEGORY 3**
**DEPARTMENT: SHIPPING**
**TASK 5:** Mark parts with the correct identification number.
**PERFORMANCE OBJECTIVE:** Given customer bill of materials, P.O. number, shipping instructions, stencil marking, and 5 felt markers, mark parts with the correct identification number.
**TOOLS/EQUIPMENT:** Customer bill of materials, customer P.O. number, special shipping instructions, stencil marking, 5 felt markers
**PERFORMANCE GUIDE:**
- Identify the parts.
- Stencil or mark with instructions.
- Place the parts in containers, skid, crate, etc.

**RELATED INFORMATION:** The part number is marked on the part according to customer requirements. Some customers require part numbers to be stenciled on the parts. These numbers can be found on a completed packing list, customer bill of material, or assembly drawing.

# LOGISTICS COMMON KNOWLEDGE TRAINING MODULE

**Logistics Training**
Module One–An Overview of Logistics

The outline below is a suggestion for what might be covered in a general logistics seminar. The modules are designed to stand alone, but can be used to provide information necessary to develop a common logistics knowledge base.

**Outline**

I. Overview of Delivery Systems
   A. Logistics
   B. Production and service systems
   C. Purchasing and materials management
   D. Transportation systems
   E. Inventory Management
   F. Financial impact of inventory

II. Inventory Management
   A. EOQ model based systems
   B. Reorder point systems
   C. Periodic systems
   D. Just-in-time (JIT)

III. Financial impact of inventory

IV. Logistics topics and techniques
   A. Warehousing
   B. Customer service in logistics
   C. order processing and order cycle
   D. Global logistics

V. Production/service topics and techniques
   A. Capacity Planning
   B. Facility Location
   C. Facility layout
   D. Shop floor planning and control
   E. Project management and control
   F. Queuing systems and models

VI. Purchasing and materials management
   A. Materials Requirements Planning (MRP)
   B. Vendor selection and elimination
   C. Negotiations

VII. Transportation systems
   A. Modes of transportation
   B. Modal selection
   C. Carrier selection
   D. Multi modal systems

**CONTENTS**
Overview of Logistics
Transportation
Warehousing
Logistics Information Systems
Material Handling
Inventory Control
Customer Service

## USING THIS MODULE

On completing this module, employees should be able to describe the logistics system and its primary components–transportation, warehousing, material handling, logistics information systems (LIS), inventory management, and customer service. They should also grasp the role of logistics in the firm and in the economy.

The module is intended for people who work in one aspect of logistics, but need a better understanding of the entire logistics system. It should be taught by someone familiar with logistics and with the logistics system of the firm in question. Presented in its most basic form, it should take 4-6 hours. Ideally, it will be elaborated upon with examples from the trainer's or employees' backgrounds. It can also be enhanced by referring to the sources listed here: *Strategic Logistics Management* by Douglas M. Lambert and James R. Stock. Chicago: Irwin, 1993; *Integrated Logistics* by David J. Bloomberg, Stephen A. LeMay, and Joseph Hanna. New York: Prentice-Hall, forthcoming; *Factory Physics* by Wallace J. Hopp and Mark L. Spearman. Chicago: Irwin, 1996.

Web sites for business and logistics terminology:
International Financial Encyclopedia
Definitions of terminology with interactive features.
http://www.euro.net/innovation/Finance_Base/Fin_encyc.html

Quicken.com: Glossary
Enter a keyword in the search field or navigate to a particular section of the glossary by clicking a letter in the alphabet.
http://www.quicken.com/glossary/

Australian Financial Review: Dictionary of Investment Terms
An alphabetical listing of terms used by investment professionals.
http://www.county.com.au/dict.htm

Glossary of Financial & Trading Terms
An A-Z listing of terms.
http://centrex.com/terms.html

MoneyWords
Glossary for business, financing, and real estate terms and phrases.
ttp://www.moneywords.com/

TermFinance
Explanations of financial terms in English, French, German, and Italian.
http://193.135.166.4/TermFinance/en/

Wall Street Glossary
List of financial terms and definitions.
http://www.wsdinc.com/pgs_idx/w_indi.shtml

WashingtonPost.com: Business Glossary
Search or manually look for a business term.
http://www.washingtonpost.com/wp-srv/business/longterm/glossary/glossary.htm

AmosWorld Economic Glossary
Search through an alphabetical listing of economic terms.
http://amos.bus.okstate.edu/glossary/search.html

Campbell R. Harvey: Financial Glossary
A listing of over 2,500 financial terms.
http://www.duke.edu/~charvey/Classes/wpg/glossary.htm

Financial Dictionary
A listing of terms and their meanings used in the financial world.
http://www.tiaa-cref.org/dict.html

## INTRODUCTION

The U.S. consumer buys millions of tubes of toothpaste every year, but seldom stops to think about how the toothpaste got on the grocery or drugstore shelf. Getting toothpaste and other goods onto retail shelves, into manufacturing plants for further processing, and to final consumers is the core of logistics. When consumers think about how goods got on the shelves, it usually means that something has gone wrong. The goods are not where they are supposed to be. The same holds true for manufacturing. Purchasing, warehouse, and production employees think more and worry more about the parts not yet in the plant or the warehouse. Effective logistics leaves everyone feeling well served, but not giving the system underlying the service a second thought. Logistics is about getting goods where they are supposed to be.

Logistics is sometimes described as getting the right goods to the right place at the right time in the right condition at the right cost to both the seller and the buyer. This description identifies the key information that must drive the system—the specific meaning of the word "right" in each case. If any one of these is incorrect, the logistics system fails to provide adequate service. The key is to understand what each of these "rights" means. Logistics gives customers access to a firm's products and services either by moving goods toward the customer or locating facilities where the customer can obtain products or services.

The right product means all of what the customer ordered—and what the customer ordered. Two primary errors might occur here: the wrong product or the wrong amount. Of course, it could also be a mixture of these two errors.

The right place means the exact address where the customer requested delivery. The right time is when the customer asked for the goods, within limits that satisfy the customer. The right condition means without damage, in the correct quantity, and with everything needed to use the product.

Communication throughout the system affects logistics systems dramatically. Sales representatives' communication with customers may create expectations about logistics service. If they tell the customer the delivery will be there Monday but fail to deliver until Tuesday, the customer is unhappy. If they tell the customer the delivery will be there by Wednesday and then deliver on Tuesday, the customer is happy. This means driving variation out of the system to make it consistent and reliable, then communicating reasonable expectations about the system's performance to key individuals–customers, sales representatives, customer service representatives, and other contact people. Presumably, they will then have realistic expectations.

The issue of variability deserves consideration. Which is preferable, delivery in ten days, plus or minus three days, or delivery in ten days, plus or minus four hours? Four hours, of course, but why? Look at the first scenario. Plus or minus three days with an average of ten means the goods may arrive this week or next week, while a variation of four hours means it may arrive this morning or this afternoon. Consistency is certainly not the only consideration, but it is extremely important. Variation causes service failures, increases inventory needs (to prevent service failures), and increases calls about arrival times and missed deliveries. If the system will deliver in ten days, plus or minus four hours, it becomes possible to schedule goods into the plant, distribution center, or retail store. With plus or minus three days, higher inventory and more storage space must be maintained in case the goods arrive early (extra storage space) or late (extra inventory). Effective logistics systems allow all the concerned parties to know what will happen next. Then the people who run the system communicate with customers, suppliers, and other parts of the target firm so everyone knows what the system can and cannot do. The elements of logistics should work together as an integrated system. Otherwise, logistics is a fragmented and often uncoordinated set of activities with differing priorities and performance measures. This can disrupt customer service and create turmoil in the organization.

The next section deals with basics about logistics systems–a definition, a discussion of components, and the introduction of broad, basic concepts.

### Definition of logistics

This module uses a simple definition of logistics: logistics is the movement and storage of goods from the raw materials source to the final consumer. This traditional definition of logistics views it as a function of manufacturing and retailing, co-equal with marketing, finance/accounting, and production. The definition deals with tangible products, although many of the

446

issues addressed in this model have implications for service organizations as well. Now examine what moving and storing goods entails.

## The Components of a Logistics System

A logistics system consists of six key elements, each one complex in itself: transportation, warehousing, inventory control, information systems, material handling, and customer service. Each of these elements can influence the others and decisions about the others. This module summarizes each of these elements briefly. Keep in mind an important point, one emphasized throughout: these components are closely linked. What happens in one usually affects the others.

Transportation by rail, water, pipeline, truck, or airplane moves the goods from the raw material source to processing, from processing to distribution or retail outlets. Safe, effective transportation requires a well-developed infrastructure, protective packaging, effective containment, and correct loading, all of which depend on well-trained managers and employees. Transportation costs should be identified in total and by vendor, customer, mode, carrier, product, and channel.

Transportation requires a path of travel or way, a vehicle, a source of motive power, and service facilities. The terms commonly used to describe the path of travel, including roadway, railway, airway, waterway, and right-of-way, contain one of these essential elements. The path of travel may be physical, like a highway, or electronic, as with much of the airway system. The vehicle contains the freight–the trailer on a large truck, a railcar, or an ocean container–while the motive power is the means to move the container. Motive power and the vehicle are often combined, as in airplanes, ships, and straight trucks, but can also be separate, as in barges and tug boats or tractors and trailers. The service facilities are essential also. There must be some place to maintain vehicles and motive power, as well as a place to refuel and refresh operators–pilots, drivers, and engineers.

*The Modes of Transportation.* Five modes of transportation are commonly described: motor carriage, railroads, air, water, and pipeline. For many freight movements, these modes are combined in some form of intermodal transportation. Each of these modes has characteristics that make it preferable for certain kinds of freight, and anything but preferable for other kinds.

Motor Carriage. Most often, this means trucking, although automobiles are used in package and express delivery services. More than 50 percent of the money spent on logistics goes to trucking–local delivery, less-than-truckload carriage, and truck-load carriage. The path of travel is, of course, the roads and highways that lace the country. They give trucks access to nearly every place in the U.S. This resulted from a long term commitment to highway infrastructure on the part of the local, state, and federal governments.

There are two basic types of motor carrier operations: truckload (TL) and less-than-truckload (LTL). A TL operation requires little more than a truck and a telephone–a way of contacting customers and vehicle to move goods. Loads are picked up at shippers' facilities and dropped off at receivers' facilities with little or no handling between. Terminals or service facilities serve maintenance and administrative purposes, but do not handle or interchange freight. LTL operations use terminals as a point to interchange traffic. A trailer usually holds several loads destined for different receivers. An LTL shipment begins with a pick-up run, usually with a smaller, straight truck. The pick-up run may be combined with a delivery run, where inbound goods are dropped off immediately prior to picking-up outbound goods. The goods are brought to a terminal, where they are consolidated with other goods headed in the same general direction. Once the shipments are consolidated into a single, large load, the truck makes a line-haul movement to the next terminal in the system. Freight destined for that terminal and its satellites is then dropped off and freight bound further down the line is added to the load.

For example, a shipment of three lawn mowers might be picked up in Tupelo, MS, bound for Austin, TX. The goods would be picked up at the manufacturer's facility in Tupelo using a straight truck that takes the goods to the Tupelo terminal. A large, tandem truck, perhaps with two short trailers, then hauls the lawn mowers, along with other goods, from Tupelo to Jackson, MS, where the firm has a hub terminal. The goods are then interchanged and loaded on a truck bound for Dallas, TX, where the firm has another hub terminal. From the Dallas, TX, terminal the goods are loaded on a truck for Austin, TX, the location of a satellite terminal. The three lawnmowers are loaded onto another straight truck for delivery to the store where they will be sold.

The greatest advantage for trucking is its flexibility. Because of the extensive U.S. highway system, trucks can deliver goods almost anywhere. The variety of equipment available means trucks can carry almost any type of freight. The greatest disadvantages for trucking, relative to other modes, are the limits on load size and the expense. Federal and state regulations limit truck weight and size, but practical matters also impose limits. Loads that are higher than the wires that support many traffic signals are impractical on trucks and loads much wider than a single traffic lane cause problems as well. Some types of freight "cube out" before they "weigh out," while others do the opposite. A truckload of potato chips is full long before the truck reaches the federal gross weight limit of 80,000 lbs., while a flatbed trailer loaded with rolled steel hardly appears to have a load at all; the load is hardly thicker than the trailer, but the truck has reached the statutory maximum weight.

Truck rates can be too high for some freight. Sand or gravel, for example, will not usually be hauled long distances in large quantities by truck. The traffic is not valuable enough to bear a high freight rate. It may be too costly to move something worth $10 per ton on a truck that will charge $20 to move a ton. Such freight is likely to move by rail or by water.

Rail. Railroads use the efficiency of steel wheels on steel rails to haul large quantities over long distances. Trains of over 100 cars each weighing, including the load, over 100 tons are not unusual. Railroads compete with pipelines and water carriers for bulk commodities. Also, the growth of intermodal transportation has put the railroads in a competition/cooperation relationship with motor carriers. Railroads haul trailers and containers as part of intermodal movements that might otherwise travel by motor carriage. This put the railroads back into competition for higher value freight.

Rail service is terminal-to-terminal, as opposed to door-to-door. This means the last leg of a journey by rail is usually in a truck, which hauls the freight from the rail terminal to the customer. Rail competitiveness is also limited by the track. Most people have a driveway, not a railway, leading into their garage. The same holds true for most businesses, so railroads must rely on some form of highway carriage to complete many deliveries. By contrast, some systems were deliberately designed for rail transportation. For example, coal deliveries to power plants usually involve unit trains–trains hauling one commodity from origin to destination without interchanges. Hopper cars can be loaded in minutes and unloaded in seconds, but keep in mind that coal is not easily damaged.

Rail yards interchange railcars in a system similar to LTL trucking but much older. A train pulling railcars bound for Dallas, Denver, and Chicago comes into Memphis and unhooks all the cars. Other trains with cars bound for the same destinations come in as well. The cars are sorted into trains bound from Memphis to Dallas, Denver, and Chicago–or points beyond.

Rail has advantages over air and motor freight transportation in cost and size of load. Rail usually costs less than either motor carriage or air transportation and the size of the load is much greater–100 tons per car or more. Its disadvantages include slower transit times and less frequent service. Also, rail covers less of the country.

Rail goes places water carriers cannot go, but usually costs more and delivers smaller loads. Rail-water competition is for lower valued freight that moves in large quantities.

Air. Most shippers view air transportation as a premium service because of its higher costs. When an item must move quickly to a distant destination, air freight offers the shortest time in transit. For distances up to 500 miles, air and truck are highly competitive. Air carriers handle high value products because air costs represent too high a percentage of the value of inexpensive goods. Air transport moves goods quickly from terminal to terminal, but freight interchange, delivery delays, and congestion reduce this advantage. The frequency and reliability of air freight service is very good between large cities, but limited between smaller markets.

Air freight may move in dedicated aircraft designed for the purpose, or in the holds of passenger aircraft. Air carriers are more likely to carry small, light packages than large heavy goods. Package express services rely heavily on air transportation.

Water. Barges, boats, and ships move freight along rivers and canals, lakes, coastal and intercostal waterways, and oceans. Water carriage competes primarily with rail and pipelines to transport bulk materials like iron ore, grains, pulpwood products, coal, limestone, fertilizers, and petroleum. Water carriers cover a limited range because waterways do not go everywhere. In the North, weather limits water carriage because the waterways freeze in the winter. Water carriage may often be the least expensive method to ship high-bulk, low-value commodities. Water carriage uses containers in intermodal logistics to reduce staffing, minimize loss and damage, shorten time in transit, and take advantage of volume shipping rates.

Pipelines. Pipelines can transport a restricted range of products. Pipelines' major advantage is high reliability, impunity to weather variation, and low cost per ton-mile. The major disadvantages are high capital costs, limited range, and product restrictions. Most commercial pipeline traffic is terminal-to-terminal, although natural gas and water are piped directly into homes.

## Warehousing

Warehousing stores goods to help meet the timing of market demand and to buffer the production line from fluctuations in market demand. More critically, warehouses and distribution centers consolidate goods into efficient transportation loads and sort them for shipment to specific destinations. Warehousing costs include all expenses that change when the number of warehouse facilities changes. Throughput costs are associated with moving goods into and out of a warehouse for sale in a market, and the fixed costs associated with the facility. Inventory storage costs change with the level of inventory held in a warehouse and tend to be negligible in a company-owned warehouse.

Warehousing manages goods and information, relying heavily on automation and computerization. Goods come into warehouses through receiving doors and then move to long term storage, the picking area, or immediately to shipping. Goods are usually stored in larger lots in long term storage and broken down into shipping-sized lots in the picking area. In cross-docking operations, goods move from a vehicle at the receiving dock immediately to a vehicle at the shipping dock.

A firm may own its warehouses (private warehousing), purchase warehousing services long term (contract warehousing), or purchase warehousing services as needed (public warehousing). The choice among these depends on which will give the firm the best return on investment. When utilization and throughput are likely to be high, private or contract warehousing usually make economic sense, while low utilization or sporadic demand push the choice toward public warehousing. Many firms use systems that blend private, contract, and public warehousing.

450

Crucial warehousing decisions include how many warehouses to include in the system and the size of each warehouse. Typically, a firm chooses between a small number of large warehouses or a large number of small warehouses, or some mixture of the two. It depends on the purpose the warehouses serve. The size of the warehouse depends on the size of the products, the number of products, the production schedules, the markets served, variations in demand, the number and type of activities included, and inventory policies. The larger the products and the larger the number of products, the larger the warehouse tends to be. Production schedules and inventory policies both influence warehouse size. Longer production runs mean higher inventories, generating a need for larger warehouses. The more markets a warehouse serves, the larger it is likely to be. Warehouses also tend to be larger when they accommodate sales, office, and computer operations in addition to the primary warehousing activities.

Higher customer service levels usually require more or larger warehouses. The size of the warehouse may also depend on whether manual, mechanized, or automated systems are used. Automated systems use higher stacked racks with narrow aisles, while manual and mechanized systems use lower racks with broader aisles. Automated systems usually make better use of the available cubic footage, but they also cost more to build.

The number of warehouse facilities depends on transportation costs, cost of lost sales, inventory costs, and warehousing costs. Inventory costs increase with the number of warehouses, as do warehousing costs. These increases must be balanced against changes in transportation costs and improved customer service, which should reduce sales lost due to a lack of available inventory.

Another important decision is where to put the warehouses. Warehouses located close to markets will improve customer service, while warehouses located close to sources of supply will reduce supply shocks and production disruptions. Warehouses located midway between suppliers and customers help balance market demands for customer service with the demands of merging the output of several plants.

Warehouses may handle specific products and serve all markets, carry a full line of products destined for specific markets, or carry a full line of products to serve all the markets in a geographic area. Theories for locating warehouses focus on minimizing transportation costs and total supply chain costs or maximizing profits. Micro location analysis seeks to pick an ideal site after the general location decision has been made.

A variety of computer models can help locate warehouses in a network, locate products in a warehouse, and lay out the warehouse for optimal operation.

## Material Handling

Material handling is the movement, packaging, and storing of goods, usually in a manufacturing plant, warehouse, or distribution center. Goods must be moved around the plant as they change form and eventually move further along the supply chain. Goods may move through a variety of production lines along the route. They must be moved from one workstation or machine to another and from one part of the manufacturing plant or distribution facility to another. Effective material handling can cut waste, improve safety and productivity, increase capacity, and improve customer service.

Material handling systems take three principal forms: manual, mechanized, and automated. Manual material handling uses hand dollies, drawers, low racks, and bins in a labor intensive system. People are the primary source of power. Mechanized material handling, the most common form, uses power devices operated by people--forklifts, cranes, storage racks, and the like. The equipment provides the power, augmented by people. Automated material handling employs few people in systems with high-rise racks, robotic pickers, conveyors, and carousels. Systems may also mix automated, mechanized, and manual elements.

In manufacturing plants, material handling moves goods from loading dock to storage, storage to the production line, between machines in the production line, and from the production line to storage or the shipping dock. The design of the production process and the frequency with which machines are reset to make different products affects the performance of the logistics system. Material handling decisions include how many items to move at a time from one production machine to another, for example. Costs associated with material handling include lot quantity costs and production preparation costs. These include set-up time, scrap, inspection, and startup costs, as well as lost capacity due to the changeover.

The broader concept of material management often includes purchasing, inbound transportation, and plant warehousing. It can incorporate all aspects of logistics, moving backward from the manufacturer toward the raw materials supply.

## Logistics Information Systems

Logistics information systems (LIS) track goods along the way from raw material to final consumption, providing decision-makers with data and information to help make good decisions about production quantities, delivery schedules, facilities, and equipment allocation. Logistics systems depend increasingly on LIS to the point that many systems cannot function without the computer. Order processing and information costs include the cost of order transmittal, order entry, order processing, related handling costs, and associated internal and external communication costs. Management should look only at relevant costs.

An LIS gathers information from many sources to assist logistics managers and employees in making decisions. It interfaces with marketing, financial, and manufacturing information systems. The order processing subsystem is the most important LIS component because it interacts with the customer. The order processing subsystem tracks the order from placement to delivery and billing, so it significantly affects customer service. Other components include the intelligence system, decision support, and the reports and outputs system. The intelligence system should connect logistics planning to corporate planning, manage interfaces with other functions, and assist external relationships. Information sources should include suppliers, customers, carriers, employees, and managers. The decision support system should contain a central file of data for analytical modeling, define the scope of decision making, and tools for optimization, heuristic, and simulation modeling. It should also maintain a file of analytical results for comparison in future analysis. The reports and outputs system should hold the structure for routine planning, operating, and control reports to assist inventory control, transportation scheduling, routing, purchasing, and production scheduling.

## Inventory Control

The standard way to refer to goods in a supply chain is as inventory. Inventory control decisions affect the performance of the logistics system in profound ways. Too much inventory adds significantly to a firm's costs. Too little inventory affects customer service; customers cannot get the goods they require for consumption or for their own businesses. This means the selling firm loses sales or customers.

Inventory carrying costs should include only those costs that vary with the level of inventory stored and that can be categorized into the following groups: capital costs (opportunity costs), inventory service costs, storage space costs, and inventory risk costs. Opportunity costs represent the value of the alternative use for the money that is tied up in inventory. Inventory service costs include insurance and taxes. If storage space costs vary with the level of inventory, then they are inventory carrying costs. If they do not, they are probably warehousing costs. Inventory risk costs include obsolescence, shrinkage, and transshipment. (A complete discussion may be found in *Strategic Logistics Management* by Douglas Lambert and James Stock, Chicago: Irwin, 1993.)

The complex issues in inventory management are how much to order and when to order it. Since production and distribution times vary, completely avoiding stockouts is expensive and nearly impossible. While no single system works perfectly, several approaches are widely used. Among the most common are the Economic Order Quantity (EOQ), Just In Time (JIT), and Materials Requirments Planning (MRP). EOQ examines products in isolation, treating them one at a time. It assumes a constant usage rate, instantaneous replenishment, and known or knowable parameters. JIT is a loose collection of tools and techniques based around the idea that less inventory is better than more inventory.

Inventory buffers the production line against supply shocks and the customer against variations in production and delivery processes. It allows for longer production runs, balances supply against seasonal and cyclical changes in demand, and permits specialized manufacturing. Inventory may be found throughout the supply chain and may be used as a buffer anywhere that uncertainty is likely to arise. It helps achieve economies of scale in purchasing, transportation, and manufacturing.

Firms usually classify inventory by its purpose. Classifications include: cycle stock – the result of the replenishment process and the need to meet known variations in demand and the order cycle; in-transit inventories – items that are en route from one location to another, and so are unavailable for use or sale; safety or buffer stock – buffers the order cycle against uncertainty in demand and lead time because forecasting rarely predicts demand accurately and demand is seldom constant; speculative stock – anticipates events that may not occur, like strikes, supply shocks, or future price increases; seasonal stock – speculative stock anticipates predictable changes in demand, but allows a firm to maintain a stable labor force and smooth production runs; a typical example would be a stock build-up of goods for sale at Christmas; dead stock – experienced no demand for a specified time, possibly due to obsolescence.

Good inventory management contributes to corporate profitability, anticipates the effects of corporate policies on inventory levels, and minimizes the total cost of logistics. Reducing back-orders and expedited shipments, purging dead stock, and increasing forecast accuracy are among the methods for decreasing inventory costs. Inventory quantities should help achieve the lowest total logistics costs possible at a given customer service level.

## Customer Service

Consumers may define customer service by the convenience store clerk that ignores them at the cash register, or by the assistant manager who places an order for a difficult to find item. Consumers approach customer service the way they approach art—they are not sure what it is, but they know it when they see it. In logistics, the definition of customer service is more precise and more carefully measured; it's more of a science. In this context, customer service can be defined in several ways: order cycle time, consistency and reliability, inventory availability, order size constraints, ordering convenience, delivery times and flexibility, invoicing procedures and accuracy, claims procedures, order status information, sales calls, and the condition of goods on arrival. To provide superior customer service, logistics managers must understand customer expectations and develop distribution channels that meet those expectations.

Successful firms increasingly compete on customer service. Although customer service means something different in each organization, the focus on satisfying customers remains constant. The order cycle and inventory availability encompass many customer service elements. The order cycle begins when the customer places an order and ends when the goods arrive in good condition at the designated destination. Inventory availability means having the goods the customer wants in the desired quantity where the customer can get them when they wish. Consistent order cycles allow a firm to promise delivery times and make effective use of facilities and equipment. They also permit lower inventories and lower inventory carrying costs. Customer service represents the output of the logistics system and the place component of the firm's marketing mix.

Customer service can be defined as an activity to be managed, a performance measure, or an element of the corporate philosophy. As an activity, customer service includes call centers, e-mail respondents, technical support units, and other customer contact functions that act independently of selling. Performance measures include on-time performance, damage rates, fill rates, billing accuracy, shipping accuracy, and potentially many more. These tie to the availability of goods, while other customer service issues relate to after-sales service and contact. As part of a corporate philosophy, customer service requires competent technical representatives and an effective system for responding to product problems and failures.

Customer service can be broken into pretransaction, transaction, and posttransaction elements. Pretransaction elements include written statements of customer service policy, definitions of service standards, system flexibility, and organizational structure. Transaction elements include stock availability, order information, order cycle, expedited shipments, order convenience, and system accuracy. Post transaction elements are installation, product tracing, warranties, claims management, and product repair and replacement.

To improve customer service, thoroughly research customer needs, set service levels realistically, use the latest technology for order processing, and evaluate the performance of each logistics activity. The idea is to keep all customers, make all sales, and avoid all back orders, but this is usually too expensive. It would mean enormous inventory, expensive transportation, and frequent expedited shipments. These may add too much to the total cost of doing business.

III. Crucial logistics concepts

The total cost concept says that the cost concern in any logistics system is not for the cost on one activity, but the total cost of the system. Put another way, a firm could maintain low inventory costs by maintaining no finished goods inventory, but it might lose sales or customers by not doing so. If one brand of toothpaste is not on the shelves, few customers will special order it. They buy another brand or go to another store that has the brand they seek. The empty shelf has zero inventory cost, but the customer service cost is high.

The cost focus of logistics is to minimize the total cost, and not just transportation, inventory, or warehousing.

Two other key concepts are postponement and speculation. Any productive or service system seeks to minimize the cost of serving customers and requires information to do so effectively. Postponement means putting off decisions about production, product allocation, and distribution until as much information as possible is available about customer preferences. Speculation means making and allocating goods in the hope that customers will buy what the firm makes available.

Take an example from the furniture industry. A large retailer like J.C. Penney, Inc. would like to postpone buying living room sets until customer preferences about style and color are known. Manufacturers like La-Z-Boy and Action Industries would like orders to come in sooner rather than later to optimize their production schedules. Since the furniture industry cannot command the textile manufacturers who make the upholstery, the furniture manufacturers must order cloth before they know what their customers will order. So the large retailers seek to postpone decisions and push the manufacturers for shorter cycle times to allow for even more postponement. Because the manufacturers cannot influence production schedules of the textile suppliers, they must speculate–buy a variety of cloth and hope that it includes the fabrics and styles that their customers want.

IV. Logistics' Role in the Economy

Because logistics is a significant component of Gross Domestic Product, it affects the rate of inflation, interest rates, productivity, energy cost, and availability of products. The infrastructure in the U.S. and Canada allows for the most sophisticated and effective logistics systems anywhere in the world. Good logistics systems allow for regional specialization, which helps to create economies of scales and lower the total cost of goods. A simple example would be growing potatoes in Idaho and oranges in Florida. Idaho lacks the weather for growing oranges, and Florida soil is less suited for growing potatoes. With efficient transportation and storage, each area can specialize in what it does best and both regions can eat both oranges and potatoes. This is not possible without an effective logistics system.

Many poor countries struggle to develop the basic infrastructure to support internal and external trade. A major difference between countries that are poor but developing and those that are poor and not developing is the fundamental investment in infrastructure to support logistics.

V. Logistics' Role in the Firm

Logistics significantly affects other functional areas of the firm. Effective logistics management enhances marketing by efficiently moving products to customers, thus adding time and place utility. By providing storage space, the logistics system allows for longer production runs to make more effective use of production capacity. Conversely, logistics can also move goods to customers quickly, thus allowing for short, focused production runs that help to maintain lower system inventory. Finance and accounting are affected by the investment in inventory, the ownership strategies followed for facilities and equipment, and the modes of transportation chosen.

Logistics is the third largest cost of doing business for most firms, behind production and marketing. This may vary however, depending on the nature of the product. For example, some mining firms spend more on logistics than on extracting ore from the ground. Rock salt, used in many chemical processing operations, often costs more to deliver than to buy. In one case, the purchase price was $10 per ton and the rail transportation cost was $11 per ton, for a total delivered cost of $21 per ton.

## VI. Other Activities Included in Logistics Management

1. Order processing: prompts the logistics system to respond to specific customer demand. Accuracy and response time are key measures of effectiveness.       (a)Distribution communication: communication takes place between the firm and its customers and suppliers, the major functional units, and the various logistics activities. This assures that customer needs are met and that customers are aware of variances.

2. Demand forecasting: anticipating the quantity of goods and associated services customers will require at specific times in the future. Used to plan transportation, distribution capacity, and production capacity and to allocate capacity to customers and markets.

3. Plant and warehouse site selection: locating plants near raw material sources may reduce transportation costs, while locating near markets may improve customer services. Proper facility location can also allow lower volume-related transportation rates in moving product from plant to warehouse, plant to plant, or warehouse to customer.

4. Procurement and purchasing: acquiring materials and services for the firm's manufacturing and logistics processes. This activity includes selecting supply sources, determining the form of acquired materials, timing purchases, determining price, and controlling quality. This topic is the subject of another module.

5. Parts and service support: maintaining adequate parts inventory, identifying sources of supply for parts, and coordinating sources for repair services clearly has major logistics implications.

6. Packaging: packaging promotes, protects, and contains products. Advertising messages and basic information about products may be imprinted on packaging. Products may need protection from contamination, the elements, or human interference. Packaging may help with all of these. Also, packaging helps keep products in unit sizes most useful to distributors and customers.

7.Salvage and scrap disposal: material that a firm needs moved away from plants and warehouses includes more than manufactured products. Waste, scrap, and salvage must also be moved.

8.Return goods handling or reverse logistics:  movement from the buyer to the seller for returns, repairs, salvage, and trade-in, among other things.  In many industries, customer service requires a willingness to accept returns for almost any reason.

# TRAINING SOURCES

# Sources of Sources for Training Programs

This section discusses sources of sources of training programs, along with some key contacts for publicly available programs and programs offered by logistics oriented associations. It is not intended to be comprehensive, but suggestive of potential sources of training content, trainers, and programs.

www.peterson.com

This web site describes education and training programs of all types. Of particular interest to this research is the Executive Education catalogue, also published in hard copy as Bricker's International Directory. Both the Executive Education catalogue and the directory outline management training and education sources by topic, by industry, and by source. It includes university-based training programs, training firms, consulting firms, and associations. Its focus is management and executive training.

Bricker's International Directory sells for $395, with a 20% discount through the Web site. Bricker's on-line is available by annual subscription

www.handilink.com/cat1/c/c1357.htm

This Web site links to corporate training and business training sources. It allows training organizations to add links, so it is regularly updated. It is free. The only problem is that some firms link services clearly not related to training. Several links offered inventory counting services, for example, when the site was checked on 6/23/99.

## Associations

This is a partial listing of associations that provide or sponsor training, training content, seminars, and certification in logistics. It is alphabetical, other than listing CLM first. The CLM Web site offers additional lists of associations, including the national logistics associations from many countries. Also, there are associations oriented to specific industries that can also be consulted. The majority of these associations offer training that focuses on managers and executives rather than operating employees.

## Council of Logistics Management (CLM)

The Council of Logistics Management is the most obvious source of management and executive training from the perspective of this research. The CLM Annual Conference and seminars sponsored by CLM have enhanced logistics education for decades. The Web site is itself an educational tool, with a substantive, searchable logistics bibliography.

Type: A professional organization in which individuals hold membership.
Number of Members: 12,000
Dues: $200.00 per person per year.

Purpose/Objective: The mission of the Council of Logistics Management is to provide:

·Leadership in developing, defining, understanding, and enhancing the logistics process on a worldwide basis.

·A forum for the exchange of concepts and best practices among logistics professionals.

·Research that advances knowledge and leads to enhanced customer value and supply chain performance.

·Education and career development programs that enhance career opportunities in logistics management.

The Council of Logistics Management is an open organization which offers individual membership to persons in all industries, types of businesses, and job functions involved in the logistics process. In recognition of diversity, the Council of Logistics Management will give priority to actively involving individuals from currently underrepresented populations in its activities. The Council of Logistics Management will operate on a not-for-profit, self-supporting basis, with emphasis on quality and in a cooperative manner with other organizations and institutions.

Chief Elected Officer:
Kathleen Strange
Director Logistics Strategy & Implementation
Staples, Inc.
500 Staples Drive
Staples Corporate Center
Framingham, MA 01701
(508) 253-7340
FAX (508) 253-7702

Chief Operating Officer:
George A. Gecowets
Executive Vice President
Council of Logistics Management
2805 Butterfield Road, Suite 200
Oak Brook, IL 60523
(630) 574-0985
FAX (630) 574-0989

E-mail: clmadmin@clm1.org
Web: http://www.clm1.org

Remarks: As with any professional organization, membership in the Council of Logistics Management is on an individual basis. The membership belongs to the individual and not to his or her company. It is not transferable. The Council of Logistics Management, as an organization, is not aligned with shippers, carriers, warehouse operators, material handling equipment manufacturers, consultants, or any other similar industrial grouping. Because its members have widespread and varying interests within the logistics industry, the Council will not get involved in legislative or similar matters in which industrial segments have contrary interests.

## Air Transport Association of America

Type: A trade association in which airlines hold membership.
Number of Members: 24
Dues: Corporate dues are on a sliding scale based on revenue ton miles. Membership is open to any US air carrier authorized to conduct passenger and/or cargo air transport service under a certificate issued pursuant to Section 604 of the Federal Aviation Act of 1958. The carrier must operate a minimum of 20 million revenue ton-miles annually and must have operated at or above such minimum level during the twelve months immediately preceding the date of membership application.
Purpose/Objective: The Air Transport Association of America is the trade and service organization of the largest airlines of the United States.

Chief Elected Officer:
Carol B. Hallett
President & CEO
Air Transport Association of America
1301 Pennsylvania Avenue, NW
Washington, DC 20004-1701
(202) 626-4000
FAX (202) 626-4181
Chief Operating Officer: Same as above.

## American Marketing Association (AMA)

Type: A professional organization in which individuals hold membership.
Number of Members:
30,000 professional members
28,000 collegiate members
Dues: $100.00 plus chapter dues (basic membership).
Purpose/Objective: The American Marketing Association is an international professional society of individual members with an interest in the study, teaching, or practice of marketing. AMA's principle roles are to urge and assist the professional development of members and to advance the science and practice of the marketing discipline.

Chief Elected Officer:
David Gordon
Chairman
American Marketing Association
250 South Wacker Drive
Chicago, IL 60606-5819
(312) 648-0536
FAX (312) 993-7542

Chief Operating Officer:
Dennis Jorgensen
Chief Operating Officer
American Marketing Association
250 South Wacker Drive
Chicago, IL 60606-5819
(312) 648-0536
FAX (312) 993-7542

E-mail: mhammer@ama.org
Remarks: Membership is based on an interest in the ethical practice of marketing.

### American Society of Transportation and Logistics, Inc. (AST&L)
Type: A professional organization in which individuals hold membership.
Number of Members: 2,000

| | |
|---|---|
| Dues: Sustaining: $280.00 | Associates: $65.00 |
| Educator: $85.00 | Affiliates: $65.00 |
| Certified: $100.00 | Full-Time Student: $25.00 |
| Founder: $60.00 | |

Purpose/Objective: To establish, promote, and maintain high standards of knowledge and professional training; to formulate a code of ethics for the profession; to advance the professional interest of members of the organization; to serve as a source of information and guidance for the fields of traffic, transportation, logistics, and physical distribution management; and to serve the industry as a whole by fostering professional accomplishments.

Chief Elected Officer:
George A. Yarusavage
Director of Technical Logistics
NBC Olympics
3 Landmark Square, Suite 401
Stamford, CT 06091

National Office:
American Society of Transportation and Logistics
320 East Water Street
Lock Haven, PA 17745-1410
(570) 748-8515
FAX (570) 748-9118

Web: http://www.astl.org
Remarks: Offers a five-part certification examination and correspondence courses on topical subjects; publishes quarterly journals and newsletters; and holds regional educational workshops and an annual meeting.

### American Trucking Associations, Inc. (ATA)
Type: A trade organization representing the interests of the trucking industry
Number of Members: 4,110 (as of 1/97)
Dues: Dues for motor carriers are assessed on the basis of revenue. Private carrier dues are based on fleet size, and supplier dues are based on revenues generated from the trucking industry.
Purpose/Objective: The American Trucking Associations, Inc., is the national trade association of the trucking industry. The ATA Federation includes the ATA nation headquarters, 50 affiliated state trucking associations, and 14 affiliated national conferences and independent organizations. The mission of ATA is to serve the united interests of the trucking industry; enhance the trucking industry's image, efficiency, productivity and competitiveness;

promote highway and workplace safety and environmental responsibility; provide educational programs; and work for a healthy business environment.

| | |
|---|---|
| Chief Elected Officer: | Chief Operating Officer: |
| Charles Ramorino (Chairman) | William B. MacCormick |
| President | President & Chief Executive Officer |
| Bob Rich Schroeder Trucking | American Trucking Association, Inc. |
| 30527 San Antonio Street | 2200 Mill Road Alexandria, VA 22314- |
| Hayward, CA 94544-7101 | 4677 |
| (510) 487-2404 | (703) 838-1700 |
| FAX (510) 487-3164 | FAX (703) 836-6070 |

## Canadian Association of Logistics Management (CALM)
Type: A professional organization in which individuals hold membership.
Number of Members: 1,000
Dues: $230.00 per person per year.
Purpose/Objective: The Canadian Association of Logistics Management is a not-for-profit organization of business professionals interested in improving their logistics and/or distribution management skills. It works in cooperation with the private sector and various organizations to further the understanding and development of the logistics concept. It does this through a continuing program of formal activities, research, and informal discussion designed to develop the theory and understanding of the logistics process; promote the art and science of managing logistics systems; and foster professional dialogue and development within the profession.

| | |
|---|---|
| Chief Elected Officer: | Chief Operating Officer: |
| Doug Carter (President) | David Long |
| Vice President and General Manager | Executive Director |
| Pacific Westeel | Canadian Association of Logistics |
| 3191 Mainway | Management |
| Burlington, Ontario L7M 1A6 | 610 Alden Road, Suite 201 |
| Canada | Markham, Ontario L3R 9Z1 |
| (905) 798-7973 | Canada |
| FAX (905) 332-5383 | (905) 513-7300 |
| | FAX (905) 513-1248 |

Web: http://www.calm.org

## Canadian Industrial Transportation League (CITL)
Type: A trade association in which corporations hold membership.
Number of Members: 420 member companies represented by approximately 1,000 member representatives.
Dues: Dues are on a sliding scale based on the number of employees.

Purpose/Objective: To develop a thorough understanding of the transportation and distribution requirements of industry; and to promote, conserve, and protect commercial transportation interests.

President / General Manager:
Pieive Caclieux
100 Allstate Pkwy #305
Markham,ON L3R 6H3
Canada
(905) 947-0575
FAX (905) 947-0585
E-Mail citl@citl.ca

Chief Operating Officer:
Maria Rehner
President
Canadian Industrial Transportation League
1090 Don Mills Road #602
Don Mills, Ontario M3C 3R6
Canada
(416) 447-7766
FAX (416) 447-7312

Remarks: Canadian counterpart to the National Industrial Transportation League.

### APICS–Educational Society for Resource Management
Type: A professional organization in which membership is extended on both an individual and corporate basis.
Number of Members: 70,000
11,500 corporate members
58,500 individual members
Dues: $80.00 per person per year, plus chapter dues.
Purpose/Objective: The Education Society for Resource Management's primary objectives are to develop professional efficiency in resource management through study, research, and application of scientific methods; to disseminate general and technical information on improved techniques and new developments; and to further develop the professional body of knowledge and through the organized resources of the profession, thereby advancing the general welfare of the industrial economy.

Chief Elected Officer:
Andrew D. Nicoll (President)
President
Caterpillar, Inc.
Building LC2236
501 SW Jefferson Avenue
Peoria, IL 61630
(309) 675-2049
FAX (309) 494-0916

Chief Operating Officer:
Jeffry W. Raynes
Executive Director and COO
American Production and Inventory Control Society
500 West Annandale Road
Falls Church, VA 22046
(703) 237-8344
FAX (703) 237-4316

Web: http://www.apics.org

**International Warehouse Logistics Association**
Type: A trade association in which corporations hold membership.
Number of Members: 550
Dues: Corporate dues are on a sliding scale based on square footage.
Purpose/Objective: To promote the general interests of persons, firms, and corporations engaged in the public merchandise warehousing industry, and to promote a high standard of business ethics therein; to collect and disseminate statistical and other information pertinent to the business of its members; to conduct research into ways and means of improving efficiency in the conduct of the business of its members; to advise its members of national legislation and regulations affecting them; and in general, to engage in all activities for the benefit of its members.

| | |
|---|---|
| Chairman & Chief Elected Officer: | President & Chief Executive Officer: |
| Darby T. Strickland, Jr. | Michael L. Jenkins |
| Shippers Warehouse | American Warehouse Association |
| 8901 Forney Avenue | 1300 West Higgins Road, Suite 111 |
| Dallas, TX 75227 | Park Ridge, IL 60068 |
| (214) 381-5050 | (847) 292-1891 |
| FAX (214) 381-5028 | FAX (847) 292-1896 |

E-mail logistx@aol.com
Web http://logistx.dartgc.com

**The Material Handling Industry (MHI)**
Type: A trade association in which corporations hold membership.
Number of Members:
200 The Material Handling Institute Division
600 The Material Handling Industry of America Division
Dues: Dues vary depending on divisional affiliations.
Purpose/Objective: Material Handling Industry is the not-for-profit umbrella organization of its two membership divisions--The Material Handling Institute (MHI) and The Material Handling Industry of America (MHIA). Since 1945, MHI has been the primary source of information on the industry. MHI members are leading the way, bringing the nation's manufacturers, users, and educators together to provide lasting solutions to today's productivity challenges through better material handling. MHIA gives its member companies a greater voice in shaping the destiny of the industry both nationally and internationally. MHIA sponsors trade events to showcase the products and services of its member companies and to provide material handling educational opportunities.

| Chief Elected Officer: | Chief Operating Officer: |
|---|---|
| Daniel J. Quinn (Executive Chairman) | J.B. Nofsinger |
| President | COO |
| Pentek Corporation | The Material Handling Industry |
| 8502 Brookville Road | 8720 Red Oak Boulevard, Suite 201 |
| Indianapolis, IN 46239 | Charlotte, NC 28217-3992 |
| | (704) 676-1190 |
| | FAX (704) 676-1199 |

Web: http://www.mhi.org

## Materials Handling and Management Society

Type: A professional organization in which individuals hold membership.
Number of Members: 1,500
Dues: $125.00 per person per year. Members must be directly involved in the field of material handling or material management in their occupations.
Purpose/Objective: The Materials Handling and Management Society is a professional society dedicated to enhancing the professional stature of its members and their fields on all levels through promoting public recognition of material handling and material management as vital professional business activities, and providing members with activities and information which facilitate acquiring increased knowledge and skills in the areas of material handling and material management.

| Chief Elected Officer: | Chief Operating Officer: |
|---|---|
| Robert Bryan (President) | F. Hal VanDiver |
| Yuasa-Exide Canada, Inc. | Executive Director |
| 329 Deerhurst Drive | Materials Handling and Management |
| Brampton, Ontario L6T 549 | Society |
| Canada | 8720 Red Oak Boulevard, Suite 224 |
| (905) 790-1212 | Charlotte, NC 28217 |
| | (704) 525-4667 |
| | FAX (704) 525-2880 |

## The National Association of Purchasing Management, Inc. (NAPM)

Type: An educational and research organization in which individuals hold membership.
Number of Members: 38,000
Dues: Dues vary, depending on which affiliate one belongs to.
Purpose/Objective: The National Association of Purchasing Management is committed to providing national and international leadership on purchasing and materials management. Through its 178 affiliated associations and over 38,000 members, the association provides opportunities for purchasing and materials management practitioners to expand their professional skills and

knowledge, and works to foster a better understanding of purchasing and materials management concepts.

| | |
|---|---|
| Chief Elected Officer: | Chief Operating Officer: |
| John D. Cologna (President) | R. Jerry Baker |
| C/O National Association of Purchasing | Executive Vice President |
| Management | National Association of Purchasing |
| PO Box 22160 | Management |
| Tempe, AZ 85285-2160 | PO Box 22160 |
| (602) 752-6276 | Tempe, AZ 85285-2160 |
| FAX (602) 752-7890 | (602) 752-6276 |
| | FAX (602) 752-7890 |
| | E-Mail: jbaker@napm.org |

Web: http://www.napm.org

### Simply Better

Type: an education organization where individuals and organizations hold
Membership: open to everyone
Dues: Simply Better is a free program provided to all organizations with the tools to run continuous improvement programs.
Purpose/Objectives: Simply Better! is a network of employment and training professionals and organizations committed to continuous improvement of their services and outcomes, to customer satisfaction, and to exceptional quality. We are creating a learning network to spread the skills and tools of continuous improvement throughout the employment and training system. This network will help us become partners in discovering new and better ways of doing our jobs and serving our customers. There is no membership process-all you need is a desire to improve, a willingness to try, and an eagerness to learn from your peers. Simply Better! Learning Network includes private industry councils, private sector service providers, state governments, employment service agencies, and U.S. Department of Labor regional and national offices.
Remarks: Simply Better is sponsored by The U.S. Department of Labor.

Web: http://www.simplybetter.org

### Transportation Research Board (TRB)

Type: An organization in which membership is extended on both an individual and corporate basis.
Number of Members:
2,200 individuals
200 corporations
4,000 committee members
Dues: Committee membership size is limited. Nominations require individual

expertise in the subject matter of a committee and approval by committee chairperson and TRB Executive Director; individual and organizational membership; and payment of required fee.

Purpose/Objective: To advance knowledge concerning the nature and performance of transportation systems by stimulating research and disseminating the information derived from research.

Chief Elected Officer:
James Van Loben Sels
Director Caltrans
MS-49
1120 N Street
Sacramento, CA 95814

Chief Operating Officer:
Robert E. Skinner, Jr.
Executive Director
Transportation Research Board
2101 Constitution Avenue, NW
Washington, DC 20418
(202) 334-2934
FAX (202) 334-2003

Web: http://www.nas.edu/trb/index.html

## Warehousing Education and Research Council (WERC)
Type: A professional organization in which individuals hold membership.
Number of Members: 3,250
Dues: $195.00 per person per year.
Purpose/Objective: WERC's purpose is to provide education and to conduct research concerning the warehousing process; and to refine the art and science of managing warehouses. WERC will foster professionalism in warehouse management. It will operate exclusively without profit and in cooperation with other organizations and institutions.

Chief Elected Officer:
Margie Costa
President
Outsource Concepts, Inc.
Granite Bay, CA

Chief Operating Officer:
Thomas E. Sharpe
Executive Director
Warehousing Education and Research Council
1100 Jorie Boulevard, Suite 170
Oak Brook, IL 60523
(630) 990-0001
FAX (630) 990-0256
E-Mail: tsharpe@werc.org

Web: http://www.werc.org

# INDEX

Decision-making skills, 55, 56,
58, 63, 67, 80, 110, 114,
116, 147-149, 170, 175,
181, 222, 227, 228
Delayering, 21, 23, 25, 26
Discrimination, 32, 33, 62, 115
Downsizing, 3, 11, 14, 21, 25,
27, 30, 34, 52, 80

**E**
EDI, 12, 68, 71, 228
Elevating processes, 44, 51-54,
63
Eliciting information, 44-46, 54,
63
Embracing uncertainty, 44, 52,
53, 63
Employee commitment, 182
Employee productivity, 111
Employee recruitment, 208
Employee retention, 2, 9, 132,
135
Empowerment, 24
Engaging complexity, 44, 45,
52-54, 63
Environmental conditions, 160,
161, 168, 181, 186, 190,
191
Equipment training, 101, 104,
109, 129, 141, 145

**F**
Flat organization, 12, 27, 251
Functional silos, 4, 10, 22, 23

**G**
Generation X, 30
GIGO rule, 74
Globalization, 21, 131

**H**
Hazardous material, 102,
139-142

Hiring process, 33
Human resource environment,
17, 20, 22, 27, 29, 32,
33, 39
Human resource issues, 1, 2, 9,
146, 205, 231
Human resource law, 6, 9, 10, 62
Human resource policies, 98, 104
Human resource practices, 9, 10,
17, 20, 22, 35, 105, 106

**I**
Industrial training, 15
Informal training, 14, 21, 36
Information exchange, 38, 90,
97, 99, 228
Information kiosk, 99, 197, 201,
202
Information technology, 10, 21,
68, 69, 75, 78, 87, 129,
217
Innovation, 84, 197
Intermodalism, 131
Internal supply chain, 177
Interpersonal expertise, 195
Interpersonal skills, 13, 18, 21,
26, 28, 38, 54, 59, 61,
67, 76, 77, 82, 90, 94,
95, 98, 100-102,
104-106, 109-111,
115-117, 129, 131, 134,
136-138, 141, 144, 145,
149-151, 160, 163,
165-167, 173, 174, 178,
179, 183, 184, 200-202,
207, 208, 216, 218-221,
225, 226, 230, 232, 238,
239, 248
Inventory databases, 169

**J**
JIT, 68, 246
Job analysis, 18, 35, 36, 58, 116,

471